Murder by Decree: The Crime of Genocide in Canada

A Counter Report to the "Truth and Reconciliation Commission"

Issued by the **International Tribunal for the Disappeared of Canada**

In conjunction with previous Citizen Commissions of Inquiry

March 1, 2016

Toronto and Brussels

Table of Contents

In Memory

To the many tens of thousands of children who died while in the internment and death camps falsely called "Indian residential schools"; To those men and women who have fought against impossible odds to recover the memory of those children and the truth of how they died, and bring to justice who and what is responsible; And to those who suffer and die today at the hands of the same criminal system. *"Earth, cover not their blood"*

And in Acknowledgment

Of the heroic efforts of three ground breaking citizen-based Inquiries into Genocide in Canada: **The Truth Commission into Genocide in Canada** (1998), **The Friends and Relatives of the Disappeared** (2005) and **The International Tribunal into Crimes of Church and State** (2010); and of Rev. Kevin D. Annett, who has fathered and led these movements from the beginning at enormous personal risk and sacrifice. What Canada and all survivors owe to him is incalculable.*

And of seven of the fallen aboriginal leaders of this movement, who died of probable foul play after naming the names of killers of children and leading protests or occupations at the Roman Catholic, Anglican and United Churches of Canada:

Virginia Baptiste, died suddenly January 29, 2004 of unstated causes while in hospital
Louis Daniels, died suddenly February 4, 2006 of unstated causes while in hospital
Harriett Nahanee, died February 24, 2007 shortly after her release from prison
Johnny "Bingo" Dawson, died December 6, 2009 after a police beating
William Arnold Combes, died February 26, 2011 after a lethal injection in St. Paul's Hospital
Ricky Lavallee, died January 23, 2012 after severe blows to the head and chest
Harry Wilson, died April 4, 2013 of unknown causes

We urge the public to read this report alongside Kevin Annett's latest book **"Unrelenting: Between Sodom and Zion" (Amazon, 2016) which gives a stirring personal account of the two decade history of this movement.* **To order:** https://www.createspace.com/6052421 . *Also see* www.itccs.org & www.KevinAnnett.com .

Preamble

This report was prompted by the enormous miscarriage of justice engineered by the government and churches of Canada known as the "Truth and Reconciliation Commission" (TRC). It is written as a corrective response to that Commission's unlawful and deceptive efforts to conceal the extent and nature of deliberate Genocide in Canada by church and state over nearly two centuries.

This report is issued by The International Tribunal for the Disappeared of Canada (ITDC), an international coalition of jurists and human rights groups. The ITDC was formed in December, 2015 to investigate the disappearance of people in Canada and prosecute those responsible. The Tribunal arose because of continued efforts by the Canadian government to obstruct and subvert justice by concealing and falsifying the truth of the genocide of native people in Canada, both past and present.

What you will read in these pages is the most definitive independent account of that genocide ever published in Canada. It encompasses the work of researchers, activists and eyewitnesses spanning over twenty years, and is based on verifiable documented evidence that was deliberately suppressed, censored or destroyed by the Canadian government's TRC between 2008 and 2015.

A genuine, non-governmental Inquiry has been operating in Canada since February of 1998: The Truth Commission into Genocide in Canada (TCGC) and its subsequent offshoots. As a grassroots, self-supporting network of native and non-native people, this movement has struggled against enormous odds to document and make public the true and uncensored story of the genocidal massacre known as the Indian residential school system. The TRC was deliberately established by church and state in response to the TCGC's independent inquiry and public protests, in order to sabotage and defuse the tremendous impact this movement has had since the spring of 1998.

This current ITDC report is based on its own original research as well as the discoveries and work of the TCGC and other independent inquiries into the Canadian Holocaust. The purpose of this report is to pull back the false narrative of genocide in Canada constructed by the governmental TRC and provide a true account of the greatest crime in Canadian history.

This report is a precious archival resource that will be used as the basis for further legal and political action; not only against individual perpetrators of this crime against humanity, but the system of power as well as the institutions that slaughtered entire nations and continue to do so.

In that regard, it was deemed appropriate to publish this report on the fifteenth anniversary of the issuing by the TCGC of the first independent study into crimes in Indian residential schools, *"Hidden from History: The Canadian Holocaust"* by Rev. Kevin Annett. Long before the TRC and other state-sponsored efforts to control and "spin" the truth, this single work began the process of shedding light on legions of missing children and giving countless survivors a voice.

The authors have composed this report for future generations of the peoples of Canada, as a first step away from a murderous legacy that is still destroying them. Canadians must know of the crime in which they are expected to live, fund and collude, if there is any hope for them to one day repudiate that system and build a new and just federation of equal nations. For *"Whoever fails to understand and embrace their own past is doomed to repeat it"*.

March 1, 2016 - Toronto and Brussels

A Critique of the "Truth and Reconciliation" Commission:

An Obstruction of Justice and Truth from Start to Finish

The Truth and Reconciliation Commission … shall not hold formal hearings, nor act as a public inquiry, nor conduct a formal legal process; shall not possess subpoena powers, and does not have powers to compel attendance or participation in any of its activities or events … shall not make any findings or express any conclusion or recommendation regarding the misconduct of any person or the possible civil or criminal liability of any person or organization … shall not name names in their events, activities, public statements, report or recommendations, or make use of personal information or of statements made which identify a person … The Commissioners shall not record the names of persons so identified. - From Section Two, "Establishment, Powers, Duties and Procedures of the Commission", Truth and Reconciliation Commission, Ottawa, 2008

I saw lots of free food and fancy suits and rock bands at the Winnipeg TRC, but they didn't have the money to pay our way down from our reserve to tell our story. What's worse, when we tried to get up at the mike and tell about all the kids we buried at residential school we were told we couldn't and the mike was turned off. That (TRC Chair) Murray Sinclair even laughed in our face, and he said, "Oh no, it's those loonies from Sandy Bay again!" - Ernie White, residential school survivor, 2011

By definition, no regime suspected of committing crimes against any people within their national boundaries may credibly undertake an investigation of those crimes. Any legitimate inquiry and any legal actions arising from it must occur through independent, neutral bodies from outside that nation. Such independent bodies must be recognized by the international community and be allowed to operate freely and conduct their investigations within that nation without interference or influencing of any kind. – Statement by Rudy James, Field Secretary for the International Human Rights Association of American Minorities (IHRAAM) at the inauguration of its Tribunal into Canadian Indian Residential Schools, June 12, 1998, Vancouver

Canada's "Truth and Reconciliation Commission" (TRC) was a rapid in-house response by church and state designed to present their own self-serving narrative of their Indian residential schools crimes. It was by any objective standard an elaborate misrepresentation of a monumental crime.

For one thing, the TRC was created by the same institutions of church and state that were responsible for the residential school crimes being investigated; this fact alone disqualified the TRC from the outset as any neutral or credible body. Indeed, the TRC only commenced its work after both institutions had legally indemnified themselves from any liability for those crimes: a maneuver that constituted an obstruction of justice under the law.

The government's formal announcement of the TRC in June of 2008 was triggered prematurely by a series of widely reported church occupations led by residential school survivors early in 2008, followed quickly by a call from a Member of Parliament for an inquiry into missing residential school children. These events forced the government to announce the TRC as part of a general residential schools "apology" issued by Prime Minister Stephen Harper on June 11, 2008.

The protests and Parliamentary exposure concerning the missing residential school children that prompted this premature announcement of the TRC had embarrassed the government and caused the churches responsible for much of the crime to panic, and insist on exerting oversight of the TRC. This in turn caused the TRC to operate in a blatantly controlled and partisan manner from its inception. The Catholic, Anglican and United churches actually nominated all three of the TRC commissioners, who were in turn approved by the government's Privy Council in Ottawa. Ironically but not surprisingly, this tag team action by the perpetrators represented the same kind of power sharing arrangement that characterized the Indian residential school system.

Similarly, the church and government lawyers who constructed the TRC mandate framed it as a legally toothless body whose findings could not be used to judge or convict any person or group *(read, church)*, and whose records were censored to exclude any evidence of criminal acts or deaths in the residential schools. The mandate even declared that the TRC *"shall not hold formal hearings, nor act as a public inquiry ... and shall not name names in their events ..."* So then, since the TRC denied that it was an inquiry, what in fact was it?

In the words of a visiting South African scholar who observed three separate TRC public events during 2011 and 2012,

"It was all an enormous pretense with very little substance to it. Its so-called 'public forums' were controlled events featuring stage-managed speakers, and were structured to prevent any damaging testimony from surfacing. I never once heard a child's death or torture even being mentioned. It was remarkable how easily the government pulled off what was such an obvious whitewash. To compare it to the South African TRC is laughable." (Dr. Neil Kruger, from an April 12, 2013 interview with Kevin Annett)

As part of its elaborate subterfuge, the TRC's name was deliberately taken from the South African government's "Truth and Reconciliation Inquiry" into crimes of apartheid , the Canadian TRC thereby giving itself the aura of a genuine investigation when it was nothing of the kind. The Canadian media assisted in the overall deception from the start, continually framing the TRC as a legitimate effort to tell the real story of the residential school crimes while never mentioning the powerless and restricted nature of the TRC as a "non inquiry".

Starved of any alternative and commanded by their own state-funded "leaders" of the Assembly of First Nations (AFN) to participate in the TRC events, many aboriginal survivors of the schools initially looked to the TRC to at least allow them the chance to publicly "tell their story". But even that opportunity was denied to them at the TRC forums.

No residential school survivor was allowed to speak at such an event unless his or her statement was first examined and vetted by the church and state-appointed "Commissioners"; the statement was then stripped of any reference to a crime, a killing or the name of a perpetrator. And thus gagged, the survivor had only ten minutes to speak, whereas no such time restriction was placed on officials from the churches that committed the crime, who were regularly allowed to use the TRC events to publicly justify and minimize the atrocities in the schools.

Shawna Green is a Cree second generation survivor who tried to speak at the TRC forum in Victoria, British Columbia during 2011, and was prevented from doing so. (Her experience is described at https://www.youtube.com/watch?v=5xb1u4S_tbs). As she recalls,

"I was disgusted by what we were all put through. I was barred from speaking, straight off, and when I challenged this I was threatened with physical expulsion from the hall. There were only a dozen or so actual survivors at the forum the day I was there, and they all looked miserable. They weren't honored or given any help or counseling or recognition at all, and they could only speak at the mike for a few minutes. But some fat cat Catholic Bishop was given a half hour to spout his disgusting crap about how they were only trying to do good in the schools.

"At that point, an old lady who had gone to Kuper Island (residential school) *started yelling out at the white church guy, "Stop lying! Tell the truth!", and* (TRC Chairman) *Murray Sinclair stood up and yelled at her to be quiet and show respect to the Bishop! Show respect to your rapist! And Sinclair's supposed to be a native. That old lady looked totally crushed. She looked like something had just been killed in her. It was like watching her get abused her all over again."*

Such re-traumatizing behavior by TRC officials was hardly accidental, considering their mandated aim to block unregulated statements, censor evidence and shield church and state from legally damaging revelations. Police were often conspicuously present at TRC events, and according to one officer at the Ottawa forum, were instructed to be on the alert for and detain "unauthorized speakers or protestors."

Such intimidation, and the clearly unlawful mandate of the TRC to deny citizens their constitutional right to speak, name their abusers and have their evidence recorded for legal purposes, actually compelled the first head Commissioner of the TRC, Judge Harry Laforme, to resign from his appointment just a few months after the TRC was launched. (See *"Chairman quits troubled residential school commission", CBC News, October 20, 2008)*

Citing differences with his two fellow Commissioners, Laforme "expressed fear that political and bureaucratic interference could compromise the panel." But Laforme referred later to the questionable practices of TRC officials and implied that his position as a judicial officer was being compromised by his association with the TRC.

Such a startling public implication by a sitting judge that the TRC was operating unlawfully did not sway the TRC in its course under the new leadership of Murray Sinclair, a Cree politician from Manitoba who took over as the TRC chairman from Judge Laforme. Although denying it was any kind of public inquiry or open forum, Sinclair and the TRC nevertheless began staging public events in major cities across Canada that were wrongly depicted by them as "truth telling" forums at which residential school survivors could freely disclose their stories. In reality, nothing a survivor said at such an event was recorded in any open, public record but rather was kept in a private archive, and the copyright to the survivor's own statement rested with the government.

This clandestine record system especially applied to any evidence of crimes or the deaths of residential school children shared at TRC events. In the spring of 2010, Sinclair stated that TRC researchers had uncovered proof that mass graves of children existed at "some" schools, but neither disclosed this evidence nor stated when it would be revealed, if ever. Later, Sinclair remarked that evidence of deaths or killings could be kept confidential "for five or ten more years". As of February 2016, neither the TRC nor the government and churches have disclosed this evidence of children's grave sites, despite the continual reference to burials and killings by eyewitnesses and in documents surfaced by independent inquires.

As in any controlled process, every TRC employee was required to sign confidentiality agreements that legally constrained them from sharing anything they uncovered in the course of their work. All of the churches that ran residential schools required a similar confidentiality statement from their employees after lawsuits by survivors commenced against them in the spring of 1995. *(See the discussion of the Brantford Anglican school excavation in the fall of 2011 in Appendix Six)*

Head TRC researcher John Milloy of Trent University was picked for his role because of his long and faithful service as a compliant scholar in several government "Royal Commissions" into aboriginal people in Canada during the 1990's. Milloy performed a similarly dissembling role for the TRC by conducting a tightly edited "research" of already-censored church documents while never revealing his findings to the public. But even Milloy was forced to admit on one occasion that his research had revealed that dead residential school children were being routinely buried "two or three to a grave" at the Anglican school in Brantford, Ontario. *(June 3, 2009)*

One of the most blatant aspects of this official cover up of evidence by the TRC was revealed in how it allowed the churches that ran the schools to edit, conceal or destroy incriminating evidence in its own records. The TRC had no mandated authority to issue subpoenas or compel disclosure of evidence or attendance at its events by the churches. And the latter were given months after the TRC commenced to re-organize their archives and remove incriminatory evidence from them.

In hindsight, and considering its nature as a creature of the parties that conducted the crime they were supposedly addressing, the TRC could be nothing other than a sanitized account of Canada's enormous Crime against Humanity. What is perhaps less understandable is why the world and so many Canadians have given the TRC even an ounce of attention or credibility.

Such organized duplicity at the highest levels of power in Canada is not confined to the TRC's obfuscation of past war crimes in Canada, but extends to the government's recent efforts to throw a similar fog and misdirection around the escalating disappearance of aboriginal women and children. Part Three of this report will examine how police, government and foreign corporate interests are not only concealing but facilitating these disappearances as part of a wider campaign to dispossess and kill off the last remaining indigenous peoples of Canada.

This report is an answer to these crimes and an urgent summons to the world and all Canadians who refuse to live any longer under a genocidal regime. To truly honor and remember those who have fallen, all people of conscience must reclaim their true history as well as their future.

Synopsis of this Report

1. Our research has established that the crimes and murders committed against children in the Canadian Indian residential school system between 1889 and 1996 were legally authorized, sanctioned and protected by every level of government, church and police in Canada. All the evidence indicates that these crimes constituted calculated mass murder under the guise of religion and education, and represented a deliberate campaign of depopulation aimed primarily at western Canadian aboriginal nations and designed to strike at their weakest link: their children. By every legal and international standard and definition, this crime amounted to deliberate genocide.

2. The primary agents responsible for this genocide were the Canadian federal government and the Crown of England, the Vatican, and Roman Catholic, Anglican and United churches of Canada.

3. At no point during this 107 year period of the residential schools' operation were these crimes ever halted or punished by authorities responsible for the schools, despite continual protests and reports documenting the crimes and a consistently enormous death rate. On the contrary, the perpetrators were routinely protected and exonerated by both government and church officials.

4. Native children began dying in droves the very first year the residential schools opened in 1889, at an average death rate of nearly 50%. The death rate in these schools was on average over ten times the mortality level on the Indian reservations from which the children had come. This death rate continued unabated for at least another fifty years, despite constant complaints and reports by doctors who inspected the schools.

5. After these huge mortality rates became public in 1903, the government stopped officially publishing any death records of students.

6. This enormous mortality was the result of a deliberate practice by all the churches that ran the schools of housing healthy children with those sick and dying from tuberculosis, and denying them medical treatment and care: in effect a regime of institutionalized germ warfare. (*See Appendix Three, The Report of Dr. Peter Bryce, Medical Officer of the Department of Indian Affairs, 1907-9*)

7. The ongoing high mortality rate was also caused by a continual denial of regular food, clothing and proper sanitation to children interned in the schools, amidst a regime of routine and systemic rapes, beatings, tortures and killings: conditions that continued unabated for over a century, from 1889 to 1996.

8. Despite these murderous conditions, attendance in the residential schools was made mandatory for all native children under a federal law enacted in 1920. Significantly, all government medical inspection of the schools was terminated that same year.

9. In the decade that followed this institutionalization of mass murder, special laws were passed across Canada that a) allowed the involuntary sexual sterilization of any residential school child, b) denied Indians the right to hire a lawyer or bring a case into court, and c) made the churches that ran the schools the legal guardian of the children.

10. In the 107 year history of the Canadian residential schools, from among the many complaints brought against staff members, clergymen and school officials there is no record of a single complaint resulting in any reprimand or disciplinary action.

11. Despite the death or disappearance of at least 66,000 children in these schools over a century and numerous statements of eyewitnesses to killings, not a single person has ever been charged or tried in a Canadian court for the death of one of these children.

12. Despite their pivotal role in these deaths and the regime of institutionalized terror in the schools, the churches responsible for the genocide – the Catholics, Anglicans and United Church – continue to operate legally, are supported by Canadian taxpayers and have been indemnified under Canadian law from any consequence for their crime.

13. Canada and its churches have never been charged with Genocide by any other nation or by the United Nations, despite their having committed this crime according to all five definitions of Genocide contained in the United Nations Convention on the Prevention of Genocide (1948), which was ratified by Canada in 1952.

14. The Canadian government and the Catholic, Anglican and United churches have engaged in a continual and illegal obstruction of justice for decades to conceal and destroy the evidence of their residential school crimes. They have done so by obliterating school records, silencing and killing eyewitnesses and survivors as well as in-house whistleblowers, destroying the remains and mass graves of children who died in the schools, and constructing a false narrative about the schools. This enormous falsification and cover up culminated in an official whitewash of their genocide established by them known as the "Truth and Reconciliation Commission" (TRC), which censored and misrepresented the residential schools genocide from start to finish.

15. In practice, Genocide has always been a legitimated and accepted tool of state and of religion. In Canada, its extermination of indigenous nations created and was a structural mainstay of the nation. Today, that extermination of indigenous nations is not only continuing but is expanding because of its continued importance to the resource extraction-based Canadian economy and its resulting institutionalization in the very fiber of government and society. Put simply, both foreign capital and domestic politics require that Indians in Canada continue to be made landless, impoverished and eradicated, and profited from in the process.

16. The Canadian state, its churches and its authorizing Crown authority are proven agents of intergenerational genocide, and as such constitute rogue powers under international law that have lost their authority and right to govern, to tax or to operate. The active replacement of these morally and lawfully nullified institutions is a duty and obligation of all citizens under the Law of Nations and such conventions as the Rome Statute of the International Criminal Court (1998) and the Nuremberg Legal Statutes of the United Nations (1950).

A Chronology of Genocide in Canada by Church and State

1840-2015

1840: The Act of Union creates a single nation of the former French and English speaking enclaves of Lower and Upper Canada. The Act establishes what will become Canada on an explicitly "assimilationist" basis dominated by the English and committed to eliminating all distinctive cultures, whether French speaking or aboriginal.

1850: Indigenous nations in eastern Canada have been decimated by deliberately-introduced diseases to barely ten percent of their pre-contact numbers. Local Indian schools run by the Church of England, like the Mohawk school in Brantford, experience enormous death rates of over 40%. Tribes west of the Lake Head remain untouched by this plague, except on the west coast where Europeans are beginning to settle.

1857: The Gradual Civilization Act is passed in the Canadian legislature, legally eradicating all indigenous people who do not "enfranchise" and surrender their land titles and nationhood.

1859: Roman Catholic missions are established throughout what will become British Columbia under Jesuit direction. Bishop Paul Durieu creates a model to exterminate traditional Indian leaders and culture and replace them with church-controlled puppet leaders: a model that will serve as the basis for the later Indian residential school system.

1862: Major smallpox epidemics are deliberately introduced among Chilcotin, Cowichan and other west coast tribes by Church of England missionaries like John Sheepshanks. Over 90% of the Indians inoculated by Sheepshanks and others will die within weeks, and land speculators like Sheepshanks' fellow investors in the Hudson's Bay Company will then occupy the land emptied of Indians.

1869-70: The first failed uprising of the mixed-blood Metis people near Winnipeg prompts the Canadian government to proclaim its sovereignty "from sea to sea" and commence the building of a national railway, along with massive European immigration onto western Indian lands.

1870: The British Crown through the Canadian Parliament establishes a "clergy reserve" system granting huge swaths of stolen indigenous land to any Anglican or Catholic missionary who settles on such land, usually near to the advancing Canadian Pacific Railway (CPR).

1873: The Royal Northwest Mounted Police, forerunner of the RCMP, is established as a para-military force with absolute jurisdiction across Canada. Its mandate includes forcibly removing all Indians from within fifty miles of the CPR and incarcerating them on impoverished "reservations".

1876: CPR lawyer and Prime Minister John A. MacDonald proclaims through Order in Council the Indian Act, which reduces all Indians and Metis people to the status of non-citizens and *"legal wards of the state in perpetuity"*. Henceforth, no Indian can vote, sue in court, own land or enjoy any civil or legal rights. This "legal ward" status of all reservation Indians continues to the present day in Canada.

1886: Following the crushing of the Second Metis Rebellion the CPR is completed, linking the west and east coasts. The same year, all west coast aboriginal ceremonies like the Potlatch are outlawed and hundreds of traditional native leaders are murdered or jailed.

1889: The Indian residential school system is launched along with the federal Department of Indian Affairs (DIA), which sponsors the "schools" in partnership with the Roman Catholic, Anglican, Methodist and Presbyterian churches (the latter two will form the United Church of Canada in 1925.) In Alberta, the death rate in such "schools" exceeds 40% in the very first year they open, compared to a mortality of barely 5% on the reservations from which the children are taken.

1891: The first official report that documents massive deaths in the residential schools is issued to the DIA by Dr. George Orton, who claims that the cause is rampant tuberculosis among children that is being "encouraged by school staff". Orton's report is ignored by the DIA.

1903: The flood of reports of an enormous death rate in the western residential schools provokes the DIA to cease publishing "total spectrum" death reports among children, meaning that many such deaths will now be officially censored by the government.
1905: Indians in western Canada has been depopulated to less than 5% of their original number. Over 100 residential schools are in operation, two thirds of them run by the Roman Catholics.

1907: DIA medical officer Dr. Peter Bryce conducts a tour of all western residential schools and issues a damning report that claims "conditions are being deliberately created to spread infectious disease." Bryce documents that an average 40% to 60% of school children are dying because of a "routine practice" of housing the sick with the healthy, and denying them all medical treatment. He claims that the staff is deliberately hiding the evidence of this genocidal practice.

November 15, 1907: *The Ottawa Citizen* and *Montreal Gazette* newspapers quote Dr. Bryce's report under the headline *"Schools aid white plague – Startling Death Rolls Revealed". (Figures 1 and 2)* Despite this, Bryce is silenced by DIA Deputy Superintendent Duncan Campbell Scott and his report is ignored.

November 1909: After conducting further investigations that confirm the murderous practices by residential school staff, Dr. Peter Bryce calls for the churches to be removed from operating the residential schools. Bryce is then fired from his position by Scott and banned from the civil service, although in 1920 he will publish his account in his book "A National Crime". *(See Appendix Three)*

November 1910: Despite Bryce's findings, Duncan Campbell Scott of the DIA institutionalizes church control over the schools through a joint contract with the Catholic and Protestant churches. This contract provides government funding and "protection" for the schools, including the use of the RCMP to incarcerate and hunt down Indian children. In return, the churches have complete day to day control of the schools and hire and fire their Principals and staff. (See *Appendix Eight for a copy of this Contract and Figure 3 for a later description of the church's control over the schools*) (1)

1910: Later government records reveal that during the first decade of the 20th century, the net population of Indians in Canada declined by over 20%, an unprecedented level "not explained by any demographic or environmental factors." (*Figure 4,* **Statistics Canada,** *Comparative Population Levels in Canada, 1900-1970*). The use of residential schools as a breeding ground for infectious disease that is then disseminated through native communities is one factor in this depopulation.

February 1919: Despite the continuing high death rates and murderous conditions in the residential schools, Duncan Campbell Scott abolishes all medical inspection in them and prohibits further studies of health conditions in the schools. Within a year, the death rates in western native communities will nearly triple. (*Figure 5*) This mortality is also caused by a routine practice of sending sick children home to infect their families with smallpox and tuberculosis. (*Figure 6*) (2)

June 8, 1920: Prime Minister Arthur Meighen states in Parliament that no provision for the health of Indians was ever included in the federal Health Act or Department. *"It was purposely left out of the Act."* (*Figure 7*)

July 1, 1920: Incarceration in the residential schools is made mandatory under a federal law passed through Order in Council. Every Indian child seven years and older must attend a school or its parents will go to jail. *(Figure 8)*

July 19, 1924: A state church is created by an Act of Parliament – the United Church of Canada – to "Canadianize and Christianize the foreign born and the heathens." This foundational genocidal purpose is affirmed not only through the church's operation of residential schools and Indian hospitals where Indian children die en masse, but in their foundational policy statements concerning their aim to "dispossess" aboriginals of their traditions. *(Figure 9)*

May 1925: Provincial laws in British Columbia and Alberta – where most "unassimilated" Indians are concentrated – strip aboriginal people of the right to consult or hire a lawyer, or even represent themselves in a court of law. Neither is any lawyer allowed to take on an aboriginal client.

1929-1933: Sexual Sterilization laws are passed in both provinces' legislatures, allowing any inmate of an Indian residential school to be involuntarily sterilized at the decision of the school Principal, a church employee. Thousands of children and adults are sexually neutered by these laws.

1929-1933: The Canadian government relinquishes its traditional legal guardianship over Indian children and grants such power to the residential school Principal, a church employee. *(See Figure 10, the Application for Admission form)*

February 1934: An attempt by the government to abolish residential schools is thwarted because of massive pressure and threats brought by all the churches running the schools.

October 1935: A genocidal "two standards of health care" system in residential schools is confirmed by Dr. C. Pitts in a letter that states "*... were I to apply the standards of health to them (Indians) that is applied to children of the white schools, that (sic) I should have to discharge 90% of them and there would be no school left.*" Pitts is referring to the Lejac Catholic School in northern British Columbia, and admits that a lower standard of health care is applied to them. *(Figure 11)*

1937-38: School records confirm that children infected with tuberculosis are admitted to west coast Indian schools, and officials refer to the fact that the Indian Affairs department "will not hospitalize Indians suffering from pulmonary tuberculosis." (*Figures 12, 13 and 14*)

January 1939: Cowichan Indian children are widely used in medical experiments conducted by "German speaking doctors" at the Catholic Kuper Island School in British Columbia. Many of them die, according to two survivors, but the RCMP suppresses inquiries by local police.

1940-45: Under the cover of war, involuntary experimental research is commenced on many residential school children by the Defense Research Board (DRB) in Ottawa. The research includes drug testing, deliberate starvation, behavior modification, pain threshold studies, chemical weapons testing and sterilizing methods. These tests are conducted in the schools, at military bases, and at special laboratories and Indian hospitals run jointly with the United, Anglican and Catholic churches, and will continue for decades. (*Figure 15*) (3)

1946-8: Hundreds of Nazi SS doctors and researchers are granted citizenship in Canada under the joint British-American "Project Paperclip", and work under cover identities and military supervision in the aforementioned experimental programs. (4)

1947: Canadian U.N. diplomat and future Prime Minister Lester Pearson helps to redefine genocide in the proposed United Nations Convention in order to make it inapplicable to Canadian Indian residential schools. Enabling legislation to allow its application in Canada is blocked in Parliament.

1958: The government again attempts to close residential schools and meets hostile resistance and threats of political action by all three churches operating the schools. The plan is dropped.

1960: Revisions to the Revised Statues of British Columbia legally define an aboriginal as *"an uncivilized person, destitute of the knowledge of God and of any fixed and clear belief in religion or in a future state of rewards and punishments"* (Figure 16)

1962: A government plan later entitled the "Sixties Scoop" covertly begins to privatize residential schools by transferring huge numbers of Indian children into non-aboriginal homes through state-subsidized foster agencies. Thousands of children have their identity and family life destroyed in this manner without setting foot in a residential school.

1965: Government document destruction teams obliterate countless residential school records related to the identity and deaths of students, in anticipation of the phasing out of the schools.

1969: Indian Affairs minister and future Prime Minister Jean Chretien affirms an "assimilationist" policy of legally exterminating native nations in a federal "White Paper" introduced in Parliament.

1970: Native protests against the White Paper, including the seizure and occupation of Bluequills residential school in Alberta by aboriginal parents, forces the government to begin the process of turning over residential schools to the control of local tribal councils.

1972: The government destroys thousands of Indian Affairs records including personnel files with information on residential school history and aboriginal land deeds, making the verification of school crimes and native land claims impossible. (Figure 17)

1975: A majority of residential schools formerly run by the churches are now either closed or under the management of local Indian band councils. Nevertheless, many of the same crimes and tortures against children continue, often at the hands of aboriginal staff members.

1982: The Government funds and establishes the puppet aboriginal organization known as the "Assembly of First Nations" (AFN), consisting of 600 self-appointed state funded tribal "chiefs". The AFN claims to "represent" all aboriginals in Canada, but it refuses all calls for indigenous sovereignty or to investigate the residential schools genocide.

October 1989: Nora Bernard, an east coast native survivor of the Shubenacadie Catholic residential school, commences the first lawsuit against both the church and the government for harm she suffered. Nora refers to "our genocide". She will be murdered in December, 2007 just prior to the launching of the government cover up known as the "Truth and Reconciliation Commission" (TRC).

October 1990: AFN head and government employee "Chief" Phil Fontaine, in response to the Nora Bernard residential school lawsuit, speaks publicly of "abuses" in the schools and establishes a benign, AFN monopoly over the issue that never mentions the death of children or genocide.

March 1994: In Port Alberni, the killing of children in the local United Church residential school is addressed by Rev. Kevin Annett and native survivors from his pulpit. Annett is told by church officers to refrain from addressing the issue and is threatened with firing.

January 23, 1995: Kevin Annett is fired without cause after reporting more stories of residential school killings and of the theft of west coast native land by his United Church employer and its business partner the logging company MacMillan-Bloedel. His unusual firing is addressed by a *Vancouver Sun* columnist that summer, as MacMillan-Bloedel issues a payoff to the United Church in Port Alberni. *(Figures 18a and 18b)*

December 13, 1995: The first account of the murder of a residential school child, Maisie Shaw, is made by eyewitness Harriett Nahanee at a rally held by fired United Church minister Kevin Annett, and is reported by the *Vancouver Sun* newspaper. (*Figure 19, "Murders alleged at residential school" by Stewart Bell, Vancouver Sun, December 13, 1995*) A week later, a second such murder, of a boy named Albert Gray, is reported by eyewitness Archie Frank, and is again reported by the *Sun*. *(Figure 20, "Beaten to death for theft of a prune" by Mark Hume, Vancouver Sun, December 20, 1995)* Both eyewitnesses claim the killer was Principal Alfred Caldwell. The RCMP refuses to investigate.

February 1, 1996: The first class action lawsuit by residential school survivors in Canada opens in the British Columbia Supreme Court, brought by fifteen former students at the Alberni School against the United Church and government. Kevin Annett is an adviser to the plaintiffs. *(Figure 21)*

February 3, 1996: The United Church begins closed, internal disciplinary proceedings against Kevin Annett to permanently expel him from the ministry, which will occur the next year at a cost to the church of over $250,000. Annett will never be charged by the church with any wrongdoing. The Church also secretly pays Annett's former wife Anne McNamee to divorce him and with the collusion of provincial court judges rob him of his two children. (*Figure* 22) (5)

1997-1998: Other Canadian newspapers begin to report eyewitness allegations of killings in residential schools, including those gathered in healing circles convened by Kevin Annett and Harriet Nahanee. *(Figures 23 and 24)*

February 9, 1998: At a public rally of over 600 people in Vancouver, many of them aboriginal, the Truth Commission into Genocide in Canada (TCGC) is established as an independent, open inquiry into residential school crimes. Kevin Annett is elected as its General Secretary. *(Figure 25)*

June 6, 1998: Justice Donald Brenner of the British Columbia Supreme Court rules that the United Church and government of Canada are <u>equally liable</u> for damages to inmates in residential schools, opening the door to thousands of subsequent lawsuits by survivors against all three churches.

June 12-14, 1998: The first independent inquiry into residential school crimes is convened in Vancouver by the United Nations affiliate IHRAAM, upon the invitation of TCGC leaders Harriett Nahanee and Kevin Annett. The inquiry hears from twenty eight eyewitnesses to these crimes and concludes that *"every act defined as genocide under international law occurred in Canadian Indian residential schools"*. None of the church and government officials subpoenaed by IHRAAM respond to or refute this claim. IHRAAM recommends to United Nations High Commissioner Mary Robinson that an international tribunal be held into these crimes, but Robinson never replies. (*Figures* 26, 27, 28 *and* 29) (6)

June 20, 1998: The *Globe and Mail* is the only media in Canada to report the IHRAAM hearings. *(Figure 30)*

Autumn 1998: A public smear and misinformation campaign is mounted for the first time against Kevin Annett and the TCGC. IHRAAM silences the inquiry participants and buries their reports.

October 27, 1998: The *Province* newspaper reports an admission by United Church lawyers that the church has engaged in a cover up of residential school crimes with the government since at least 1960, and that church officials kidnapped child to bring them into the schools. *(Figure 31)*

January 1999: The residential school crimes and the IHRAAM - TCGC inquiry are reported for the first time outside of Canada, in the British magazine *The New Internationalist.* But the publication is pressured by Crown lawyers to desist from any subsequent coverage of the issue. *(Figure 32)*

March 1999: In response to the IHRAAM inquiry and escalating lawsuits, the Canadian government creates an "Aboriginal Healing Fund" (AHF) that is used as a hush fund for survivors. Any of the AHF recipients must first agree never to sue the government or churches that ran the schools.

April 26, 2000: In the first of many "spin doctoring" of residential school atrocities, Health Canada admits that it conducted "limited" experiments on school children during the 1950's by denying them dental care, food and vitamins, but provides no details. (*See Figure 15)*

2000-2001: Facing over ten thousand individual lawsuits by school survivors, the government under church pressure legislates a limit on the scope of such lawsuits and assumes primary financial liability for residential school damages, ignoring the Brenner joint-liability legal decision of 1998. Crown courts in Alberta and Ontario impose similar restrictions and deny survivors the right to sue church and state for genocide. *(Figure 33)*

February 1, 2001: The TCGC publishes the first documentation of deliberate genocide in Canadian residential schools, *"Hidden from History: The Canadian Holocaust"* by Kevin Annett. Over 1,000 copies are sent to the media, politicians and many residential school survivors. *(Figure 34)*

August 14, 2001: The British Columbia Court of Appeals, under government pressure, reverses the 1998 Brenner Decision and places the entire financial liability for residential school damages on the federal government and taxpayer, absolving the churches of any financial liability.

2001-2004: The TCGC mounts a broad public education campaign about the residential schools genocide, picketing the churches responsible and holding public forums across Canada at which survivors tell their stories and name names. The Commission begins its own radio program on Vancouver Co-op Radio, "*Hidden from History*", hosted by Kevin Annett. The program will air for nine years until it is terminated from government pressure.

December 29, 2004: After being contacted by Kevin Annett, a federation of Mayan indigenous groups issues a "*Denuncia*" or official demand to the Canadian government to disclose its evidence of the genocide of native people in Canada. Receiving no reply, the Mayans take their *Denuncia* of the Canadian Genocide to the United Nations. *(Figure 35)*

April 15, 2005: The TCGC and its affiliate The Friends and Relatives of the Disappeared (FRD) hold the first "Aboriginal Holocaust Remembrance Day" in Vancouver outside Catholic, Anglican and United churches. For the first time speakers issue a call for the repatriation of the remains of children who died at the residential schools. The event is widely reported in the media.

March-October 2006: Numerous accounts of mass graves of children at or near former Indian residential schools are received by the TCGC and FRD, prompting the production of the first documentary film on Genocide in Canada: *Unrepentant*. The film is based on Kevin Annett's research and work with survivors. On October 1 the TCGC merges with FRD into one organization.

January – May 2007: *Unrepentant* is released worldwide to hundreds of thousands of viewers, and wins Best Documentary at the Los Angeles Independent Film Festival. (*Figure 36*) FRD and Kevin Annett commence high profile occupations of Catholic, Anglican and United churches in Vancouver, Winnipeg and Toronto, which are widely reported in the media. A report surfaces that residential school documents were deliberately destroyed by the government. *(Figures 37 and 38)*

April 2007: After seeing *Unrepentant*, Member of Parliament Gary Merasty calls on the government to begin repatriating the remains of residential school children. Indian Affairs minister Jim Prentice announces a "Missing Children's Task Force" that never convenes. But Prentice also hints at the formation of a "Truth and Reconciliation Commission" to investigate residential school deaths.

April 24, 2007: Based on interviews with Kevin Annett and his network of survivors, the *Globe and Mail* newspaper publishes a front page article confirming the 50% death rate in residential schools. *(Figure 39, "Natives died in droves as Ottawa ignored warnings", Globe and Mail, April 24, 2007)*

January – March, 2008: As the government stalls, FRD launches a new wave of church occupations and declares its intent to begin an action in international courts of justice against Canada and its churches. Eviction notices are issued against the Catholic, Anglican and United churches by aboriginal elders across Canada. (*Figures 40, 41 and 42, "Native group warns of international court action", The National Post, February 13, 2008; "Show us where dead buried, natives ask", Toronto Sun, February 5, 2008; "Protesters storm church in bid to learn fate of aboriginal children", The Globe and Mail, March 10, 2008; "Native protesters disrupt Easter services in Vancouver", The Globe and Mail, March 24, 2008)*

April 10, 2008: Kevin Annett and FRD release to the world media a list of twenty eight mass grave sites at or near former Indian residential schools across Canada. Neither Annett nor any FRD member is ever contacted by the police or government about the grave sites. *(See Appendix Five)*

April 15, 2008: On the FRD's fourth Aboriginal Holocaust Memorial Day, the government issues a statement that although "enormous numbers of deaths" occurred in residential schools, no criminal charges will be laid against the churches that ran the schools, thereby legally indemnifying them from any prosecution. The churches then all quickly endorse the proposed "Truth and Reconciliation Commission".

June 1, 2008: The Truth and Reconciliation Commission (TRC) is launched by the government after its officers are nominated by the three churches and approved by the Prime Minister's office. Its restricted mandate forbids it from laying criminal charges, issuing subpoenas, investigating homicides or taking down as evidence the names of any residential school perpetrators. And over half of all school survivors are disqualified from any compensation by the government.

June 11, 2008: Prime Minister Stephen Harper issues a formal "apology" in Parliament for Indian residential schools, not mentioning the deaths of students or the involvement of churches in the schools. But Bloc Quebecois leader Gilles Duceppe refers to the "mass graves" of Indian children.
June 15, 2008: FRD calls on all Canadians and school survivors to reject the "apology" and boycott the

TRC, and seek instead an international criminal tribunal into Genocide in Canada with the power to sub-poena, arrest and prosecute.

January 2009: *Unrepentant* is now viewed worldwide and prompts human rights groups in Europe to invite Kevin Annett and FRD members to speak at public forums in London, Dublin, Paris and Rome. The government's TRC responds to each new action by the FRD by holding public forums for survivors, but the latter are discouraged from naming names or describing crimes other than physical and sexual "abuse".

October 2009: Italian politicians, including the provincial government of Liguria in Genoa, agree to sponsor an inquiry into Genocide in Canada after an FRD delegation including Kevin Annett presents them with the evidence and wins their endorsement. *(Figures 43 and 44)* On October 11, Kevin conducts a public exorcism outside the Vatican. The next day, a tornado strikes the center of Rome. *(Figures 45 and 46)* That week, European media first begin to report the personal complicity of Pope Benedict, Joseph Ratzinger, in concealing crimes against children in the Catholic Church.

December 14, 2009: FRD organizer and residential school survivor Bingo Dawson is beaten to death by three Vancouver policemen, according to eyewitness Ricky Lavallee. The cause of death is listed as "alcohol poisoning" although an accompanying toxicology report states that no alcohol or drugs were found in his bloodstream. Bingo is the first of six FRD members who will die of foul play between 2009 and 2012. *(Figures 47 and 48, including Coroner's Report)*

April 1-4, 2010: Sponsoring Italian politicians host Kevin Annett and an FRD delegation of residential school survivors at a major press conference in Rome. But their support is suddenly curtailed and the FRD delegation is detained by the police just before they are to protest outside the Vatican. A Canadian government-paid operative has infiltrated the FRD and discredited it to media and FRD supporters with false stories. *(Figure 49 – the operative, Charles Cook, is on far right in the picture)*
April 15-16, 2010: Kevin Annett holds high profile protests with Irish survivors of Catholic Church torture outside the Irish Parliament in Dublin, and calls for the public prosecution of Pope Benedict. *(Figures 50 and 51; "Abuse in Canadian residential schools identical to here, says clergyman", The Irish Times, April 16, 2010; "Survivors demand truth panel probe claims on care institutions", The Irish Independent, April 16,*

2010. Kevin's trip was sponsored by three groups of Irish survivors of church crimes.)

June 15, 2010: The International Tribunal into Crimes of Church and State (ITCCS) is established in Dublin by six organizations and survivors of church tortures. Its mandate is to prosecute both church and state for crimes committed against children, and disestablish such unlawful authorities. The Canadian government's TRC issues a statement the same week that its research has uncovered evidence of the graves of children at residential school sites, but gives no details.

August, 2010: The film *Unrepentant* is broadcast in four languages to over ten million viewers on Swiss and German television. Kevin Annett's new book **Unrepentant: Disrobing the Emperor** is published in London. But on August 9, Kevin's long standing radio program *Hidden from History* is canceled without cause or explanation by Vancouver Co-op radio, which is government funded.

April 10, 2011: Ten Mohawk elders invite Kevin Annett to their territory at Brantford, Ontario to assist them in recovering the remains of children in mass graves next to the oldest residential school in Canada, the Mohawk Institute, and run by the Church of England. (*Figure* 52) The next month, on May 29, while doing archival research in London, Kevin is deported from England without cause. *(Figure 53)*

October-December 2011: The ITCCS and Mohawk elders begin their joint investigation into the missing children at the Brantford school by employing grand penetrating radar. Suspected grave sites are located almost immediately based on surviving eyewitness account. Actual excavation of such a site commences in November, and uncovers buttons off school uniforms and sixteen bone samples, one of which is confirmed by forensic experts to be from a small child. This first recovery of bones from a residential school grave goes completely unreported in the Canadian media, despite a Mohawk press conference in November. *(Figures 54 and 55; see Appendix Six for the full report and http://itccs.org/mass-graves-of-children-in-canada-documented-evidence/)*

January 2012: The Mohawk excavation is sabotaged by paid government agents in the local tribal council. But two remaining elders and the ITCCS publish their findings before the world. The same month, the government's TRC releases its "interim report" that confirms that an unstated number of children died in residential schools without naming the names or who is responsible.

July 1, 2012: Encouraged by the Brantford dig findings, the ITCCS convenes the International Common Law Court of Justice (ICLCJ) in Brussels. The court commences a criminal trial that charges Canada and its churches, the crown of England and the Vatican with Genocide and crimes against humanity, and engaging in a criminal conspiracy. Thirty defendants are named and subpoenaed, including Queen Elizabeth, Pope Benedict and Prime Minister Stephen Harper; none of them respond to or contest any of the charges or evidence brought against them in the court. *(See http://itccs.org/common-law-court-documents/)*

February 11, 2013: The chief defendant in the ICLCJ trial, Pope Benedict (Joseph Ratzinger) resigns suddenly from his office just five days after the Vatican receives a diplomatic note from the Spanish government announcing that, based on the ICLCJ court material, an arrest warrant against Ratzinger could be issued if he enters Spanish territory.

February 25, 2013: The ICLCJ court and jury find Joseph Ratzinger and all of the other defendants guilty as charged of crimes against humanity and engaging in a criminal conspiracy. Defendants are sentenced *in absentia* to twenty five years in prison without parole and a loss of their assets and authority. Arrest warrants are issued against the guilty on February 25. (*Figure* 56)

April-August, 2013: Three other Vatican officials who are named as defendants in the ICLCJ case and eventually found guilty under its verdict will resign from their offices: Tarcisio Bertone, Vatican Secretary of State; Irish Cardinal Sean Brady; and eventually, Jesuit leader Adolfo Pachon.

April-July, 2014: The ICLCJ convenes a second case to charge three top Vatican officials with aiding and abetting child trafficking and homicide: Pope Francis (Jorge Bergoglio), Jesuit head Adolfo Pachon, and Archbishop of Canterbury Justin Welby.

Based on the testimonies of 29 eyewitnesses linking all three defendants to the 9th Circle cult, all are found guilty as charged and sentenced in absentia to life imprisonment. Common law arrest warrants are issued. *(See http://itccs.org/2014/07/24/sheriffs-move-to-arrest-convicted-church-leaders-bergoglio-*

pachon-and-welby-vatican-crown-plan-counter-attack/)

January 15, 2015: Based on the conviction and legal nullification of the authority of the Crown of England resulting from the ICLCJ verdict of February 25, 2013, patriots in Canada declare the establishment of a sovereign Republic of Kanata under the authority of international and common law. Stand down Orders are issued to all crown agents in Canada and a Constitutional Convention is announced. (*http://itccs.org/2015/01/07/debts-taxes-nullified-in-new-republic-of-kanata*)

June 3, 2015: Canada acknowledges that genocide occurred within the Indian residential school system and that thousands of children died as a result. (*New York Times, 3/6/2015*) In response, the ITCCS convenes a new coalition that will establish the International Tribunal for the Disappeared of Canada (ITDC) the following December, 2015.

March 1, 2016: Counter Report to the TRC's misinformation is issued by the International Tribunal for the Disappeared of Canada (ITDC) and Kevin Annett.

Footnotes - Chronology

(1) *"While the property, including the buildings, belongs to the Government, the management of the institution, which is a Roman Catholic school, rests entirely with the church authorities who have the privilege of nominating the principal and appointing the other members of the staff."* - from a letter of Duncan Campbell Scott, DIA Deputy Superintendent, November 8, 1920 to James McGuire, Oblate Principal of Kamloops residential school.

(2) *"I herewith beg to submit a report upon the outbreak of smallpox in this Agency, which started by girls being sent home from St. Mary's (Catholic) Mission School suffering from the disease."* - from a letter of H. Graham, Indian Agent for Lytton, British Columbia, to DIA in Ottawa, October 20, 1919.

(3) A sanitized account of some of these experiments involving the government's selective deprivation of dental care, food and vitamins to "some" residential school children was reported by the Canadian Press on April 26, 2000, based entirely on information released by the Anglican Church, a participant in the tortures!

(4) See **Always Remember Love: Memoirs of a Survivor of Nazi Medical Experimentation in post-war Canada** by Sara Hunter for an account of a lone survivor of one of these programs. (Bibliography)

(5) These facts are affirmed by Ms. McNamee in divorce court documents and in this letter to the editor of the *Vancouver Courier* newspaper dated September 28, 1997. A complete account is found in the documentary film ***Unrepentant*** (*www.hiddennolonger.com* and *www.itccs.org*)

(6) IHRAAM is an acronym for The International Human Rights Association of American Minorities, an NGO with "consultative status" at the U.N. IHRAAM officials have falsely claimed, after the fact, that they never sponsored the Vancouver inquiry, despite documents showing that IHRAAM convened the event, paid for the hall where it was held and issued Public Summonses under their own letterhead to those persons subpoenaed by the inquiry. See Figures 26-29.

Part One: The Crime

To invade, search out, capture, vanquish and subdue all Saracens and pagans whatsoever, and other enemies of Christ wheresoever placed, and to reduce their persons to perpetual slavery. - Papal Bull **Romanus Pontifex** that authorized the conquest and genocide of the non-Catholic world (1455). This Bull has never been revoked.

Genocide does not necessarily mean the immediate destruction of an entire nation ... It is rather a coordinated plan of different actions aiming at the destruction of essential foundations of the life of national groups, with the aim of annihilating the groups themselves. – Raphael Lemkin, **Axis Rule in Occupied Europe** (1944)

The culture that made the Nazi death camps possible was not only indigenous to the West but was an outcome of its fundamental religious traditions that insist upon a dichotomous division of mankind into the elect and the reprobate. - Richard Rubenstein, **The Cunning of History** (1978)

Colonization is civilization. If we, the superior race, take the land of other races, we must utterly destroy the previous inhabitants ... The disappearance of our local Indians is of little consequence.
- Sir Edward Bulwer-Lytton, co-founder of British Columbia and Member of the Legislative Assembly, 1868

I just got a blanket well-infected with smallpox and put it between my saddle blanket and a sweat pad. I went into all their villages with it and I succeeded. All of the savages died of smallpox.
- John McLain, Hudson's Bay company trader and land speculator, on his sojourn among the Chilcotins of British Columbia, **Only in Nazko** (1908)

I believe the conditions are being deliberately created in our Indian schools to spread infectious diseases. The death rate often exceeds fifty percent. This is a national crime. - Dr. Peter Bryce to Indian Affairs Deputy Superintendent Duncan Campbell Scott, April 12, 1907, prior to his dismissal by Scott.

It is quite within the mark to say that fifty per cent of the children who passed through these schools did not live to benefit from the education which they had received therein. - Indian Affairs Deputy

Superintendent Duncan Campbell Scott in 1913 referring to the mortality in Indian residential schools, 1913 (*CBC news, June 3, 2015*)

If I were to choose to kill off half the Indian children under our care, there is no better instrument to use than your typical residential school. - Neil Parker, Indian Affairs Superintendent, 1949

The fact that European powers deliberately exterminated millions of non-Christian indigenous people in the New World is historically undeniable, constituting as it does the numerically largest genocide in world history. (7) The participation of Canadian church and state in the same crime has been and continues to be denied, especially by Canadians, despite overwhelming evidence.

Broadly speaking, it would be a strange paradox indeed for Euro-Canadians not to have conquered, de-populated, legally constrained and eradicated the Indian nations they encountered after 1497, operating as they were from precisely the same mentality and practice of "Superior Christian Dominion" (8) that animated every other Vatican-authorized nation. Those who would claim a "Canadian exceptionalism" to the norm of European genocide have yet to produce any evidence to show that indigenous nations somehow fared better under Canadian rule.

On the contrary, a simple peeling back of the Great Canadian Myth of benevolence towards Indians reveals a rancid, hidden history of war crimes and mass murder on par with any criminal regime in the world. The outcome for native nations has been the same, whether in Canada, America or Brazil. And yet the process of extermination played out differently in Canada.

The sheer vastness of the country, for one thing, and the slower, more gradual colonization process, meant that the usual genocidal sequence of Conquest, Containment and Long term Annihilation took place over more than four centuries, making its reality less obvious in any given generation.

From the first Labrador landfall of Cabot and his slaughter of the Beothuk people around 1500 to the final smallpox wars that decimated most west coast Indian tribes by 1920, British and French imperialism employed a mixture of strategies of how to eliminate indigenous nations. The economic importance of eastern woodland tribes like the Huron and Iroquois to the Canadian fur trade and their usefulness as military allies ruled out a Spanish Solution of outright extermination of these Indians. But when such usefulness passed, their eradication proceeded just as thoroughly.

The very fact that the conquering Europeans had to be more circumspect and strategic in their treatment of their brown skinned targets made the role of religion all that more crucial to the success of the Canadian genocide, which can truthfully be described as a religious enterprise from start to finish. Indeed, the predominance of the churches in forming and operating colonial policy towards Indians, and in establishing and maintaining, against periodic government opposition, the murderous Indian residential school system for over a century, is unique when compared to most other nations' genocide track record. (9)

The fact that the Canadian Holocaust occurred in prolonged waves under the leadership of Roman Catholicism and Anglicanism – and their offshoots – and did so under "benevolent" guises of education and missionary proselytizing, has done much to fog and camouflage the reality of Genocide in Canada, and not accidentally. British imperialism always presented itself as a "civilizing" force wherever it exterminated local populations, a "hammer in a velvet glove" approach epitomized by General George Maitland, who in 1843 described British treatment of African tribes as "A good thrashing followed by great kindness". (10)

That said, the sheer vastness of the western half of Canada placed the occupying power at a real disadvantage, making it much harder for Indian nations to be physically corralled and snuffed out. Force alone wouldn't work on the prairie expanse, as was proven by the nearly-successful Metis and Cree guerrilla war of 1885 against a bumbling Canadian militia. Even with the linking of the country by the Canadian Pacific Railway the next year, many western tribes, especially on the west coast, evaded reservations and "assimilation" for decades afterward. And even the early Indian residential schools, devised by Jesuit missionaries as the "final solution" of the predominantly western Indian Problem, failed for many years to attract and hold very many children. (11)

The solution to this impasse was a simple one: church missionaries were to be armed with the full powers of the state and the law, and given an absolutely free hand in their task of subverting, containing and de-populating the untamed tribes west of the Lake Head: a job they enshrined with a halo of religious legitimating that made genocide seem like a charity mission. (12) And they and their church sponsors achieved this eradication with remarkable ruthlessness and efficiency by first going after the aboriginal children.

"Give us a child for seven years and he will be ours for life" said the 16th century Jesuit founder Ignatius Loyola – and it should be added, in the Canadian context, *"at least, if he survives."*

The full gamut of genocidal crime in Canada is outside the scope of this report. Instead, we are scrutinizing that specific Group Crime called the Indian residential school system – again, a term designed to deceive – by which all of the indigenous nations in Canada were finally brought down and decimated by the church and state and their corporate sponsors.

A) Understanding the Killing Machine

As with the concept and application of Genocide itself, the Indian residential school system has been so falsely framed and misunderstood that we must return to the source of what that arrangement was, including its foundational purpose.

The idea behind it all is very old, harking back to the late Roman Empire and its Byzantine counterpart, which was simply to conquer an enemy by kidnapping and re-educating their own children to destroy their former nation, as the programmed mercenaries of the conquering power. In effect, the "salvageable" young ones among the enemy would be saved and assimilated into the Empire, and used to infiltrate and annihilate the rest in a form of "selective redemption".

The system always worked, since it struck unexpectedly at the Achilles' heel and vital, vulnerable center of any culture: its next generation. (13)

With the incorporation of the Roman Imperium into the Roman Catholic Church, this practice of Selective Redemption became a religious dogma and an institutionalized part of the foreign policy of the Vatican and every European nation.

Since non-Catholics anywhere in the world were deemed to have no souls or rights of any kind, they had to be conquered and destroyed for their own good. But these non-people could avoid slaughter and acquire a limited slave status by being baptized. In this way, the conquest of the world by the Catholic Imperium could proceed on both an efficient and a "morally legitimate" basis – especially since in the Papal doctrine of Indulgence, Holy Warriors killing on behalf of Rome were spiritually cleansed into a state of original grace. (14)

Genocide, in short, was good for both conquered and the conqueror alike: an idea that became deeply imbedded in the psyche of the western world.

In response to the Protestant Reformation, the Jesuit Order was established in 1543 as a secret military order to crush all opposition to the Pope. It refined this system of Conquest through Salvation by creating a model for sabotaging an enemy culture from within. The Jesuits did so through the classic divide and conquer method of winning over a few leaders and provoking internecine tribal warfare, like they did in Canada among the Hurons by arming Catholic chiefs with muskets and smallpox blankets to wipe out their "pagan" brothers.

Key to the success of this strategy was the re-education of the children of those converted chiefs in special Jesuit-run "schools", from where the next generation of brainwashed Holy Papal Warriors could complete the destruction of their former nation. (15) Obvious present day analogies come to mind.

This Jesuit weapon was often used successfully on any monarch or government that opposed or dissented from papal rule. But to see its particular efficacy in the New World we must jump forward to the mid 19th century on Canada's west coast, still largely unsettled by Europeans save for Catholic missionaries; usually Jesuit-trained ones, like a priest named Paul Durieu.

In his work among the coastal Salish Indians, Durieu came up with the prototype for what would become the Indian residential school system in Canada. Using the time honored system of converting and then inciting aboriginals against each other, Durieu targeted youths and relocated them into church-run camps where as "Watchmen" they would spy on one another and punish any backsliding "heathens" in their ranks, as in any Inquisition.

"It is remarkable how soon our young acolytes have learned to root out heresy and impiety within their own families and discipline the recalcitrant" wrote Durieu to his superiors in Montreal in 1868.

Not coincidentally, the same year witnessed the first major smallpox outbreak among the traditional Indians in the lower Fraser river region where Durieu worked: a plague assisted by Church of England missionary John Sheepshanks during 1864 when he infected the Chilcotin Indians with smallpox using inoculations, depopulating over 90% of them. (16)

Durieu's approach seemed to impress his Oblate missionary bosses. Soon, they adopted his work as the basis for the first Catholic Indian residential schools, which institutionalized Durieu's method of pitting of children against each other to weed out and destroy the "heathens". By 1889, this system spawned similar efforts by Protestant missionaries and eventually, the government of Canada itself, which formally sanctioned the Durieu-like "Watchmen" camps that would be eventually called "Indian residential schools". (17)

Significantly, over one half of the children began dying in these "schools" *the very first year they were opened*: especially in areas like the Prairies where traditional indigenous identity remained strong. For example, in the Fort Qu'appelle Catholic Indian school that opened in 1896, seven of the thirteen students were either dead or dying after one year; in another school in Regina, eight out of twelve died. In comparison, the average mortality on the surrounding prairie Indian reservations in the same period was barely 5%. (*Figures 57, 58, 59 and 60*) (18)

These facts suggest that, in keeping with papal ideology, killing off non-Christian, unassimilable Indians was an accepted part and parcel of the residential schools project.

The instantly high death rate at the very inception of the Indian residential school system in areas targeted for ethnic cleansing is a fact never mentioned in official historical accounts like the government's TRC report, <u>since this one fact goes far to prove a genocidal intent behind the "schools"</u> and thereby undermine the mainstream position that the system was a basically benevolent effort gone wrong. In the same way, the fact that this mortality level stayed constant for over a half century – between at least 1889 and 1949 – without any action to reduce it by either church or state, irrefutably points to the conclusion that Indian residential schools were a deliberate killing machine from their inception. (19) Their primary and unstated aim was to de-populate "untamed" indigenous nations by at least one half: an aim proven in the result. *(See the enormous death rates in western Indian schools documented following, in Figures 61 and 62).*

By 1909, nearly half of the children in Indian schools were dying from deliberately introduced diseases like tuberculosis, according to DIA Medical inspector Dr. Peter Bryce who had conducted an exhaustive study of health conditions in the schools. (*Figures 61 and 62*) This mortality rate stayed at the same level for decades thereafter because of a routine practice by staff of infecting healthy children through forced contact with children dying of tuberculosis, and then denying them care. This practice was done by all of the churches that ran the schools, according to Bryce.

Between 1907 and 1909, Dr. Bryce made two separate tours of nearly every Indian school in the west. Bryce continually found that school staff and their church bosses were routinely concealing the enormous number of deaths among children caused by their disease-spreading practices. He also documented how children consistently died at a much higher rate after entering residential schools, and that no effort was made to separate healthy children from the infected ones.

Bryce did not mince his words: "*I believe the conditions are being deliberately created in our Indian schools to spread infectious disease. The death rate often exceeds fifty percent ... This is a national crime.*" (20)

Bryce was not alone in identifying the deadly environment being maintained in the residential schools. Indian Agent A.W. Neill of the West Coast Agency wrote to Indian Affairs less than a year after Bryce's final report describing conditions in Vancouver Island residential schools.
"These people have lived for centuries in the open air. A child is taken into a school at 8, spends ten years in the school. After that its constitution is so weakened that it has no vitality to withstand disease."
(Figure 63; April 25, 1910 Letter to Duncan Campbell Scott)

Both Bryce and Neill were ignored by the government, the good doctor being dismissed and blacklisted for his report, which called among other things for the churches to be removed from operating the residential schools because of their "manslaughter" of the children.

In fact, after firing Dr. Bryce and burying his report, Indian Affairs responded to his expose by actually institutionalizing church control over Indian children, making it mandatory for every Indian child to be incarcerated in the deadly schools, and taking many other steps to increase the death rate. These measures included:

1. November 1910: The government signs a formal contract with the Catholic, Anglican, Methodist and Presbyterian churches giving them full operation of all Indian schools. (21)

2. January 1911: The government stops publishing any follow-up reports on the health and death rate of children after leaving the schools, implementing a 1903 recommendation.

3. 1914-1918: War time emergency powers grants to residential school Principals the power to impress Indian children *of any age* into "labor battalions" and be shipped as unpaid workers anywhere in Canada to do heavy manual labor.

4. March 11, 1919: Despite soaring death rates in the schools, an Order in Council abolishes all medical inspection therein. *(See Figure 5)*

5. April 1920: An Act of Parliament makes it mandatory for every Indian child seven or old to be interned in a residential school, on pain of fines and imprisonment. *(See Figure 8)*

6. Spring 1926: Governments in Alberta and British Columbia – where nearly half of the schools are concentrated – pass laws denying Indians the right to appear in court, file petitions or hire a lawyer.

7. December 1929: The federal government relinquishes its traditional role and makes the churches and residential school Principal the legal guardian of all children therein. *(See Figure 10, above)*

8. 1929-1933: Alberta and British Columbia governments pass Sexual Sterilization laws allowing any Indian school inmate to be involuntarily sterilized at the whim of the Principal. *(Figures 64, 65, 66, 66a)*

The devastating impact of the residential schools on all native people is testified by the demographic records of the Canadian government itself, which shows that during the two decades after the residential schools were first launched and after these special measures were adopted, the net population of Indians across Canada actually *declined*: by over 20% from 1901-1911, and by almost 5% from 1931-1941. *(See Figure 4, above)*

The residential schools not only targeted their imprisoned children for germ warfare and de-population, but the surrounding native communities as well, using the schools and special Indian hospitals as breeding grounds for communicable disease. For it was also a standard practice for children sick with tuberculosis or smallpox to be sent back to their homes to infect their families.

Such a case occurred in October 1919, at a Catholic Indian school in central British Columbia, where the local Indian Agent, H. Graham, wrote to Indian Affairs,

"I herewith beg to submit a report upon the outbreak of smallpox in this Agency, which started by girls being sent home from St. Mary's Mission school suffering from the disease. These were practically all sent into the lower portion of this Agency with the result that I had no less than twenty-seven cases of smallpox ... Owing to these cases there were no less than fifty five who were in these quarantine camps ..." (See Figure 6)

This deliberate infecting of the healthy by the sick never abated. Thirty years later, a petition from aboriginal parents reported that children at the Lejac Catholic School were not kept separate from the sick. *(Figure 67)* Later, an Indian Agent from the same area admitted that during any epidemic in the same Lejac school, "*it is impossible to segregate the pupils.*" *(Figure 68)*
The earlier records from the residential schools show clearly that children sick with tuberculosis were being admitted to the school. *(Figures 69 and 70)*

This germ warfare carried on to modern times. As Delmar Johnny, a survivor of the Catholic Kuper Island residential school relates from his experience as a boy there in 1961, "*They made us sleep and play with all the kids who were sick with T.B. They never tried to separate us.*" (22)

This kind of institutionalized biological genocide is rooted in a "two standards of care" system that allows a certain "tolerable" level of death among the targeted group.

"If we are to operate these schools, we must accept the fact that an inordinate number of Indian children will die within them" declared Deputy Superintendent Duncan Campbell Scott in response to Dr. Bryce's damning report of 1909. In this way, the top civil servant in Indian Affairs legitimated the death rate and even encouraged it by offering a shield of justification over the disease-breeding schools. This same attitude was voiced by other Indian Affairs officials. (*Figures 71 and 72*)

That this double standard thinking and practice was a structural part of the residential school system was revealed in October 1935 by Dr. C. Pitts, who treated children at the Lejac Catholic school in British Columbia. In a letter to the local Indian Agent, R.H. Moore, in which he explained why he hadn't made a complete medical examination of the Indian children at Lejac, Pitts wrote, *"Where is the point of this, when I know that, were I to apply the standards of health to them that is applied to children of the white schools, that I should have to discharge 90% of them and there would be no school left ..." (Figure 73)*

This acknowledgment of a practice of accepting a lower standard of health care for Indian children is a sure indication of a genocidal intent, and calls into question every official announcement, whether then or now, that residential school children were "generally healthy and well fed" - a phrase often repeated in school correspondence and Indian Agent reports. "Healthy", that is, <u>according to the standards applied to Indians</u>, which was a far lower standard than the norm, and allowed countless children to suffer and die at an "acceptable" level that was not considered worthy of reporting. This illuminating strand in the genocide web is never mentioned in the government's TRC report, which operates under the false assumption that official correspondence is reflecting the truth of what was being done to generations of Indian children. On the contrary: rather than mere duplicity, the automatic cover up of the residential schools genocide was <u>structurally integral to the entire system at work</u> simply because no-one causing the crime considered it to be a crime.

This sort of systemic genocide is a killing machine that is unlikely to be turned off while the system that spawned it endures, since it reflects the values and interests of that system. The continued routine killing of aboriginal people at the hands of Canadian police who are never reprimanded is but the most obvious aspect of this grisly historical reality of "acceptable Indian deaths".

B) How many Children Died?

It is quite within the mark to say that fifty per cent of the children who passed through these schools did not live to benefit from the education, which they had received therein. - DIA Deputy Superintendent D.C. Scott, July 1913 (*CBC News, June 3, 2015*)

We couldn't begin an investigation of deaths in the residential schools. It would be too huge an investigation. - Constable Gerry Peters, RCMP "E" Division, Vancouver, July 9, 1997

The odds of a residential school student dying in the early years of the program were one in two. So okay, fifty percent is a fair estimate of the mortality. - Murray Sinclair, TRC Chairman, March 3, 2011

Long before the Canadian government was forced to begin closing Indian residential schools in the early 1970's, it commissioned special "document destruction teams" to gather and shred any files related to the deaths, accidents or registration of students, according to the Canadian press and Member of Parliament Gary Merasty. (23) Conveniently, the same government and its handpicked TRC spokesmen can now claim ignorance of the total number of deaths in the schools over more than a century: inevitably, perhaps, when the perpetrator of the crime is still in power.

While it is true that no reliable figure of total deaths can be deduced from the archival records alone – especially since even the documents not destroyed never accurately report and usually censor accounts of the death of children – the extensive record of death rates from the early reports of Indian Affairs doctors like George Orton and Peter Bryce does provide a foundation for an informed and extrapolated estimate.

Our research team calculated a total figure for deaths in the residential school system, based on records, government statistics, conditions in the schools and extensive testimonies. We initially attained a low figure of 32,000 deaths and a high figure of 73,000 out of 150,000 total attendees in the schools over 107 years (1889-1996), or a death rate of somewhere around 30%. But since these estimates are based on the government's conservative figure of 150,000 students, rather than the more likely figure of 200,000, the number of dead was probably much higher. (24)

Our final calculations are based on examining the following factors: 1. the total number of Indian residential schools, 2. the average number of students in each school, and the length of their stay, and 3. the average mortality rate in each school by decade, commencing 1890-1900 and continuing to 1990-2000, since the last school closed in 1996.

Factor 1: The number of schools across Canada varied from 77 during the period 1900-1930, to a maximum of 130 by 1950 and declining to less than 50 by 1975, giving an average for the century of **103 schools across Canada.**

Factor 2: Calculating the average turnover rates and class sizes across all of the schools, the average residential school had 65 students each year attending for an average 6.8 years, causing between 11 and 14 separate "generations" of attendees.

Factor 3: The average mortality rate in the schools varied between four different time periods, being highest in the early years (1889-1929) and lowest in the final (1975-1996). The mortality rate averaging in each period was calculated as follows: Period 1 (1889-1929): **55%** ; Period 2 (1929-1949): **39%** ; Period 3 (1950-1975): **25%** ; Period 4 (1975-1996): **10%. The total average mortality rate over the entire period was therefore calculated to be 32.2%, or almost exactly one third of all students.**
Since the total number of attendees was likely about 200,000 students, (say one third higher than the official count of 150,000), a simple calculation of the total number of dead comes to 66,600 children over 107 years, or 650 deaths per year, or ten deaths per school every year. But even this figure is still a conservative one, considering that several school records show that far more than ten children had died there in less than one year.

Nevertheless, 66,000 deaths far exceeds the absurdly low level cited by the government's TRC, of no more than 3,200 total deaths, or less than 5% of the actual likely number. Defying both the archival record and simple logic, the TRC would have us believe that only thirty or so children died every year in the schools, or one child every year in every third residential school, for a mortality rate of barely 1.5% - even when the government's own records cite an average death rate of 30% to 50% for many decades! *(See Figures 61 and 62)*

Sixty six thousand unsolved deaths are tantamount to purposeful genocide, while 3,200 deaths can be rationalized as mere negligence and human error. If you were a guilty nation seeking to avoid exposure and prosecution, which figure would you prefer? And yet the truth has no room for expediency or vested interest. The dead require only the truth.

C) The issue of Intentionality, and the exceptional case of Group Crime

The Canadian government and churches, like all parties caught in their own crime, have relied on the "loophole" provision inserted into Section Two of the United Nations Genocide Convention that states that genocide is intent to commit the crime, not the crime itself. This loop hole has allowed regimes guilty of genocide to evade prosecution, Canada included, since it is nearly impossible to uncover a specific intent behind an array of historical actions by a state power.

Fortunately, as early as the publishing of Raphael Lemkin's seminal work on Genocide, in which the term was first coined – *"Axis Rule in Occupied Europe"* (1944) – it has been recognized that the normal legal criteria pertaining to criminal acts by individuals do not apply to such acts that emerge from Group Crime, as in the case of a genocidal regime and culture.

In particular, the normal common law judicial requirement of proving both an act and a preceding intent to commit the act does not apply when entire groups of people are engaged in systemic and habitual crime against another group.

Accordingly, Raphael Lemkin's original definition of Genocide made no mention of "intentionality" regarding this crime. For him, intent was not a factor; genocide meant simply an action - "the destruction of a group" - and that act of destruction by itself demonstrated and implied the intent to commit the crime simply because so many people engaged in it so consistently, and with an obvious murderous result.

Ironically, such a clear and uncompromising understanding of Group Crime indicted not only the Nazis after the war, but also those western powers that committed genocide against their own indigenous peoples, including the governments and churches of Canada and the USA. This was recognized by the future Prime Minister Lester Pearson, who stated in 1952,

"If the original draft definition of genocide introduced in the (U.N.) General Assembly had have remained, we in Canada would have had to close every Indian school in our country, and since that was an impossibility, the Genocide Convention had to be modified." (**Report to the House of Commons,** August 12, 1952)

Both the Canadian and American governments worked hard to revise Lemkin's original definition to protect themselves for prosecution for their own home grown war crimes. The main way they accomplished this was by inserting the following phrase into the draft definition of Genocide:

***"Genocide means the intent to destroy, in whole or in part, any national, ethnic, racial or religious group …"*(our emphasis)**

In short, genocide was re-translated to mean not an action, but an intention: a position as absurd and legally unsupportable as to claim that when a man kills someone and then robs them, the crime wasn't the killing but the man's intent to kill.

This self-serving re-definition was adopted in the final United Nations Convention on the Crime of Genocide (1948). Ever since then, governments and churches implicated in genocide have heavily relied on the "intent loophole" as a safeguard against their own prosecution: especially in North America. Suddenly, the act of genocide itself was not necessarily a crime, and not one that could be prosecuted, unless it could be proven beyond any doubt that the intent to commit these acts was also present. But how does one prove intent by entire institutions?

Proving intent, as any lawyer knows, is always difficult, since it requires inferences about a person's state of mind, something that is to some degree always speculative, and shrouded in doubt and ambiguity: a doubt that allows guilty parties to often walk away free. Nevertheless, when it comes to

Group Crime and Genocide in particular, intent is much easier to discern because it is contained within and inherent in every aspect of the Group's laws, treatment and habits regarding those meant for destruction.

That is, intent is not necessary to prove when it comes to systemic genocide; for such intent can be assumed on the basis of the act itself because of the legitimacy of the act within the genocidal culture. In this regard, the American prosecutor at the Nuremberg trials Robert Jackson, observed,

No regime that wages wars and crimes against entire peoples can be relied on to record their aims in any detail, since the purpose of what they did is inherent in the murderous acts themselves and is demonstrated by the daily operation of their regime. Mass murder requires no justification or rationale by a nation committed to it. For the defense counsel to demand proof of intent in regard to the actions of the defendants is spurious and misleading, since intent is a mental attitude by which an individual acts, and therefore cannot be directly proved but must be inferred from the circumstances. These criteria do not apply to criminal regimes bent on mass murder. In the latter case, the proof of their crime lies not in assumed attitudes or motives, but in the corpses and ruination caused by the daily operation of the regime itself, its laws, and the behavior of its citizenry. (September 30, 1946)

In summary, the entire issue of intentionality in relation to Group Crime and Genocide is a politically motivated issue arising from the need of guilty powers to find legal loopholes through which they can avoid not just prosecution but their lawful disestablishment as criminal regimes.
The bare existence of genocidal crimes indicates an inherent intentionality which is proven in the legal protection, consistency and institutional complicity associated with the crimes.

Echoing the Nuremberg precedent, then, it is not necessary today to prove the intent behind the Canadian Genocide, since by its very nature such a crime intends to exterminate inassimilable indigenous people. This crime has not emerged from random acts by individuals but rather from carefully planned programs and their underlying ideologies basic to Christian Canada. For any such Group Crime proves its own intent, and can and must be prosecuted on that basis.

D. Homicide

After my brother got better he didn't go back to the Mush Hole ... and he said, 'You know what happened to all of those kids who were there? You know what happened to them?' And I said no, and he said, 'They called in the army and they took them to the Army base, and they shot them. They stood them along this big hole and they shot them. When the bullets hit them they fell into the hole. – Lorna McNaughton, survivor of the Anglican Mohawk residential school, Brantford, Ontario

It was scary, finding those little skulls in there. What were those little skulls, where did they come from? Just lying there in that furnace. They were tiny, little ones. Two little skulls. Tiny baby ones. I still feel that fear, running out of there." – Lillian Shirt, survivor of the Catholic Bluequills residential school, Edmonton

But when you enter through these doors, you're like a dead kid walking, a dead man walking. You are not human. Your history means nothing. Your childhood means nothing ... There was absolutely no reason for these places except one thing: Genocide. – Peter Yellowquill, survivor of the United Church residential schools in Brandon and Portage la Prairie, Manitoba.

"Looking for individual cases of murder in the residential schools is like asking why fetuses are killed at an abortion clinic"- Harriett Nahanee, Alberni school survivor, February 9, 1998

In a system designed to "kill the Indian in the Indian", to quote Duncan Campbell Scott, and to also kill the Indian, death was the norm; and to search out individual cases of homicide recalls again the words of Nuremberg prosecutor Robert Jackson, who observed early in those war crimes trials:

"The prosecution need not prove the individual culpability of the death camp guard or of the high state official when the system itself was geared to mass destruction. Any single individual serving such a system is assumed to be complicit and guilty by the fact of his association with it."

That said, individual killings of children by staff, clergy and other students were routine occurrences in the schools, according to many eyewitnesses who saw the murders happen or dug the graves of the victims. Homicide reports even turn up in the heavily-censored official school records, invariably accompanied by a routine vindication of the accused and the refusal by local police to investigate further.

Beatings, gang rapes, forced confinement without food, "disciplinary" tortures like electric shock, exposure to tuberculosis and even formal executions were the usual homicidal methods of school staff and clergy who were literally beyond the law and protected by RCMP and Indian Agents. (25) The first eyewitness to the killing of a residential school child went public on December 18, 1995, at a public protest organized by Kevin Annett at United Church offices in Vancouver. Harriett Nahanee was a ten year old at the United Church school in Port Alberni when, on Christmas eve 1946 she saw Principal Alfred Caldwell kick a student, Maisie Shaw, to her death.

"I was at the bottom of the stairs in the basement. I always went to the bottom of the stairs to sit and cry. I heard her crying, she was looking for her mother. I heard (Caldwell) yelling at the supervisor for letting the child run around on the stairwell. I heard him kick her and she fell down the stairs. I went to look – her eyes were open, she wasn't moving. They didn't even come down the stairs ... I never saw her again." (*Figures 74 and 74a*) (26)

This first report was immediately shrouded in cover up and official denial by police and church alike, who both claim Maisie was "hit by a train", which is what Caldwell told her parents. But in January, 1996 researcher Kevin Annett recovered a provincial death certificate for Maisie Shaw that states she died of "*Acute Rheumatic Pericarditis*": heart failure. (*Figure 75*) But further examination revealed that this certificate had only been entered into the provincial archives the month before, shortly after Harriett Nahanee's account appeared in the *Sun* newspaper.

In a telephone conversation and when asked about this anomaly, Brian Young of the Provincial Coroner's office stated that "There was no death certificate for a Maisie Shaw before last month."

"Is that normal, no death certificate?" Kevin asked him.

"With Indians it is. It probably meant she was just shoved in the ground somewhere."

Nor does the information on the newly-deposited "official" death certificate agree with live witnesses. There is no record for a Maisie Shaw at the Port Alberni funeral home the certificate claims buried her. The fact that the Coroner's report was issued the day after she died is "bizarre and unusual ... that never happens", according to Louise, the Director of the same funeral home.

"I've seen these things before," commented *Vancouver Sun* reporter, Stephen Hume, on Maisie's "death certificate" later in 1995. *"It's just a crude forgery."*

Yet another crudity was the national press release issued by the United Church of Canada – Caldwell's employer – the day after Harriett Nahanee spoke to the media. The church claimed pre-emptively that it "has not engaged in any form of cover up or deception in relation to this sad occurrence". But at that point, no-one had accused them of covering up anything.

A second murder by Principal Alfred Caldwell was reported just one week after Harriett's story went public, by another eyewitness, Archie Frank.

A former inmate at the United Church School in Ahousaht, Archie told *Sun* reporters that he saw Caldwell beat a boy named Albert Gray senseless for taking a prune out of a jar. Albert died the next day and was buried in secret.

"He got strapped to death. Just for stealing one prune, Caldwell strapped him to death. Beat the s..t right out of him ...The day after he got strapped so badly he couldn't get out of bed. The strap wore through a half inch of his skin. His kidneys gave out. He couldn't hold his water anymore ... They wouldn't bring him to a doctor. I don't think they wanted to reveal the extent of his injuries." (Figure 76, "Beaten to Death for theft of a prune" by Mark Hume, The Vancouver Sun, December 20, 1995)

After Albert died, Archie and another boy named Stanley Sam were ordered by Principal Caldwell to bury him in the woods behind the school. Two days before he was to be video interviewed by Kevin Annett, Archie Frank died of undisclosed causes, in January of 2000: the same week that another key witness died - Willie Sport, who was also scheduled for an interview with Annett.

Another former inmate at the United Church School in Port Alberni, Harry Wilson, went public in 1997. He described in an affidavit how when he was fourteen he stumbled across the body of a dead girl on the grounds of the school, and what happened to him when he reported it.

"In 1967, I discovered a dead body behind the Caldwell Hall at the school. Two kids from the Tseshaht reserve and me found a young girl, she was about 16, lying dead, completely naked and covered in blood. There was blood everywhere. I ran and told (Principal) Mr. Andrews, and he said he was calling the RCMP. But I never saw them show up, and the girl's body disappeared ... Less than two months later, after I told Andrews about finding her body, I was shipped out to Nanaimo and put in the hospital there for three months ... I was expelled from the school in 1970. I was sent to the Bella Bella hospital then ... the Mounties had me committed and I was strapped down in bed. I was in there like that for months." (September 17, 1997) (*Figure 77*)

Harry's story gets even more interesting. Recruited by human rights investigators from the U.N. group IHRAAM to speak at a public forum in Port Alberni the following year, Harry was approached by two aboriginal officials of the state-funded Nuu-Chah-Nulth tribal Council, Ron Hamilton and Charlie Thompson. In a signed statement of March 31, 1998, Harry describes,

"Just before I was to talk about the girl I found Ron Hamilton comes up to me and says, 'I wouldn't talk about her if I was you. If you say anything about it, you'll be sorry ... As Nuu-Chah-Nulth Tribal Council official Charlie Thompson left our Circle, he walked by me and said to me, 'Harry, you have half a brain and no-one will miss you if you're found floating face down in the water.' "(Figure 78)

Naturally, Harry didn't say a word at the forum. When he was later found dead on a Vancouver street, Harry Wilson's death received the same attention as had the young girl whose body he found when he was eleven.

Harry's friend Dennis Tallio, another Alberni school inmate, also found a dead body on the grounds of the same establishment, in 1965. According to Dennis, *"We even found a dead body at the school. It was in the fall of 1965. We were playing soccer in the back field behind the school, where it was really covered in weeds ... in those weeds I came across the remains of a body, maybe three feet long. It was decomposed and you could see a lot of skeleton ... I ran to the school, and then we had to call the RCMP ... After that, the RCMP came to us and told us not to say anything about what we had discovered in the field. I thought this was strange. Why would they want us to keep quiet?"* (Figure 79)

The forested hills behind the Alberni residential school hold many of the graves of the dead children, according to Harry, Dennis and other witnesses. In April, 2008 a forensic specialist and his team conducted a survey of the suspected mass burial site in these hills identified by survivors. His survey confirmed what they had reported.

"The land has all the classic signs of multiple burials, the telltale vegetation and the presence of regular sinkholes and the undulating terrain. It covers more than a hundred square meters. That kind of disturbance means that a lot of digging's gone on there. I've examined mass graves in Kosovo and Bosnia and what I saw behind the Alberni School bears all the same features." (Statement of Dennis Ball to Kevin Annett, April 3, 2008; See his survey map in ***Figure 80*** *- sinkholes are circled)*

Based on the Port Alberni evidence and other surveys and eyewitness accounts of burials, on April 10, 2008, Kevin Annett released to the world media a list of 28 suspected mass graves near former Indian residential schools across Canada. *(Appendix Five)* Not a single Canadian media outlet responded to the release, nor did the police.

Another suspected mass grave in British Columbia is on the grounds of the former Catholic Kamloops Indian School: one of the "special treatment" centers where children who ran away more than once tended to be concentrated for particular discipline and punishment. William Combes, who was incarcerated at the Kamloops facility from 1962 to 1964, saw a priest bury a child there one night, in the orchard south of the main building.

"My friend Jessie Jules and me were out scavenging for food for all the little ones since they never fed us regular. It was night but we could see from the moonlight that Brother Murphy was dragging this bag out into the orchard. We watched and he turned it over and a small little body fell out, and he kicked it into the hole with one boot. Then he started throwing the dirt in." (27)

William also witnessed other horrors.

"They had a furnace going twenty four seven that was totally out of bounds. And me and a friend witnessed the sisters and brothers taking what looked like little bodies under white wrappings or white cloths and putting them in to the furnace. The Queen came and visited us for three days and a lot of children went missing then. Many children that weren't cooperative like myself, I wasn't cooperative, they were put with the children who were sick with the tuberculosis. They put me and my brother Ernie in with the ones who were sick because we wouldn't comply." (ibid)

Lorna McNaughton is a survivor of the Anglican Mohawk Indian School – "the Mush Hole" - in Brantford, Ontario. Lorna claims that a group of several dozen young inmates from that school were shot and killed by Canadian soldiers during 1943 or 1944. Her brother Rufus was an eyewitness to the killings, according to Lorna.

"After my brother got better he didn't go back to the Mush Hole ... he said, 'You know what happened to all of those kids who were there at the Mush Hole? You remember that?' And I said, 'Yeah! Our dorm was just filled with girls!' And he said, 'Yeah, so was ours full of boys ... You know what happened to them?' And I said no, and he said, 'They called in the army and they took them to the Army base, and they shot them. They stood them along this big hole and they shot them. When the bullets hit them they fell into the hole. And when they were all done those that hadn't fallen into the hole, some of them were still alive, and some of them were still alive in the hole', and he said they came along and, I want to say a bulldozer, that's what comes to my mind, but I'm not really sure that my brother had said a bulldozer. They came along with a big machine anyway and they shoved them all in that big hole and covered it up. And he says that's what happened to them. I must have been about eight I guess, seven or eight ... let's see, that must have been in forty three or forty four." (From a January, 2012 interview. See https://www.youtube.com/watch?v=RBUd3UXt6fI)

East of Kamloops in Cranbrook, British Columbia stood the Catholic St. Eugene Indian School. Before she died suddenly in early 2004 after confronting the local Catholic Church over the missing children there, survivor Virginia Baptiste described the reign of terror and the local mass grave.

"We called St. Eugene's 'boot hill' 'cause so many kids were dying there from disease. Every second or third kid. I saw a nun lock up a little girl in a closet and she just left her in there to starve to death. They all ended up in that

big grave not far from the school ... After we started our protests and made a big stink, guess what? The feds came in and spent a million bucks covering the graves with a new golf course. The Chief was in on the deal. Everybody knew what was in that ground, but now everyone wants to forget." (See Figure 81) (28)

Virginia's friend Helene Armstrong of the local Osoyoos Indian tribe also attended St. Eugene and knows lots of local history, including where some of it all started.

"I know a lot of the local Doukhobours and they tell me that the first whites into this area got the land from our people after showing the Indian Agent the fingertips of the Indians they'd killed off. That would have been around 1910 or 1920. All of the Naramatas were chased out of Arrow Lakes by bounty hunters hired by gold mining companies. There are mass graves all over the Arrow Lakes region. When all the rez school kids started dying off, they just shoved them in those graves that were already there." (29)

One of the Doukhobours, and a member of the Osoyoos Nation, is Pierre Kruger, who lives near Penticton.

"We spent years documenting all the graves around here because we wanted the world to know. Our mistake was to trust the whites. In 1992, we contacted the provincial government and asked the Heritage Conservation Branch to come out and inspect the mass graves we mapped. We found more than twenty of them between Cranbrook and Nelson. The government people showed up on a Thursday and by Sunday they'd brought in the backhoes and wiped out most of the sites. Completely gone. Since then we don't tell nothing to nobody." (30)

The same pattern repeated itself in Alberta residential schools. A nine year old girl, Vicky Stewart, was killed with a two-by-four one morning in April, 1958 at the United Church's Edmonton residential school. The killer was a school supervisor named Anne Knizky.

Little Vicky's sister Beryl saw it happen.

"We were running in from the yard and, just because we were running, that's why (Knizky) hit Vicky" Beryl told the Vancouver Province newspaper in May, 2009. *"First she got me in the back with the two-by-four and then she got Vicky over the head. Then by next morning they told us she had died."* (See

Figure 82, *picture, and* **Figure 83**, *"Family says school staffer killed 9 year old girl sister" by Sam Cooper, Vancouver Province, May 28, 2009*)

The "official" cause of death for Vicky was tuberculosis. The RCMP and the United Church still stick by that story, and refuse to investigate further, despite Beryl's eyewitness account. Significantly, the Edmonton school Principal when Vicky was killed was the same Alfred Caldwell, who killed two children on the west coast years before according to witnesses Nahanee and Frank. (*Figure 84*)

Interviewed for Kevin Annett's award-winning documentary film *Unrepentant (2007)*, another Edmonton residential school survivor, Doug Wilson of the Haida nation, describes burying kids at the same school in 1961.

"I don't know how all the other kids died, but I know we dug a lot of graves. Lots from the school, but also from Charles Camsell (Indian hospital) ... I couldn't figure out after that why I couldn't remember anything. Then I read in your book about shock treatment ... All I remember is they had me down and I kept seeing these flashing lights and then nothing. I guess it was to make me forget." (31)

Sylvester Green was another student at the United Church's Edmonton school, and was also interviewed for *Unrepentant*. In the fall of 1962, he and three other students buried an Inuit boy who was beaten to death by Principal Rev. Jim Ludford, according to Sylvester's companion Mel Patzie who witnessed it.

"There were four of us who dug the grave: myself, my brother, Mel Patzie and Albert Cardinal. It was right next to the staff garden. The boy was from up north somewhere ... Every Sunday in church Mr. Ludford used to preach to us and he always ended by saying, 'Remember: the only good Indian is a dead Indian.' And we all had to repeat his words." (32)

Lillian Shirt was an inmate of the nearby Catholic Bluequills Indian School.

"Late one night there were three tiny little ones that were brought in by their mother. And they cried so much that the nun took them and put them in this room here. This was the storage room for our winter coats and our rubber boots. And those little ones were brought in there. We heard them cry for a long time. All of a sudden you'd hear them gasp like "uuhh!" and we never heard them after that. Never saw them the next day. We don't know. We asked what happened to them but nobody knows what happened to those three little ones. "

James Whitehawk, a Cree man who lives in Regina, saw a priest drown a small boy in a cattle trough and then bury him behind the Catholic Indian School in Camstock, Saskatchewan in the spring of 1965. When James mentioned the incident to other children at the school, he was committed to the TB sanitarium in Boissevain, Manitoba for several years, despite being healthy. *(From a June 4, 2001 interview)*

The total number of homicides in residential schools can never be known, considering their systemically violent environment and the continual official secrecy surrounding children's deaths. In a basically homicidal system, no death can or should be considered accidental or unintended.
What is certain is that none of those who killed innocent children at these schools were ever arrested, charged or tried before a court of law. Rather, the killers were shielded and protected by those courts, by their church employers, and by every level of government in Canada.

In the words of Doug Wilson, *"The only reason I survived that place was I learned to use a knife when I was a very young boy, and I stole food whenever I could. It turned me into something I wasn't, but that's what makes a survivor."* (33)

Other Contributory Causes of Death

As we have described, the primary cause of the enormous mortality rate in residential schools was the staff's deliberate spreading of tuberculosis and smallpox between sick and healthy children, accompanied by a denial of all care and treatment for the infected. Any of the deaths arising from this murderous practice could only have been deliberate, for the simple reason that human beings do not die easily or immediately from tuberculosis.

Tuberculosis is a wasting and debilitating disease that only kills after many weeks, once the host's immune system has collapsed. Logically then, for so many children to have died so consistently from T.B. they had to have been deliberately denied proper food, warmth and other of life's essentials for long enough to allow the germs to have their deadly effect. And such indeed were the standard conditions deliberately maintained in every residential school across the country, as doctors, Indian Agents and public records continually reported.

The fact that this policy of deliberately creating sickness among residential school children was emanating from the highest level of government was described by the Indian Affairs medical officer, Dr. Peter Bryce, who had first reported on the enormous death rates in the schools.

In his book **A National Crime,** published in 1922, Bryce claims that 93% of Indian children suffered from tuberculosis after entering a residential school, but that only ten cents per Indian was spent by the government on combating T.B., compared to over $3.00 for every white Canadian with T.B. He also claimed that the federal government deliberately encouraged the overcrowding and poor conditions in the schools and successfully pressured the Canadian Tuberculosis Association to ignore the whole issue. *(Appendix Three)*

Years before Bryce's report, a chief inspector for Indian Affairs summed up how residential schools were a threat to the health of all its young inmates when he said in an official letter,

"Whatever good the children may receive through residence in a boarding school will be at the expense of the health of all and the lives of some. Of the truth of this statement we have the indisputable proof of long and uniform experience." (Figure 85)

Even the most diehard proponents of residential schools, like Principal A.R. Lett of the Anglican St. George's school in Lytton, British Columbia concurred with this estimate when he arrived at the school.

"The children were lean, anemic and T.B. glands were running in many cases ... The children were ill clothed and turned out into the cold to work and without leadership ... Dormitories in bad repair, no

cleaning had been done for years, floors worn out in many places, ventilation poor, beds absent or broken down. Small wonder parents had to be forced to place their children here." (34)

Mabel Sport, a survivor of the Christie school on Meares Island between 1935 and 1944, recalls:

"The food was always rotten and inedible, the dorms were always cold, and we were never even given winter clothing. They starved us and froze us until we all came down sick... I can't even stand to look at nuns anymore. They were trying to deliberately infect us with TB because they always made me sleep in the same bed with girls who had it. One on each side of me. I was so scared, so I slept turned away from them, even under the bed sometimes. I'd always open the windows, too. But then the nuns would come and close them and even nail them shut." (35)

Photographic proof of this practice of mixing the sick with the healthy is found in Figure 86, taken from John Miller's book **Shingwauk's Vision** (1996). The photo shows a class of Sarcee Indian children in the Anglican school on their reserve early in 1912. Two of the students who are sitting among healthy children are wearing bandages around their heads, and the caption states they are suffering from "active and open tubercular sores." *(Figure 86)*

It's significant that the two infected, bandaged boys in the photograph - Reggie Starlight and Ronald Big Bear - were both the children of hereditary tribal chiefs, according to a relative of Reggie. As Harriett Nahanee, Steve Sampson and other witnesses have described, the offspring of the "blue blood" traditional leaders were the primary targets of rape and killing in the schools, in the same way that many of the missing aboriginal women today come from hereditary clan mother tribal leaders.

Eyewitnesses experienced this practice of deliberate exposure to children sick with tuberculosis. Besides William Combes' aforementioned description of being housed with TB infected kids as punishment, others attest to this practice.

"They put us in the same room with people who had TB. They didn't separate us" describes Delmar Johnny in the 2007 film *Unrepentant*, from his days at the Catholic school on Kuper Island, British Columbia, during the late 1950's.

Virginia Baptiste describes the same thing at a Catholic school in eastern British Columbia during the 1960's.

Then we were forced to play with them. The nuns made us play with those kids. We didn't want to get sick either but the nuns were forcing us to play with those kids. And also they made some of them sleep with the other kids. (Unrepentant, 2007)

Besides maintaining the unhealthy environment needed to lower immunity and breed tubercular infections among children, the staff of residential schools uniformly terrorized their little inmates with routine, habitual violence. Hourly bed checks during the night, random beatings and organized gang raping of students of every age were the norm. (*See Appendix One*)

This reign of terror is described by survivor Del Riley.

I spent five years in what the Canadian government calls residential schools but they were really prisoner of war camps. I was in the one they called the Mohawk Institute. They starved us, beat us, they froze us. It was horrific. There were no controls in the place. Kids were always getting beat up or being put through various torture rituals. A lot of the kids were tortured in there. They were made to hold onto hot pipes until they couldn't hold on anymore, or they just fell to the floor from the roof. They were beaten when anyone felt like it, and made to hold onto electric fences ... I would love to see the perpetrators severely punished for all of this. The greatest thing I would want to see is the Church of England to get barred from practicing in Canada. (From an October 9, 2011 interview)

And similarly, in the words of Peter Yellowquill, who endured years at the Brandon and Portage la Prairie United Church schools in Manitoba,

"But when you enter through these doors, you're like a dead kid walking, a dead man walking. You are not human. Your history means nothing. Your childhood means nothing. They had their choice of victims. Here in the washroom the molestations would go on in here also. There was absolutely no place to run, the children were absolutely defenseless. The RCMP even if they were told they wouldn't have come. There's no record of the RCMP ever laying one charge against the pedophiles, against the people who assaulted us and assaulted our friends, I mean beat them down. This isn't just a few slaps on the wrist. Boards, two by fours, whips, anything: even shovels. And not one charge has ever been laid. We don't know where the graveyard is, we don't know where the bodies are. But if it's like Brandon we know that there's bodies out there. There was absolutely no reason for these places except one thing: Genocide." (From a videotaped interview with Peter on location at the Brandon school on March 5, 2007) George Brown, who survived the Catholic Coqueetza school in British Columbia, says, *"When we got to the residential school we never did go to school. We were never fed. We were always starving. And the mental abuse was there, the physical abuse. And they treated us like animals. They'd throw food at us. Kids would be screaming throughout the night, and the screams never stopped. So we lived in constant fear."*

In addition, every staff member was expected to carry on them at all times a "prescribed leather belt" with which to flog students. Those who refused to carry it were often fired on the spot by the Principal, normally a clergyman, who under church regulations had absolute power to hire and fire staff, censor their letters and phone calls and have them arrested by the local, compliant RCMP. *(From a list of regulations at the United Church Alberni school circa 1962, see Appendix Nine)*

The existence of this military-style hierarchy in every residential school was necessary in order to maintain the high degree of secrecy and information control required in a killing zone. The outside world could not be allowed to know the fate of so many suffering children. Accordingly, humane staff members who showed sympathy for the children tended to be weeded out quickly and fired.

Marion MacFarlane was one such staffer. Speaking at a public forum in Vancouver in early 1998, she described her experience at the United Church School in Port Alberni in the mid 1960's.
"I only worked at the school for nine months until I got canned by the Principal, Mr. Andrews. It happened because I saved the life of a little girl ... One morning I came across one of the other matrons

beating this girl viciously with a piano leg. The blood was flying, it was terrible. So I grabbed the woman and I belted her and knocked her cold. But then I got called before Andrews and he fired me for hitting the woman. Me, not the one beating the girl!

"When I objected to Andrews and said how she was killing that little girl, Andrews just smiled and said, 'Nothing that would have happened to that little squaw would have been as bad as losing your colleague. She plays the organ in church on Sundays.' *That showed me where the children ranked in the scheme of things. We were expected to go along and let them die if we wanted to keep our jobs."* (36)

As mentioned, records show that T.B. infected children were routinely admitted into residential schools without any screening or examination. Examples of such admissions occur in the documentary record in the years 1919, 1924, 1937 and 1952, in different schools across B.C. and Alberta: the two provinces where germ warfare, medical experimentation and sexual sterilization against Indian children were especially concentrated throughout the 20th century.

Many of these murderous actions also occurred in state-funded and church-run Indian hospitals, especially in isolated west coast communities like Sardis, Bella Bella, Nanaimo and Prince Rupert. These hospitals operated as fronts for grisly experiments under the guise of tuberculosis sanitariums. Children were deliberately infected with TB and then studied as they died, or used as involuntary test subjects for drug testing.

In 1963, Joan Morris of the Songhees nation on Vancouver Island was imprisoned in the Nanaimo Indian Hospital. She was just five years old. Joan was held there for over six years and experimented on by military doctors.

"They told my mother I had tuberculosis but I didn't, I was perfectly healthy. That was their excuse. They shipped me off to the Nanaimo Indian Hospital after that ... They used me like a guinea pig. I was strapped down in a bed for months at a time. They took out some of my rib bones and parts of my lungs, and they even broke all the bones in my feet; I've got X rays of that.

"They also injected me with drugs that made me sick all the time. They made me drink something that

later I learned was radioactive iodine. After I was there awhile I did come down with TB but they must have infected me with it because nobody there had TB when they arrived.

"I saw lots of other Indians kids in there too, all of them like me: healthy when they arrived, then they all got TB and a lot of them died off. The doctors and nurses let it happen ... I remember the doctors there, Dr. Weinrib and Lang, Schmidt and Connelly, they never helped the kids, just stood around and took notes. They'd give kids the shots and they'd get the TB and die." (37)

The Indian hospitals relied on the residential schools as a source of easily obtained experimental subjects whose disappearance could go unquestioned. Kenny Quatell was one of those disappeared.

Kenny is an Indian from northern Vancouver Island who was abducted from a local hospital in Campbell River in 1964 when he was five years old. His parents were told he had died during an operation. He was incarcerated in the Nanaimo Indian Hospital for years, until he was a teenager. *"They had me in the dark room all the time, giving me shocks to my head. My brain still gets a kick from that now and then. I was given drugs that made me sick but then I had to eat whatever I threw up. It went on like that for years. I got the sense it was the army running things. Later during my treatment, my doctor in Campbell River told me I couldn't see my medical records because it was a matter of national security.*

"I have to say that I saw a lot of other Indian kids pass through there. They were dying like flies all the time. I saw them burying them in the woods west of the hospital." (From a videotaped interview in Nanaimo on August 12, 2005)

The disposal of children's' bodies at both the Indian hospitals and residential schools was handled routinely either by incineration in school furnaces, mass burials or dumping bodies in nearby lakes or oceans.

Marie B., a survivor of the Catholic Shubenacadie Indian School in Nova Scotia, witnessed the dumping of children's remains in a large reservoir lake west of the school grounds.

"Those bones must still be there, they were dumped around 1962 sometime. I remember it because Sister Gilberta had just ordered me to burn all of the leather straps the staff carried around with them. The school was getting closed down and they were getting rid of the evidence I suppose. But I hid one of the straps and I still have it." (From an interview on October 12, 2015)

The mass graves at the Catholic school in Mission, British Columbia described by survivor William Combes are known to local police, who refuse to investigate. In a letter to Kevin Annett dated February 3, 2008, a Mission news reporter and former city councilor named Ron Taylor stated, *"For over a decade I have known of the babies buried behind the old girls' dormitory in Mission Heritage Park. I was actively discouraged by several parties from pursuing this issue ... I am painfully aware that pursuing this to a conclusion will be extremely unpopular with certain parties – the Sto:lo chiefs, the RCMP, Mission Council and of course the Roman Catholic Church ... Others are aware of the mass graves you mention, including even some of the Sto:lo chiefs and their former archaeologist Gordon Mohs, although they do not want the issue pursued. There has been no attempt to disinter ... The RCMP DO have some evidence. But they almost pleaded with me not to pursue it. One of them said, "Please leave this alone. Nobody responsible is still alive, so what is to be gained?"*

E. Imposing Measures to Prevent Births and Conception

"You're a good Christian, Ed. Have lots of children. I only sterilize the pagans"- Dr. George Darby sr., United Church missionary doctor, to Ed Martin of the Hesquait Nation, Bella Bella, B.C., 1952

There is no more clear an act and intention of genocide than attempting to stop a targeted group from procreating, by preventing both conception and births, and by killing the newborn. The existence of laws to legitimate these crimes and to allow involuntary sterilizations of a specific group confirms the intent of a government and nation to wipe out that group.

Canada passed such laws between 1929 and 1933 (*Figures 64-66a, above*) and they were aimed specifically at Indians and Metis people. Within dozens of residential schools, Indian hospitals and special research centers on military facilities, many thousands of Indians were made infertile simply because they were Indians, or for "disciplinary" or experimental purposes. These programs sprung from a wider Eugenics movement that originated in America during the 1880's and spread like wildfire through Canada as the 20th century dawned. Many of the leading Eugenicists practiced on Canadian Indians and residential school children, including Nazi researchers brought into Canada after World War Two under the infamous Project Paperclip. (38)

According to author Edwin Black, in his book **War against the Weak: Eugenics and America's Campaign to Create a Master Race** (2003),

"In Canada, eugenics passions became inflamed over many issues, including the birth rate of French Canadians ... Following the example of America's hunt for mongrels, Alberta disproportionately sterilized Indians and Metis, who constituted just 2.5 per cent of Canada's population, but represented 25 per cent of Alberta's sterilized." (39)

In effect, any step designed to disrupt or destroy the ability of a group to perpetuate itself can be considered genocidal eugenics, including by separating males and females at a young age and alienating them from their families, traditions and normal sexual and biological functions. All of these crimes were intrinsic to the Indian residential school system.

Sterilizations

Intrusive, radiological and chemical sterilizations of residential school children began in earnest after the passing of the Sexual Sterilization Acts in British Columbia and Alberta between 1929 and 1933, and continue to the present day. The operations were normally performed at Indian hospitals or even in clinics of larger Catholic, Anglican and United Church residential schools.

Jackson Steene is a Dene Indian man who was sterilized as a child at the Carcross Anglican residential school in the Yukon, one of the last schools to close, which it finally did in 1996.

"I guess it would have been sometime around 1969 or 1970. They did the procedure to me and all ten of my brothers when we were at the school, just before we reached puberty. One after another. I was taken into the infirmary and strapped down onto a gurney and wheeled under an X ray machine. They

positioned it over my pelvis and left it on me for at least ten minutes. I didn't know what it was at the time; they told me they had to scan me for tuberculosis. But I was never able to have children. Neither could any of my brothers who got done that day. I tried suing the Anglican Church years later but my lawyer wouldn't raise the sterilization thing in court." (40)

Another Anglican school in Alert Bay also sterilized children. Cambel Quatell, a Kwakiutl man from Campbell River, B.C. was made infertile in the local church-run St. Joseph's hospital.

"I could never talk about this shit for years but now more of the truth's coming out. I led the fight for compensation around here but everyone's too chicken shit to talk about the sterilizations. Well it happened to me and all seven brothers of mine except James, he's the only one of us who could have kids. They gave me some vile shit to drink and then gave me a shot and I don't remember anything after that. I hurt pretty bad after that but I never put two and two together. One of the priests used to call us his 'lab rats'. Something went on there around 1962 that made me infertile; me, and a lot of other kids too." (41)

Especially intelligent indian children with high marks, or those who were more independent or confrontational with the white authorities, tended to be targeted for sterilization. Sam Adolph went to the Catholic Kamloops School and was sterilized there in 1959 when he was fourteen.

"They called us the 'red tag' boys. At the end of each term they'd hand out the red tags and if you had one you had to report to the clinic. That's where I got cut. I don't know who the doctor was, he was from somewhere else and we never saw him again. But he fixed me so I could never have a kid." (42)

The R.W. Large Hospital in Bella Bella, British Columbia, which is still in operation, was a major sterilization center for at least forty years. Established as a United Church missionary clinic by Rev. Dr. George Darby senior, (1889-1962) the hospital has received major federal government funding. Dr. Darby and his son, Dr. George Darby junior, personally sterilized many hundreds of aboriginal women at the facility between 1930 and 1962, often simply because they weren't Christians or wouldn't attend church. *(See Figure 87)*

The late Ethel Wilson was one of his victims.

"Darby was king in Bella Bella and Waglisla, and his word was law. He sterilized a lot of us. He used to watch who wasn't going to church in the village. He said to me once, 'Ethel, you'd better go to church if you don't want the treatment.' That was around 1949.

"Well, I had my appendix out the next year and that's when Darby did me when I was under. I knew something was wrong when I woke up. My insides really hurt and all my gold teeth were missing. Later I found out in Vancouver I'd had my tubes tied. That went on all the time with the women on our reserve, even recently." (43)

Ed Martin, another resident of Waglisla, spoke to the IHRAAM Tribunal in 1998 about Dr. Darby.

"I went to Darby around 1952 to get a vasectomy 'cause I couldn't feed all my children, but he just laughed and he said, 'Ed, you're a good Christian. Have lots of children. I only sterilize the pagans.'
I guess he liked me 'cause I went to his church. Later he told me the government was paying him $300 for every Indian woman he sterilized." (44)

The R.W. Large Hospital kept annotated records of all the sterilizations, until many of them were destroyed in 1995 soon after the residential school atrocities began to make news in British Columbia. According to Christy White, a former hospital employee, all of the sterilization records were "*dumped in the ocean*" by an administrator named Barb Brown.

Steve Sampson, a traditional Chemainus elder on Vancouver Island, claims to have seen samples of the Bella Bella sterilization records when he and other members of the Red Power movement occupied Indian Affairs headquarters in Vancouver during the summer of 1973. Perhaps not accidentally, Steve's own two sons were subsequently sterilized.

"They got my eldest son in 1975, when he was just four. The cops took him to Victoria General Hospital and fixed him so he couldn't carry on our line, which is royalty, we are the Siem of our people. They've always been trying to destroy us. My second son was sterilized when he was nine, in 1981. Both times they were grabbed by the Mounties when I was away. It was Dr. Bowen-Roberts and Dr. Boaker who

supervised the operations. They were both Indian Affairs doctors who worked for the government. They're buddies with the Harris family on our reserve, the sellouts who were set up by the Crown as puppet chiefs many years ago. I also learned that our local doctors in Duncan were sterilizing our people, Dr. Styles and Dr. Henderson, right on Ingram street. It's all out in the open but nobody will talk about it." (45)

Traditionally, any aboriginal person could be targeted for sterilization under the law. Sterilizations especially occurred in regions of rich natural resources still occupied by Indians, or in areas more densely populated by off-reserve or traditional indigenous groups. Sarah Modeste, who lives not far from Steve Sampson in Duncan, B.C., was sterilized by a government-funded doctor in 1951 after she married a non-assimilated, traditional chief.

"Doctor Goodbrand heard that I was going to marry Freddie, and he got so mad. He came to my home and said, 'Sarah, if you marry Freddie I'll have to do an operation on you.' I was really scared after that and I tried to get away, but we couldn't leave the reserve without a pass back then. But the next year after Freddie and I were married I got pregnant with our daughter. Goodbrand was the only doctor we were allowed to see. So when I gave birth it was Goodbrand who did the delivery, in the King's Daughters Clinic in Duncan.

"When I woke up I was bleeding a lot and it wouldn't stop ... Later I learned that my tubes had been tied. He did it to me when I was unconscious I guess ... I couldn't have any more children after Dr. Goodbrand did that to me. But that happened a lot to our women. It was still going on in the seventies and eighties." (46)

Eliza Stewart, a Gitk'san woman living in Vancouver, has confirmed that Indian women were still being sterilized by the government in the 1980's. In 1987, she was forced to undergo a tubal ligation by order of a social worker named Sally Heather in North Vancouver.

"The Ministry had already taken my daughter from me, and my worker, Sally Heather, told me that if I ever wanted to see her again I'd have to have my tubes tied. She said, 'You Indians have too many children as it is. This is for your own good.' So it was done in a north shore hospital after two mounties

came to my home and took me away. I've never gotten over that. No lawyer will touch my case, and none of the doctors who did it will talk about it." (47)

Finally, an insider in the system of hospital-based sterilizations, a former nurse named Pat Taylor, shared her knowledge with the IHRAMM inquiry in June, 1998.

"I worked for two years as a relief nurse at the Prairie Training School (PTS) in Red Deer, Alberta. That would be 1956 to 1958. The school was a front really, a place where all the scooped up kids were brought for sterilizing: lots of vagrant and runaway kids, unwed teenage moms, really just ordinary people. And PTS policy was to sterilize all of them if they'd reached puberty, no exceptions. There was no consent involved. That included a lot of Indian kids. The Mounties used to bring them to us in big batches, mostly from the Edmonton (United Church) residential school. They all got sterilized." (See Pat's separate affidavit in Figure 66) (48)

In Ontario, aboriginal women have been routinely used as involuntary test subjects in clinics to try out experimental birth control devices like the IUD, and in the process have been sterilized. Lynn Sharman, an aboriginal community worker in Thunder Bay, has documented these experiments over many years.

"The aim has always been to stop Indian women from conceiving. Starting in the fifties, Cree and Ojibway women were locked up in the Lake head Psychiatric Hospital and pumped full of experimental birth control drugs. I have a list of over three hundred of them who died from these experiments and were never reported buried. The Crees around Fort Albany found a death register, all of them with the names of women who died "under surgery". It was when they needed guinea pigs for the IUD. They'd insert it and watched what happened, looking for the best way to stop procreation among the savages. All the doctors used to talk like that. They're just more discreet now." (49)

These individual cases are tips of a much bigger iceberg of crime. *The Globe and Mail* reported in December, 1979 that Health Canada was distributing birth control pills to pre-menstrual Inuit and Dene girls without their knowledge; and that the government had an "unofficial" policy of sterilizing Inuit women after a certain number of childbirths. (*Figure 88*)

In addition, government doctors have employed a lactation suppressant known as "Agalactia", a "non-intrusive sterilization method", against native women for decades, according to Renee la Fortune. Renee was a doctoral student in Toronto whose academic career was cut short after she made her discovery of Agalactia public. Similar accounts abound. (50)

The growing body of literature on the ongoing sterilization of "third world" peoples indicates that since 1980 as many as one third of all aboriginal women in some western American states have been chemically sterilized by vaccines as part of tribal" public health programs". Independent studies also claim that sterilizing agents have been found in World Health Organization (WHO) serums used to immunize Asians, aboriginals and Africans against polio and other diseases. (51)

And straight from the "horse's mouth", the Director of the WHO's Expanded Immunization Program, and architect of the Vietnam War, Robert MacNamara, told a Paris journal in 1996,

"One must take draconian measures of demographic reduction against the will of certain populations. Reducing the birth rate has proved to be impossible. One must therefore increase the mortality rate. How? By natural means: famine and sickness." (52)

Earlier in his career, President Obama's chief scientific adviser John Holdren stated,

"A program of compulsory sterilization of women after their second child might be easier to arrange than the mass sterilization of men ... Alternatively, adding a sterilant to drinking water or staple foods can only be effective if it was uniformly applied." (53)

Murder of Newborns, Forced Abortions and Segregation

"And they took the baby into the furnace room and they threw that little baby in there and burned it alive. All you could hear was this little cry, like 'uhh!'..." (54) - Irene Favel, survivor of the Catholic Muscowequan residential school, Saskatchewan, 1944-1949, from a CBC TV interview, July 3, 2008

"When I was in Senior B, the girls would get pregnant but they'd never have their kids, you know. They'd bring in someone who'd do an abortion. It was scary, we'd hear the incinerator door being opened and

hear the big clang, and we'd know they'd be getting rid of the evidence ... We'd wonder how many kids got thrown into that incinerator."- Eddy Jules, survivor of Catholic Kamloops residential school, quoted in Behind Closed Doors: Stories from the Kamloops Indian Residential School, Secwepemc Cultural Education Society, 2000

"I'll never forget those little skulls we found inside the furnace - tiny ones, like from babies."- Lillian Shirt, survivor of Bluequills Catholic Indian school, Alberta, 1949-1958

By definition, the late night killing of unwanted newborns or fetuses will not be recorded in any record besides the memory of those who witnessed it. There are many such bystanders, who as children were pressed into service by priests or staffers who buried or incinerated the evidence of their impregnation of Indian girls. But the bystanders included insiders who have talked.

Former Port Alberni school employee Marion MacFarlane, mentioned earlier, witnessed regular child trafficking of Indian girls who would end up pregnant.

"We used to call the school 'The White House' because of all the big shots who'd show up to pick out little boys and girls. Sometimes I recognized a local cop or judge. It was just like a slave auction, they'd line up the children and some would be picked and taken away. Often the girls would come back pregnant, and we'd drive them to the West Coast Hospital for an abortion. Sometimes the girls would make a fuss and you wouldn't see them again. I think they're buried out past the old water pipeline in the hills behind the school, them and those newborns." (55)

Local hospitals near to the residential schools were regularly used to dispose of newborns or fetuses from native girls, or even from impregnated nuns. These hospitals included West Coast General in Port Alberni, St. Paul's catholic hospital in Vancouver, St. Joseph's Anglican hospital in Alert Bay, the R.W. Large Hospital in Bella Bella, B.C., the Charles Camsell hospital in Edmonton, the Lake Head Psychiatric hospital in Thunder Bay, and many local church-run clinics.

In the same way that tuberculosis sanitaria provided the institutional cover for deliberately infecting or experimenting on Indians, regular hospitals became child disposal centers: not just for body removal but, as child trafficking from residential schools became more lucrative, to circulate children for sale to the highest bidding pedocide. (56)

The enslavement of children to grueling labor and as sexual chattels was a structural feature of the residential schools. Their trafficking provided a source of young bodies for sex rings and medical experimentation. But it also served a broader genocidal purpose in permanently destroying kinship ties and estranging the aboriginal generations and sexes from one another: a prime aim of any genocidal regime. This intergenerational estrangement is a structural feature of aboriginal families in Canada and a primary cause of the ongoing destruction of native societies.

The alienation of native siblings and relatives from each other was as fundamental to the residential schools as was the suppression of all native languages, and was even reflected architecturally in the standard "H" block design of most Indian residential schools whereby the sexes were kept strictly segregated. Unlawful mixing of the sexes was often punished severely. *(See **Figure 89** for a blueprint of the standard "H" architecture of an Indian residential school)*

Nan Johnson never saw her little brother for the entire seven years they were both incarcerated in the catholic school on Meares Island during the 1960's.

"I didn't recognize my brother Tom when I saw him again, it had been so long ... We were never allowed anywhere near the boys or into the boys' dorm, it was locked away from us anyway. But one of the girls couldn't stand not seeing her brothers and she tried creeping over to them one night. But she was caught and the next day we had to give her the Gauntlet treatment ... We were all given belts and heavy sticks by the nuns and we had to beat her as she ran down our line. She couldn't even walk after we were done with her." (57)

The long term consequences of such inter-generational estrangement have been catastrophic on aboriginal families. Child abuse, marital violence, divorce and incest are between ten and fifteen times higher among natives than non-natives. The continuing epidemic of child trafficking on and off Indian reservations, often aided and abetted by state-funded tribal council chiefs themselves, is as big a threat to native survival as is the drug trade-related gang violence on many reserves today.

The late Harriett Nahanee, who survived the Alberni residential school, described the child trafficking trade operating from her Squamish Indian reserve to Vancouver establishments.

"The same black stretch limousine will pull up late on Friday nights, usually after midnight. This one night last year I saw two little kids loaded into the back. They were maybe eight or ten years old and all dressed up fancy with make up on. They were stumbling like they'd been drugged.

"So I got my son to follow the limousine and it dropped the children off at the back of the Vancouver Club. A reporter with the Aboriginal Drum newspaper named Noel, he staked out the back door of the Club and at 3 am or so the kids came out the door, looking all dazed and mixed up. Noel started interviewing them and then he got hit on the head. When he woke up his recorder was gone and so were the kids. They never showed up on the reserve after that. Nobody knows what happened to them." (58)

A year after the IHRAAM Tribunal, in the summer of 1999, a UNESCO report on pan-pacific child trafficking named Vancouver and Bangkok as major hotspots for the crime, *"where organized pedophilia (sic) goes on with extensive police, judicial and political protection . Of particular abuse is the widespread trafficking of indigenous children who are abducted off their traditional territories, often as part of a bigger strategy to intimidate and control aboriginal families in order to seize their lands and resources"* (59)

F. Forcibly Transferring Children from one group to another

"Every Indian child between the ages of seven and fifteen years who is physically able shall attend such day, industrial or boarding school as may be designated ... The Superintendent General may appoint any officer or person to be a truant officer to enforce the attendance of Indian children at school, and for such purpose a truant officer shall be vested with the powers of a peace officer, and shall have authority to enter any place ... Any parent, guardian or person with whom an Indian child is residing who fails to cause such child ... to attend school as required by this Section ... shall be liable on summary conviction to (a) fine and imprisonment ..."

- from the amendment to the Indian Act establishing Indian Residential Schools, 10-11 George V, Chapter 50, July 1, 1920, Parliament of Canada

"Sawyer has not sent his two children to the local Residential School. Constable Burroughs will assist the Indian Agent in having Sawyer's children removed to the Residential School at Kuper Island under sec. 35 of the Indian Act. Sawyer will be prosecuted if he does not comply."

- Telegram from Inspector C.R. Peters, Commander, RCMP Vancouver Island Section, December 11, 1942 to Indian Agent, Cowichan Agency, Duncan, B.C.

Since the autumn of 1948, the act of forcibly transporting children from one group to another is considered to be genocide and an indictable crime under international law. Yet until 1996 within the residential schools, and still to this day through foster care and government "child welfare" agencies, this genocidal act against aboriginal children occurred and continues with impunity at the hands of the government, churches and private corporations. (60)

Such a forcible transfer and alienation of Indian children from their culture was the very *raison d'etre* and fiber of the residential school system. The bare existence of that system itself is enough to condemn it as genocidal. Its massive kidnapping and incarceration of nearly a quarter of a million native children between 1889 and 1996 was always coercive, involuntary and violent.

As Harriett Nahanee recounted in 1998,

"My parents hid me before the Mounties arrived, and I watched everything from under the steps of our house ... They had their guns drawn and they were clubbing down all the men and rounding up every child in our village, even the three and four year olds. Everyone was running around and screaming ... They had all the children tied together by a rope and they dragged them off onto the RCMP gunboat. The cops kept grabbing and slapping the children who were screaming and crying for their mothers. I couldn't watch it ... Later when I got taken I found out that two of my cousins had died on that boat. They just threw their bodies overboard." (61)

The violence of the residential schools' round up of children was deliberate and flowed from the insistence by the churches that children be incarcerated year-round in residential or boarding schools rather than day schools.

In an 1888 letter from Alexander Sutherland, head of the Methodist Church in Canada, to Indian Affairs in Ottawa, Sutherland said "… *we think it most important that provision should be made for Boarding Schools, and also for Industrial Institutions, where the children can be kept for a series of years away from the influences which surround them on the Reserves* ..." (*Figure 90*) (62)

The churches were assisted in their plan to rob Indian nations of their children by force. Aboriginal chiefs themselves often aided the rounding up of young natives, with the guarantee that their own children would be spared the ordeal of residential school if the chiefs collaborated. Chief Paul White of the Nanaimo band was one such quisling. On December 4, 1935 he was paid $54 by the local Indian Agent to transport reserve children into the Nanaimo day school. Chief Thorne of the Cowichan band near Duncan was paid to do the same hatchet job for many years. As a reward, none of his children ever had to go to a residential school. (*Figures 91 and 92*)

Upon entering the average residential school, all aboriginal children regardless of their age were uniformly stripped, their hair shaved off completely as noxious and poisonous DDT powder was showered on them, and they were given a standard prison-like uniform with a number on it. They could no longer use their real name but had to respond to the number. In many cases, mandatory rape was inflicted on every child, especially those who would not cooperate. And any child who continued to use their native language was beaten and tortured mercilessly. (63)

Older native students collaborated with the school authorities and were trained to supervise and even assault arriving groups of children. Vera Hunt of the Ahousaht nation remembers the day she arrived at the United Church School in Port Alberni in the fall of 1963.

"*There were three hundred of us lined on the beach in the rain. We were all shivering and crying. The white people weren't even near to us, just watching from in the school. These guys carrying whips walked up and down the lines, and whenever we spoke our language they started beating us and screaming. It turns out they were Indians too, but you couldn't tell that at first. Later I learned to use a knife when I was just eight years old and that saved my life.*" (64)

As a masquerade of legality over the abduction of their children, all native parents were forced to sign an "Application for Admission Form" that legally surrendered legal guardianship to the residential school Principal, normally a clergyman. This form proved the ultimate legal liability of the churches for the crimes and damages within their Indian schools. *(Figure 93)* (65)

The conditions in residential "schools" were more akin to labor camps than educational facilities. A letter from a Deputy Indian Affairs official to an Indian Agent in Fort Fraser, B.C. *stated "the Department considers the boys should be at work six and a half days per week"*, and outlined the heavy labor students as young as ten should be engaged in on residential school lands, including tree cutting and clearing, farm and field work, and construction. The "primary aim" of educating Indian females should be towards training them as domestic servants and kitchen help. (66)

A United Church policy statement from its General Council meeting in October, 1935 confirms this genocidal aim of creating a race of aboriginal "hewers of wood and carriers of water":

"In our residential schools we are teaching our young wards to be successful farmers. Nothing will so dispossess the Indians of their nomadic habits and traditional ways than to bind them to the soil and make them practical artisans, since it is their attachment to their culture and traditions that has created the Indian Problem in the first place." (See Figure 9)

In keeping with this goal of de-educating natives, teachers in the residential schools were rarely qualified. Schooling was minimal and irregular, confined on average to some two or three hours of instruction a day, and then on largely religious topics and rudimentary learning. Higher education was deliberately shut off to Indians as a matter of unwritten policy. (67)

A clear example of this policy is referred to in a letter from Indian Agent Edward Frost to Indian Affairs in Ottawa, dated August 18, 1934, in which Frost urges the Department not to provide funds for the higher education of five Alberni residential school students who are "above the ordinary run of intelligence".

States Frost,

I fail to see where a High School training is going to benefit them, as all classes of employment are now over stocked with white students ... I am not making these remarks as pertaining to the above mentioned pupils only, but I consider they apply generally to Indian pupils, at least in this Agency ..." *(Figure 94)*

According to Lillian Shirt, a survivor of the Bluequills Catholic school in Alberta,

"*We weren't allowed to laugh. We weren't allowed to read. We had no books. If we were ever caught reading ... whew! Look out! We weren't even allowed comics. All we ever got in class was long lectures about the Virgin Mary from some stupid old nun. That was it. We were never educated at all.*" (68)

This explicit policy of deliberate de-educating and "dumbing down" of a conquered people is a basic feature of genocide everywhere in the world, and was foundational to the Indian residential school system in Canada.

Like any battlefield, residential schools were the same kind of mixture of the mundane and the quickly violent. These conditions often caused children to run away. The RCMP was deputized by the government during the 1930's to act as the police arm of the schools, and its officers tracked down and returned the runaways. But any private citizen could be deputized to do the same, and school Principals often hired private vigilante "slave hunters" to find the missing children.

These vigilantes had unlimited power to break into any home and seize anything and anyone without a warrant, and then charge the runaways with juvenile delinquency, which allowed any native child to be jailed and criminalized like an adult.

When runaways were returned to the residential schools they faced mandatory, extreme and sometimes deadly punishment. At the United Church's Alberni School, returned children were routinely locked in a basement cold storage locker for days without food and water. If they survived, they were stripped naked and beaten in front of the other children as an example and a warning. (69)

At the St. George Anglican School in Lytton, British Columbia runaways faced a medieval-like brutality, as admitted by a former Principal, Canon Charles Hives in a letter dated June 21, 1942:

"... two girls ran away and they were chained together and driven home in front of the Principal. They used the shackles to chain runnaways (sic) to the bed. They also had stocks in the playgrounds. And they were used." (Figure 95)

According to another former employee at St. George's, *"First offense was just a flogging. Second offense, the kid got the stocks and then was manacled to their bed for a week. Sometimes we'd find a dead child in the stocks, especially in winter. No allowance was ever made for the weather. Mr. Lett, the Principal, he used to parade the children around the school in chains."* (70)

The late Virginia Baptiste of the Osoyoos Nation ran away several times from the St. Eugene catholic school in Cranbrook. Each time she was captured she was beaten unconscious by nuns holding wooden brushes. After her third escape at the age of nine, she was given an "ice water" torture.

"Those bastard nuns made me stand in ice for hours. I lost all feeling in my feet and legs and I still haven't recovered from it. After I passed out they beat me until I woke up. The damage was permanent. I was just nine then and I'm fifty eight now and I can never seem to get warm. I've never been able to walk right since that day." (71)

In 1942, Willy Sport had his feet deliberately deformed as a child in the United Church School in Port Alberni by the Principal, Mr. Pitts, in order to prevent him from running away.

"The second time they caught me Pitts made me wear these shoes that were too small. He never let me take them off. I was just six and still growing. My toes got all twisted and the bones got bent. I could only hobble around. Been that way my whole life. But some other kids had their feet smashed with a hammer after they got caught, so I consider myself lucky." (Figure 96) (72)

One of the most torturous aspects of children's incarceration in the residential schools was the vicious "divide and conquer" system of management used by the school staff. Children were incited to inform on, attack and molest one another. Those who informed on their fellows received better food and less punishment.

"We called them the Goon squad" said the late Delmar Johnny of the Cowichan nation to researchers in the fall of 2006. He was recounting his years in the Kuper Island catholic school.
"They were always better dressed than the rest of us. They were in the protected group. Nobody else was protected, we were all fair game for the rapists on staff. The goons got the pick of any of us too, just for ratting on us whenever the staff needed to know who was planning what." (73)

Ominously, these "goons" often went on to receive a better education and acquire political power in the local native hierarchy, becoming tribal council officials who often continue to terrorize their own people for the same white masters.

"Things in the aboriginal world never change" reflected Haida native and Edmonton school survivor Doug Wilson at a University of Victoria forum on Genocide in Canada in the fall of 2007.

"The very same people who used to abuse us as lackeys for the white man in residential school are doing the same thing today on our tribal councils. They tell all of us to heal and get our lives together, but they've never dealt with their own shit. They're ordered by Ottawa to sell us out and give away our land for nothing, and they do it. That subservience is still wired in to them. Our so-called leaders are our biggest roadblock to progress, and that's mostly because of residential school. It was set up that way to debilitate us over the long run and make us incapable of governing ourselves." (74)

G. Inflicting conditions designed to cause long term destruction

"I have before pointed out that the Indian death rate is terribly high; that our medical advisers attribute the frightful mortality to tuberculosis ... that in my opinion, we are taking no effective steps to reduce the death rate ..." (Figure 97)- West Coast Indian Superintendent Dr. Ian MacRae to Indian Affairs Deputy Superintendent Duncan Campbell Scott, February 6, 1903

" ... if matters are allowed to proceed, as they are proceeding today, it will be but a short time before the Indians are wiped out of existence by this disease." (Figure 98) - Letter of Dr. C.J. Fagan to Dr. Peter

Bryce, Chief Medical Officer for Indian Affairs, July 7, 1909

"If the schools are to be conducted at all we must face the fact that a large number of the pupils will suffer from tuberculosis ... While it is true that they die at a much higher rate after entering the schools, such is in keeping with the policy of this Department, which is geared towards the final solution of the Indian Problem."- Letter of Indian Affairs Deputy Superintendent Duncan Campbell Scott to Major D. McKay, Inspector of Indian schools, British Columbia, March 7, 1910

Genocide is never a series of isolated acts but a continuum of purpose, which is clearly evident in the physical conditions in which a targeted group is forced to live and die. These conditions are the template for the future, eventual destruction of that group.

We have observed how the residential schools were deliberately maintained in a substandard condition to foster and spread tuberculosis and other communicable diseases: a practice that can account for the enormous number of deaths from the normally containable and treatable tuberculosis. This "contaminant imperative" required that all of the physical and psychological conditions in the schools be equally as destructive to the long term survival of Indians.

"In no single instance in any school where a young child was found did it not show signs of tuberculosis, made worse by the practice of admitting children suffering from the disease ... What is unfortunately too certain is that whatever good the children may receive through residence in a boarding school will be at the expense of the health of all and the lives of some." (See Figure 85)

When an Indian school Inspector named William Chisholm wrote these words on September 22, 1905, he was recognizing that *all* the Indian children had tuberculosis, and that *all* of them in the system were unhealthy just by being there. But despite this awareness, lower level officials like Chisholm acted as if they did not understand the genocidal purpose of the residential schools.

Like the proverbial elephant in the living room, the proof of this purpose has always been before Canadians in stark detail. For like the enormous death rate, the examples of unhealthy and deadly conditions in the residential schools remained unchanged, decade after decade, despite warnings, protests and calls for improvement.

These examples abound in the residential school documentary record from 1896 to the 1960's *(Some original documents are too faded or illegible for reproduction in this report):*

April 24, 1896: *"It is remarked that many children apparently healthy on their admission to the different schools, are affected with tuberculosis"* (Hayter Reed, Ottawa) *(Figure 99)*

September 3, 1903: *"Our charges lack the most elementary requirements of sanitation and any fresh food whatsoever"* (Donald Jamieson, File Hills, Alberta)

February 14, 1909: *"Nothing is being done to provide for the children, who are even forced out of doors in the winter"* (Sr. Ruth Cluharty, Regina)

October 1, 1915: *"Of 163 students, 98 of them are sick with the pox and the rest are too ill to attend classes"* (C. C. Baker, Lytton)

June 13, 1922: *"Since the Home started forty-nine had died and fifty were still alive"* (RCMP Cpl. R.W. Clearwater, Ocean Falls to RCMP Command, Prince Rupert) *(Figure 100)*

April 10, 1923: *"The children were lean, anemic and T.B. glands were running in many cases"* (Rev. A.R. Lett, Lytton) *(Figure 101)*

May 6, 1927: *"...during the past winter thirteen pupils of this school have died, four of whom were buried within the past three weeks ... " (C.C. Perry, Indian Agent, regarding the Anglican school in Lytton, BC) (Figure 102)*

February 8, 1929: "The nature of *the present water supply and the so called toilet system is a positive menace to health ... And it is not to be wondered that there has been in recent years a very unusual number of deaths ..."* (Rev. W. Wood, Ahousaht) *(Figure 103)*

June 30, 1938: *"this building can only be described as a fire trap and a menace to health ... sanitary arrangements are terrible"* (P. D. Ashbridge, Port Alberni)

March 27, 1939: "*Children in residential schools are inclined to grow away from the life of the Indian band and are unable to fit anywhere as functioning citizens*" (Conference of United Church clergy, Ottawa) *(Figure 104)*

September 30, 1942: "*Under the present arrangements the school does not remotely satisfy the usually accepted standards of sanitation ... I have therefore decided to condemn the buildings of the residential school as unsuitable ...* " *(Dr. F. Burns Roth, M.D., regarding the Anglican Carcross school, Yukon) (Figure 105)*

January 6, 1946: "*when children were sick at the residential school at Lejac they were not kept separate from the other children*" (Nautley Indian Band petition) *(See Figure 67, above)*

March 2, 1953: "*Morale was very low among the children who are generally sick, listless and withdrawn no doubt because of the harsh regime of punishments they must endure ...* " (Mrs. E. Riley, Alert Bay)

June 1, 1960: "*the overcrowded and unhealthy quarters in which the boys are expected to live have not improved since our last inspection over a year ago*" (A.L. Smithe, St. Mary's Mission)

In the course of the research that went into preparing this report beginning with the earliest healing circles and public forums in Vancouver in the spring of 1997, a total of over twelve hundred residential school survivors in seven provinces were interviewed at some point. Of these, three hundred and fifty eight survivors agreed to have their statements made public and be quoted.

A survey of the latter's statements found this commonality of experience when it came to the conditions they endured between the years 1932 and 1981 in thirty eight different residential schools run by the Catholic, Anglican and United Church: (*See Appendix One and Two*) (75)

- Rancid or contaminated food
- Insufficient clothing
- Unheated and unventilated dormitories
- Permanent isolation from family, friends and love

- A daily environment of indiscriminate violence, racism, random and undeserved punishment, and unalleviated stress
- Regular exposure to sick children and those suffering from the flu or tuberculosis
- No regular medical care or examinations
- No regular visits by government agents or care workers
- Continual physical and sexual assaults
- Regular deaths of fellow students that were never investigated
- Punishment for speaking their native languages, including extreme tortures
- Forced, unpaid labor

Reflecting on these monstrous conditions, Edmonton school survivor Sylvester Green said in March, 2007, *"We can never recover from what they did to us and now what we're doing to ourselves. The worst part is we passed on everything to our children: the alcoholism, the drugs, the violence and rape. All this 'healing' talk is just for white people."* (76)

Echoing Sylvester, Kevin Annett observed in his testimony before the IHRAAM Tribunal that the majority of native men and women he encountered in the local Vancouver "healing circles" had never attended an Indian residential school– they were the offspring of school survivors – and yet they bore exactly the same degree of dysfunction, addiction and shortened life expectancy as their parents. This pattern is found everywhere across Canada. (77)

The long term destructiveness established among all Canadian aboriginals by the schools' brutalities is clear to anyone who visits and Indian reservation or the poverty-stricken urban ghettos in which three fourths of Indians live: conditions that are permanent and inter-generational. Even Canadian government studies confirm this.

On October 12, 1998, an Indian Affairs study reported in *The Globe and Mail* revealed that, if grouped as a nation, aboriginal people on reservations in Canada had a standard of living sixty third in the world, below that of Mexico and Thailand. Off reserve natives ranked thirty fifth. (*Figure 106*) (78)

Similarly, contrary to popular belief, tuberculosis has never been eradicated in Canada. As of 1985, TB rates among Indians were over forty times greater than in non-Indians, afflicting between 29.4% and 44.5% of aboriginals, or an average of more than one third of them. (*Figure 107*)

According to Carol Martin of Vancouver's Downtown Native Women's Center, *"You're fifty times more likely than a white person to die from poverty or disease if you're an Indian in Canada, and over two hundred times more likely to be in prison. Nearly half of the inmates in Canada are Indians, and we're just two percent of the population. Hundreds of our women have gone missing and their disappearance is being covered up by the police. And they say genocide is a thing of the past!"* (79)

This level of suffering among aboriginals is in truth on the rise. And this isn't simply because of a genocidal legacy; Indians are being deliberately kept dependent and powerless, and thereby even more open to destruction, by government policies and Canadian law.

In the words of Raphael Lemkin, the original author of the U.N. Genocide Convention,

"The targeted group must be rendered and then maintained politically stateless and powerless as part of its long term destruction".

The Indian Act of Canada, which is still in effect, has traditionally been the primary means to ensure aboriginal statelessness.

Under that Act, all reserve Indians are legal "wards of the state in perpetuity", meaning forever, at least as long as "Crown" authority endures. As "wards" Indians have no legal identity or self-governance, and are in the same category as a child or mentally incompetent individual. Reserve Indians cannot even refuse medical treatment or elect their own autonomous band council, since the latter can be dismissed at any time by the federal Indian Affairs minister.

In addition, reservation children can be seized at will, whether on or off reserve, without any legal recourse: a fact that accounts for the startling fact that more aboriginal children are in white foster homes today than were ever in residential schools, with the same destructive consequence on their health and cultural identity. (80)

If Canada really was trying to put away its genocidal past and "never repeat the mistake of residential schools" (to quote the flaccid words of Prime Minister Stephen Harper in his official "apology" of 2008), then why is it structurally and legally maintaining Indians in genocidal conditions today? The truth is that the actions of state and church in Canada are today exactly as they were a century ago when it comes to Indians: deceptive, self-serving, and murderous.

H. Causing Bodily and Mental Harm

"They were always getting us to fight each other and rat each other out. The older boys all wanted to be like the whites and carry their own leather strap to beat up anyone they wanted. Everybody knew that you could get attacked or molested at any time. When you grow up around that you let it take over you because there's nothing else you can do. There was nowhere to hide in residential school. You either became a slave or a sellout."- Harriett Nahanee, December 1, 1995

The entire Indian residential school system was a single, enduring act of violence designed to cause permanent bodily, spiritual and mental harm to its inmates. This essential reality can become lost in its details: a reality that is ongoing because it has forever marked its victims. For example, Harry Lucas, a Vancouver Island Indian who endured the Kuper Island Catholic School as a boy, was arrested many times as a man on charges of indecency and prostitution. As he explained in 2006, as part of his appearance in the documentary film *Unrepentant,*

"I didn't know why I liked dressing up like a woman and doing it like I was one until I started my therapy and I remembered what went on in Kuper Island ... The nuns used to dress me up like a girl and prepare me for the priests by shoving broom handles and plungers up my ass. You had to go along with them or you'd be beaten to death. I saw it happen to other boys who they did the same thing to ... I just blanked out after the first time and never fought them after that. Now I can't look at myself in the mirror." (81)

This kind of psychological trauma was as severe as the physical, and started the moment children were abducted by school clergy or the RCMP. According to Larry Lavoie, a Cree elder from Alberta,

"I was just eight years old, which would have been in 1959. They grabbed me right out of my mother's arms and locked me in a closed grain truck, shoved in like cattle with lots of other boys. We drove a hundred miles to the Ermineskin rez school in that sweltering and dusty tank and by the end some of the boys were dead. But that wasn't the worst. The first time I cried for my mom a nun slapped me around and tied fish twine to my penis. She'd tighten it whenever I cried. Sister Denise her name was. She loved to smash our heads against concrete pillars. My cousin Jackie died that way. He went crazy first. The Sister told me after Jackie died, 'I'd do that to every one of you stinking little savages if I could." (82)

According to church "punishment logs" entered into court by government lawyers during the first lawsuit of 1996, routine tortures were used against children as young as four by staff and clergy in all of the denominational Indian schools.

Based on this evidence, Judge Donald Brenner of the British Columbia Supreme Court made the remark that *"the Indian residential schools were part of a system of institutionalized torture and pedophilia." (From his judgment of June 6, 1998)*

The evidence reveals that these routine tortures used on residential school children by all of the churches included the following acts: (83)

Shaving of heads with dull razors, beatings with brass knuckles, leather straps and pieces of metal, floggings with a whip, rape by individuals and organized gangs, confinement in small closets for days without food and water, forcing students to eat regurgitated or rancid food, outright starvation, electric shocks to the head, genitals and gums, forcing students to throw their pet mice into furnaces or beat their pets to death, extracting or filling teeth without painkillers, shoving needles and nails stuck through tongues, hands and limbs, forcing students to stand naked in the snow, the use of manacles and public stocks, confining students for days in the rain or snow, forcing students to watch others being raped, beaten, tortured and killed, and forcing them to commit these acts on others and then burying their dead bodies.

This is but a sample of the organized atrocities inflicted on residential school children, as elaborated in Appendix One. These tortures were not random but calculated and prescribed, and were as prevalent in 1960 as they were in 1930.

For example, at the June 1998 IHRAAM hearings, two different school survivors from the same United Church's Alberni school – Harriett Nahanee and Dennis Tallio - described having their teeth extracted without painkillers by school dentists more than thirty years apart. Alberni school staffer Marion MacFarlane confirmed in 1998 that local Port Alberni dentists "*were given the option of cutting their cost by not using Novocain when they yanked or filled our students' teeth.*" And a fourth eyewitness, Alia Point, says the same practice went on at her Chehalis reserve near Sechelt in the late 1960's. *(Figure 108)*

Records confirm this torturous practice on children, and that is actually spanned at least over a half century. For documents from the Indian Affairs archives contain a report by a dentist, Dr. E. Fraser Allen of Vancouver, dated May, 1924, in which Allen carefully annotates the names and ages of those Indian children to whom he administered anesthetic when he pulled or filled their teeth, and those whom he denied painkiller. There were seventy of them, aged between seven and fourteen years, and they were all inmates at the St. Paul's Catholic Indian school in North Vancouver. *(Figures 109 and 110)*

Electric chairs were used in the basements of the United Church's Alberni residential school and in Fort Albany, Ontario in the St. Anne's Catholic school to punish children and to "entertain visiting dignitaries", to quote a *Globe and Mail* article of October 21, 1996. Two surviving victims of the St. Anne's school chair described their ordeal. (*Figure 111*)

In their words, as cited in the *Globe and Mail* article:

"They would put children in it if they were bad. The nuns used it as a weapon. It was done to me on more than one occasion. They would strap your arms to the metal arm rests, and it would jolt you and go through your system." (Mary Anne Nakogee-Davis, tortured in 1963)

"I was six years old. There was no sense of volunteering or anything ... Once the thing was cranked up, I could feel the current going through me ... Your legs are jumping up, and everyone was laughing.

(*Edmund Metatawabin, tortured at the same facility in 1953*)

For these same dental and electrical tortures to be inflicted on children decades a part in the same facilities indicates a standardized method and policy regarding discipline and punishment – and apparently, entertainment for white people – rather than simply being random sadistic acts by individuals. It was an accepted norm in the residential schools to torture children, even to death.

The daily mental torture was, as Harriett Nahanee described earlier, just as brutal and destructive in the long run; especially when inflicted on helpless and dependent children at a formative age. Once again, there was a purpose behind this assault: to not only psychologically break children into obedient slaves, but to identify and mold those from among them who would one day act as the "assimilated" political stooges of the government and corporate interests.

Turning native children into these kinds of "*ab-originals*" - "*those not from an original group*", according to Webster's Dictionary – involved a sophisticated and systematic brainwashing program requiring unrelenting terror and trauma. In that sense, the Indian residential schools were not simply extermination centers, but heavily monitored re-education camps to weed out "expendable" from "salvageable" Indians, and to train the latter as future neo-colonial puppets.

Experimental Mind Control, MKULTRA and the residential schools

School survivors' therapists have long pointed out the prevalence of "Stockholm Syndrome" characteristics among many of their patients, whereby those who suffered the most extreme tortures and deprivations in residential schools nevertheless identify with and even defend the system, and avoid confronting their torturers. But this tendency is part of a larger pathology deliberately engendered by church and state in these schools, especially after World War Two, when military researchers flocked to the isolated and secure environments of residential schools to exploit the perfect young test subjects interned there.

In hindsight, the creation of a large pool of such human guinea pigs, preconditioned into split personalities by the degree of their torture at a young age, became a Cold War purpose behind the residential schools. After 1952, the CIA MKULTRA program required such a population of prepared test subjects for their extensive research into mind control and how to fashion unquestioned obedience in soldier and civilian populations. For its experimental human fodder, the Agency drew heavily on captured populations found in prisons, asylums and Indian schools. (84)

Two documented examples of this military-led research involving Indian children include the "Sara Hunter" case and the activity of Nazi-trained medical researchers at the Kuper Island Catholic School before and after World War Two. The Sara Hunter story is told separately in the book by that name - listed in our Bibliography – and is a remarkable account of the extent to which Nazi researchers penetrated Canadian political and military circles during the 1950's and '60's. For our immediate purposes, the Kuper Island account is most relevant.

In 1932, responsibility for the Catholic Indian School on Kuper Island on the west coast was given to the Montfort Order, a Dutch-German Catholic sect with ties to fascist movements in Europe. In January 1939, the Montforts brought to Kuper Island a group of *"about a dozen German speaking doctors"*, according to eyewitness Dennis Charlie, who survived what happened next.

"They took us out in batches of twenty five, boys and girls" recounted Dennis in an interview in June of 2005 on his Penelakut Indian reservation near Duncan, British Columbia.
"I was ten at the time. There were boys in our group a lot younger than that. They marched us into the infirmary and lined us up so the Germans could examine us. The German doctors weren't from around there, they needed translators to ask us questions ... Then they gave us injections in our chest. Two needles, near each nipple. We started falling down right away. It made us sick, dizzy, some of us passed out ... Two of us got so sick they died later from the shots. One of them was my friend Sandy Mitchell. But they took him over to some hospital in Vancouver and studied him before they died. Another boy told me he'd seen Sandy on the ward with him: he was all bloated up and oozing some bad shit. But they told us he died of pneumonia." (85)

Soon after this incident, three boys who had been injected ran away from the school, and local police were informed of the experiments. Unusually, the police refused to return the boys to the school, and a week later all of the Montfort Brothers resigned and were replaced by the Oblates. The

German doctors vanished until 1947, when some of them appeared again. Arnold Sylvester, who had been one of the boys in the original group injected, recognized one of the doctors living in the town of Duncan. But the tight security around Kuper Island prevented any further inquiries.

While not going into detail about the Sara Hunter case, it is relevant to note that one of the children who was killed at the Calgary air force base when Sara was held there from 1956 to 1958 was a boy named Sandy Mitchell: the name of the Kuper island boy supposedly killed "at a Vancouver hospital". According to Sara, among the test subjects tortured and killed by the head doctor at the Calgary base were *"lots of local Indian kids, and some even were brought from the west coast from some Catholic school there."* (86) The doctor's official name was Major Bob Armstrong, and he carried the SS tattoo designation 091374 SS. (87)

Much of this covert experimental research using aboriginal children was coordinated by the Canadian military's Defense Research Board through its two major facilities: the National Defense Medical Center (NDMC) in Ottawa and the Defense and Civil Institute of Environmental Medicine (DCEM) in Toronto. Both facilities were supervised by Dr. Roger LaFortune of McGill University in Montreal, who worked closely with the CIA's post-war Project Paperclip and many Nazi scientists and researchers smuggled through Canada.

Dr. LaFortune's adopted daughter, an aboriginal woman named Renee LaFortune, was used in experiments at both facilities when she was a young girl. In an interview in Victoria, British Columbia in the spring of 2006, Renee described,

"Originally I was part of a batch of children from the western Arctic who were transported by military airplanes to the (Catholic) Shubenacadie residential school in 1962. We were designated as 'sick', but none of us were. They farmed us out from there to local Catholic convents where kids were being starved and killed all the time, like at St. Michael's convent near Newcastle, New Brunswick. There's still a big grave there of all the children who died after being locked away without food and water. It was some weird experiment.

"Eventually I was sent to the NDMC in Ottawa where I met my adopted father Roger. I was given a lot of drugs there, used like a guinea pig. They inserted experimental birth control devices in me even though I was only eight. I met some of the German scientists at the NDMC including an SS doctor. They were all working under RCAF (air force) covers. (Note: See testimony of "Sara Hunter" concerning the RCAF air base at Lincoln Park near Calgary) *I saw them kill children in decompression chambers and during the ice water immersion tests. That would have been in the mid sixties.*

"Later in my life I couldn't let it rest and I did my own research when I was doing my Anthropology degree in Toronto. I came across lots of evidence from Roger's files that a massive program to sterilize Inuit and western native women had kicked in right after the war. It was a military driven thing but the Catholic Church was heavily involved through its German order called the Montforts (Note: See testimonies of Kuper Island survivors including Dennis Charlie). *But my faculty wouldn't approve my thesis and I got blackballed in the academic world after that.*

"By the way, I got in touch recently with an alumni group of former students at the Shubenacadie school. Of their 1971 graduating class of two hundred children, only two are still alive." (From an April 16, 2006 interview)

Another survivor of these experiments is Bea Maguire. Now in her eighties, Bea was used in the McGill University mind control experiments run by Dr. LaFortune's colleague in crime, Dr. Ewen Cameron. During the 1940's when she was still a child, Bea was abducted from her Catholic school and transported to the Montreal Neurological Institute (MNI) where she was imprisoned until her teen years. According to Bea, like many other children she was used sexually and experimentally by the leading Canadian neurologist and much lauded "humanitarian" Dr. Wilder Penfield. In her words, *"Penfield had two sets of cages for his experiments: one cage for the white kids and the other for the Indians. Those were from the local reservations and Indian schools. They never lasted long. I saw Penfield actually strangle one of the Indian boys on the operating table when he kept fighting back. But my father had been in the military and he was a member of something called The Club, so Penfield went easier on me.* (Note: "The Club" is a designation for a suspected Satanic network among Anglo-Canadian elites in Montreal).

"Penfield was trying to erase and control memory and thinking. He pioneered brain surgery and was linked up to all that CIA funding coming out of the MKULTRA program. He did everything on us, electric shocks, surgery, drug induced seizures. That kind of thing went on constantly at the MNI, there's even been lawsuits by the Duplessis Orphans over what happened to them there, but of course they didn't go anywhere. It was all heavily protected and government funded from at least the 1940's. Penfield's own grand daughter Wendy used to talk about it openly with me because she'd been part of it too. She said her grand father had told her she was making a great sacrifice for the free world or some such nonsense." (From an interview in March of 2013)

On October 2, 1998, shortly after the IHRAAM Tribunal, Kevin Annett received an anonymous phone call from a man who claimed to be a retired member of the Canadian civil service. The call came from an unlisted number. At one point the recorded conversation reads:

Caller: You're just scratching the surface but it still has a lot of people here concerned.

Kevin: Concerned about what exactly?

Caller: You had some people from Kuper Island at your thing ... (undecipherable) can't let them talk about the German connection.

Kevin: What connection?

Caller: ... the whole thing, uh ... the gentlemen's agreement, with the Americans and the churches. They provided the kids, the Force brought them to us ...

Kevin: By Force you mean the RCMP?

Caller: Yeah, that's correct. Kuper Island was isolated and perfect. Lots of the DND (Department of National Defense) research money went there. And to Calgary, the Lincoln Park thing you mentioned, that was bang on.

Kevin: With Sara Hunter?

Caller: Correct. It all came from the Pentagon originally. How to make the perfect obedient soldier. The Germans had started up the research before and during the war, and we perfected it. The churches were cooperative from the start. The agreement was they'd provide a quota every year and have them delivered ...

Kevin: Are you talking about children from the Indian residential schools, just so we're clear?

Caller: Correct. It went on for years, at least from forty six to the seventies, well, maybe earlier, the Catholics had their own thing going too but lots of that is classified ... (undecipherable) ... known to lots of people. But there'll never be an official acknowledgment, no way in hell. That's why we never spoke. This is for only you, understood?

Kevin: Okay.

Caller: Hell, nobody'd believe you anyway. (88)

The Indian schools were one aspect of an enormous crime against humanity involving social engineering, where violence and terror were used to fashion a permanent slave class of compliant aboriginal "leaders" and a majority of traumatized, impoverished underlings: the two tiered aboriginal society across Canada that is really a model for a future, globalized Corporatocracy. The residential schools were one laboratory in which this new world order began to be fashioned.

The Genocide is enduring. And now it affects all of us.

I. Destroying indigenous ways of life, cultures and souls

"We often talked about our right as strangers to take possession of the district, especially as it was evident that we had taken the land not simply through the work of our missionaries but at the point of a cannon ... There is little doubt that colonization has meant the displacing and extinction of the native population. But this impending execration of a vanishing race should stimulate the English settler to acts of humanity towards them ... The whole question of the right of any people to intrude upon another and to dispossess them of their country, is one of those questions to which the answer is always the same."- Gilbert Sproat, Provincial Government Land Commissioner, British Columbia, 1883

"When the Mounties came in and deliberately shot over 30,000 of our sled dogs during the sixties, it destroyed our nomadic way of life as a hunting people. All our men started drinking. In not even a generation our people fell apart. After that, everybody went on welfare. We just lost our reason for living." - Alice Joamie of Iqaluit, speaking before the independent Qikiqtani Truth Commission of the Inuit nation, June 2008

"You want to know what really killed all my friends at residential school? They died of broken hearts." - Virginia Baptiste, survivor of St. Eugene catholic school, Cranbrook

Genocide tears up the identity of a targeted people by its roots by driving them off their land and the traditions that form the cornerstone of their means of survival. From its beginning in the 16th century, the Canadian holocaust of Indians aimed to do exactly that, and it has never ceased.
The banning by law of the west coast tribal Potlatch redistributive feats in 1885, the same year colonial Canada was linked by railway, was perhaps a more obvious example of this intent. But the uprooting of tribal ways of life involved as well the extermination of the buffalo that sustained tribes on both sides of the border, the banning of all aboriginal salmon fishing on the west coast, and the prohibition of traditional shamanistic practices of the plains Indians. And of course the violent elimination of native languages was a major coup against genuine indigenous self hood.

The assault continues. Of the more than fifty aboriginal languages still in use in Canada in 2015, only three will still be alive by mid century, or even sooner. And since under Canadian law, no funds allocated to Indian reservations are allowed to be used there to create long term employment or alternative economic practices, the gradual extermination of any traditional people still on their land seems virtually guaranteed. (89)

Even more blatantly, the RCMP and corporate interests are today waging an unrelenting war against traditional tribes still on their land. The Uranium cartel Cameco, closely tied to the American military and both the ruling Liberal and Conservative parties, has displaced and poisoned thousands of northern Indians, just as it has done in the Black Hills of South Dakota against the Lakota nation. And on the west coast, where notorious collaborating "chiefs" like Ed John have signed away huge tracts of native land to water and mining conglomerates in both America and China, not only aboriginal women but entire villages are disappearing into the night. (90)

No doubt because of the severity of this escalating genocide, Canada has gone out of its way since 2008 to create the appearance of "healing and reconciliation" and a "new deal" with aboriginal people: claims that, like Vatican announcements of reform, change nothing in practice. Ignorant of their own history and society, most Euro-Canadians accept the claim uncritically.

However, an appreciation of real Canadian history is the best antidote to both ignorance and complicity: a fact that should compel people of conscience to begin teaching these facts in Canadian classrooms. For even a cursory look at this hidden history reveals the deliberate and ongoing nature of the Canadian genocide, in as simple a matter of how the diet of children in every Indian residential school was designed to cause sickness and death, and long term destruction.

This "dietary imperialism" within residential schools was examined by the IHRAAM Tribunal of June, 1998. After most of the witnesses who spoke to the Tribunal described never being fed regularly while in residential schools, and of consequently developing serious health and diabetic problems in later life, some of the IHRAAM judges focused on the basic issue of why children were being denied food and care so routinely and deliberately.

On the final day of the Tribunal, residential school survivor Sharon Blakeborough was asked why she and none of her fellow students were ever fed properly. Blakeborough, a survivor of St. Mary's Catholic school in Mission, B.C. from 1961 to 1969, replied,

"They wanted us dead, that's the short answer. Why else would they starve us, and then give us rotten baloney and maggot filled porridge while the white staff and the priest ate steak and eggs? I always tried to get on the garbage detail so I could scoop out their throwaways. I was just five at the time. I've got diabetes now and I'm only forty one. That's normal among my people." (91)

Government statistics show that, paradoxically, after the 1920's and in all denominations, the annual expenditures for residential school supplies, including food and clothing for students, tended to diminish the longer a school was in operation, and the larger it was. That is, children got less care and worse food the more "successful" and financially solvent the school became.

This pattern was due not only to the clear genocidal purpose of these places, but because of the nature of the residential schools as big money making operations for all of the churches involved. Originally, many of these schools were situated purposely on or near valuable resources and lands, including rich fishing grounds, mining deposits or pastures desired by white settlers.

For example, a May, 1919 letter from the top Indian Affairs bureaucrat, Duncan Campbell Scott to the local Member of Parliament for Port Alberni reveals that the Alberni residential school was deliberately relocated to allow access by white people to the local lands they coveted for settlement. *(Figure 112)*

In addition to this big land and resources grab, residential school Principals made money by hiring out students as slave labor to local farmers in return for kickbacks, and sexually trafficking young girls and boys to local wealthy whites. (92) As well, school staff members were expected to conceal the deaths of children in their schools to maximize the governments grants allotted to them each year, which were calculated according to the number of children in attendance in each school.

It was hardly surprising, then, that all of the churches fought tooth and nail against the closing of these "cash cow" schools, especially when the government attempted to do so and take over their operation, during the 1930's and again in the early 1960's. In one irate letter from 1948, a top United Church official threatens to close a residential school if Ottawa curtails its share of funding for the school. (*Figure 113*)

Profiteering off child slave labor as they did, the churches also cut financial corners by often simply starving large numbers of children to death: a practice that was necessary to weaken children's' immune system to allow a massive die-off from tuberculosis, as was described earlier. Germ warfare and starvation were the two prime killers in these death camps.

Along with Sharon Blakeborough, eyewitness survivors like Sylvester Green, Ricky Lavallee, Peter Yellowquill, William Combes and Harry Wilson describe how they obtained regular food in their respective Catholic, Anglican and United church schools only by rummaging at night through garbage cans and staff throwaways. The fact that their schools were located many hundreds of miles apart, in

British Columbia, Alberta and Manitoba, reveals the systemic nature of these conditions of deliberate starvation.

According to William Combes,

"If it wasn't for me stealing food and bringing in the garbage at night, none of the little ones would have made it through the year. The nuns would decide who would eat and who wouldn't, then they'd blame the kids they starved by saying they'd been bad and didn't deserve to eat. I saw lots of kids waste away and die that way at Kamloops." (93)

And Peter Yellowquill states, *"At the Brandon (United Church) school it was just everyday business that the strong kids ate and the weak ones starved and died. We were deliberately pitted against each other that way, fighting over the scraps thrown to us like we were dogs. The minister and his cronies ate steak and we ate what we could scrounge when the maggoty mush ran out. That was done to five year olds."* (94)

The very extent of this institutionalized murder compelled both church and state to increasingly surround their crimes with a halo of beatific purpose while routinely burying the truth and the bodies. This culture of the Big Lie generated an enormous myth about the Indian residential schools as being a "basically good intention gone wrong by a few bad apples": a lie that still constitutes the official residential school narrative in Canada.

However this account has been cast, the underlying purpose of these camps remained to uproot and exterminate every vestige of traditional indigenous life and thought, by killing off half of the next generation of Indians and traumatizing the rest into conformity. The entire so-called Indian residential school system thereby amounted to a deliberate genocide that has never ceased, manifested then and now in the same enormous and accompanying deception that kills while it claims to heal.

Footnotes: Part One - The Crime

(7) A conservative estimate of the demographic reduction of New World aboriginals between 1500 and 1900 is 50 to 75 million people, or from 25 percent of the world's population to two percent.

(8) See **Pagans in the Promised Land** by Steven Newcombe (Fulcrum Press, 2008).

(9) In the United States, by comparison, "free church" missionary groups and the Roman Catholic Church were the main instigators of the Indian boarding schools, but most of them were taken over by the federal Bureau of Indian Affairs by the early 20th century, with the notable exception of Jesuit-run schools in the west.

(10) As quoted in the ***London Illustrated News,*** June 9, 1843.

(11) See the following discussion of the "Durieu system" imposed on aboriginal tribes. The early residential school archives between 1890 and 1910 are filled with letters from clergy imploring the government to make attendance in the residential schools mandatory.

(12) West coast Presbyterian missionary John Ross, for example, who worked among the Ahousaht people, was made the local judicial magistrate, doctor and school supervisor by the provincial government in 1903.

(13) See **The Kindness of Strangers** by John Boswell for a discussion of the history of church abduction of children.

(14) *"The crusader, in turn, was the beneficiary of many special privileges, both temporal and spiritual, above all the Crusade 'Indulgence', which was commonly understood to wipe away all one's former sins and to restore one to a state of spiritual innocence."* (**A History of the Christian Church** by Williston Walker et al, 4th ed., p. 285, Scribners, 1918)

(15) See **A World Lit only by Fire** by William Manchester (Little, Brown, 1992)

(16) Sheepshanks is discussed in more detail in Appendix Ten.

(17) Durieu's history is remarkably sugar-coated by academics as well as, of course, the church. This report was able to uncover Durieu's "Watchmen" model only by accessing documents from a source in the Oblate Order in Montreal.

(18) See the complete documentary evidence of this discrepancy at *http://itccs.org/the-international-common-law-court-of-justice-case-no-1-genocide-in-canada*

(19) Ibid.

(20) Dr. Peter Bryce to Duncan Campbell Scott, Ottawa, November 5, 1909. (RG 10 series archives, File 7733)

(21) See a copy of this agreement in Appendix Eight.

(22) From the statement of Delmar Johnny made in the documentary film ***Unrepentant*** at www.hiddennolonger.com . Delmar led the movement of Kuper Island survivors to win recognition until his sudden and untimely death.

(23) *"Residential school docs pulped: MP"*, 24 Hours News, April 25, 2007. **See Figure 38.**

(24) The government's figure is based strictly on the assumption that only children seven years and older were incarcerated in the school, which was the law; but it is well established from many eyewitnesses and school correspondence that it was a common practice for children as young as three or four to be included when Mounties and others would scoop them from their villages. Considering the prevalence of this practice, we assume that the total number of children in the school had to be at least one third higher than the government estimate, or around 200,000.

(25) This fact was admitted by United Church lawyers during the first class action trial culminating in the Brenner legal decision of June, 1998 in the B.C. Supreme Court. But reference to this admission

was stricken from the media.

(26) *"Claim of Murder goes back to the '40's"* by Karen Gram, *The Vancouver Sun*, December 18, 1995.

(27) From an interview on *"Hidden from History"*, Vancouver Co-op radio, March 8, 2007.

(28) From an interview on August 12, 2002 in Penticton, British Columbia.

(29) From a joint interview with Virginia Baptiste and Helene Armstrong, recorded by Kevin Annett on August 12, 2002 in Penticton.

(30) From an interview given by Pierre Kruger to Kevin Annett on August 14, 2002 in Osoyoos, British Columbia.

(31) From the extended interview with Doug Wilson given on June 4, 2006 in Victoria, BC. Doug is also featured in the film *Unrepentant.*

(32) From the extended interview with Sylvester Green given on August 2, 2006 in Vancouver.

(33) Wilson, ibid.

(34) Report from A.R. Lett to Indian Affairs, Ottawa, April 10, 1923 (RG 10 series, INAC, Vol. 6462, file 888-1, Part 2.

(35)From the extended interview given by Mabel Sport on March 29, 1998 in Port Alberni, BC. Mabel's husband Willie Sport's accompanying and invaluable testimony about his deliberate exposure to TB at the hands of Principal Pitts at the United Church School in Port Alberni can be found in Appendix Two, containing additional testimonies.

(36) From Marion's talk at the Circle of Justice public forum held in the evening of February 9, 1998 at the Simon Fraser University downtown campus. Marion prefaced her remarks by saying to Kevin

Annett, *"I heard about your work and I drove here all the way from Ontario to help expose this thing. I was threatened and warned not to come here."* She declined to say who had threatened her.

(37) From the extended interview given by Joan Morris on September 3 and 16, 2004 in Victoria and Nanaimo, BC. Joan is today still being denied access to her medical files, as is Kenny Quatell and other survivors of medical experimentation at the Nanaimo Indian Hospital, who have been told by their doctors that they cannot see their own records "for reasons of national security". This seems to confirm the military involvement in the hospital. Many of the records of the Indian Hospitals are held in the National Archives in Ottawa. Until the spring of 1999, they were accessible to the public, but less than six months after the IHRAAM Tribunal into residential schools in Vancouver, all of the hospital records were classified and placed in a National Security restricted area of the Archives requiring government permission to enter.

(38)For a restricted account of Project Paperclip see the book by Annie Jacobsen, **Operation Paperclip: The Secret Intelligence Program that brought Nazi Scientists to America** (Little, Brown and co. 2014)

(39) From Edwin Black, ibid., pp. 242.

(40) From an interview given by Jackson Steene on Denman Island, BC on August 24, 2005.

(41) From an interview given by Cambel Quatell in Campbell River on March 4, 2005. Cambel is the brother of Nanaimo Indian hospital victim Kenny Quatell.

(42) From an interview given by Sam Adolph on June 4, 2007. Sam was a friend of fellow Kamloops survivor William Combes, and also confirmed the secret late-night burials at the Kamloops school. Sam died of unstated causes the year before William was killed in St. Paul's Catholic hospital in Vancouver.

(43)From an interview given by Ethel Wilson on June 10, 1998 in Vancouver, shortly before Ethel spoke at the IHRAAM Tribunal of June 12-14, 1998.

(44) From the record of testimonies given at the IHRAAM Tribunal and independently recorded by Eva Lyman and Kevin Annett. Ed Martin spoke at the Tribunal on June 13, 1998.

(45) From an interview with Steve Sampson given in Chemainus, British Columbia on November 9, 2005.

(46) From an extended, two hour interview with Sarah Modeste in Duncan, BC on September 12, 2002. Some of her statement can also be viewed in the film *Unrepentant.*

(47) Some of Eliza's statement is featured in the film *Unrepentant* and on this link: https://www.youtube.com/watch?v=RBUd3UXt6fI

(48) From a telephone interview with Pat Taylor on November 3, 1999.

(49) From a telephone interview with Lynn Sharman on February 3, 2006.

(50) From a series of interviews with Renee la Fortune in Victoria, B.C. during September, 2007. Renee was also the adopted daughter of Roger LaFortune, a military researcher who used native children from residential schools in grisly experiments in Toronto during the 1960's.

(51) http://healthimpactnews.com/2014/mass-sterilization-kenyan-doctors-find-anti-fertility-agent-in-un-tetanus-vaccine/

(52) From an interview on March 1, 1996, featured in *J'ai Tout Compris (Pairs, spring 1999)*

(53) http://zombietime.com/john_holdren/

(54) Irene's entire statement, given at a CBC TV "Town Forum" in Regina on July 3, 2008, reads: *"I'm Irene Favel, I'm seventy five. I went to residential school in Muscowequan from 1944 to 1949, and I had a rough life. I was mistreated in every way. There was a young girl, and she was pregnant. And what they did, she had her baby, and they took the baby and wrapped it up in a nice pink outfit, and they took it downstairs where I was*

cooking dinner with the nun. And they took the baby into the furnace room, and they threw that little baby in there and burned it alive. All you could hear was this little cry, like 'uhh!". You could smell that flesh cooking." To view Irene's interview, which was removed from the CBC website within 24 hours of it being posted, see: **https://www.youtube.com/watch?v=CReISnQDbBE**

(55) From Marion's talk, delivered at the Circle of Justice forum, Vancouver, February 9, 1998.

(56) The present study relies on the more accurate term "pedocide", meaning the killer of children, rather than the misleading term "pedophile", which means "friend of children".

(57) From a statement made to Kevin Annett on August 12, 2001 in Tofino, B.C.

(58) From a statement made to the IHRAAM Panel of judges, June 13, 1998, Vancouver.

(59) Cited by Dr. Jennifer Wade of Amnesty International in a lecture she gave in Vancouver on August 12, 1999.

(60) For example, the privately-owned "Children's Aid Society" of Ontario, while posing as a state agency, makes on average $100,000 for every child they apprehend from its family and deliver to orphanages or foster care homes. This lucrative human trafficking system is replicated in every province.

(61) From Harriett's remarks made at the Circle of Justice public forum of February 9, 1998 in Vancouver where she, Kevin Annett and others established the Truth Commission into Genocide in Canada (TCGC) See the Chronology above.

(62) Sutherland's use of the term "Industrial Institutions" is significant, since under the Industrial Schools Act, any inmate could be legally incarcerated as in a prison for an indefinite period, and eventually, subjected to involuntary procedures including sexual sterilizations.

(63) See Appendix One for a complete list of offenses committed on Indian residential school

children.

(64) From a statement by Vera Hunt at the IHRAAM Tribunal in Vancouver on June 14, 1998.

(65) This standard Admission form was discovered by Kevin Annett in his archival research at the University of British Columbia early in the spring of 1996, and was successfully used in court to convict the United Church and government of joint liability for residential school crimes. The Admission form was established in 1929 after the government transferred legal guardianship power over Indian children to the churches that ran the residential schools.

(66) All of the churches reaped huge financial profits from this system of exploiting students as forced and unpaid labor, and was one of the main reasons these churches lobbied continually to keep the residential schools operating.

(67) Countless survivors refer to the lack of formal teaching hours in the schools and how their predominant time was spent in manual labor.

(68) From Lillian Shirt's statement of February 8, 2006 recorded in part in the film *Unrepentant*. This practice of not funding Indian students past a certain grade is enunciated in the letter in Figure 94 in which funds for the higher education of Indians *is explicitly denied as a matter of policy.*

(69) This practice is described in the testimonies of Harriett Nahanee and Vera Hunt *(ibid).*

(70) This witness was a former dorm supervisor at the Lytton school who requested anonymity. See an interview with this employee in Appendix Two, Testimonies, *"Even War Criminals go to Church"* by Kevin Annett (2002).

(71) From the statement of Virginia Baptiste made in Penticton on August 12, 2002.

(72) From an interview with Willie and Mabel Sport on March 29, 1998 in Port Alberni. See a picture of Willie's deformed feet in Figure 96.

(73) From a statement made by Delmar Johnny at a public forum at the University of Victoria on October 12, 2007.

(74) From an oral statement made by Doug Wilson at the same University of Victoria forum where Delmar Johnny spoke on October 12, 2007. At the same event, Charlie Thompson, one of the state-funded tribal council chiefs who in 1998 had threatened eyewitness Harry Wilson with death if he spoke about the dead body he'd found at the Alberni school, also threatened Doug Wilson. The latter refused to make any more public criticisms of the government Indian chiefs after this event.

(75) For an earlier citation of these conditions see also **Hidden No Longer: Genocide in Canada, Past and Present** (2010) at www.hiddennolonger.com .

(76) From an oral statement made by Sylvester Green to the Vancouver media at a protest organized by Friends and Relatives of the Disappeared (FRD) on March 31, 2007.

(77) See Kevin Annett's statements in this regard at www.hiddennolonger.com, in the film *Unrepentant*, and in his many books, including ***Unrelenting*** (2016).

(78) *"Canada's squalid secret: life on native reserves – Income, education, life expectancy worse than in 62 countries"* by Erin Anderssen, *The Globe and Mail*, October 12, 1998, page 1.

(79) From a statement made by Carol Martin on *Hidden from History*, Vancouver Co-op radio, on March 12, 2010.

(80) See the **Indian Act of Canada,** Revised Statutes of Canada (RSC) 1985.

(81) From the extended interview of Harry Lucas made during the filming of *Unrepentant* in the spring and summer of 2006.

(82) From the oral statement made by Larry Lavoie at the Circle of Justice forum in Vancouver on February 9, 1998.

(83) See Appendix One.

(84) From the extensive literature on the MKULTRA program, see especially a personal account by experimental survivor Ann Diamond of Montreal, in her book **My Cold War** (Diamondback Books, 2005)

(85) From an oral interview with Dennis Charlie. See also Dennis' abridged statement in *www.hiddennolonger.com* .

(86) See Sara's book **Always Remember Love** for a complete account. This quote was taken from the first oral interview with her conducted at her Salt Spring Island home by Kevin Annett in the spring of 2005.

(87) A Sergeant Dan Gasseau of the NCIS, Canada's military intelligence agency, confirmed the existence of this person in a phone call to Sara's husband in January, 1994.

(88) This recording is held in the personal archives of Kevin Annett and a copy is held by the ITCCS. In the fall of 1998 and throughout 1999, copies of the recording were offered by Kevin to reporters with the Canadian Broadcasting Corporation (CBC), the *Globe and Mail* and the *Vancouver Sun*; all of them refused once they were told of its content.

(89) This same policy of disallowing funds to be used to create long term employment among aboriginal recipients has also applied to all recipients of the government's so-called "Aboriginal Healing Fund", which arose in response to and to deflate the impact of the 1998 IHRAAM Tribunal revelations of residential schools genocide.

(90) This matter of deliberate and continued genocide in Canada is discussed in more detail in Part Three of this Report. Ed John's particular role in this crime, and in the suppression of incriminating evidence by residential school survivors, is also highlighted in Part Three.

(91) In her statement to the IHRAAM panel, Blakeborough also referred to her brief employment on

the RCMP's "Residential Schools Task Force" in North Vancouver from 1995-1997. "The whole thing was a farce, a big show with nothing behind it. All we did all day was to push paper around and look busy but we were never supposed to respond to actual survivors and their stories. To give you an example, the Task Force's top guy, Gerry Peters, got a call from some chiefs up on the north coast about a big grave they'd found of children's bones near one of the old residential schools. Some of them wanted to give their testimonies about what they'd suffered in the school. Gerry flew up there but he was back the next day. He never took one statement from the chiefs. That's the way we dealt with the issue."

(92) This practice has been documented as occurring at the Coqualeetza (United) school in Sardis, British Columbia by Principal George Raley during the 1920's and at the Mohawk (Anglican) school in Brantford, Ontario by Principal John Zimmerman during the 1940's and '50's.

(93) William Combes, from a statement made on the *Hidden from History* program at Vancouver Co-op radio on August 22, 2010.

(94) From an interview with Peter Yellowquill made on July 13, 2008 in Portage la Prairie, Manitoba. Peter is a traditional Anishinabe elder who is also featured on documentary footage used by the International Common Law Court of Justice and its case against Canada and its churches for genocide, found at these sites: https://www.youtube.com/watch?v=UvhfXAd08TE *and* https://www.youtube.com/watch?v=OPKFk_L7y9g .

Part Two: Concealment, Containment and Deception

As this was the property of, and conducted by, the church, care was taken to avoid too close (an) inquiry. - Indian Agent Gerald Barry, regarding a fire and the death of children at the United Church Ahousaht residential school, February 3, 1940 *(Figure 114)*

The policy of the Department is not to interfere with the work of any church on an Indian Reserve ... - Indian Affairs Deputy Superintendent Frank Pedley, January 21, 1904 *(Figure 115)*

Nobody wants to prosecute the churches or see them go bankrupt. - Truth and Reconciliation Commission Chairman Murray Sinclair, October 8, 2012

The Truth and Reconciliation Commission ... shall not hold formal hearings, nor act as a public inquiry, nor conduct a formal legal process; shall not possess subpoena powers, and do not have powers to compel attendance or participation in any of its activities or events ... shall not make any findings or express any conclusion or recommendation regarding the misconduct of any person or the possible civil or criminal liability of any person or organization ... shall not name names in their events, activities, public statements, report or recommendations, or make use of personal information or of statements made which identify a person ... The Commissioners shall not record the names of persons so identified ... - From Section Two, *"Establishment, Powers, Duties and Procedures of the Commission"*, Truth and Reconciliation Commission, Ottawa, 2008

The active concealment of the Canadian Genocide has always operated hand in hand with the crime itself.

As early as 1891, just two years after the opening of the first state-authorized, church run Indian residential school, the federal government began mimicking the missionaries' practice of concealing deaths of children in the schools by altering and deleting records of such mortality. This tag team operation continued unchecked during the history of the crime, and culminated in 2008 when both Canadian church and state established the misnamed "Truth and Reconciliation Commission" (TRC) to pretend to examine their own torture and killing of residential school children.

"They've granted themselves de facto immunity again, just like they always have when it comes to their slaughter of our people" summed up traditional Anishnabe elder and survivor Peter Yellowquill, soon after the TRC was launched. *"I predict that the TRC will not find a single white person or a single church guilty of any crime."* (95)

Peter's Yellowquill's prediction was accurate. How could a body without any legal power do anything but comment on a crime while letting the criminals go free? The TRC mandate was crafted by the guilty to protect themselves while creating the appearance of an actual investigation: a continuation of the same dissimulation that governed the operation of the residential schools.

The evidence of this deception runs throughout the official record of the schools. Perhaps the earliest cover up of residential school crimes came from the top of the government system, in June of 1903, just a few years after the opening of the schools. In that month, Frank Pedley, Deputy Superintendent for Indian Affairs, authorized a new practice of deleting from residential school reports the names and numbers of all Indian children who had died after leaving the schools. Clearly, that number was very high. *(Figures 116 and 117)*

For example, the June 19, 1903 letter to Pedley requesting such a change in policy, from the Indian Commissioner for western Canada, stated that 191 pupils from the Qu'Appelle Indian School had died the previous year. This was an astounding **61%** of the students at that school. (96)

In short, at the dawn of the 20th century and the residential school system, the top civil servant for Indian Affairs in Canada ordered the concealment of mortality rates among former residential school students by censoring them from all school reports after 1903. After that, no official account of school deaths could possibly reflect accurately the real level of mortality among Indian children; nor was it intended to. And yet today's TRC erroneously relied on such whitewashed accounts as its sole "evidence" of a barely one percent death rate in the residential schools!

This pattern of the government's official fogging of conditions in the schools remained constant over the life of the system, especially after those conditions were threatened with exposure by honest officials, civil servants or doctors.

The classic example of this was the government's suppression of the damning report of Dr. Peter Bryce in 1909, and his subsequent railroading out of the civil service, after Bryce discovered that tuberculosis was being deliberately and routinely spread among healthy students. (97) But in general the residential school system's very structure was designed to allow institutional secrecy and easy concealment of whatever occurred within it.

As late as the 1960's and '70's, residential school Principals retained absolute control not only over the children but the school staff, including the power over the latter to censor their letters and monitor their phone calls, fire them without cause and withhold their salaries. (*See Appendix Nine*) This military-like, pyramidal power structure was set up from the start to control information in and out of the schools as any system of wrongdoing does in anticipation of any possible "leaks".

The efficiency of such control was demonstrated by how completely the crimes in the Indian residential schools were concealed from public scrutiny, including by the most senior government officials. Some of the latter used open duplicity, like Prime Minister Arthur Meighen, who in Parliament in 1920 lauded the "phenomenal success" of the very File Hills Indian school in Saskatchewan whose undisclosed but actual death rate the previous year, was 69%. (*Figure 118*) (98)

Others, like Duncan Campbell Scott who headed Indian Affairs until the 1930's, openly legitimated the enormous death rates with statements like *"If the schools are to be conducted at all we must face the fact that a large number of the pupils will suffer from tuberculosis in some of its various forms."* *(Figure 119)*

The same Duncan Campbell Scott did more than provide a broad justification for the deliberately-spread tuberculosis epidemic among students. He also actively exonerated and protected those who colluded in the infecting of Indians with the disease, in accordance with his concern about protecting the churches that he revealed in his March, 1910 letter depicted in Figure 119.

In November, 1919 a Dr. A. J. Stuart who was medical inspector for Indian schools near Vancouver was criticized harshly by a lower level Indian Affairs official for not detecting and stopping the spread of smallpox from the catholic St. Mary's Indian school in Mission to many local tribes.

The official implied that Stuart had even facilitated the infecting of these Indians and demanded an explanation. But D.C. Scott quickly intervened and exonerated the doctor, and even apologized to him in writing, despite the fact that smallpox had definitely been spread by children under his care to all the surrounding Indian villages. (*Figures 120 and 121*) (99)

Despite the meddling consciences of occasional employees of the system, it was demonstrated by the top officials like Scott that complaints of the residential schools were to be disregarded, and – as with today's TRC – the churches largely responsible for the sickness and death of children were to be shielded and automatically exonerated of any wrongdoing. No-one summed up this policy of official cover up more clearly than West Coast Agency Indian Agent P.B. Ashbridge in February, 1940, when, after investigating the death of children after a fire at the United Church School in Ahousaht, stated,

"As this school was the property of, and conducted by, the Church, care was taken to avoid too close (an) *inquiry."* (*See Figure 114*)

However, it must be remembered that the real cloaking of this massive institutionalized extermination of Indians occurred through a mindset and practice of "Two Standards of Care", common to any genocidal system, and adhered to by all residential school employees if they were to keep their jobs.

Dr. C. Pitts, a medical inspector for British Columbia residential schools, described that Two Standards system in a letter of October 22, 1935 to Indian Agent R. H. Moore, in which he wrote,

" ... were I to apply the standards of health to them (Indian children) that is applied to children of the white schools, that (sic) *I should have to discharge 90% of them and there would be no school left"* (*Figure 122*)

This lower standard of care for Indian children allowed a massive sickness and death rate among them to be considered "acceptable" by the government and churches, and was in that manner camouflaged: part of the normalization of genocide that makes it invisible to its perpetrators.

Significantly, this same Dr. Pitts was also involved in a blatant state cover up of the death of four boys from the Lejac Catholic school barely a year after he wrote his "two standards" letter: a case that continues to reverberate down through the decades.

The best justice we can do to this story, and the four dead boys in question, is to reprint the following news article that appeared in June, 2015 across Canada.

Why is Canada still lying about how four Indian boys died? A Post-Mortem Study of how a Crime Carries On

By Kevin D. Annett

"I have been placed in the awkward predicament of sustaining the claim that the boys were fully dressed in winter garments, when of course they were discovered clad only in light summer clothing lacking even overcoats and footwear. To allege they were merely trying to visit their parents over the holiday does not correspond with the facts of their deaths." - Dr. C.W. Pitts to Indian Agent R.H. Moore, January 4, 1937, after the Coroner's Inquiry into the deaths

Two days later: *"(The) Inquest showed (the) boys did not run away from school because of ill treatment but to spend holidays with parents."* - Dr. C.W. Pitts to Moore, January 6, 1937

The picture of their corpses appeared on the internet suddenly and conveniently this year. It was in fact the first time an image of dead residential school children was ever shown to the Canadian public, which says a lot. But why now, and why this particular photograph? Hold on to that question.

There are only three Indian boys in the picture, but four of them were said to have died: frozen to death on January 2, 1937 after fleeing from the Lejac Catholic school in central British Columbia. In the photo, the features of the three boys show no trauma, but are composed, their hair combed, and their arms tied neatly across their chests. Their corpses are also garbed in heavy winter clothing.

Someone dressed them up that way after they died, and posed their bodies for the camera.

The first Coroner's report claimed that the boys were not found in winter clothes but rather in "light summer clothing, lacking even overcoats and footwear." Clearly, something terrible enough caused these boys to flee from the Lejac Indian school in the depth of night, in a blizzard, with only the clothes on their back. A cover story of their wanting to "visit their parents" was made up after the fact.

The same Coroner also reported that one of the boys had still been alive when their bodies were found.

But the final Inquiry report says that all the boys were dead when discovered. So what happened to that fourth boy?

All of these inconsistencies were quickly concealed by government and church authorities in the days following their death. A fake story was issued. And that lie is still being propagated today, in accounts of the boys' deaths published as recently as January, 2014 in the National Post.

So, why is there this continuing Big Lie? And why is this photograph being issued, right now?

The runaway boys' names were Allen Willie, Andrew Paul, Maurice Justin and Johnny Jack, and they were all eight or nine years old. I know their story well, because I first came across it in the spring of 1999 as a doctoral student in Vancouver. The documents I unearthed then from Indian Affairs archives showed a clear cover up of what happened to the boys. And for sixteen years, not surprisingly, nobody in the media, government or academic world has wanted to look at what I unearthed.

That said, the evidence suggesting foul play and concealment is even more damning, when we consider the identity of the Coroner who kept changing his account of the boys' fate. The man's name was Dr. C.W. Pitts, the Indian school medical inspector for central B.C. He was also the son of a residential school Principal who was accused during the same period of torturing children at the Port Alberni facility. *(See the 1998 statement of Willie Sport in Appendix two)*

Dr. Pitts the younger wrote a remarkable letter to the local Indian Agent barely one year before the four boys died, in which he admitted that a genocidal "two standards of care" system operated in the residential schools, including at Lejac. Referring to his examination of Indian kids at Lejac and stating that such regular medical care of these children would "serve no purpose", Pitts explained that,

"Were I to apply the standards of health to them that is applied to children of the white schools, I should have to discharge 90% of them and there would be no school left." (October 22, 1935)

In short, a lower standard of care for Indian children means that lots of them could die or suffer at an "acceptable level", and it would never be reported or dealt with. This "two standards" was an effective and legal way for massive killings of children to occur. Two months after the death of the runaway boys, for instance, the same Dr. Pitts reported that children were routinely being admitted to Lejac who were suffering from "active tuberculosis": a practice still reported a dozen years later at the same school, in 1948.

It's clear now that the Lejac school was a "Special Treatment" facility in which germ warfare and experimental research was conducted routinely on Indian children by church and military doctors, just like at the Catholic Kuper Island school, the Anglican Mohawk school in Brantford, and the United Church facility in Port Alberni. And so it's not surprising that the Lejac runaways of 1937 were driven to their deaths and that one of them was killed to keep things quiet.

As part of Canada's big genocidal secret, the official story of these four boys' fate is an "approved", sanitized account of residential school deaths; and as such, it is one required and usable these days by the government's Holocaust-Denying "Truth and Reconciliation Commission" (TRC).

The TRC, after all, has publicly acknowledged that thousands of children died in the system. Now, they have to produce the evidence behind their claim: but only the right kind of evidence, which will incriminate nobody and continue the veil of secrecy over the "Special Treatment" programs. And that's why we are allowed to see only this one manufactured image of three dead Lejac boys, and none of the other pictures in the hidden military archives from which this picture emerged.
I still find it mind boggling how controlled a land is Canada, when not a single image of the dead is allowed to emerge for decades, and only then at the hands of the perpetrators.

To say that the church and state criminals still have a firm monopoly on official truth is an understatement. What is truly remarkable is how unchallenged they continue to be in the eyes of otherwise "aware" Canadians.

But "one man and the truth makes a majority", I have learned: and this latest exposure of how Canada has continued to mask a cover-up of murder 78 years old shows that the residential schools Genocide is hardly a dead issue, or a "resolved" one. The hunt for the assassins continues.

....

(See Figure 123 for the staged photo of three of the four dead boys that appeared in the National Post in January, 2014, and Figures124 and 125 for additional evidence related to this cover up.)

A Legacy of Lies

The archival record from the Indian residential school record abounds in fragments of evidence of a habitual and systemic deception to mask the true extent of death and criminality in the system. School records were not only continually destroyed but censored, especially when the deaths of children occurred.

For example, the May 1948 death record of a student named Reggie Allan at the St. George's Indian Hospital in Alert Bay, British Columbia reports that the boy died of a "Fracture Skull", and yet no cause of death was recorded underneath it. (*Figure 126*) Similarly, school attendance records would often list a student as simply "dead" without any explanatory note, as in the case of Louie Johnson, a Grade 4 pupil at the Sechelt Catholic school in early 1938. *(Figure 127)*

Indian Agents themselves acknowledged the concealment that was part and parcel of the Indian schools. In June 1993, agent E. H. Newham quoted a residential school Principal, one F. Arnfield, who said that a government commission in Winnipeg was *"always receiving complaints and took no notice of them." (Figure 128)*

This history of concealment is evident in the remaining archival records from the Indian schools. In ***Figure 129,*** for example, a search for a listing in the RG 10 series concerning deaths of children in residential schools in the earliest years (1883-1898) resulted in the remark "no file found". This pattern continues to the present day.

Continued Concealment

The continuity of the residential school cover up by church and state across the generations is starkly revealed not only by the Lejac story, but from numerous firsthand accounts of survivors.

Kenny Quatell, a Kwakiutl Indian on Vancouver Island, is a survivor of involuntary medical experiments at the United Church-affiliated Nanaimo Indian Hospital during the 1960's. In 2005, he described the continuing secrecy surrounding what was done to him as a child.

"They told my mother I'd died on the operating table when I was five. Then they took me off to the Nanaimo hospital and they had me there for years and did all sorts of tests on me. They made it so I couldn't have children. I was given drugs that made me sick and black out all the time. Then for God knows how long I was in the dark room (note: sensory deprivation tests). I remember these wires in my head, I had on a kind of metal hat and they'd give me shocks and I'd black out. I still get those twitches in my head.

"Finally when I was a teenager they let me out, I don't know why. I guess they were done with me. They just dumped me on the street in Nanaimo and I was homeless for a long time. But one day a relative of mine spotted me and I got home but most of my family was dead and gone by then.
"For years I've been getting therapy for my problems in Campbell River, but the shrink who's treating me will never tell me anything. Whenever I ask to see my chart he says no, I can't show that to you, it's because of national security.

"One day I told him I was going to go to another doctor and he laughed and said, if you try that you'll just get arrested. He kept saying the same thing; my case was about national security." (100)

Harry Wilson, who discovered the dead body of a young girl at the United Church's Alberni residential school in 1967, was incarcerated in the same Nanaimo Indian Hospital for over a year after he reported the corpse to Principal John Andrews. He was given electric shocks to make him forget. Years later in 1998, when Harry attempted to speak of the incident at a Port Alberni forum, two state-funded natives threatened to kill him if he spoke. (101)

Irene Starr discussed the concealment of children's remains at a Vancouver Island Anglican school during the June, 1998 IHRAAM Tribunal. In her statement she said, *"I saw rows of little skeletons behind the walls of the Alert Bay School when they tore down the old building in 1970. Why would they have buried those bones behind the walls unless they were trying to hide something?"* (102)

Such stories abound in hundreds of personal accounts of residential school survivors that make up this report. The cover up continued unabated long after the formal closing of the schools by 1996, and is present even in the court settlement process governing reparations to school survivors.

For example, in a March, 2008 letter to his client, Christie catholic school survivor Trudy Smith, Victoria BC lawyer Scott Hall stated, *"... by signing the Acceptance Letter you release Canada and the Church for responsibility for the pain and suffering caused to you by the conduct of their employees or agents while you were at the residential School ... This is final and means that you cannot bring a claim in the future against Canada and the Church ..." (See Figure 130).*

This legal absolving of the guilty for their crime is a structural part of the residential school survivors' "compensation" program in Canada and another form of concealment of that crime. This charade has been accompanied by even more blatant masking of the wrongdoing by lawyers, including survivors' advocates. The lawyer for survivors Harry Wilson and Dennis Tallio, David Patterson, refused to include in their court statements any mention of the dead children both of them discovered on the grounds of the Alberni residential school.

According to Kevin Annett, who questioned Patterson later,

"He was extremely self-defensive and even threatened to sue Harry and Dennis if they kept pressing him to include their full statement about the dead bodies. Finally, I called him at his office in the fall of 1997 and asked him why he wasn't fulfilling his clients' wishes. Patterson evaded the question for awhile but then finally blurted out in anger, 'Look, I'm not just their lawyer! I'm also an officer of the Court and there are some things I'm not allowed to raise'!" (103)

Sure enough, not one of the thousands of lawsuits eventually filed against the government and the Catholic, Anglican and United Church ever addressed incidents of murder or other criminal acts in the residential schools, confining the litigation to tort or damages related to "physical and sexual abuse" or "neglect of duty of care". And on two occasions in 1999 and 2002, provincial Supreme Courts explicitly denied the right of native plaintiffs to sue Canada and the Crown of England for genocide, claiming that such a charge was *"ultra vires"* and beyond the "jurisdictional competence" of their courts. (104)

This institutionalized cover up extends to the Canadian media reportage – such as it is - of residential school crimes. A stark example followed the Globe and Mail headline of April 24, 2007 that confirmed a fifty percent death rate in the schools*: "Natives **Died in Droves** as Ottawa ignored warnings"*. But after the government's TRC concluded its whitewash of the genocide in 2015, the same headline had the words "in Droves" removed and reads in that edited version in today's internet archives: no doubt to conform to the TRC's "official" claim of a mere one percent death rate in the Indian schools! (***Compare Figures 131 and 132***)

Such an institutional cover up also extends to the police. An entire separate report could be issued about the long history of concealment and obstruction of justice by the RCMP as the police arm of the Indian residential school system. But some recent examples will highlight this pattern.

After the first media reporting of an eye witnessed murder in a residential school, in the *Vancouver Sun* in December 1995, a spokesman for the RCMP stated publicly *"If killings occurred in these schools it's definitely within our mandate to investigate them."* (*Sgt. Paul Willms, "E" Division, Vancouver*) But three months later, after a flurry of more reported killings and the formation of an RCMP "Task Force" into the schools, the successor to Sgt. Willms, Constable Gerry Peters, said, *"We have never had a mandate to investigate alleged homicides in residential schools."* (105)

On several occasions during this same period, RCMP officials including Willms and Peters refused to investigate reports of killings brought by eyewitnesses to murders at the Alberni school while lying publicly that "nothing had turned up" concerning such murders. Both officers also personally threatened Kevin Annett and warned him of "consequences" if he persisted in making statements to the media about killings of residential school children. (106)

The first eye witnessed killing – of Maisie Shaw by Alberni School Principal Alfred Caldwell, as seen by Harriett Nanahee – triggered the issuing of a falsified death certificate for Maisie by the B.C. Government's Provincial Archives. After stating to Kevin Annett on December 12, 1995 that there existed no death certificate for Maisie Shaw anywhere in the provincial registry, archivist Brian Young contacted Kevin two weeks later – after the *Vancouver Sun* article reporting her murder had been published – and notified him that a death certificate for Maisie now existed.

Young claimed that the document had "gone missing" after having been entered into the archival system "only just recently", even though it was dated fifty years earlier: December 26, 1946. The document contains erroneous and highly suspect information.

For example, it claims that Maisie Shaw – whom Harriett Nahanee saw kicked to her death down some stairs by Caldwell - died of heart failure, and that she was buried the next day, the same day the death certificate was signed.

"That never happens" stated Louise, a senior employee at the Alberni funeral home where Maisie was allegedly handled, in a January, 1996 interview with *Vancouver Sun* journalist Stephen Hume. *"We have no record of a Maisie Shaw. And nobody ever dies and is processed in twenty four hours like that. Also, the death certificate would have been entered early in 1947, not 1995, if it was genuine."*

In a subsequent phone call with Kevin Annett on January 20, 1996 in which he described the funeral home employee's words, Stephen Hume said, *"I've seen these fake certificates before. They're easy to cook up ... The girl was probably just stuck in the ground somewhere and then when Harriett's story broke in the press, somebody quickly stuck this fake one in the system."*

Meanwhile, despite Harriett's eyewitness account and thirteen other reports to the RCMP of deaths at the Alberni school, the RCMP continue to falsely claim that "no one was ever reported a killing at the Alberni residential school", while the United Church alleges that Maisie Shaw died after being "hit by a train." (107)

For policemen and civil servants to dissimulate so freely and without apparent concern of any consequence indicates that they are being protected and encouraged to do so. The same behavior was present in residential school staff and Principals who routinely tortured and killed children without fear for decades, knowing that the system authorized and exonerated their behavior. This continuity of complicity reflects a systemic evil and not one originating merely from individuals.

That system is evident at the highest level of church and state – and within the institution primarily responsible for the residential school genocide – in the Vatican policy called *Crimen Sollicitationas,* which has been called a "blueprint for deception and concealment". (108)

Crimen has been in effect as a governing policy over all Roman clergy since 1929, and over all Catholics since 1962. It is a papal decree that was only revealed in August, 2003 by the London based *Observer* newspaper, obtained through a contact in the Vatican Library archives where it was stored. *Crimen* imposes a papal oath of "perpetual secrecy" on all victims of priestly rape and on the rapist, on pain of excommunication. It also prohibits the reporting of the crime to the police and prevents the rapist from being tried in a civil court.

Thanks to *Crimen*, all Catholic clergy – the main perpetrators in this crime - are automatically and institutionally protected for any act of rape or violence towards a child. *Crimen* embodies an enormous, global criminal conspiracy. (109)

The present Pope Francis, Jorge Bergoglio, despite his "reform" rhetoric, has reaffirmed the *Crimen* policy in speeches to Italian and American Bishops, and in papal pronouncements. Bergoglio's own role in trafficking children during Argentina's "dirty wars" while Archbishop of Buenos Aires no doubt gives him a personal motive in continuing *Crimen*'s policy of silencing and cover up. (110)

In short, since 1929 and undoubtedly before that, every Catholic priest in the world, and in two thirds of Indian residential schools in Canada, knew that he could rape and harm children with impunity and would not face prosecution or reprimand. This papal "law" of official concealment was a green light for pedocides to flock into the already unmonitored and isolated Indian schools, knowing that every staff member and fellow clergyman was <u>obligated</u> to stay silent.

It is significant, in that sense, that the very same year that *Crimen* was formally adopted by the Vatican, in 1929, the Canadian government surrendered official guardianship over residential school children to the primarily-catholic Principals of those facilities. That is, once that official secrecy and impunity was guaranteed by the church, the government could safely surrender to them the absolute control over the Indian children they and their early missionaries always sought.

Considering the preponderant influence of Roman Catholicism in the civil service and government of Canada, this collusion between the Canadian state and the primarily catholic-run residential school system is hardly surprising. That influence ensured that the original Jesuit model for the residential schools, the so-called Durieu system, was copied by the government and other churches.

But that leverage also arose from the Vatican's traditional monopoly over Quebec society and its strategic voting bloc that has ensured, for example, that every Prime Minister since 1968, save one, has been a Roman Catholic, despite the minority status of the latter in the Canadian population.

In general, this stranglehold of monarchical and papal absolutism over the legal, political and cultural life of Canada down the centuries has made official dissembling by the ruling elite not only easy but the norm when it comes to the crimes of church and state. There is no independent judiciary or watch dog agency in Canada, no structural "checks and balances" or accountability available at least formally to citizens of a constitutional Republic. The old colonial system of one man governance is embodied in Canada's official "head of state", the crown-appointed Governor General, and in the fact that the Chief Justice of the Supreme Court of Canada is also a member of the Executive inner circle known as the Privy Council.

Two historic incidents illustrate this link between absolutism and genocide, and its concealment:

- Within two years of the defeat of the 1837 rebellion that tried winning democracy in both English and French Canada, and to suppress free thought and dissent, the British Crown granted total authority over education, including the right to establish the first Indian residential schools, to the Anglican and Roman Catholic churches;

- The same day that the government's "Truth and Reconciliation Commission" (TRC) issued its careful whitewash of the residential schools atrocities, in May of 2015, Supreme Court Chief Justice Beverley MacLachlan publicly endorsed the TRC report despite its unlawful procedures, obstruction of justice and blatant concealment of evidence.

The Hindu philosopher Krishnamurti said that it takes only one man to commit a crime but an entire community to conceal it. Canada has proved that time and again when it comes to its own homegrown genocide. The ready cooperation of all levels of Canadian society with this crime and its obfuscation is ultimately a reflection of a political body whose neo-feudalist absolutism and unaccountability allow fraud to become an operative principle.

This malaise of endemic silence across Canada is perhaps best summarized by a recent remark of a local television programming director on Vancouver Island, who cancelled a scheduled interview with Kevin Annett with the remark, ***"the program** airs at all different times of day and the content with Kevin could be quite disturbing. Asking that you consider someone else." (February 15, 2016)*

Fashioning the Deceptive Narrative and the Language of Normative Genocide

Pope Francis this week canonized the 18th century missionary Junipero Serra, who led the conquest and enslavement of California Indians, and who caused the death of thousands of them on church mission plantations. In proclaiming Serra an official saint of the Roman Catholic Church, the Pope declared "We are inspired by his zeal". – Turtle Island News, September 25, 2015

The policy of the Dominion aims at a concentration of Indians upon Reserves with a view of weaning them by degrees from savage life, and of gradually leading them to adopt habits of peace, honesty and industry. – Report on Indian Reserves, Department of the Interior, Ottawa, Vol. 2, p. 58 (1868)

All men must die. The Indians obeyed the mandate perhaps a little earlier than otherwise they might. The diseases that were introduced not only killed many but made the living diseased and their women barren. This is the real and sole cause of their disappearance. Their death was of little consequence; politically, it does not seem they were intended to set the world on fire. Our ultimate service to them was to improve their breed by crossing their survivors with a superior race, as we are now doing. – Dr. John Helmcken, Speaker of the British Columbia Legislature and Hudson's Bay Company director, from his book Reminiscences (1898)

The so-called ill treatment and torture in our detention centers, stories of which were spread everywhere by the people, and later by the prisoners who were freed, were not, as some assumed, inflicted methodically, but were excesses committed by individual prison guards, their deputies, and men who laid violent hands on their detainees. We did everything possible to make the inmates' stay with us livable and humane. – Rudolf Hoess, SS Commandant at Auschitz, at his trial in 1945

The abuses done to students at our Indian residential schools were almost benign in nature, and generally random. They were not the result of a deliberate policy but rather the isolated acts of certain individuals. – Brian Thorpe, Secretary of the British Columbia Conference of the United Church of Canada, March 3, 1996

Institutionalized criminality is rarely if ever considered a crime by its participants, who see their system as benign and necessary, and rationalize their involvement in it with a special language designed to legitimate and normalize that system. Missionaries "save" the savages, who are "civilized" or "assimilated" rather than exterminated. Death camps inmates are "relocated" or "processed"; enemy soldiers are "pacified", not killed; and victims of genocide are "abused".

Every system of oppression requires such a doublethink language and an accompanying deceptive narrative to justify itself and ensure the continued loyalty of its members. Nowhere was this truer than in the European effort to subordinate the world to its Christendom, or Universal Christian Empire, by which all of humanity had to come under the rule of the Roman papacy, or perish.
The Canadian genocide, as one expression of this imperial purpose, was devised and expressed from the beginning as an essentially religious enterprise, with its own built in theological language and rationale. It was implicitly understood that no traditional indigenous person or nation could be allowed to survive outside of Christendom and its "white" nation.

Each conquering nation applied this imperative differently. To the early Catholic missionaries with their eyes on quick profit, "converting the savage" meant "Whatever is required for the Faith and the Fur Trade", to quote Jesuit leader Jean de Brebeuf. To the later Dominion of Canada with its halo of Anglo-Saxon benevolence, the Indians were to be "*Canadianized and Christianized*", to quote the declared aim of the government-created United Church of Canada in 1925.

Regardless of the approach to genocide or the parlance employed, the aim was ultimately the same, namely – in modern terminology – to "assimilate" any Indians who survived their own conquest into the body politic of Christendom. Every approach shared the same deceptive narrative that painted genocide as a sacred quest and an act of charity towards lesser beings. (111)

The remarkable aspect of the language of normative genocide is that the double meaning within its words not only shrouds the murderous intent and nature of the crime, but convinces members of the genocidal nation that no such crime occurred. Three good examples of this phenomenon can be found in the continually misleading use by the Canadian media, church and state of the terms "*abuse*", "*reconciliation*" and "*apology*" in the wake of the residential schools atrocity.
In reality, this trio of terms quickly became a bulwark against the possibility of truth entering into the "official" discourse surrounding the crime. Their deceptive nomenclature appeared at the very

beginning of this discourse, when in the spring of 1990 state-funded "chief" Phil Fontaine of the government created Assembly of First Nations (AFN) referred in the media to his "abuse" in a Manitoba residential school. After this staged statement, "abuse" became the operating and accepted term to cover all of the wrongdoing within Indian residential schools, even when those wrongs included killings, torture and clear crimes against humanity.

"This use of the meaningless word 'abuse' was deliberate, and part of the government's legal strategy to contain the inevitable litigation from the victims within tort law rather than criminal law. As mere 'abuse', anything that had happened to children was defined as tort 'damage' rather than a criminal act; rape, murder and torture could then be 'compensated' like one would do over damages to a broken window. This deception was all designed to protect the churches and government from any legal consequence for their crime. Control the language and you control the outcome." (112)

Significantly, Phil Fontaine's use of the benign and vacuous term "abuse" in relation to residential schools and the uniform adoption of this word by the media and academia thereafter occurred in direct response to the launching of the first lawsuit by a residential school survivor named Nora Bernard, a former internee of the catholic-run Shubanacadie school in Nova Scotia. Bernard acted on her own, and in the fall of 1989 opened her own discourse into the residential school era with what her legal Statement of Claim called the "*deliberate murder of our people*". Fontaine's rapid public response was an obvious government counter-spin to contain the issue. (113)

This state-sponsored damage control became even more obvious when the second term in the Obfuscating Trilogy, "reconciliation", appeared quickly on the heels of Fontaine's statement. Even before details of the residential school crimes were elaborated, politicians and editorial columnists across Canada began parroting the same call for a process of "healing and reconciliation". The two terms quickly became synonymous in any discourse around residential schools, even when in practice they turned out to be mutually antagonistic.

In the words of the late Delmar Johnny who led a movement of survivors of the catholic Kuper island school, "*You couldn't speak about your residential school experience without hearing that word 'reconciliation' all the time, from your doctor, the cops, the newspapers. You can't heal without being reconciled, that was the line we got from the beginning. It never made any sense to me. How am I supposed to be reconciled with the people who destroyed my life and my brother's life?"* (114)

The meaning of "reconciliation" is in reality the exact opposite of its vernacular usage and understanding, as "the end of a disagreement and the return to friendly relations" *(Oxford Dictionary, 2002)*. Even such a common understanding of the word is absurd when applied to the conquest of Indians by Europeans; genocide was hardly a mere "disagreement", and nothing has been especially "friendly" in aboriginal and white relations.

In reality, the word "reconciliation" is derived from the Latin term "*reconcilia*" which means *to re-establish the domination and control of a ruler over his subjects.* It is a term implying resignation and defeat before the inevitability of a conquest, as in, "be reconciled to your fate".

For example, the papal Inquisition often employed the term to describe the sentences imposed on "heretics" and other enemies of the Roman church. According to medieval historian Henry Charles Lea, a record from the Spanish papal court in 1549 describes how three men who were accused of Lutheranism were "reconciled to the church through a loss of property". Other religious dissidents "were subjected to reconciliation for Judaism and committed to the galleys as slaves". (115)

Catholicism inherited this understanding and practice of "reconciliation" from its parent body, the Imperial Roman Empire. For beginning in the first century it was the practice of Emperors to parade those captured chieftains who had rebelled against Rome through the Forum, and to have them kneel in supplication before the Emperor and beg his forgiveness. The rebel leaders were then ritually strangled to death in an elaborate public ceremony known as the "reconcilia". Imperial records make continual reference to this "act of reconciliation". (116)

Understood in this light, the "reconciliation" between white Canada and its aboriginal victims becomes much clearer: not as an act of friendly, mutual recovery but of a reassertion of Canadian authority and domination over Indians who had dared to accuse and sue their tormentors of church and state. The very fact that not one person has ever gone to trial in Canada for the death of any of the 50,000 and more Indian children killed in residential schools proves that these deaths are not considered a crime. The real crime is to reveal what happened, and such rebellion must be "reconciled" through the public humiliation and admission of wrong by the rebel, not the rulers.

And that is indeed what has happened in Canada throughout the entire process surrounding the residential schools exposure, and of subsequent litigation, "compensation" and "apology": school survivors have been publicly humiliated and re-subordinated as subjects of the Crown by legally absolving their torturers in writing from all wrongdoing in exchange for a few token dollars and a pat on the head.

By openly flouting domestic and international law through this arranged pardoning of themselves of proven criminal wrongdoing, and by establishing the terms of reparations and self-indemnification, the Canadian government has imposed its own "*Reconcilia*" on its subject peoples under the familiar guise of benevolence.

As part of this process whereby Christian Canada re-imposed its authority over aboriginal people, the government justified itself through a formal "apology" to residential school survivors in parliament on June 11, 2008. Once again, this word has a double, contradictory meaning: both an expression of regret, and a defense of one's actions.

A classic "apologia" was a written vindication of a scholar's work or ideas, or in court, of a legal argument. Under the law, a statement of "apology" is part of a legal settlement whereby the "apologist" is released from all obligations towards an injured party through the apology. In reality, Prime Minister Stephen Harper was saying publicly to every residential school survivor, "It's unfortunate what you suffered but we were justified in doing it, we are not at fault, and the matter is hereby officially resolved." (117)

By accepting the Harper apology on "behalf" of the consulted survivors whom they had never consulted, the AFN chiefs and other subordinated Indians completed this ancient process and ritual of *Reconcilia* by showing that native nations had once again accepted the supremacy of the Crown and Canadian laws, as in the government-run "treaty" process where the "Crown" is recognized as the true owner of the land.

Ultimately, even without such recent "apologetic" measures by their own government, Canadians – like all citizens of a genocidal regime – had already been raised with and conditioned by a carefully modified definition of the crime designed to normalize it and prevent legal action against the institutions responsible. This modification occurred quite deliberately at the United Nations, and was engineered by American and Canadian diplomats during 1946 prior to the adoption of the final version of the Genocide Convention in 1947.

Indeed, this historic re-conceptualization of Genocide both under the law and in the popular consciousness has been a key factor in creating the present culture of normalized genocide in Canada; a culture that has allowed the concealment and continuation of the crime.

Redefining Genocide: The Ultimate Deceptive Lens

By genocide we mean the destruction of a nation or of an ethnic group. – Raphael Lemkin, 1944
Genocide means any of the following acts with the intent to destroy ... a national, ethnic, racial or religious group. – United Nations Convention on the Crime of Genocide, 1948

A Polish Jewish refugee named Raphael Lemkin lost over fifty members of his family in Nazi death camps during the Second World War. After fleeing to America in 1943, Lemkin, a jurist, helped draft the Nuremburg Declaration and post-war human rights conventions, including the much-quoted but rarely-enacted United Nations Convention on the Crime of Genocide (1948).

Lemkin had a very broad notion of the crime. In his 1944 book, Axis Rule in Occupied Europe, he wrote,

"Generally speaking, genocide does not necessarily mean the immediate destruction of a nation, except when accomplished by mass killings of all members of a nation. It is intended rather to signify a coordinated plan of different actions aiming at the destruction of essential foundations of the life of national groups, with the aim of annihilating the groups themselves." (118)

To Lemkin, anything that a conquering group does to the conquered which tries to cause their eventual demise is genocide, including the banning of their language, disrupting their normal family patterns, or placing children of the conquered group in the homes of others so that the children forget who they are.

Obviously, this kind of sweeping sense of the crime created huge potential problems for the very nations that conquered Nazi Germany, including Canada and the United States, who for centuries had been doing just such eradication against indigenous nations across their own continent. And so not surprisingly, Lemkin's broad understanding of genocide never survived post-war political realities. Thanks to pressure brought by Canadian and American diplomats at the United Nations, genocide was fundamentally redefined in two ways: 1. it constituted not simply actions, but intentions, and 2. it meant primarily the physical killing of a people. This new understanding of genocide de-emphasized those aspects of the crime that might indict western governments and their partner churches, including for what was occurring at that very time in Indian boarding schools in both Canada and the United States, as well as in Australia, South Africa and many other settler states.

The centuries-old efforts by every European and North American government and their churches to wipe out indigenous peoples' language, identity and nationhood clearly fell under Lemkin's original definition of genocide. But more than post-war political expediency prompted this kind of revision of Lemkin's understanding of genocide. Because that crime emerged from the very religious and philosophical fabric of European culture, and commenced specifically with the rise of Christian Empire, or Christendom, in the fourth century, "western" culture as a whole was indicted by the Lemkin understanding of genocide.

To quote author Richard Rubenstein, *The culture that made the (Nazi) death camps possible was not only indigenous to the West but was an outcome ... of its fundamental religious tradition that insists upon the dichotomous division of mankind into the elect and the reprobate.* (119)

The "religious tradition" Rubenstein refers to emerged from a Greco-Judeao-Christian culture that equated one's religious faith with the conquest and destruction of other people. Its two main roots are in the Hebrew Bible and Greek philosophy, both of which were foundational in the formation of the Roman Catholic church and the culture it spawned, and that formed the United Nations.

Lemkin had originally defined genocide as any act that caused the eventual destruction of a people, including efforts to eradicate a peoples' language, culture or nationhood, as well as displacing them from their homeland: a definition that could easily be applied to North Americans' treatment of aboriginal peoples. Armed with this broad view, Lemkin wrote an initial "Draft Declaration" in October, 1946, and won sponsorship for it in the Economic and Social Council of the U.N. from Cuba, India and Panama. It also won initial support from the United States, which in hindsight appeared to be a way for that nation to situate itself on the sub-committee in order to re-write the Draft that had been produced by the Legal Committee of the U.N. General Assembly.

Sometime between October of 1946 and the final approval of the new version of the Draft in the General Assembly on December 11th of that year, the sub-committee altered the definition of genocide provided by Lemkin to make it inapplicable to crimes occurring domestically in North America and other countries, and to shift the emphasis in the U.N. document's definition of genocide away from the action itself to its intentionality. The chairman of the sub-committee, Charles Fahy, was a lawyer for the U.S. State Department and the American delegate to the U.N. One of his first acts, according to Lemkin, was to try to change the word "genocide" to the more legally vague term "extermination": an attempt that failed. (120)

As Lemkin describes in his unpublished work *Totally Unofficial Man: The Autobiography of Raphael Lemkin*, in the wake of his failed attempt, Fahy dispatched the Canadian U.N. delegate, Dana Wilgress, to try to win over Lemkin to the United States position that a revised version of the Convention was needed: one that de-emphasized cultural genocide and left ambiguous the application of the Convention to national legal systems.

In short, Canada and the United States – and by then with the support of Great Britain – wanted to make the Convention not only inapplicable to their nations and to their own acts of genocide, but have it remain a general statement that could not be implemented in their own domestic legal and political systems.

One of the ways they eventually ensured such immunity was by a legal formalism that shifted the focus in the definition of genocide from an action to an intention; a redefinition that created enormous ambiguity and gave any criminal regime a huge loophole through which to escape prosecution. For example, in Lemkin's original opening sentence in his book Axis Rule in Occupied Europe (1944), he stated simply and boldly,

By genocide we mean the destruction of a nation or of an ethnic group.

But in the final Genocide Convention, passed by the U.N. General Assembly, Lemkin's statement was altered to read,

In the present Convention, genocide means any of the following acts committed with the intent to destroy, in whole or in part, a national, ethnical, racial or religious group.

Lemkin's original definition automatically condemns any practitioner of certain acts. But the revised U.N. Convention only allows such prosecution *if it can first be established that there was an intention to commit those acts.* And yet how can the intent of genocidal regimes to wipe out certain groups ever be established beyond any reasonable doubt? Clearly, it is much more difficult to ascertain intent than results.

Thanks to the pressure brought by these "Big Three" nations (USA, England, Canada), this loophole became part of the redefinition of genocide that protected these three nations and others from prosecution for their genocide of foreign or indigenous peoples. The final debate on the Genocide Convention defeated Lemkin's position and excluded most of his definitions of cultural genocide from the final draft, in order to narrow the notion of genocide to a primarily physical destruction. In addition, it left it up to each individual nation to decide whether or not to enact enabling legislation to allow the Convention to be applied to crimes within their own borders: precisely like asking the accused criminal whether or not he's willing to be prosecuted.

In justifying its actions, the Canadian delegation wrote unconvincingly in a September, 1948 External Affairs publication:

Canadian opposition to the inclusion of "cultural genocide" in the convention was prompted by the consideration that it was neither within the Economic and Social Council's terms of reference, nor properly included in a convention designed for protection of human life. (121)

This narrow attitude – that safeguarding a peoples' culture had no connection to saving their lives – reflected the re-conceptualizing of genocide being foisted by Canada, the USA and Britain on the United Nations: namely, that this crime consisted essentially of the outright physical extermination of a people, and that, contrary to all the evidence, *destroying the culture or social life of a group was not genocide.*

The Canadian government took immediate advantage of this new restricted and emasculated version of the Genocide Convention to ensure that even this diluted document could never be applied to its own actions within its borders. The government did so by blocking any domestic enabling legislation that would have allowed the Convention to be applied within Canada.
Speaking in Canada's House of Commons on May 21, 1952, External Affairs Minister - and future Prime Minister and liberal paragon - Lester B. Pearson actually argued that such legislation was unnecessary in Canada:

I am further of the opinion that no legislation is required by Canada at this time to implement this convention, inasmuch as I cannot conceive of any act of commission or omission occurring in Canada as falling within the definition of the crime of genocide contained in this convention. (Hansard, Spring Session 1952, House of Commons, Ottawa)

Pearson made this statement at the same time that hundreds of aboriginal children were being deliberately starved, tortured and killed every month in Canada's Indian residential school system. Later that week Pearson commented again, echoing a statement by a Parliamentary human rights committee and explicitly stating that residential schools "must not be considered to be a crime".
In Pearson's words,

The concept of genocide must be limited to physical destruction of a group since otherwise it is an offense to transfer children from one group to another in order to destroy them. Could it then not be argued that the proposals to impose integrated education on the children of Doukhobors or Indians for example might fall within this prohibition? Clearly, this must not be considered to be a crime. (122)
In other words, we don't want to be tried for genocide, even though it's happening here; so let's just redefine genocide to get ourselves off the hook! And that's precisely what happened.
Not surprisingly, while ratifying the Genocide Convention "in principle" in 1952, Canada did not pass any enabling legislation related to the Convention at that time, and didn't do so for another half century, during the spring of 2000.

However, this law, entitled "The Crimes against Humanity Act" actually prohibits the prosecution of any crime of genocide that happened within Canada if it occurred before the year 2000, thereby barring any prosecution for genocide in the residential schools, which closed in 1996. By such self-serving actions, Canada has consistently protected itself from being prosecuted for actions within the country that were clearly genocidal, like transferring children to another group, preventing births, causing deaths and the long term destruction of a group, and other acts that were planned and occurred throughout the entire Indian residential school system.

It is therefore not surprising that mainstream Canadians have not been capable of recognizing that what happened to native children in these schools constitutes genocide, since their understanding of the latter has been conditioned to not recognize it when it occurs in their own country.
Nevertheless, this attitude does not lessen or restrict the guilt and liability of Canada and its Christian churches for their proven crimes against humanity. Under domestic laws, genocide was legal in Canada, as it was in Nazi Germany. But under the principle of *"post ipso facto"* justice employed and established at the Nuremburg Tribunals after World War Two, even if a crime was legal under the laws of one country at the time they were committed, it still constitutes a crime under international law and can be prosecuted. Generally speaking, these examples go far to demonstrate that normative genocide is not only a matter of legal custom and language. For as a hegemonic system of control, it is invisible to its participants, whether they are the conquerors or the dominated nations. Such indeed is the experience of genocide in Canada, and of how that destruction is continuing.

Footnotes: Part Two: Concealment, Containment and Deception

(95) From the July, 2008 interview with Peter Yellowquill.

(96) Correspondence of June 19 and 24, 1903. RG 10 series, File 7733. (Figures 116 and 117)

(97) See the discussion of the Bryce report in Section One of this report, and in its entirety in Appendix One and at *www.hiddennolonger.com* .

(98) From the **Hansard Parliamentary Reports,** Ottawa, June 8, 1920, p. 3278. The average of a 69% death rate at the File Hill School was first reported in the Ottawa Citizen on November 15, 1907 in its discussion of Dr. Peter Bryce's report (*see Figure 1*). That is, a two thirds die off rate had not diminished at the File Hills School in thirteen years.

(99) The November 6, 1919 letter criticizing Dr. Stuart states clearly that a local smallpox epidemic was deliberately spread from the St. Mary's Catholic Indian school in Mission to the surrounding reservations.

(100) From an extended interview with Kenny Quatell in Nanaimo on May 8, 2005. Some of Kenny's remarks can also be viewed in the film *Unrepentant.*

(101) Harry's affidavits describing these incidents are in Figures 77 and 78.

(102) From a statement of Irene Starr to the IHRAAM Tribunal, June 14, 1998.

(103) From a statement by Kevin Annett at a Vancouver public forum on February 9, 1998.

(104) These rulings by the Alberta and Ontario Supreme Courts were followed quickly by federal legislation that restricted the scope and conditions of any future residential school lawsuits, and even denied "healing funds" to survivors engaged in litigation against the government or the churches.

(105) See **Hidden No Longer: Genocide in Canada** , Appendix 4. (*www.hiddennolonger.com*)

(106) For a transcript of these incidents and statements, see Appendix Two.

(107) These allegations were made as recently as June 5, 2014 (RCMP) and October 9, 2011 (United Church). The RCMP desk sergeant in the Port Alberni detachment even claimed to Kevin Annett during a phone call that "There never were any reported deaths in the residential school here". Annett then asked him if he reads the newspapers.

(108) See "*Vatican told bishops to cover up sex abuse*" by Antony Barnett, *The Observer*, August 17, 2003 (London)

(109) A complete transcript of **Crimen Sollicitationas** can be found in Appendix Four, along with a copy of the London *Observer* article reporting its discovery.

(110) See *http://humansarefree.com/2014/03/pope-francis-charged-in-trafficking.html and http://itccs.org/2014/02/02/pope-francis-is-named-by-former-argentine-junta-insider-as-prime-mover-in-child-trafficking-network-francis-concealed-vatican-crown-of-england-holyrood-agreement/*

(111) The language of benevolent extermination goes back centuries in British culture to the time of Thomas Hobbes and Francis Bacon. "Assimilation" literally means to eat another person, or people, and to thereby extinguish and absorb them into the "body" of the State. See Hobbes' work **Leviathan** (1659) for the context behind this term.

(112) From a speech given by Kevin Annett on August 30, 2008 at the International Humanist Convention in Carlingford, Ireland.

(113) Of equal significance is the fact that Nora Bernard was murdered on December 30, 2007, on the eve of the government's major spin and containment operation known as the "Truth and Reconciliation Commission" (TRC). No motive was ever ascribed to her killing besides an undisclosed "family dispute", and the media quickly buried the story despite its topical nature.

(114)From an interview with Delmar Johnny on August 4, 2005 in Duncan, British Columbia.

(115) Lea, Henry Charles, **The Inquisition of the Spanish Dependencies** (1908), p. 421. See Bibliography.

(116) This Imperial custom of "reconciling" the conqueror and conquered on the terms of the former entered into Roman catholic theology as one of its so-called sacraments, "the penitential act of reconciliation", otherwise known as the "confessional", whereby sins are supposedly absolved by a priest acting for the "divine emperor", ie, God. The message of re-subordination to a higher power remains the same. See Lea, ibid.

(117) For a discussion of the Biblical origin and nature of an "apologia" as a "reasoned defense of an argument" see *http://biblehub.com/greek/627.htm* .

(118) **Axis Rule in Occupied Europe** by Raphael Lemkin (Washington, 1944), pp. 3-4

(119) **The Cunning of History: The Holocaust and the American Future** by Richard Rubenstein (1978), p. 31.

(120) Much of this account of the events at the United Nations are taken from **Raphael Lemkin and the Struggle for the Genocide Convention** by John Cooper (Herald Press, 2008) and from Lemkin's own self-published account in his **Totally Unofficial Man** autobiography.

(121) This incident and Lester Pearson's remarks are discussed extensively in Cooper, ibid.

(122) Cooper, ibid. p. 141.

Part Three: The Ongoing Crime

A former official of the Indian Affairs Department who spent two years in Eskimo communities charged that there is an unofficial policy of recommending sterilization of Eskimo women … - The Globe and Mail, January 12, 1979, *"Native women told birth control pills vitamins: nurse".*

An organized system of abduction, exploitation, torture and murder of large numbers of women and children appears to exist on Canada's west coast, and is operated and protected in part by sectors of the RCMP, the Vancouver Police Department (VPD), the judiciary, and members of the British Columbia government and federal government of Canada, including the Canadian military. - From the Memorandum on West Coast Human Trafficking, Issued by the Friends and Relatives of the Disappeared (FRD), May 26, 2006, Vancouver (*See Appendix Seven*)

Social services can grab an Indian mother's kids anytime without a warrant or any procedure. More Indians die in prison here than any other group, and a third of the inmates are aboriginal. Hell, the prison officials are given twice the amount of money by the government for a native inmate than a white one. Every hospital in town has an unofficial "do not resuscitate" policy when it comes to Indians in Emergency. And practically every homeless Indian is there because he lost his land up north somewhere to some fat cat company. You learn all these things as a cop right away, but like in the residential schools, everybody's supposed to look the other way and just go along with the genocide.
- Former RCMP Constable George Brown, Vancouver, April 18, 2005

It's not just our women who are going missing. Whole families are disappearing, starting with the children. Our northern indigenous communities are being terrorized and wiped out for their land by big corporations and their hired RCMP thugs. It's the residential schools genocide taken to its next step. – Vancouver native activist Carol Martin, June 5, 2009

Genocide has always been a necessary tool of state and of religion. The extermination of indigenous nations established Canada and has ensured its prosperity. Today, that same annihilation of indigenous nations is not only continuing but is expanding.

The simple reason for this is because such genocide continues to profit the resource extraction-based Canadian economy, and consequently, has become institutionalized in the very fiber of government and society.

Put simply, both foreign capital and domestic politics require that Indians in Canada continue to be made landless, impoverished and eradicated, and profitably milked in the process. The foreign corporate-driven plundering of Canadian resources is hardly a new phenomenon, anymore than is the fact that traditional native people stand in the way of that huge land grab. Yesterday, Indians were annihilated so that British and American companies could harvest the furs, lumber and minerals of Canada. Today, this plundering is led by Asian capital and the American military-based Uranium industry that is poisoning and killing northern Cree and Inuit peoples off their lands. (123)

The different manifestations of this crime and its social consequences need to be seen in this context and not viewed separately or in isolation, as the corporate media does when it examines, for instance, "the disturbingly high rates of teenage aboriginal suicide", or "the prevailing poverty rates among on-reserve natives." Such conditions are neither accidental nor unconnected to the continued genocidal requirement of, to quote article two of the U.N. Genocide Convention, "fostering conditions designed to cause the long term destruction of a group".

The clues lie everywhere concerning the deliberate Canadian state policy of fostering such destruction of aboriginal nations. The very existence of the apartheid Indian Act, that denies citizenship rights to Indians on reservations and makes them legal wards of the state, is the most obvious example. Such legal segregation of a targeted group is a tell tale sign of genocidal policy. Its aim of keeping Indians poor and dependent is evident in such policies as the Indian Act statute that forbids local band councils from using government money to make their tribe economically self-sufficient by creating local jobs or businesses on reservations.

Significantly, the same restriction applies to any "compensation" money given to Indian residential school survivors by the government. Such money can only be awarded to individuals in the form of a cheque rather than as a group endowment that, for example, could go towards building proper drinking water, sewage and sanitation facilities on the over half of reservations across Canada that still lack such basic necessities.

The Indian Act also restricts the amount of money a band council can spend on children on their reserve, and even denies the right of reserve Indians to modify or improve their homes, causing many aboriginal homes to become moldy, disease-breeding firetraps. "They can put us in jail if we try ventilating or insulating our own homes" said Harriett Nahanee to Kevin Annett in December, 1995 during his visit to her Squamish reservation slum dwelling in North Vancouver.

The obvious question is, if Canada is not trying to make Indians permanently unhealthy and impoverished, then why would it continue to impose on them by law such draconian, unhealthy conditions?

Another sign of this intentional ongoing genocide by the Canadian state is the institutionalized practice of "two standards" when it comes to aboriginal health care, child protection and civil liberties.

"My social worker Sally Heather told me I had to have a tubal ligation if I ever wanted to see my daughter again after they took her from me" describes Eliza Stewart, a west coast aboriginal woman in Vancouver. "Two Mounties came to my house and grabbed me and brought me to a north shore hospital. That's where they did it to me. It's not like I had a choice or anything. Then I had to sign a form saying I'd never sue them for what they did to me." (124)

Such forced sterilizations and assaults on native women are routine across Canada, and are allowed by the subordinate, second class status of Indians under the law. Under provincial child protection protocols, children in native families can be seized without a warrant or the kind of review and appeal process that applies to non-aboriginal families on social services.

"The child welfare system is just another residential school, only worse" says Chief Peter Yellowquill of the Long Plains Anishinabe Nation in Manitoba. *"Today, there are more of our children in government institutions or white foster homes than were ever in residential schools. They're still trying to wipe out our culture and our families."* (125)

Yellowquill is not exaggerating. Even Canadian government statistics show that growing numbers of aboriginal children are being incarcerated in non-native homes or institutions, including by their deliberate criminalization at a young age by the police and court system across Canada. Over half of all children in foster care in Canada are aboriginal, despite being barely 2% of the population. (126) Other government statistics reveal that of the approximately fifty indigenous languages still in use in Canada in 1996, only three will still be in existence by 2025. (127)

The general picture of aboriginal life expectancy and standard of living in Canada is equally dismal, and is not improving. In 2007, mortality rates among Indians were five times the national average, infant mortality three times higher, tuberculosis eight to ten times higher. Only one third of native communities had adequate housing or regular sewage disposal. None of these figures had improved, and tuberculosis levels had actually worsened, since a similar survey was conducted by the Department of Indian Affairs (DIA) in October, 1998. (128)

The DIA study of 1998 was discussed in a front page *Globe and Mail* article of October 13, 1998 entitled *"Canada's squalid secret: life on native reserves; Income, education, life expectancy worse than in 62 countries."* Aboriginal people's standard of living in Canada ranked below Thailand and Brazil when grouped as a nation. Native children in British Columbia have the same chance of dying as an Indian child in Guatemala, according to the study.

The telling fact is that life in Canada is becoming constantly worse for Indians despite an annual expenditure of over $6 billion towards "Indian affairs". None of these funds are reaching most Indians for they are not meant to. In the words of former Assembly of First Nations (AFN) chief Wilfred Price of the Haida Nation,

"The whole system is structured to benefit a handful of aboriginal insiders, the AFN chiefs and their families on reserve. We calculated that over 96% of the government 'Indian Affairs' money ends up either in their hands or is used up in the DIA administration, which is run entirely by white bureaucrats. Nothing gets down to the people on reserve who are dying off quicker every year. That's no accident either. The local chiefs are supposed to starve their own people off their land and off the reserve with a minimum 'cut off quota' every year. That's why I quit." (129)

Wilfred Price's description of the destructive role of reservation Chiefs towards their own people has been confirmed by Les Guerin of the Musqueam Nation in Vancouver and by AFN documents surfaced by him in October of 2004. The documents are transcripts of a closed, top-level AFN gathering in Calgary from October 20 and 23, 2003 that discussed how to implement what AFN leaders called "the Agenda 21 agenda" on their own reservations.

In the words of the Chairman of the meeting, Wendy Grant, *"There's a whole new society coming and we're going to be running it. We've got to get rid of the dead wood and all the useless mouths, Agenda 21 and all that"* (130)

"Agenda 21" is the designation of a program launched at the United Nations "Sustainable Development" Conferences during the 1990's which aims at limiting and reducing human population levels under the guise of "environmental sustainability". In keeping with the aims of this Agenda, Wendy Grant – an official as well of the Musqueam band council – has since 2003 forced over one third of all Musqueam families out of their housing on the reserve and denied them education and health subsidies in order to expel them from Musqueam land altogether. (131)

Under the language of normative genocide, "sustainable development" is a code word for the de-population of indigenous and poor people. Numerous advocates of Agenda 21, like former US Defense Secretary Robert MacNamara, are proponents of the massive sterilization of black and aboriginal people, and of imposing "austerity measures" on the same groups of the kind enacted at Musqueam and many Indian reservations across Canada.

Two former members of the Carrier-Sekani Tribal Council in Prince George, British Columbia confirmed this practice in their testimony before the IHRAAM Tribunal into residential schools in June, 1998 in Vancouver. According to that testimony, Frank Martin and Helen Michel were forced into exile from their traditional lands after Chief Ed John – Wendy Grant's husband – arranged the murder of their family members and terrorized them to surrender their land title.
"I heard Eddie John say it himself at the Council meeting in the spring of 2002, how they had to consolidate the Nation, is how he put it. That meant throw half of us off our land and cut lots off the band's welfare rolls. Where did all those people end up? I'll tell you where, homeless and dying down here on the streets. And then the chiefs made a bundle selling off our land to B.C. Hydro and Interfor. Anyone who tried opposing Eddie got a one way trip to the lake." (132)

Such band council-led terrorism and neo-genocide against indigenous people is closely tied to the corporate agenda and geo-politics of the 21st century, especially in the resource-rich, strategically vital economy of British Columbia and northern Canada.

Merv Richie is a former newspaper publisher in Terrace, British Columbia whose publication, the *Terrace Daily News*, was shut down in 2015 after it began reporting the genocide of local Indians and the crimes of the Catholic Church. According to Richie,

"It was the local Knights of Columbus who scared off all my advertisers, one after another. I even know the guy who did it. But that wasn't just because of my editorial criticisms of the Vatican. For months I was reporting the Chinese connection to all the disappearances around here, and how China is heavily invested in the present day genocide. I also showed the RCMP's involvement. The harassment's never stopped since then." (133)

Richie describes how he discovered that aboriginal lands and their resources in northern British Columbia are being bought up by Chinese cartels and colonized by Chinese settlers under secret agreements with the provincial government and Beijing that have been in place since at least the 1990's. RCMP officers, native politicians and private mercenaries working for Chinese cartels are killing and terrorizing Indians off their lands to make way for this new wave of immigration.

"I was the only media covering this stuff. I covered the trial in 2007 and 2008 where it came out how Rio Tinto and Alcan through the provincial Premier Gordon Campbell had made secret deals with the Haisla Indian band to sell off their lands for nothing. I even discovered secret military maneuvers going on up north. I guess I just pushed too many buttons." (134)

The corporate reign of terror against traditional tribal groups occupying rich resources has been continual and deliberate. In a September 2, 2002 email letter, a man named Pete MacLean, a former insider with Alcan in northern British Columbia, wrote to Kevin Annett, *"The Kemano project in the late 1970's was based on an earlier document for the water rights signed sometime in the 1950's giving Alcan the water rights for 50 years. But what happened was that the people living where Cheslatta Falls now is were more or less coerced into signing it. The Alcan officials that wanted the water rights showed up in the fall when most of the men were hunting. The village at that time of the season consisted of young children, women and the old. From what I remember they told the people that they had to sign this. The village asked if they could get a hold of the men who were away hunting but the Alcan officials said no.*

"The saddest part of all is that the village could not discuss this amongst themselves since Alcan gave them no alternative. They basically told them that if they didn't sign they would flood their land anyways. In signing this document they would at least be moved to another area ... But after the signing they were given only so many days to leave the area. When the men came back from hunting they were told what happened. There was nothing they could do now but pack up and leave.

"The area that Alcan gave them was deplorable. There was not enough game to hunt and many starved. Some tried to stay at their old village but sickness and disease swept the area. How many died I can't remember."

As mentioned, local tribal council chiefs have normally assisted this massive land theft and dislocation of their own people. Sharon Tootchie, a Cowichan Indian from Vancouver Island, described in an interview on November 2, 2006,

"Our family is from a traditionalist line and so as the oldest daughter I was set to inherit our land and pass it on to my son Rick. But right after he came of age he was picked up by the RCMP and beaten badly, then he kept getting targeted for midnight rides so he went into hiding. But it didn't stop. When I found out how the local tribal council chief, Harvey Alphonse, was stealing our land I tried making a stink and I get the treatment too. I had to flee to Saskatchewan if I wanted to live.

"It turns out that during 2005 Harvey had stolen not just our land but over 36,000 acres of Cowichan land and given it cheaply to his friends in the Timberwest company, who own practically all of Vancouver Island now. Harvey's payoff was a new fishing boat, a yacht and two new cars."

Peter Yellowquill in Manitoba describes a similar regime of official terrorism against his people by the state-funded "chief and council" on his Long Plains reserve.

"The elected chiefs like Dennis Meeches are the ones dealing the drugs on our reserve and ripping off all the money. The feds use them to keep the rest of us in line. That's why Meeches and his kind are put and kept in power by the government, to control and help wipe out their own people. Our house was burned to the ground and my kids got arrested and then targeted by the band council to force me to go along with their scams. Anybody who isn't part of their crooked game gets chased out or rubbed out." (135) Devoid of any authentic leadership and kept in fear by the "official" chiefs, aboriginals in Canada are kept defenseless against whatever violence and depredations church and state, the police and corporations choose to inflict on them, in the manner of any third world banana republic.

This neo-colonial reality partly explains the level and ferocity of the ongoing institutionalized violence towards them, which is and has always been aimed specifically at aboriginal women and children.

Disappeared Women and Children

(This section of the Report should be read in conjunction with Appendix Seven)

The genocide of our people began and it carries on with the targeting of our women and children for destruction, because once the occupying powers break the aboriginal family that way, we will have no more future.

– Dr. Douglas Wilson of the Haida Nation speaking at the University of Victoria, March 3, 2007

There is a pattern to the disappearances of all these women. We found they're mostly related by blood to the clan mothers from up north who are the original holders of the land. This is planned racial targeting to get the land.

– Former RCMP Constable George Brown of the *Community Inquiry into Missing People*, Vancouver, January 5, 2002

For many years the RCMP and corporate media contained and camouflaged the fact that hundreds of aboriginal women and their children were vanishing along the corridor known as the "Highway of Tears" in northern British Columbia: Highway 16 between Terrace and Prince George.

Since the late 1980's when stories of missing west coast native women first appeared in cursory media coverage, the RCMP has consistently ignored missing persons requests filed by aboriginal families. Under pressure, the RCMP eventually produced a media cover story that claimed that only sixteen women could not be accounted for: a number that stayed constant for years, despite escalating reports of disappearances not just along Highway 16 but all over the province.

Even as recently as 2014, the RCMP have claimed that over thirty two years, between 1980 and 2012, only 40 unsolved aboriginal female murders and 36 missing cases in which foul play was suspected have occurred in British Columbia. (136) And equally remarkable is the fact that at no time did the RCMP identify where these disappearances were clustered: along Highway 16 and in Vancouver's slum-ridden Downtown Eastside community.

George Brown, a now-retired aboriginal RCMP officer, ran afoul of his commander in Chilliwack, British Columbia when he began probing into the missing women as early as 1999.

"Their official line bore all the typical signs of an organized cover up, like right out of the old residential schools. I knew right away that an order was coming down to steer attention away from where and why the killings were happening because a wall of silence came down whenever I tried finding out these things, to trace a pattern behind the disappearances. None of us was ever allowed to go past a certain point even after we started investigating the missing women. That woke me up that somebody was being covered for." (137)

Frustrated and alarmed, George Brown and a handful of friends began their own "Community Inquiry into Missing People" in the spring of 1999. Their investigation began in Vancouver's downtown east side among the mostly-aboriginal street people and prostitutes who not only were related to many of the missing women, but who themselves were prime targets for going missing. Indeed, dozens of east side prostitutes, over 90% of them aboriginal, simply vanished without a trace during this same period.

Brown and his colleagues quickly encountered Kevin Annett and his work with residential school survivors, some of whom were the very women being interviewed by Brown's group. Annett had worked in the downtown east side as a street minister since 1985 and had just helped convene the historic IHRAAM Tribunal into residential schools the previous summer in the same neighborhood. Brown and Annett soon uncovered startling new evidence. According to Brown, "*Cops were involved, for one thing. That was confirmed by many independent sources, and not just the women on the street who I assumed had a natural bias against any cop. I was told by fellow officers that they'd witnessed Indian women getting abducted by other Mounties and then gang raped in the lock up or out on a road somewhere. The ones who did it would actually joke about it. But then the woman would never turn up again, ever."* (138)

Based on their own investigations in Vancouver, the New York group Human Rights Watch issued two separate reports in 2007 and 2013 that confirmed that aboriginal people, especially prostitutes and the homeless, were being systematically targeted by Vancouver police for rape, torture and other attacks. But these reports never drew the connection between such deliberate assaults and the accompanying disappearance of native women. (139)

Brown's group also began to do background checks into the actual women going missing. The majority of them in Vancouver and along Highway 16 who were documented by Brown were related by kinship to traditional chiefly families or clan mothers who were matriarchal "keepers of the land" among the northern tribes. These disappearances were clearly not random.

In Brown's own words from an interview in January, 2002 while he was still engaged in the investigation, *"There is a pattern to the disappearances of all these women. We found they're mostly related by blood to the clan mothers from up north who are the original holders of the land. This is planned racial targeting to get the land."*

One of the women interviewed by Brown and Annett was Carol Martin of the Haida Nation who worked at the Downtown East side Women's Centre. Martin described how the disappearances were engulfing more than aboriginal women.

"It's not just our women who are going missing. Whole families are disappearing, starting with the children. Our northern communities are being wiped out for their land by big corporations and their hired RCMP thugs. It's the residential school genocide taken to its next step." (140)

Martin described how the common pattern involving disappeared native families was for children to first be unlawfully abducted on a flimsy pretext by the provincial Ministry of Children and Families (MCF) – an agency actually run by accused child trafficker Chief Ed John between 2000 and 2002 – and then, in response to complaints or non-cooperation by either or both parents, all of the children and then the parents would be apprehended, usually by the RCMP. The family would then vanish. In more overt cases, native families driving in rural areas would simply disappear and the local police would claim to have no record of them. (141)

Kevin Annett has observed how a similar pattern characterized the systematic disappearance of homeless people and prostitutes in Vancouver during "Expo 86".

"Dozens of people just vanished from the streets during Expo and were never seen again. In most cases these were homeless people and prostitutes who had no money or mobility, and so would have found it impossible to simply take up and leave on their own. The majority of them were also aboriginal. I've spoken with locals who saw people being loaded into police vehicles and driven away and then never return. When we checked with the Vancouver police about these people, they'd continually claim they never heard of them and had no record of a disappearance." (142)

The targeting of traditional aboriginal women for murder is evident in the disappearance of Wendy Poole during the late 1990's. Wendy was an early victim of the Vancouver downtown eastside serial killing. She was not only a hereditary chief but related to a politically militant family that had fought the government for years over their land rights; her uncle Art Napoleon had attempted to establish sovereignty for his Moberly Lake Cree band and reclaimed much of the land in that territory.

After she disappeared, Wendy's body was eventually found dismembered and mutilated in a Vancouver dumpster. Her body was missing body parts, suggesting death by torture and possible even ritual slaying. But a veil of silence descended on her killing and neither the police nor media investigated it, even when her family petitioned the government to do so over ten years after her murder.

At this time, between 2005 and 2009, the growing Canadian media coverage of Annett's Vancouver-based campaign to confront local churches over their residential school crimes brought renewed attention on the missing aboriginal women and children. By 2006, downtown east side activists and native women – many of whom like Carol Martin appeared on Annett's *Hidden from History* program - were conducting annual "Remember the Sisters" marches on Valentine's Day that received wide media attention. Growing political pressure forced the federal government to begin making noises about conducting an inquiry into missing women while avoiding any actual investigation.

Craftily, in the same manner that the Indian residential schools genocide was reduced in the public mind to a benign and manageable issue of "apology and compensation", the continued slaughter of aboriginal women and children was reduced by the government and media to the issues surrounding the trial of the alleged serial killer Willie Picton. *(See Addendum to Appendix Seven, Witness No. 7)*

According to sources like former Canadian Security Intelligence Service (CSIS) operative Grant Wakefield, Picton had been made a deliberate scapegoat by the courts and government to distract attention from the wide network of police, judges and politicians who were preying on and killing native women and children on the west coast. The overt corruption and manipulation surrounding the Picton trial, and the demands of victims' families to reopen that case, completely dominated the public discourse about missing women just as the Brown-Annett independent inquiry began gaining steam. This was not coincidental. (143)

Independent commentators noted that the number of aboriginal women going missing continued to rise after Picton's arrest: a stark indication of a bigger crime that all of the corporate media ignored as they restricted their coverage to the "lone gunman" Willie Picton. In reality, as Wakefield and other police sources have confirmed, Picton and his brother Dave were merely low-level members of a body disposal crew unconnected to the actual kidnappings and killings.

Building on this big deception and the discontent of many victims' families, the newly elected Liberal government and its Prime Minister Justin Trudeau announced a national "missing women's inquiry" early in the new year of 2016. While making all of the politically correct noises including promising to "consult" victims' families, the Liberals created the same restricted and controlled "inquiry" that relied upon the very groups that had concealed and been implicated in the crime – including the RCMP and the Vancouver Police Department - in the manner of a latter day TRC.

It will be the aim of the ITDC to not only conduct its own independent inquiry into missing aboriginal people across Canada but to monitor this latest attempt by Canada and its police forces to misrepresent and conceal the ongoing genocide.

Child trafficking beyond the aboriginal world

It is clear that the massive underground industry in child trafficking is not confined to the aboriginal world, although admittedly native children are especially easy to steal and made to go missing because of the declassed, colonial status of Indians in Canada. Any marginal group, especially young pregnant girls, low income families and targeted families are susceptible to child abduction.

Modern child trafficking begins in the womb. A massive west coast baby adoption racket operating through the Roman Catholic Church, church-funded hospitals and the provincial government's social services was revealed by one of its victims, Hanne Andersen, in 2007.

In June, 1983 in Vancouver, Hanne was fifteen years old and became pregnant. She was then coerced by her mother, a social worker and her parish priest, a Rev. Mika from Holy Rosary cathedral, to enter into a special facility run by the church where her baby was slated for eventual adoption. That facility was known as the Maywood Home for Unwed Mothers at 7280 Oak Street. At that point Hanne was only six weeks pregnant. She had no say in the matter and at the Home was subjected to what she calls "a constant regime of brainwashing and intimidation" to agree to give up her baby while it was still in utero. *"I was locked up like I was a prisoner and given drugs day and night. The matrons were abusive and kept the fridge locked up so none of us could eat without their oversight. We had to watch these Catholic propaganda films and were constantly told we were unfit to be mothers. They were making us brainwashed to hate the idea of being mothers. They even made us write letters saying we didn't want our babies and starved and beat us until we signed them."*

The priest who engineered Hanne's incarceration in this church-run prison worked closely with a Dr. Bertha Brisco and the staff of St. Paul's Catholic hospital. Dr. Brisco was a member of the Holy Rosary parish. She forced a series of drugs on Hanne including seconal, oxycontin and other barbiturates to induce depression and to speed up labor, and parladol, a lactation suppressant. According to documents provided by Hanne, Dr. Brisco operated according to a "BFA Protocol" – "Baby for Adoption" – by which hospitals designate a specialized and secretive program of medication for young girls whose unborn babies have been targeted for adoption.

"The BFA designation appeared on the hospital records so it was an institutional protocol, not just Brisco's thing. She even mentioned to me once that the Catholic Church was expected to provide a quota of newborns to the adoption agencies they had contracted with, using the 'pro life' movement to justify it. The BFA protocol operates in many Canadian hospitals to this day. I was just one of many girls that are still hunted and targeted by a black market in babies." (From a May 3, 2007 interview)

The direct collusion of senior Canadian politicians in these Catholic-run child rape and trafficking networks has been revealed by a former Cornwall, Ontario policeman named Perry Dunlop. In the early 1990's, Constable Dunlop stumbled across an extensive network of child rapists among local social workers, judges, businessmen and priests, but was ordered by senior police officials to refrain from pressing his investigation. When he did so anyway, Dunlop was reprimanded, harassed by his department superiors, and eventually expelled from his job and sentenced to six months in prison for refusing to cooperate with an elaborate cover up of the Cornwall child trafficking ring.

In the course of his investigations, Dunlop found that the Vatican's Papal Nuncio Ambassador to Canada had intervened personally to silence victims in Cornwall and pay off policemen. He also discovered that the Cornwall child abuse ring spanned the border and was part of a much bigger network.

On his own during the spring of 2000, Perry Dunlop pressed for a government inquiry into the Cornwall ring by writing to the Attorney General of Ontario, Robert Runciman. Dunlop included in his letter the evidence of the ring and local police involvement in its cover up.

An assistant to Attorney General Runciman, John Periversoff, replied to Dunlop in a letter that stated, in part, *"I appreciate your concerns but I have to protect the minister (Runciman) and he could lose his seat if he views the evidence you provided. I can accept your letter but not the package that came with it.* ***We have no authority to investigate****."* *(Our emphasis)*

Perivseroff never explained why the senior legal officer in Ontario lacked the authority to investigate crimes against children. Perry Dunlop eventually retired to the west coast of Canada and lives in semi-seclusion.

It is estimated that over 15,000 children either going missing or are unaccounted for every year across Canada. Police agencies, social services and the media have yet to provide any explanation for these continuing disappearances.

Summary

It is apparent that the genocidal norm in Canada in modern times is closely determined by the structural needs of its economy and its global and especially trans-Pacific partnerships. The apparent corporate-sponsored colonization of Chinese migrants into rural and northern areas of British Columbia and the interests of resource-hungry Chinese cartels is becoming a major factor in the continued disappearance of aboriginal families in those areas. Evidence exists that private, corporate-funded death squads operating alongside the RCMP are responsible for these continued disappearances and killings of native people.

Generally, Genocide as an unofficial policy of a corporate-driven Canadian state is escalating, especially in the traditional "killing zones" of heavily concentrated aboriginal populations in western Canada, such as northern British Columbia, Vancouver Island and urban hotspots like Vancouver, Edmonton, Regina and Winnipeg.

The deliberate targeting of native women tied to traditional tribal and matriarchal leaderships is evident, and has become institutionalized through the so-called Agenda 21 policy of the Assembly of First Nations (AFN) by which – whether on or off reservations - these targeted traditional individuals and their families are assaulted, killed, marginalized and forced into poverty, illness and homelessness. This form of neo-colonial self-slaughter is even more evident on the feudal-style Indian reservations across Canada.

These reserves are in fact internal refugee camps, which are dictatorially ruled by government-run "chiefs" often engaged in drug and child trafficking with the open compliance of the RCMP. These chiefs were programmed and prepared for this role of eliminating their own people within the Indian residential school system that identified and rewarded collaborators at a young age: a conditioning that was one of the central purposes of these schools.

Because this continued eradication of traditional aboriginal people is a structural feature of Canadian society and is highly lucrative for domestic and international capital, such genocide is unlikely to diminish either through government legislation, "official inquiries" or public petitioning. The climbing mortality among native people in the resource-rich regions of Canada is simple testimony to this hard truth.

Clearly, a more fundamental change is required.

Footnotes: Part Three - The Ongoing Crime

(123) See *http://www.watershedsentinel.ca/content/first-nation-struggle-maintain-environmental-sustainability* and *http://www.vice.com/en_ca/read/a-dene-alliance-formed-to-resist-uranium-and-tar-sands-mining-in-saskatchewan-892* . Besides the Alberta Tar Sands desecration, the operations of companies like Cameco, the uranium mining giant, are direct threats to the lives of many northern Canadian tribes. Cameco's directors and shareholders include leading Liberal and Conservative politicians.

(124) From an interview on October 12, 2010 in Vancouver. Eliza is the sister of a child murdered at the United Church's Edmonton residential schools. She tells some of her story at ***https://www.youtube.com/watch?v=RBUd3UXt6fI*** .

(125) From an interview in Portage la Prairie, Manitoba on August 4, 2012.

(126) See the Annual Review of Statistics Canada, Ottawa, 2015 at *http://www.statcan.gc.ca/pub/89-503-x/2010001/article/11442-eng.htm*. See also this Canada newswire article from May 8, 2013, "*'Tragic' number of aboriginal children in foster care stuns even the experts*", *http://www.canada.com/health/Tragic+number+aboriginal+children+foster+care+stuns+even+experts/8354098/story.html*

(127) *"Languages are dying in Canada's Aboriginal communities at an alarming rate. As of 1996, only 3 out of Canada's roughly 50 Aboriginal languages had enough speakers to be considered secure. Between 1951 and 1981 the percentage of Aboriginal people reporting an Aboriginal language as a mother tongue declined from 87.4% to 29.3%". Mary Jane Norris,* "CANADA'S ABORIGINAL LANGUAGES", **Statistics Canada — Catalogue No 11-008** *(1998)*

(128) The statistics cited are taken from a University of Ottawa study and the aforementioned *Globe and Mail* article dated October 13, 1998. See *http://www.med.uottawa.ca/sim/data/Aboriginal_e.htm* *and* *www.hiddennolonger.com*

(129) From an interview on January 9, 2010. After his interview was broadcast Wilfred was threatened by the RCMP in Vancouver. Wilfred's extended interview is part of the ITCCS archive and appears in part in *Unrepentant.*

(130) From the transcripts of the Calgary AFN meeting, pp. 32 and 33, copies of which are in the possession of Les Guerin and in the ITCCS archive. Wendy Grant is a DIA employee and the wife of the aforementioned accused child trafficker and killer Chief Ed John who is also highly placed in the Canadian government. Grant and John are both residents of the Musqueam reservation in Vancouver and have been personally responsible for the eviction and death of numerous Musqueam families, according to Les Guerin and other residents. Guerin's role in identifying the buried remains of aboriginal women on the same Musqueam reserve is described in Section Two of this report.

(131) According to Les Guerin, from his recorded statement of November 5, 2004 and held in the ITCCS archives.

(132) From the June 14, 1998 videotaped testimony of Helen Michel to the IHRAAM Panel in Vancouver, held in the ITCCS archives.

(133) From a videotaped interview with Kevin Annett made in Vancouver on December 31, 2015, to be published.

(134) Ibid. The ITDC is conducting and will publish a separate inquiry into this "Chinese connection" to disappearances.

(135) From a videotaped interview with Kevin Annett made in Portage la Prairie on May 5, 2006.

(136) See the *Vancouver Sun*, November 3, 2015.
http://www.vancouversun.com/news/many+missing+murdered+aboriginal+women+from/11490141/story.html

(137) Taken from a videotaped interview with George Brown in Chilliwack on April 17, 2006, held in the personal collection of Shawna Duckworth. See an earlier videotaped account of Brown's story recorded in Vancouver on January 5 and 6, 2002 by Kevin Annett and held in his personal collection and in the ITCCS archives.

(138) From George Brown's April, 2006 interview.

(139) The first Human Rights Watch report was issued in the fall of 2007 but was subsequently withdrawn without explanation. A second, sanitized report that deleted some of the earlier accusations against the RCMP was issued in February, 2013. See *https://www.hrw.org/report/2013/02/13/those-who-take-us-away/abusive-policing-and-failures-protection-indigenous-women* and also *http://www.cbc.ca/news/canada/british-columbia/rcmp-accused-of-rape-in-report-on-b-c-aboriginal-women-1.1305824* . It should also be noted that Human Rights Watch was established and is funded by the multi-billionaire George Soros, who has been accused by two Dutch women of having participated in ritual killings of children at cult gatherings outside Brussels during the first decade of this century. See http://itccs.org/2014/09/10/breaking-eyewitness-evidence-of-child-killing-by-dutch-royalty-george-soros-and-others/ *and* https://www.youtube.com/watch?v=SbhMfZRhsXw&feature=youtu.be

(140) From an interview with Carol Martin on *Hidden from History*, Vancouver Co-op Radio, September 12, 2008.

(141) Carol Martin was herself abducted by three Vancouver policemen just before Christmas of 2008, soon after she began speaking about the disappearances over the airwaves of Kevin Annett's radio program *Hidden from History*. Carol was beaten and threatened with rape by the policemen until her cries drew attention and she was released. Subsequently, after bringing a complaint against the police, all of Carol's children were seized by the MCF and held incommunicado for weeks.

(142) From a lecture given by Kevin Annett at Capilano College in North Vancouver on September 22. 2005.

(143) In Grant Wakefield's words, *"Pickton was the straw man set up for everyone to gawk at and hate while the real culprits got away"*. See Wakefield's account in Appendix Seven.

Summary and Conclusions: A Consequential Course of Remedy and Action

You already know enough. So do I. It is not knowledge we lack. What is missing is the courage to understand what we know and to draw conclusions. - Exterminate All the Brutes: The Origins of European Genocide by Sven Lindquist (1992)

A proven genocidal regime like Canada has lost its right to govern or to expect allegiance from its citizens. No-one is obligated to fund or collude in crimes by either church or state, or to be part of such criminal bodies - From A Judicial Declaration for a New Republic, June 5, 2014, Toronto

A crime occurred across Canada that claimed the lives of tens of thousands of children - and yet it is not considered a crime by that nation and its courts for the simple reason that no body of law may indict a sovereign for a crime under its own law. And thus the Indian residential schools and the wider genocide they represent are deemed within Canada to constitute merely a private breach of duty by the state towards its Indian "wards", despite the proven killings, tortures and planned extermination by agents of Canada that occurred within their walls for over a century. And the churches that birthed and perpetrated much of the crime are not even considered.

Black is black, and this crime is a crime, it seems, only in the court of morality and public opinion, and under different systems of law. And these other tribunals have in fact indicted and convicted Canadian church and state, and their sponsors, for what was and continues to be Crimes against Humanity. The verdicts of these higher courts stand, as do the consequences that follow. [www.itccs.org]

If Canada was unlike other regimes and was capable of convicting its own sovereign power for its criminal acts, then justice, proper redress and "healing" would be possible within its borders. But such is not the case, and so these remedies must occur through the separate tribunals that have independently found Christian Canada guilty for its planned slaughter of Indian children and their nations. And these tribunals have also declared that, in the words of a June, 2014 Declaration, "*A proven genocidal regime like Canada has lost its right to govern or to expect allegiance from its citizens.*"

In short, a far reaching social revolution is the required response and just remedy decreed by the higher law: nothing less than a disestablishment of Canada, its churches and their sponsoring powers in London and Rome. Anything less than this step is neither remedy nor justice, under a system that continues to perpetrate the same genocidal crimes.

This report is not the place to enunciate every aspect of that revolution, except to note that unless the attitudes and guiding spirit that account for Canada's normalized genocide are overcome and replaced with a new ethos and sense of nationhood, even the most fundamental political change will not alter the problem. The possibility of such an inward moral revolution is in the hands of ordinary Canadians.

That said, this report has specific conclusions and recommendations that flow from its findings and the requirements of International Law when it comes to Canada's proven genocidal crimes.

1. The corporate entities known as Canada, the Crown of England, the Vatican and the Roman Catholic, Anglican and United Church of Canada, and their fiduciary officers and agents, are guilty of planning and executing the deliberate genocide of indigenous nations and their children, and of deliberately concealing that crime and obstructing justice. This offense constitutes a massive criminal conspiracy to wage an unrelenting war against humanity. The same corporate and human persons are also guilty of sustaining that genocide today through their policies and actions.

2. Accordingly, these corporate and human persons represent a clear and present danger to the peace, security and sovereignty of the world community and its children, as well as to the indigenous nations within Canada, and therefore must be regarded as rogue terrorist powers under the Law of Nations. These powers must be condemned, shunned and subjected to diplomatic and economic sanctions as a step towards their political and legal disestablishment.

3. Within Canada, all citizens and agents of any of these criminal powers are absolved and released from any allegiance, duty or obligation owed to them. The power of the Canadian state, its crown courts and the aforementioned churches to legally operate, tax and make laws is forever nullified.

Canadians must therefore not only refuse to pay taxes to or otherwise fund or cooperate with these institutions of church and state, but must actively disassociate themselves from them. To do so they must establish the political and legal framework for a new sovereign Republic that repudiates the genocidal policies and practices of Canada through the creation of common law courts and self-governing legislative assemblies.

4. Under such a new political and constitutional arrangement, the Republic will be capable and judicially competent to try, judge and enforce the verdicts brought against the genocidal bodies herein named, and thereby actively bring about the justice presently denied to Canada's victims. Until then, the ITDC will continue to assist this process of political reclamation through its investigations and by helping to convene common law courts in Canada to adjudicate the crimes against humanity that continue to occur on Canadian soil.

5. Towards these ends, copies of this report and plan of action will be circulated widely to world leaders, the media and the general public. The report will also be submitted as evidence in upcoming common law court actions against Canada, its churches and their corporate allies and sponsors on behalf of those targeted by the Canadian genocide.

The ITDC wishes to thank all of the people who have assisted in preparing this report. May its evidence serve as a beacon and a reliable historic archive in the years to come, as the fate of all of the Disappeared of Canada is brought to light and avenged through the law and popular justice.

Respectfully submitted by the Executive Council of the International Tribunal for the Disappeared of Canada (ITDC)

March 1, 2016

Toronto and Brussels

disappearedofcanada@gmail.com

How are you going to do that? How are you going to get a person who was responsible for all these deaths, this mass genocide, how are you going to get them to investigate themselves? Because it's not going to happen unless you take it outside of Canada and go in the higher level and charge them internationally because that's the only way I believe these criminals are going to be brought to justice.

– Rob Morgan, Nishga nation and second generation residential school survivor, during a protest of Friends and Relatives of the Disappeared (FRD) in Vancouver, March 4, 2008

It's just insane. You don't murder children and get away with it. I work every day to protect children and it just really bothers me that so many of our children have been killed. And nothing's ever been done about it. You read about it and there's information about it all over but nothing's ever been done about it. So why should these people, the churches and the government and Indian Affairs, they were all in on this as well, why should they get away with killing our children? It's just not right and something needs to be done about it.

– Cheryl Squire, Mohawk elder, Brantford, Ontario, October 9, 2011

Documentation from the Text

[...]NG CITIZEN GREAT FAMILY JOURNAL

[...]DAY, NOVEMBER 15 1907—12 PAGES Price One Cent.

[...]ALCONER,
[...]versity of Toronto,
[...]wa this afternoon
[...]iversity club in
[...] this evening and
[...] at luncheon in
[...] at 1.30 p.m. to-

[...]MATEUR

[...]nes of Lon-
[...]nd Skating
[...]tition.

[...]ams sends to the
[...]om the "amateur
[...]up by the commit-
[...]ames of London,
[...] to the skating
[...] winter is coming
[...]ating competitions
[...]ce very shortly, it
[...]o give the extract
[...] possible.
[...]he Olympic games
[...] follows:
[...]g Union—A skater

COMES OUT FOR TARIFF REFORM

Epoch in Conservative History in Britain.

MR. BALFOUR'S SPEECH

Declared for Mutual Preference amid Enthusiasm.

(Canadian Associated Press.)

London, Nov. 14.—Ex-Premier Balfour aroused tremendous enthusiasm at Birmingham tonight by giving utterance to a speech wherein he disregarded the advice of the Times and the wishes of the Unionist Free Traders. He made a strong declaration on the fiscal question. After alluding to the absence of "the immortal statesman," Mr. Chamberlain, and appealing for the unity of the Conservative party, which meant everything, he referred to tariff reform, and, amid uproarious cheering, he asked had the fiscal proposal lost its force? "No," came the answer. Had it gained force? "Yes," was the reply. "You have given me your answer; I agree with that," answered Mr. Balfour. (Tumultuous cheering.) He admitted that originally he had fears as to whether the policy of promoting free trade within the empire, which was the most important to our commercial interests, and must appeal to every member of our world-wide empire, could be carried out with so many units interested, but after the last imperial conference no misgivings were possible. (Cheers.) If the Conservatives were in power tomorrow their first duty would be the summon-

LOCAL BRIEFS

—The annual meeting of the Ottawa City Hockey league will be held on the evening of the 26th inst., at the O. A. A. C.

—In the list of aldermen attending the meeting in the board of trade room last evening, the name of Ald. Little was inadvertently omitted.

—The annual congregational at home of St. George's parish will be held next Tuesday evening in the parish hall at 8 o'clock, under the auspices of the Woman's association.

—William Bisson, sent up for trial from the city police court, came before Judge Gunn and elected to be tried by a judge. His case will be heard on Monday morning.

—Detective McCaskill, Montreal, who was injured yesterday afternoon while attempting to board a street car opposite the Russell house, is reported to be a little better at the Water street hospital today.

—The boxing classes at the O. A. A. C. under the able tuition of Prof. Clem Austin, are doing a record business at the popular local athletic club. Almost double the number of young men are in the class this year than formerly, and are in earnest training for the Canadian championship next spring.

—The O. A. A. C. will open a handicap pool tourney for members on Monday. While Alex. Graham may not enter the competition, McBride, Laflamme, a new man from Montreal; Oscar Mather, Guy Smith, H. Edwards, G. Johnstone, G. Burgess, A. and J. McLaughlin, P. White, Chas. Graham and others will be in line.

PERSONAL

Mr. Hugh Guthrie, M.P., South Wellington, is in the city on departmental business.

Hon. Wm. Harty, M.P., Kingston, is here on business with the department of railways and canals.

Hon. Adelard Turgeon, M.L.A., Bellechasse, is in the city and had an interview today with Sir Wilfrid Laurier.

Mr. C. L. Owen, M.P., of Campbell-

SCHOOLS AID WHITE PLAGUE

Startling Death Rolls Revealed.

AMONG INDIANS

Absolute Inattention To Bare Necessities of Health.

In his report upon the Indian boarding schools in Manitoba and the Northwest, Dr. P. H. Bryce, chief medical officer of the Indian department, emphasizes the absolute necessity for greater care in the selection of pupils and for sanitary precautions in the schools to prevent the spread of disease. During his recent tour of inspection Dr. Bryce instructed the principals of all the schools to report to Ottawa direct upon the past history and present condition of the health of the children who have been pupils at the schools.

Summarizing the statistical statement thus obtained Dr. Bryce says, after alluding to the defective records of the schools: "It suffices for us to know however, that of a total of 1,537 pupils reported upon, nearly 25 per cent. are dead, of one school with an absolutely accurate statement, 69 per cent. of ex-pupils are dead, and that everywhere the almost invariable cause of death given is tuberculosis."

Dr. Bryce's description of the schools shows them to be veritable hotbeds for the propagation and spread of this disease. In fact in only one school which the medical inspector visited was attention paid to the most ordinary requirements of ventilation of the dormitories.

Figure 1: Huge mortality rate and genocidal practices in Indian residential schools is reported in the *Ottawa Citizen* newspaper, November 15, 1907

Dr Peter Bryce

Chief Medical Inspector for the Department of Indian Affairs

Figure 2: Author of the first comprehensive report on genocidal practices and enormous mortality in Indian schools. Bryce was subsequently fired from the civil service and blacklisted.

November 8th. 1920.

Dear Father McGuire,

I have your letter of the 20th. ultimo with further reference to the management of the Kamloops Industrial school. In reply I would state that this communication makes quite clear the purport of your letter of the 4th. ultimo.

While the property, including the buildings, belongs to the Government, the management of the institution, which is a Roman Catholic school, rests entirely with the church authorities who have the privilege of nominating the principal and appointing the other members of the staff. The Government provides a per capita grant and is under obligation to keep the buildings and plant in proper repair. With this grant supplemented by funds from any other source, such as farm proceeds, charitable donations, etc., the church authorities are held responsible for feeding and clothing the children, the payment of staff salaries, and for the provision of proper class-room education for the pupils, as well as instruction in farming, gardening, care of stock and other industries suitable to the local requirements. You will thus see that the amount of salary to be allowed any member of the staff is a matter of arrangement between you as principal and the church authorities. The Department assumes no monetary obligation beyond the grant and maintenance of plant as above referred to.

In conclusion I may again state that I am very pleased with the present management of the Kamloops Industrial School.

Yours very truly,

Deputy Superintendent General.

Rev. James McGuire, O.M.I.,
Principal,
Kamloops Industrial School,
Kamloops, B. C.

Figure 3: Letter of Indian Affairs Superintendent Duncan Campbell Scott confirming that churches have operational control of Indian schools, including appointing the Principal and staff (1920)

Series A125–163. Origins of the population, census dates, 1871 to 1971 (concluded)

Series no.	Origin[1]	1871	1881	1901	1911	1921	1931	1941	1951	1961	1971
154	Asiatic	4	4,383	23,731	43,213	65,914	84,548	74,064	72,827	121,753	285,540
155	Chinese	–	4,383	17,312	27,831	39,587	46,519	34,627	32,528	58,197	118,815
156	Japanese	–	–	4,738	9,067	15,868	23,342	23,149	21,663	29,157	37,260
157	Other	4	–	1,681	6,315	10,459	14,687	16,288	18,636	34,399	129,460
158	Other origins	52,442	173,527	177,062	157,847	153,451	157,925	189,723	354,028	462,630	518,850
159	Native Indian and Inuit (Eskimo)	23,037	108,547	127,941	105,611	113,724	128,890	125,521	165,607	220,121	312,760
160	Negro	21,496	21,394	17,437	16,994	18,291	19,456	22,174	18,020	32,127	34,445
161	Other	348	2,780	145	18,310	[illegible]	681	36,753[9]	170,401	210,382	171,645[10]
162	Not stated	7,561	40,806	31,539	16,932	21,249	8,898	5,275			
163	Total	3,485,761	4,324,810	5,371,315	7,206,643	8,787,949	10,376,786	11,506,655	14,009,429	18,238,247	21,568,310

[1] The data for 1871 refer only to the four original provinces of Canada. The data for 1951 and later years include Newfoundland.
[2] Includes Bohemian, Bukovinian and Slavic.
[3] Included under Scandinavian.
[4] Includes Lithuanian and Moravian.
[5] Includes Bulgarian.
[6] Includes Finnish and Polish.
[7] Since 1921 Scandinavian has been divided into Danish, Icelandic, Norwegian and Swedish.
[8] Includes Bukovinian, Galacian and Ruthenian.
[9] Includes 35,416 Métis.
[10] Origin 'not stated' cases in 1971 were computer assigned.

Series A164–184. Principal religious denominations of the population, census dates, 1871 to 1971

Year	Anglican	Baptist	Congregationalist	Evangelical Church	Greek Orthodox[1]	Jehovah's Witnesses	Jewish	Lutheran	Mennonite[2]	Methodist	Mormon
	164	165	166	167	168	169	170	171	172	173	174
1971	2,543,180	667,245	–[3]	–[4]	316,605	174,805	276,025	715,740	181,800	–[3]	66,635
1961	2,409,068	593,553	–[4]	27,079	239,766	68,018	254,368	662,744	152,452	–[4]	50,016
1951	2,060,720	519,585	–[4]	50,900	172,271	34,596	204,836	444,923	125,938	–[4]	32,888
1941	1,754,368	484,465	–[4]	37,064	139,845	7,007	168,585	401,836	111,554	–[4]	25,238
1931	1,639,075	443,944	694[5]	22,239	102,529	13,582	155,766	394,920	88,837	–[4]	22,041
1921	1,407,780	421,730	30,730	13,905	169,832	6,689	125,197	286,458	58,797	1,159,246	19,622
1911	1,043,017	382,720	34,054	10,595	88,507	938	74,564	229,864	44,625	1,079,993	15,971
1901	681,494	318,005	28,293	10,193	15,630	101	16,401	92,524	31,797	916,886	6,891
1891	646,059	303,839	28,157	–	–	–	6,414	63,982	–	847,765	–
1881	574,818	296,525	26,900	–	–	–	2,393	46,350	–	742,981	–
1871	501,269	243,714	21,829	4,701	18	–	1,115	37,935	–	578,161	534

Year Pentecostal Presby- Roman Salvation Ukrainian United Other Not No Total

Figure 4: Government record of the De-Population of Aboriginal peoples across Canada, especially during the first decade of the 20th century when Indian schools became established nationally

INDIAN AFFAIRS
CANADA

Ottawa, March 11, 1919.

521...

His Excellency

The Governor General in Council.

The undersigned begs to refer to the Order of Your Excellency in Council of 12th February, 1919, under the authority and from the date of which the position of Medical Inspector for Indian Agencies and Residential Indian Schools was abolished.

The undersigned would recommend that from the date of the said Order in Council the incumbent of the office, Dr.O.I.Grain of Selkirk, be granted two months' leave of absence, with full pay, in consideration of the abolition of his office.

Superintendent General
of Indian Affairs.

TB rate: Aboriginal and total population, British Columbia, 1918-29

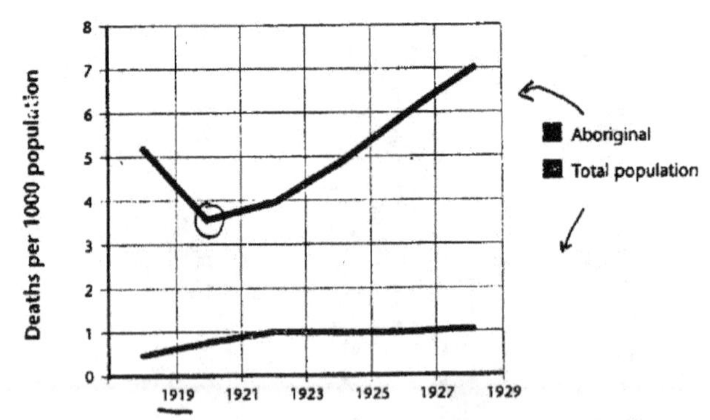

Source: British Columbia, Vital Statistics, 'Reports,' 1918-36, *Sessional Papers, 1919-1937.*

Figure 5: The abolition of government medical inspection in Indian schools (1919), and the subsequent rapid rise in deaths from tuberculosis among Indians in British Columbia

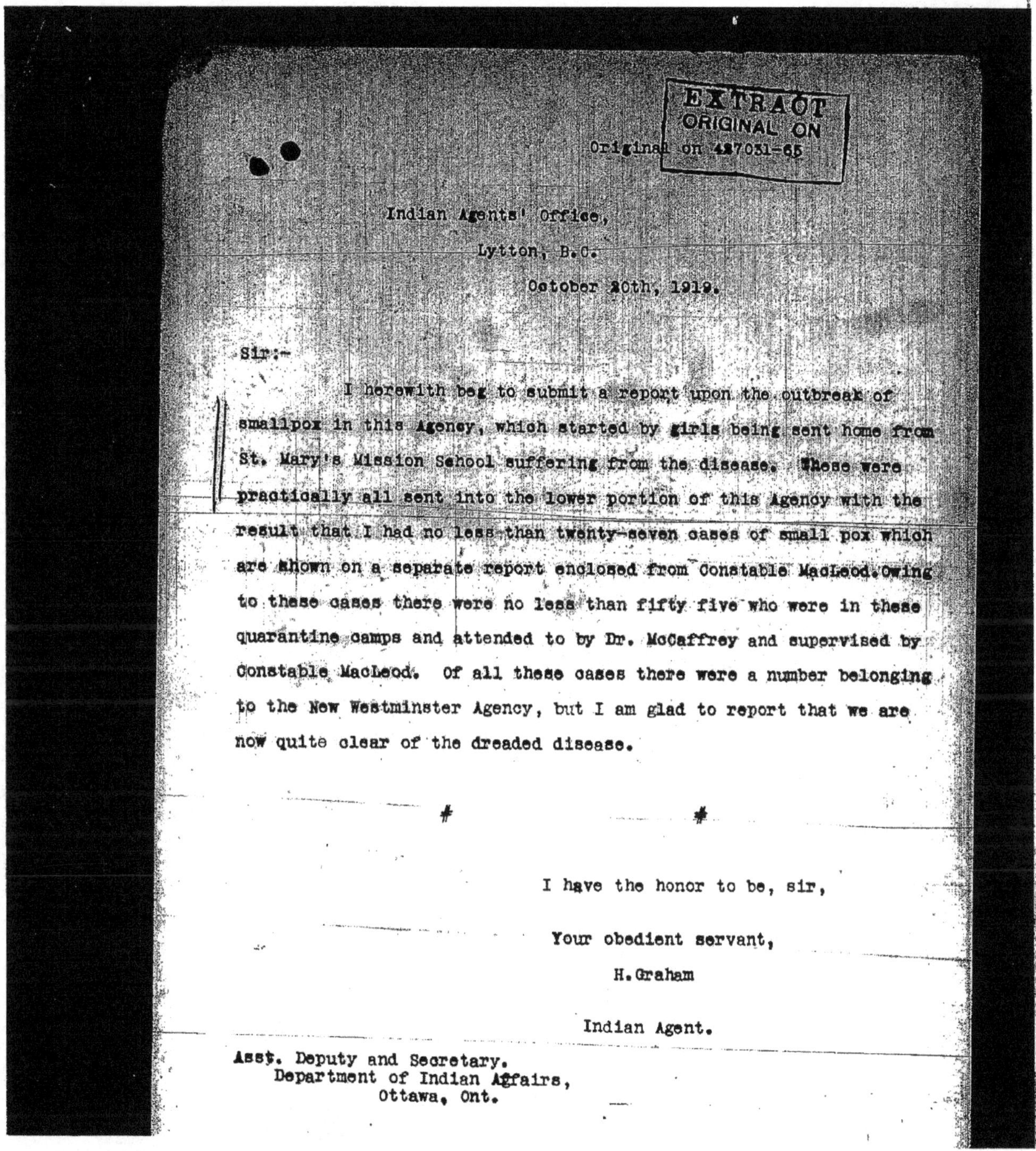
EXTRACT
ORIGINAL ON

Original on 427031-65

Indian Agents' Office,

Lytton, B.C.

October 20th, 1919.

Sir:-

I herewith beg to submit a report upon the outbreak of smallpox in this Agency, which started by girls being sent home from St. Mary's Mission School suffering from the disease. These were practically all sent into the lower portion of this Agency with the result that I had no less than twenty-seven cases of small pox which are shown on a separate report enclosed from Constable MacLeod. Owing to these cases there were no less than fifty five who were in these quarantine camps and attended to by Dr. McCaffrey and supervised by Constable MacLeod. Of all these cases there were a number belonging to the New Westminster Agency, but I am glad to report that we are now quite clear of the dreaded disease.

# #

I have the honor to be, sir,

Your obedient servant,

H. Graham

Indian Agent.

Asst. Deputy and Secretary.
Department of Indian Affairs,
Ottawa, Ont.

Figure 6: Description of the routine practice of sending sick Indian children home to infect their families with smallpox and tuberculosis (1919)

House of Commons, Ottawa

That is the provision
rrender of land for sale
provide for the payment
he proceeds to the indi-
is is an appropriation to

ı Indian reserve in On-
ed some time ago. Was
mpleted, or is it still

A surrender of a reserve
e occurs about once a
Does the hon. member
erve this was?

Sarnia.

I am informed that the
et been completed. The
aid.

is being held for pur-
time? Until such time
ay for it? What are the
overning a sale of that

The Indians have sur-
e. We are not holding
ospective purchasers go
urchase, all right, they
, they do not get it.

e Indians have surren-

To the Crown for pur-

w long will the Crown
not paid for it?

Until they sell it.

t might be fifty years.

It might be. We can-
buy it, but we have to
with the terms of the
no reason to think the
el company, is it not—
s establishing a big in-
going ahead with the
bes not, of course it will
the land will be avail-
else.

at are the terms of the

I have not the terms
very lengthy, and I
them on the table of
n. member so desires.
reserve are a very in-
ians; they have a very
f their business, and

they looked carefully after their interest in fixing the terms of the surrender.

Mr. CAHILL: If the minister will put the terms on the Table to-morrow, that will be satisfactory.

Mr. McKENZIE: In this appropriation there is an item of $10,000 to prevent the spread of tuberculosis. I am sure that throughout Canada a great deal of sympathy is felt for the Indians on account of the ravages that tuberculosis and smallpox are making amongst them. I was going to suggest to the minister that this is a possible opportunity of handing over this branch of the work of the Indian Department to the Health Department, unless that has been done already. I do not know that there is any phase of the work of the Health Department that is more important than that of making proper provision for the health of the poor Indians. I understand that frightful ravages are being made amongst them by tuberculosis, and their conditions of life are certainly not such as to preserve them from the ravages of that deadly disease. I should be pleased to know that at the earliest possible moment that that branch of the department was going to be transferred to the Department of Health and that proper steps would be taken to look after these Indians. I am sure that even though we are striking hard for economy now, if more money is wanted for this purpose the people of this country would be willing to spend it.

Mr. MEIGHEN: The Health Department has no power to take over the matter of the health of Indians. That is not included in the Act establishing that department. It was purposely left out of the Act. I did not think, and I do not think yet, that it would be practicable for the Health Department to do that work, because they would require to duplicate the organization away in the remote regions where Indians reserves are, and there would be established a sort of divided control and authority over the Indians which would produce confusion and insubordination and other ill effects among the Indians themselves. However, we get every possible assistance from the Health Department. The deputy minister advises me that Dr. Amyot, the Deputy Minister of Health, and his officers have been enthusiastic in their co-operation with the Indian Department in connection with the recent ravages and health matters generally.

Mr. McKENZIE: I am not so much concerned, nor are the people of this country, as to which department does this work, as that it be done. I am not speaking for myself but for a great body of Canadian people.

Mr. ROSS: What is the policy of the department in regard to the employment of medical attendants for the several reserves throughout the country? Is the policy the same in every province? If not, what is the policy in regard to this matter in the province of Ontario? Are the medical men who are employed paid fixed salaries? Who appoints them? Upon whose recommendation are they appointed, and what is the policy generally?

Mr. MEIGHEN: They are usually, though not always, paid a fixed salary. It depends upon the circumstances, the amount of work there is to do, and the availability of a man to do it. There may be a man available whom you can get to do the work incidentally, and not a man available whom you can get to do the work on salary. These two factors control. The Civil Service Commission in every case appoints the salaried men.

Mr. ROSS: These medical men?

Mr. MEIGHEN: Yes.

Mr. ROSS: Since how long?

Mr. MEIGHEN: Since the Act came into effect. There is no patronage.

Mr. BUREAU: The second item under the head of "General" is "relief to destitute Indians in remote districts, $65,000." There is a similar item for all the provinces where provision is made for the Indians. For Ontario and Quebec I find an item of $42,700 for "relief, medical attendance and medicines," and for Manitoba, Saskatchewan, Alberta and Northwest Territories an item of $149,000 for "supplies for destitute." Then there is an item of $11,000 for "relief in Nova Scotia, $10,000 for "relief" in New Brunswick, $13,000 for "relief and seed grain" in Prince Edward Island, and $22,000 for "relief to destitute" in British Columbia. Now I understand that in all the provinces except the Northwest Territories there is a regular organization to take care of these Indians. The remote districts would only be in the Northwest Territories, I presume, where the Indian population, according to the figures that have just been given, is only 3,369. Yet we find the sum of $65,000 allotted for relief to destitute Indians in remote districts. That relief work seems to be covered by item No. 263.

Mr. MEIGHEN: Not exactly. This item is intended to look after the Northwest Ter-

Figure 7: Prime Minister Arthur Meighen admits in Parliament that any provision for the health of Indians was deliberately left out of the federal Health Act (1920)

10-11 GEORGE V.

CHAP. 50.

An Act to amend the Indian Act.

[*Assented to 1st July, 1920.*]

2 Chap. **50.** *Indians.* 10-11 GEO. V.

Annuities and interest applied to maintenance.

"(6) The Superintendent General may apply the whole or any part of the annuities and interest moneys of Indian children attending an industrial or boarding school to the maintenance of such school or to the maintenance of the children themselves.

Children from 7 to 15 to attend school.

"**10.** (1) Every Indian child between the ages of seven and fifteen years who is physically able shall attend such day, industrial or boarding school as may be designated by the Superintendent General for the full periods during which such school is open each year.

Proviso as to religions.

Provided, however, that such school shall be the nearest available school of the kind required, and that no Protestant child shall be assigned to a Roman Catholic school or a school conducted under Roman Catholic auspices, and no Roman Catholic child shall be assigned to a Protestant school or a school conducted under Protestant auspices.

Truant officers and compulsory attendance.

Power to investigate cases of truancy.

"(2) The Superintendent General may appoint any officer or person to be a truant officer to enforce the attendance of Indian children at school, and for such purpose a truant officer shall be vested with the powers of a peace officer, and shall have authority to enter any place where he has reason to believe there are Indian children between the ages of seven and fifteen years, and when requested by the Indian agent, a school teacher or the chief of a band shall examine into any case of truancy, shall warn the truants, their parents or guardians or the person with whom any Indian child resides, of the consequences of truancy, and notify the parent, guardian or such person in writing to cause the child to attend school.

Notice to parents, guardians, etc.

Penalty for guardian, parent or others failing to cause child to attend school, after notice.

"(3) Any parent, guardian or person with whom an Indian child is residing who fails to cause such child, being between the ages aforesaid, to attend school as required by this section after having received three days' notice so to do by a truant officer shall, on the complaint of the truant officer, be liable on summary conviction before a justice of the peace or Indian agent to a fine of not more than two dollars and costs, or imprisonment for a period not exceeding ten days or both, and such child may be arrested without a warrant and conveyed to school by the truant officer:

Figure 8: Federal law making attendance in Indian residential schools compulsory for all native children seven years and older (1920)

genocide

"In our Residential Schools we are trying to give the Indian boy and girl instruction that is practical, and such as will prepare them to be successful farmers. No occupation will so soon dispossess him of his nomadic instincts and fix upon him a permanency of habitation as gardening, care of stock and farming. If in the next generation or two he can be made self-sustaining, our fondest hopes will have been realized.

"Many of our graduates surrender their treaty rights and become naturalized and for them and their children, the Indian problem is for ever solved, since it is the Indian massed in tribes and kept on reserves which creates the problem.

"The enrolment of Muncey, Norway House, Brandon, Edmonton and Coqualeetza, totals 700 pupils and the schools are all filled with the exception of Edmonton, which was opened during the year. We expect it to be filled by the end of June.

"During the year the Government has built and equipped a beautiful frame building at Morley, Alberta, with accommodation for sixty pupils and we expect to open it, filled to capacity, in the month of May."

From Rev. S. R. McVitty, of Mount Elgin Institute, Ontario, comes the following cheery word:

"We are closing the very best year in our history and are surrounded by the best staff we ever had. Attendance—full capacity; conduct—excellent. Every pupil in school has voluntarily pledged not to lie or steal."

Medical:—With reference to medical work among Indians, Rev. Thompson Ferrier reports:

"Our medical work is carried on by doctors, nurses and field-matrons on some of the reserves, and in our hospitals situated at Hazelton, Port Simpson and Bella Bella, with Rivers Inlet and Port Essington as summer hospitals during the fishing season. The Government has built a fine hospital at Norway House and the cost of maintenance is met by the Indian Department and the Church is given the right of nominating the doctor and lady superintendent.

"Our schools and hospitals are all managed by a competent staff of consecrated workers. Such fields of labor have proven the truth of the saying: 'Men are great, not according to the number of their servants, but according to the number whom they serve.'"

Of the advantage of the X-ray machine, Dr. Darby, of Bella Bella, gives an illustration:

"The X-ray has already been of great use. The other evening, a young man brought in his three-year-old son, who had just swallowed a silver quarter dollar. Ordinarily it would have been a difficult matter to tell where the coin was. But it took only a moment to get the machine going and the fluroscope showed the money well down in his throat. I went after it and out it came."

Rev. W. Sager, B.A., M.D., of Port Simpson, writes:

"The records of twenty years ago reveal that we are now treating twice as many patients as we did then and have twice as many days' treatment. For thirty-five years, this hospital has served the people on the coast of Northern British Columbia and we are convinced that we still have a work to do here. Most of our patients are indigent Indians."

Dr. H. C. Wrinch, M.P.P., of Hazelton presents a very gratifying report:

"In the four years from 1922 to 1925 inclusive, the increase in attendance amounts to nearly seventy per cent.

"On account of the hazardous character of much of the work carried on in the district, e.g., mining, tie and pole cutting, lumbering, accidental injuries comprise a large number of the cases treated—hence, surgical treatment has been more required than medical—and, for the same reason, more men than women make use of the hospital."

HOM

In the nine hospitals su
accommodation for 230 patie
we have reports, 2,912 patien
there were 5,605 treated in f
given were 46,451. The lowe
the highest $4.62. The tot
hospital fees was $67,348.13;
municipalities $1,215.70; fro
Society $36, 850.40; and from
for the year on Maintenance

THE MISSI

STATEMENT OF INCOM
EN

Maintenance and Extension Fund to
Interest on Legacies..............
Interest from National Campaign Fu
Miscellaneous Receipts............
Woman's Missionary Society for Bible

Total Current Income..........

Home Missions, Indian Missions, For
Toronto Conference...........
London Conference............
Hamilton Conference..........
Bay of Quinte Conference......
Montreal Conference..........
Nova Scotia Conference........
New Brunswick and P.E.I. Conf
Newfoundland Conference......
Manitoba Conference..........
Saskatchewan Conference......
Alberta Conference...........
British Columbia Conference...

Immigration..................
Superannuation Fund..........
Summer Supply................
Canadian Ranok..............
Home Missions Council........

Foreign Missions—
Japan—appropriation..........
West China—appropriation.....
Miscellaneous.................

Superannuation Fund..........
Lay Missionaries' Superannuatio

Administration:
Salaries, etc., General Officers...
Office salaries and expenses.....
Travelling expenses............

Cultivation—
Publication account............
Young People's Forward Movem
Juvenile Rewards..............
Missionary Education..........
Centenary Celebration—1924-25
Maintenance and Extension Fun

from 2nd Annual Conference (1926)

Figure 9: Genocidal aim to "dispossess" Indians of their traditions is stated by the Second General Council of the United Church of Canada (1925)

APPLICATION FOR ADMISSION

To the
Deputy Superintendent General
of Indian Affairs,
Ottawa, Canada.

1 wk. later

November 4 th 1933 19

Sir,—

I hereby make application for admission of the undermentioned child into the Kuper Island *Residential School; to remain therein under the guardianship of the Principal for such term as the Department of Indian Affairs may deem proper:*

Indian name of child

English name Laurence

Age 9 years

473

Name of Band Chemainus Bay

No. of ticket under which child's annuity is paid

Father's full name and No. Charlie Harris

Mother's full name and No. Juliane

Parents living or dead Father living , mother dead

State of child's health good

Religion R.C.

Does applicant speak English ? little

Previously attended none school for years.

Charlie X Harris (his mark)
(Signature of Father)

NOTE—If mother or guardian signs, agent must forward full explanatory note.

I hereby certify that the above application for admission has been read over and interpreted to the parent or guardian and that the contents were understood by him or her and that I witnessed his or her signature to this document.

* [signature]
(Signature of Missionary or other Witness)

I recommend the admission of the above child, who is of good moral character and is eligible to be admitted as a grant-earning pupil.

H. Graham
Agent

*Principal or other official of the school must not sign as witness.

NOTE—All the above particulars must be fully given, especially the "Name of Band," "No. of ticket under which child's annuity is paid" and "Religion." The minimum age for admission is seven (7) years, except in the case of an orphan, destitute or neglected child. When application is made for the admission of such cases, full particulars should accompany the application.

Figure 10: The *Application for Admission Form* that bestowed legal guardianship over Indian children to the residential school Principal, a church employee. This form established a joint legal liability by both church and state for all residential school children. (1933)

Fraser Lake, B.C.,

October 22nd. 1935.

R.H.Moore, Esq.,
Indian Agent,
Vanderhoof, B.C.

Dear Sir:-

Your letter of October the 18th. received with complaints of attention I am giving the Indians. These complaints have been so frequent lately and so unjustified that I begin to believe they are promoted by personal feeling against me rather than an interest in the welfare of the Indians. This may be on your part but I prefer to think it comes from Rivet, for whom I have little use and who probably guesses that I feel so toward him.

Since my father is principal of an Indian School and I have had opportunity to meet the principals and medical attendants of other schools, I happen to know that the attention I am giving the Lejac School is as good or better than in any other place in the province. As for the general medical examination you speak of, this is not done in any other school that I have any knowledge of. This would bear no weight with me if I thought that any purpose would be served by doing so, but I do not think so. Where is the point of this, when I know that, were I to apply the standards of health to them that is applied to children of the white schools, that I should have to discharge 90% of them and there would be no school left; and when I know that they are under the constant observation of a staff who have the opportunity of reporting any ill health to me either on my weekly visit to the school or by phone. If the department makes this a regulation applying to all schools I have nothing to say, otherwise I shall use my own judgement.

As for dental work, anyone knows that there is always dental work in such an institution. I have asked for a dentist on two previous occasions and am surprised that the department does not arrange for an annual attednance of a dentist, rather than wait for the doctor to examine the whole school and tell them a dentist is required (which everyone knows). I am only too pleased to facilitate his work, when I know he is coming, by going over the children and picking out the ones who require work done.

In conclusion, I feel that I am doing everything that experience and commonsense dictates for the welfare of the children. If any more complaints emanate from the school through you I shall put it up to the department at Ottawa, giving them a statement of just how I am carrying on the work and let them decide whether it should be satisfactory or not.

Yours,

Signed:- C. Pitts, M.D.

Figure 11: A genocidal practice of operating a separate and lower standard of health care for aboriginal children is admitted by Dr. C. Pitts, medical inspector for Indian schools (1935)

163-1-13.

EX'D.

Ottawa, February 17, 1937.

Dear Sir:

The Department has recently received a report indicating that Paul Shorty will have to be removed from the Lejac Indian Residential School, as he has never been cured of the tubercular infection from which he was suffering at the time of his admission.

A review of our files indicates that several children from the Stikine Agency who were admitted to the Lejac Residential School have developed tuberculosis and the available information shows that they were probably infected at the time of their admission.

At the present time I do not think there are any children from your Agency in the Lejac Residential School with the exception of Paul Shorty, but, in future, if you receive requests from any Indian parents to send their children to the Lejac School, the Department considers that such children should be very carefully examined and pronounced physically fit before being allowed to go.

I realize that a medical examination may be difficult at certain points owing to no doctor being available, but the only way to handle the matter is to start some months in advance of the time any child is to be brought out and to arrange that such child receive the most searching examination possible in their own district. If such examination is not obtainable at home, they should be thoroughly examined at the nearest point where there is a doctor.

Yours truly,

Philip Phelan,
Chief, Training Division.

T. F. H. Reed, Esq.,
Indian Agent,
Telegraph Creek, B.C.

Figure 12: The practice of routinely admitting children infected with tuberculosis into Indian schools is described by an Indian Affairs official (1937)

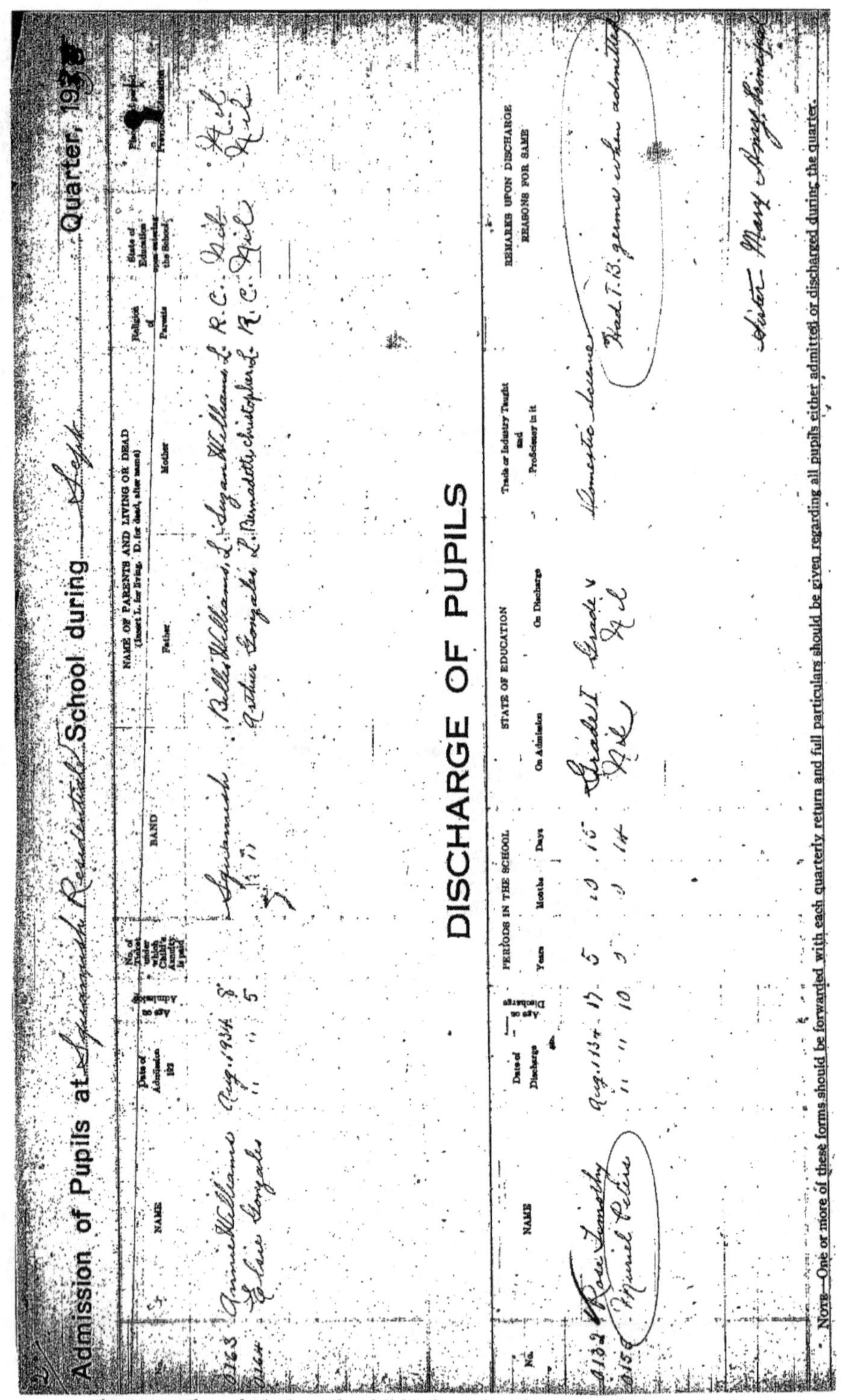

Admission of Pupils at Squamish Residential **School during** Sept **Quarter, 1938**

No.	NAME	Date of Admission 193	Age on Admission	No. of Ticket under which Child's Annuity is paid	BAND	NAME OF PARENTS AND LIVING OR DEAD (Insert L. for living, D. for dead, after name) Father	Mother	Religion of Parents	State of Education upon entering the School	Previous Education
363	Annie Williams	Aug. 1934	8		Squamish	Bill Williams, L.	Susan Williams L.	R.C.	Nil	Nil
364	Elsie Gonzales	" "	5		" "	Arthur Gonzales L.	Bernadette Christopher L.	R.C.	Nil	Nil

DISCHARGE OF PUPILS

No.	NAME	Date of Discharge	Age on Discharge	Periods in the School: Years	Months	Days	State of Education: On Admission	On Discharge	Trade or Industry Taught and Proficiency in it	Remarks upon Discharge Reasons for Same
0182	Rose Timothy	Aug. 1934	17	5	10	15	Grade I	Grade V	Domestic Science	
0150	Muriel Peter	" "	10	3	3	14	Nil	Nil		Had T.B. germs when admitted

Sister Mary Agnes, Principal

NOTE—One or more of these forms should be forwarded with each quarterly return and full particulars should be given regarding all pupils either admitted or discharged during the quarter.

Figure 13: The admission of a child infected with tuberculosis is noted in the records of the Squamish Catholic Indian school (1938)

COPY.

Fraser Lake, B. C.

January 28th. 1938.

R.H.Moore, Esq.,
Indian Agent,
Vanderhoof, B. C.

Dear Sir:-

RE: DOROTHY PAUL, LeJac.

Father Grant has asked me to write to you concerning the above. as she has a fair amount of sputum it endangers the infant child of Harry if she goes home.

policy

While I am aware that the Indian Dept. will not hospitalize Indians suffering from Pulmonary tuberculosis, Bishop Coudert has offered to arrange for her hospital treatment at Smithers if the Dept. refuses to do so. In view of this I would recommend hospital care for Dorothy. It would also be nice if she could have a chest-plate to confirm my diagnosis.

Yours truly;

John C. Poole.

Figure 14: Reference by a local residential school official to the government practice of not hospitalizing Indians infected with tuberculosis (1938). This same practice is noted in 1953.

A12 THE VANCOUVER SUN, WEDNESDAY, APRIL 26, 2000 NATION

Native kids 'used for experiments'

A church magazine says federal health tests were conducted in B.C. and Ontario residential schools in the 1940s and '50s.

SOUTHAM NEWS, VANCOUVER SUN

OTTAWA — The federal government conducted health experiments on First Nations children in residential schools in the late 1940s and early '50s, a church magazine has reported. One of the four residential schools was located in Port Alberni.

Native children were deliberately denied basic dental treatment at the United Church-run Port Alberni school and scientists also "tinkered" with the children's diets at other schools, the *Anglican Journal* reports.

The government did not inform many of the parents of the research the government was conducting on their children.

In a letter on Oct. 3, 1949, Dr. H.K. Brown, chief of the dental health division of the federal health department, requested staff halt some dental treatments at the Port Alberni school, the *Journal* reports.

"No specialized, over-all type of dental service should be provided, such as the use of sodium fluoride, dental prophylaxis or even urea compounds," he wrote in his one-page letter. "In this study dental caries and gingivitis are both important factors in assessing nutritional status."

The *Anglican Journal* story quotes the doctor who headed the five-year research program, now a 90-year-old nursing-home resident.

"It was not a deliberate attempt to leave children to develop caries [tooth decay] except for a limited time or place or purpose, and only then to study the effects of vitamin C or fluoride," said Dr. L.B. Pett, former chief of the nutritional division of the health department.

Pett acknowledged that "parental consent was not always obtained for those children involved in the study".

The revelation shocked George Erasmus, head of the Aboriginal Healing Foundation, which aids victims of residential-school abuse. He told the *Journal* the experiments were unknown to him.

The objective of the research at Indian residential school children was "to evolve methods for improving health, not only of the school children but of the whole population," Pett said in the story.

In dietary experiments, federal health officials supplied flour with added vitamins in 1949-50. Then the vitamin supplements were halted so the results could be studied.

Figure 15: Sanitized report of involuntary "health experiments" performed on Indian school children by church and state, including starving children and denying them dental care (2000)

Vol. 2 Revised Statutes of British Columbia, 1960

case shall be decided upon such evidence alone, and such evidence shall be corroborated by some other material evidence. R.S. 1948, c. 113, s. 6.

Person charged and wife or husband competent.

7. Every person charged with an offence, and the wife or husband, as the case may be, of the person so charged, is a competent witness whether the person so charged is charged solely or jointly with any other person. R.S. 1948, c. 113, s. 7.

Parties to civil causes and their wives may be witnesses.

8. (1) The parties to any action, suit, petition, or other matter of a civil nature in any of the Courts of the Province, and their wives or husbands, are, except as hereinafter excepted, competent as witnesses, and compellable to attend and give evidence in like manner as they would be if not parties to the proceedings, or wives or husbands of such parties, but no plaintiff in any action for breach of promise of marriage shall recover a verdict unless his or her testimony is corroborated by some other material evidence in support of such promise.

(2) Notwithstanding any rule to the contrary, a husband or wife may in any proceeding in any Court give evidence that he or she did or did not have sexual intercourse with the other party to the marriage at any time or within any period of time before or during the marriage. R.S. 1948, c. 113, s. 8; 1949, c. 22, s. 2.

Communications made during marriage need not be disclosed.

9. No husband is compellable to disclose any communication made to him by his wife during the marriage, and no wife is compellable to disclose any communication made to her by her husband during the marriage. R.S. 1948, c. 113, s. 9.

In actions by or against lunatics.

10. In any action or proceeding by or against a person found by inquisition to be of unsound mind, or being an inmate of a lunatic asylum or hospital for insane, an opposite or interested party shall not obtain a verdict, judgment, or decision therein, on his own evidence, unless such evidence is corroborated by some other material evidence. R.S. 1948, c. 113, s. 10.

Corroboration in certain actions.

11. In any action or proceeding by or against the heirs, executors, administrators, or assigns of a deceased person, an opposite or interested party to the action shall not obtain a verdict, judgment, or decision therein, on his own evidence, in respect of any matter occurring before the death of the deceased person, unless such evidence is corroborated by some other material evidence. R.S. 1948, c. 113, s. 11.

Indian testimony receivable in certain cases.

12. In any proceeding over which the Legislature has jurisdiction, it is lawful for any Court, Judge, Coroner, Gold or other Commissioner, or Justice, in the discretion of such Court, Judge, Coroner, Gold or other Commissioner, or Justice, to receive the evidence of any aboriginal native, or native of mixed blood, of the continent of North America or the islands adjacent thereto, being an uncivilized person, destitute of the knowledge of God and of any fixed and clear belief in religion or in a future state of rewards and punishments, without administering the usual form of oath to such aboriginal native, or native of mixed blood, as aforesaid, upon his solemn affirmation or declaration to tell the truth, the whole truth, and nothing but the truth, or in such other form as may be approved by the Court, Judge, Coroner, Gold or other Commissioner, or Justice. R.S. 1948, c. 113, s. 12. * exact wording in 1874 law

Figure 16: Legal definition of an Indian as "an uncivilized person" in a separate legal category, from the Evidence Act of British Columbia (1960)

Department of
Indian Affairs and
Northern Development

Ministère des
Affaires indiennes et
du Nord canadien

Vancouver 2, B. C.
September 22, 1972

Isabel Crowe
Membership Clerk
Fraser Indian District

Transfer of Personal Files to
Indian Bands

As there seems to be some confusion in this area I have extracted Motion 8, regarding Personal Files, from minutes of the Advisory Council Meeting held on August 4th, 1972 in Vancouver. Motion 8 follows below:

"Personal Files

Individual Indian personal files in the District are going to be destroyed. A commitment was made to the UBCIC to have these destroyed by September 1st and there should be Indian involvement in scrutinizing. Clarence Joe made a motion for each Band Council to decide on the selection of a scrutineer to oversee the destruction of that particular Band's personal files. Motion seconded by Joe Mitchell, question called, the motion was carried.

There is classified information on these files and each scrutineer should be made aware of this.

A list will be kept of files destroyed."

I think it is important that when we are sending out such personal files that we should set up a register listing the documents forwarded from each file.

J. R. Mooney
District Head of Administration
Fraser Indian District

JRM/sh

c.c. I.S. Wilson
Fraser Indian District

Figure 17: Government destruction of Indian Affairs records as part of the cover up of residential school crimes (1972)

AT LARGE

Vancouver Sun, July 10, 1995

Minister who tried to bring natives into the fold fired by his church

STEPHEN HUME

PORT ALBERNI

Nuu-Chah-Nulth peoples have associated with the United Church since it dispatched fervent missionaries to snag souls in remote settlements a hundred years ago.

Yet Rev. Kevin McNamee-Annett, newly arrived in Port Alerberni from an activist street ministry in Toronto, observed that almost no natives attended his new church.

"They never set foot in our church. I found that strange."

George Hamilton, a young native, returned from Vancouver's tough East Side streets to raise his kids. He says he felt the lash of Port Alberni's unspoken prejudice while he was growing up.

"As a kid, I don't remember one Indian face working in any of the stores in town. I still don't see any Indian faces working in any of the stores. But Kevin, Kevin didn't just have compassion for Indians. He had compassion for all the poor and weak."

Hamilton became one of McNamee-Annett's parishioners.

McNamee-Annett says he did set out to change things. He counselled abuse victims at the native friendship centre. He ran workshops. He started a food bank. Many of its users were native and he says he became close to them.

"In the poor part of the town and on the reserve some of the housing is the worst I've ever seen — and I've done urban ministries in Toronto, Vancouver and Winnipeg.

"I was involved in taking several slum landlords to arbitration and helping set up tenants' advocacy groups — that didn't sit well."

The new reverend began baptizing the poor, marrying the neglected, burying the dispossessed. His ministry took him into the wretched strip that natives call The Ghetto. It still seems invisible to Port Alberni's comfortable middle-class.

"When nobody else spoke out," says Hamilton, "there was Kevin."

McNamee-Annett says he simply sought to ground lost souls in his church, welcoming them. Sunday attendance doubled. He told his flock to "learn to love them, up close. For love of the stranger is the *only* measure by which you and I will be judged."

Some of the congregation didn't like it. Loving strangers was okay in theory, it seems, but not in practice.

"To bring the natives into the pews was explosive," McNamee-Annett says. "The traditional congregation was fairly uptight."

McNamee-Annett says some families he encouraged to begin attending church services ran into a chilly climate. When he suggested at one board meeting that Ahousat elder Nelson Keitlah serve on a church committee the silence was "deafening."

One day a young woman from the poorest part of Port Alberni brought her little son to church. The baby cried, as babies do. This, McNamee-Annett says, did not bother him. But for some members of the congregation, it was a final, infuriating straw.

"Two women went to her and told her to get out. They said her baby was a little brat, 'Why did you bring him here, we don't want you.' They later came to me and threatened to leave if she stayed."

It was, he says, a dilemma to test his faith.

"It was 'suffer the little children to come unto me' versus good relations with the congregation."

He chose the young mother. One of his parishioners quit. On Jan. 8, he notified the church of his intention to resign effective June 30. Two weeks later, he says, he was summarily fired at the behest of six parishioners.

"The only reason church officials have given for this sudden, harsh action is that certain unidentified members of St. Andrew's had criticisms of my sermons and ministry."

At one point, the minister wrote a strong letter supporting the Ahousat band's objection to the church's sale, for substantial profit, of a property it had been more or less given by the native community for a school.

That, Keitlah believes, was the real source of his lack of support from the church hierarchy.

Church authorities decline to comment on the reasons for the firing. Authorities do confirm that it was not a disciplinary matter and that it had nothing to do with moral misconduct. They claim it was not connected to his ministry to poor natives.

"It's important to remember that there are good people here," says Keitlah. "People were kind to me."

But he admits he has stopped attending the church since McNamee-Annett was dismissed.

"My faith in God isn't shaken," Hamilton says, "but it is certainly shaken in the church. It was, 'Get them out of here! We don't want them here!' It was gross.

"I wouldn't paint the entire congregation with the same brush — there is a silent majority. It's an indictment of them that they were silent. I have no desire to attend that church."

"I think it's just atrocious what they did to him," says Jack McDonald of Port Alberni's Metis Association. "His actions spoke louder than words — so do theirs."

As for the jobless reverend?

McNamee-Annett says he will be preaching the gospel, church or no church:

"They've taken away my job but not my calling." □

Figure 18a: First media report of the firing without cause of Rev. Kevin Annett for bringing aboriginal people into his St. Andrew's United Church in Port Alberni, British Columbia (1995)

THE GRANT REPORT (Centre for Philanthropy, Ottawa, 1995)

Second Harvest Food Support Committee, Toronto, ON, *Poverty Relief)*	$7,500
Second Mile Club of Toronto, Toronto, ON, *Social Services*	$7,500
Views-for the Visually Impaired, Etobicoke, ON, *Blind*	$6,255
United Way of Greater Toronto, Toronto, ON, *United Ways*	$6,000

SPORTS AND RECREATION

Canada Israel Athletics Fund, Concord, ON, *Sports*	$20,000

527 Lynch Foundation; Walker

Grant information not available.

528 M.Q.L. Foundation

1993 Grants

EDUCATION

McGill University, Montreal, PQ, *Universities*	$10,000

529 M.S.I. Foundation; The

Grant information not available.

530 MacDonald Foundation for Animal Welfare; The A.J.

Grant information not available.

531 MacDonald Foundation; Richard and Mary

Grant information not available.

532 Macdonald Stewart Foundation; The

Grant information not available.

533 Machan Charitable Foundation Inc.; The George

534 Mackenzie Memorial Foundation; The Ada

1993 Grants

SOCIAL SERVICES AND ISSUES

Canadian Wheelchair Sports Association, Vanier, ON, *Physically Disabled*	$50,000
Ontario Track Three Ski Association for the Disabled, Etobicoke, ON, *Disabled*	$20,000
CNIB, National Organization, Toronto, ON, *Blind*; Ontario Visually Impaired Golfers Association	$12,000

535 MacKinnon Foundation

1993 Grants

RELIGIOUS ORGANIZATIONS

Providence College & Seminary, Otterburne, MB, *Religious Education*	$8,800
Bethesda Church, Winnipeg, MB, *Churches*	$6,000

536 MacLennan Foundation; The Charles and Mary

Grant information not available.

537 MacMillan Family Fund; The

1993 Grants

EDUCATION

University of British Columbia, Vancouver, BC, *Universities*; Faculty of Forestry	$20,000
Western Canadian Universities, Marine Biological Society, Victoria, BC, *Universities*; Re: Bamfield Marine Station	$20,000

* 1994-95

RELIGIOUS ORGANIZATIONS

First United Church, Port Alberni, BC, *United Churches and Organizations*	$8,000
Salvation Army, Public Relations	$5,000

Figure 18b: Payoff by MacMillan-Bloedel logging company to its business partner the United Church of Canada for receiving stolen land of the Ahousaht Indian nation (1995)

Murders alleged at residential school

NDP leadership candidate claims 2 Indians killed in Port Alberni in '40s and '50s.

STEWART BELL
Vancouver Sun

At least two students were murdered at Indian residential schools in the Port Alberni area in the 1940s and '50s, a candidate for the leadership of the New Democratic Party alleged Tuesday.

Jack McDonald, who led a demonstration outside the United Church offices in Vancouver to protest the church's treatment of aboriginal people, called for a public inquiry into the deaths.

However, the head of an RCMP probe investigating abuse at Indian residential schools says he knows nothing about the allegations.

"To me that's a totally new allegation, and I'm familiar with all the information that's come in from Port Alberni," said Sgt. Paul Willms.

"I haven't even heard a rumor or second-hand information of that nature."

McDonald said former students at residential schools in Port Alberni and nearby Ahousaht have recently come forward with stories about the deaths.

In one case, a boy is said to have bled to death after he was beaten as punishment for breaking a jar at the school in Ahousaht in the '40s.

A second death is said to have occurred in the early '50s, when a girl was kicked down a flight of stairs at the Alberni Indian Residential School.

"We've held personal interviews with natives who were in the residential school who will tell you they carried bodies out of the school," said McDonald.

The incidents could not be found in police or coroners' records and attempts to research the alleged deaths were met with "roadblock after roadblock" by the United Church, he said.

"They wouldn't let us see the records," said McDonald, a Port Alberni funeral planner who is the only declared candidate so far for Premier Mike Harcourt's job.

He also said the United Church removed Rev. Kevin McNamee-Annett from Port Alberni last January because he was "getting close to those facts, because more and more natives were opening up to him about these atrocities at the United Church."

McDonald wants Attorney-General Ujjal Dosanjh and Aboriginal Affairs Minister John Cashore to order a public inquiry and police investigation.

Art Anderson, personnel minister for the B.C. conference of the United Church, said the church is cooperating fully with the police investigation into residential schools.

He said he invited the demonstrators to his office to discuss their concerns, which they did. "There's no attempt to dodge communication or hide anything."

Anderson said he was unable to comment on the reasons for McNamee-Annett's dismissal. "That matter is before the church courts so it would be inappropriate to discuss that at the moment."

McNamee-Annett said the stories about the killings were told to him while he was working with Nuu-chah-nulth Indians in the Alberni Valley.

He said he will not reveal the names of the victims.

But he said he had urged the witnesses to take their accounts to authorities.

In a letter to McNamee-Annett dated Nov. 15, the head of human rights and aboriginal justice for the United Church of Canada called the murder allegations "deeply disturbing."

"If you have evidence related to such allegations, I trust you have reported this to the appropriate police authorities and will encourage others to do so as well," wrote John Siebert.

"It is worth repeating that the United Church of Canada fully supports the investigation of any and all criminal actions alleged to have taken place in residential schools."

Siebert said in an interview from Toronto Tuesday he isn't aware what requests have been made for documents related to the Alberni Valley schools, but he doubts they would be useful in investigating abuse.

"These are records that probably aren't going to record these kinds of stories from the aboriginal people's perspective," he said.

Willms suggested it may be that former students are now recalling deaths that were ruled accidental at the time. He said the deaths would certainly fall within the mandate of the police investigation.

CENTRE OF PROTEST: Rev. Kevin McNamee-Anett details allegations

The RCMP formed the probe almost a year ago to investigate allegations that large numbers of Indian children were sexually and physically abused at church-run schools.

Beginning in the 1880s, Indian children were removed, sometimes forcibly, from their homes and sent to residential schools in an attempt to assimilate them.

The policy was abandoned in the '70s, but the lingering effects of residential school abuse are blamed for a variety of ills on Indian reserves, including high rates of suicide, substance abuse and family breakdown.

Figure 19: First media account of the murder of students at west coast Indian schools, Vancouver Sun, December 13, 1995

Beaten to death for theft of a prune

Indian elder recalls strapping of 15-year-old boy at Island residential school in 1938 by United Church minister.

MARK HUME
Vancouver Sun

A 15-year-old boy who stole a prune from a jar in the kitchen of a United Church residential school was strapped so relentlessly his kidneys failed him and he later died in bed, says a native Indian elder who was there at the time.

Archie Frank, now 68, was just 11 years old when his school mate, Albert Gray, was caught stealing in the Ahousat Residential School kitchen one night in 1938.

Frank, a retired commercial fisher, says he's never forgotten what happened to Gray, a husky youngster from the remote Vancouver Island community of Nitinat.

"He got strapped to death," said Frank in an interview on Tuesday.

"Just for stealing one prune, [Rev. A.E.] Caldwell strapped him to death.

"Beat the s— right out of him."

Frank's story, told after a 57-year silence, crystallizes much of what the furore over residential schools is all about.

For the past year the RCMP has been probing a series of alleged abuses at church-run residential schools. So far they have found evidence that 54 people were victims of abuse at the hands of 94 offenders. The investigation is concerned with 14 residential schools operated by the Anglican, United and Roman Catholic churches from the late 1800s to 1984.

The First United Church has come under scrutiny by the RCMP this week because of new allegations that two children were killed while at the residential school in the Port Alberni area in the 1940s and '50s.

Frank said Caldwell left Ahousat after the residential school burned down in 1940 and went on to be principal of the United Church school in Port Alberni.

Please see SCHOOL, A2

SCHOOL: Beaten to death for theft of a prune

Continued from page 1

Frank said Gray was caught with his hand in the prune jar by the night watchman at the Ahousat school.

"The day after he got strapped so badly he couldn't get out of bed. The strap wore through a half inch of his skin.

"His kidneys gave out. He couldn't hold his water anymore," said Frank, who has never told his story to the police.

He said Gray lay in his bed for several weeks after the beating, while he and another boy at the school cared for him, bringing him meals, and changing the urine-soaked sheets on his bed.

"They wouldn't bring him to a doctor.

"I don't think they wanted to reveal the extent of his injuries," said Frank, who still lives in the tiny village of Ahousat, just outside Tofino on the west coast of Vancouver Island.

Frank said he spent several years attending the First United Church residential school in Ahousat, and for the most part found it to be a good place.

"I had a very good experience in that school.

"That was the only one [bad incident] I experienced," said Frank of the death of his friend.

He said he never thought of reporting the death at the time because he was only 11 years old and because the principal of the school was seen as the ultimate authority.

When he grew older he sometimes remembered Gray, he said, but didn't go to the police because his philosophy was: "Keep out of harm's way — and learn to forgive."

Frank was asked why he thought a boy would be beaten so severely for such a minor offence.

"I don't know how you guys operate. That's not the Indian way," he replied.

Frank also said there seems little point because Caldwell is now dead.

"There's no use having hard feelings for a dead man. If he was alive, I'd still be angry," he said.

Rev. Bruce Gunn, the United Church minister in Ahousat, said Frank's attitude of forgiveness is typical of the older generation of Indian people.

"Their tradition was to get along because they lived in survival cultures. They knew how important it was to forgive," he said.

But Gunn said younger Indian people feel it's important to get to the bottom of what happened, and they are pressing for inquiries into crimes that may have happened more than 50 years ago.

Gunn said he has been talking to elders in Ahousat, trying to confirm some of the stories that have been going around.

He hadn't talked to Frank, but said he would.

Attention was drawn to the United Church residential school system on Vancouver Island earlier this month when Jack McDonald, a candidate for the New Democratic Party leadership, called for a public inquiry into alleged deaths at schools in the Port Alberni area.

McDonald said he'd heard of at least two deaths, one of which was in Ahousat.

Sgt. Paul Willms, who is heading the RCMP investigation into abuse at B.C. residential schools, said he hadn't heard any allegations about deaths in the Port Alberni area until McDonald brought them up.

The police in Port Alberni this week began questioning witnesses and promised a thorough investigation.

Meanwhile, Kevin McNamee-Annett, a former United Church minister, issued a statement Monday saying he's going on a fast to protest against the church's handling of the issue.

Vancouver Sun, December 20, 1995

Figure 20: An eyewitness account of one of these killings, of student Albert Gray by United Church Principal Alfred Caldwell at the Ahousaht Indian school (1995)

The Vancouver Sun

THURSDAY, FEBRUARY 1, 1996

15 Indian men seek millions

Rapes, beatings 30 years ago at Island residential school are the basis of a lawsuit against Ottawa, United Church.

MARK HUME
Vancouver Sun

A series of rapes and beatings that shocked a B.C. Supreme Court judge are the basis for a massive lawsuit by 15 men against the federal government, the United Church of Canada and four administrators.

The case, filed in Vancouver on Tuesday, claims unspecified damages for a series of brutal physical and sexual assaults that took place at the Port Alberni Indian Residential School during the 1960s.

Vancouver lawyer Peter Grant said that he could not put a specific dollar figure to the claim, but believes it will become the biggest suit of its kind ever filed in Canada.

"For any one of the victims the claim would be for a large amount of money. For all of them it would be massive," he said.

"We have 15 individuals here whose lives have been destroyed."

By way of comparison, Grant said that his clients would be seeking "a lot more" than the $50 million former prime minister Brian Mulroney is seeking in a libel suit against the federal government.

"I wonder what he would have sued for if he'd lost 30 years of his life," said Grant.

"When you look at the pleadings in this case, the destruction to each of these people is immense. One of the victims was beaten so much he became deaf. Most never finished school because of what happened to them. They've suffered the problems of divorce, alcohol abuse, drug addiction. One described today how he can't control his bowels whenever he's under stress, because of what happened to him."

The suit follows the conviction last March of Arthur Henry Plint, who was given 11 years in jail for a series of sexual assaults that took place 30 years ago at the Alberni residential school.

Plint, who was supervisor of the boys' dorms at the school, repeatedly abused the children in his care.

The courts heard that when some the children complained to oth school officials, they were ostracized beaten.

When B.C. Supreme Court Justice Douglas Hogarth heard the case against Plint, he said he was shocked.

"I must say that I have now been this business since 1950 as a lawyer and primarily in criminal law, and also on the bench, and I have never se

Please see LAWSUIT

Figure 21: Report of the first class action lawsuit brought by residential school students against the United Church and government of Canada (1996)

To the editor:

As Kevin Annett's former wife, I feel compelled to respond to certain inaccuracies contained in Clodagh O'Connell's article *Maverick Minister* (Sept. 21 issue).

Contrary to what O'Connell wrote, at no time did I ever meet or talk with a lawyer or any other person representing the United Church regarding my divorce action. My lawyer did seek out and receive a report regarding Mr. Annett's suitability for ministry prepared by Comox-Nanaimo Presbytery, available to anyone interested in the matter.

ANNE MCNAMEE,
VANCOUVER

(The Vancouver Courier, Sept. 28, 1997)

Figure 22: Admission by ex-wife of Kevin Annett that she colluded with the United Church of Canada to divorce Kevin and deprive him of his children (1997)

PORT ALBERNI

Victoria Times-Colonist, September 24, '97 p. A4

Police told of death at residential school

By Dirk Meissner
Times Colonist staff

Port Alberni Mounties may have a 30-year-old unsolved murder on their hands.

A former Alberni Residential School student said Tuesday he discovered the naked, bloodied body of a young aboriginal girl in 1967, but never heard from the police.

Harry Wilson said he was 10 years old when he and two friends made the grisly discovery behind a school building. He immediately reported the body to the school principal, who said he would call the RCMP. Wilson said he saw police at the school, but was never interviewed and less than a week later was transferred to a residential school in Nanaimo.

Wilson said the girl appeared to be about 16 years old. He said she was a new student who had been at the school for about two weeks. He said he did not know her name.

Wilson said he was readmitted to the Alberni school about three months later, but nobody said a word about the body.

Mounties in Port Alberni and officers working on an RCMP task force investigating abuses at B.C.'s aboriginal residential schools said they will investigate Wilson's allegations.

Sgt. Dale Djos, Port Alberni's investigation section chief, said he did not recall any police investigation involving the 1967 death. "What we have to do is work backwards on this," he said.

Const. Gerry Peters, who is part of the residential school task force, said the girl's death should be investigated. "It is definitely worthy of our attention."

The task force was formed in November 1994 to investigate reports of physical and sexual abuse at B.C.'s 15 residential schools. Five schools were on the Island.

Peters said 18 officers are part of the task force, which has so far identified 115 victims and spoken to 400 people.

Officers investigated two reports of murders at Island residential schools, but both turned out to be deaths due to sickness, he said.

It was reported that Maisie Shaw died in 1946 when she was thrown down a flight of stairs at the Alberni school. Police discovered she suffered rheumatic fever and died.

It was also reported that Albert Gray was beaten to death at the residential school in Ahousaht. Peters said police could not confirm his cause of death, but are reasonably certain he died in hospital in Port Alberni suffering from pneumonia.

Kevin Annett, a former Port Alberni United Church minister, spoke to Wilson about the girl's death. Annett was fired by the church in June 1995.

He is currently working on a doctoral thesis at the University of B.C. that examines the impact of the Island's two United Church-run residential schools on the aboriginal community and the church.

Annett said he heard many stories about deaths and violence involving Port Alberni area aboriginals when he was with the church. "I do think it happened," he said. "It's hard to say how many."

Figure 23: Media report of Harry Wilson's discovery of a dead girl at the Alberni residential school (1997)

RESIDENTIAL SCHOOL ABUSE

Former minister alleges officials killed students

By Nelson Bennett
Daily News

Beatings and rape weren't the only crimes committed at the Port Alberni Indian Residential School, says a former United Church minister.

Kevin Annett, who was removed from the pulpit in 1995, says at least four children at the Alberni Residential School may have died under suspicious circumstances. He's convinced they were murdered.

He says witnesses are only now beginning to come forward with stories of children being beaten to death.

Four of those witnesses will speak at a seminar being organized by Annett tonight, starting at 6:30 p.m., at Simon Fraser University's Harbour Centre Campus in Vancouver (515 West Hastings St.)

Annett served as minister at St. Andrew's United Church in Port Alberni from 1992 to 1995.

When he started asking local native people why they didn't attend church, he was told the incredible history of sexual and physical abuse at the Alberni residential school, which had been run by the United Church.

"All the visits I did in native homes, they all said the same thing," Annett said. "And they said even worse. They said that kids are buried out behind the Alberni school.

"I found it incredible. But I couldn't deny what people were telling me and what I was increasingly finding out."

Annett began inviting former residential school victims to speak at Sunday services about the abuses they experienced.

Annett was dismissed in 1995, and though he said he was never given a reason for his dismissal, he suspects it was because he was digging up history the church would rather keep buried.

Annett is convinced one former residential school employee was responsible for the deaths of two students.

The first was Albert Gray, who was allegedly beaten to death in 1938. And according to one former student, a 14-year-old girl named Maisie Shaw died in 1946 after being kicked down a flight of stairs by the same employee.

> **"I found a 16-year-old native girl beaten to death, with no clothes on,"**
>
> Harry Wilson

More recently, Dennis Tallio – who is one of the plaintiffs in the ongoing Alberni Indian Residential School trial – told Annett he accidentally stumbled across the partially decomposed body of a girl in 1965 while he was student at the school.

Harry Wilson, who is also a plaintiff in the trial, reported a similar incident occurring in 1967.

Wilson, who had snuck out of the school around 6 a.m. one morning to meet up with two friends from the nearby reserve, said he came across the body of a girl who had only recently come to the school.

"I found a 16-year-old native girl beaten to death, with no clothes on," Wilson said in a phone interview Sunday.

He said he told the principal. He was soon sent away to hospital in Nanaimo. He never did find out what happened to the girl.

Annett said the deaths have never been satisfactorily explained by either police, school or church officials, and he thinks he knows why.

"They're trying to protect reputations of senior people," said Annett, who is currently pursuing a PhD. at the University of British Columbia.

Stories of children who died mysteriously at residential schools have been rumored within the native community for some time. Only recently have eyewitness began to go public with their testimony.

Annett hopes tonight's meeting will encourage others who may have knowledge of mysterious deaths at residential schools to come forward.

"It requires more people coming forward," he said. "These things are not going to be written down on a document somewhere."

The Nanaimo Daily News, Feb. 9, 1998

Figure 24: Other media reports of killings at Indian schools (1998)

- **Witness to murder:** Harriett Nahanee, a survivor of the Alberni Residential school, will describe the killing of a fellow student by Church officials, and the abuses she suffered.

- **Cover-up by RCMP:** Dennis Tallio and Harry Wilson, survivors of the Alberni Residential School, will discuss their discovery of dead bodies at the school in the 1960's and their mistreatment by the RCMP after they reported the bodies.

- **Profiteering off Native lands and resources:** Reverend Kevin Annett, former United Church minister in Port Alberni, will describe how that church illegally sold Native land at its residential schools to white business interests and MacMillan-Blodel, with the collusion of the provincial government.

- **Welcome:** Bob George, Burrard Band

This Forum is Sponsored by the Simon Fraser Public Interest Research Group

Monday, February 9th
6:30 p.m.

Fletcher Challenge Lecture Hall, Room 1900
Simon Fraser University, Harbour Centre Campus
515 West Hastings, Vancouver

It Is Strongly Recommended You Reserve Your Seat
For Reservations Call: (604) 251-3048 (604) 251-2542

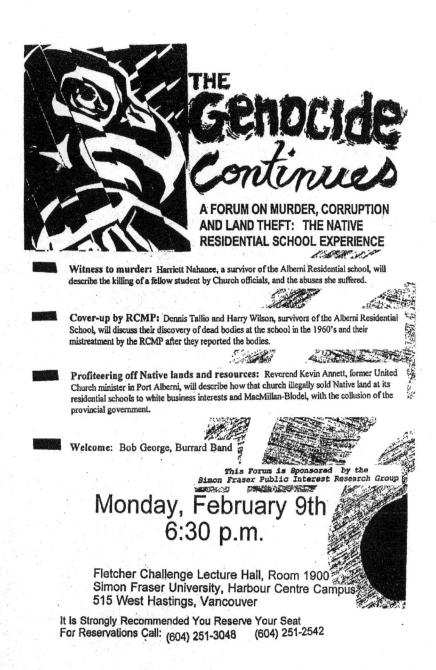

Figure 25: Public forum on Indian residential school crimes that established the independent Truth Commission into Genocide in Canada (TCGC), Vancouver (1998)

INTERNATIONAL

HUMAN RIGHTS

ASSOCIATION OF AMERICAN MINORITIES

An International NGO in Consultative Status (Roster) with the Economic and Social Council of the United Nations

You are invited to add your testimony about native residential schools to the voice of many, at an International Human Rights Tribunal, June 12-14, 1998, in Vancouver, B.C.

The *International Human Rights Association of American Minorities* (IHRAAM), an affiliate of the United Nations with consultative status, is conducting an inquiry into allegations of murder and other atrocities at native residential schools in British Columbia. This inquiry will include a panel of international human rights experts, who will receive testimony and examine all evidence.

The panel will come to a verdict about the guilt or innocence of church, government and police officials in the reported deaths and torture of native children at the residential schools. Their findings and verdict will be forwarded to the Secretary-General of the United Nations, the Human Rights Commission and to the international media.

If you have personal, family or any kind of knowledge of the abuse, torture and murder of native people at the residential schools and the inter-generational legacy of the residential school system, please attend this tribunal so that the full truth of the schools can be made known and healing can begin. Testimonies can be made either in full confidence at the public tribunal or in private.

The Tribunal will be held at the Maritime Labour Centre, 1880 Triumph St., in Vancouver, commencing at 9:00 a.m. each day. For more information, contact the *International Human Rights Association of American Minorities*, c/o Rudy James, at 425-483-9251 or, in Vancouver, contact The Circle of Justice c/o Kevin at 462-1086 or Harriett at 985-5817.

Thlau Goo Yailth Thlee Rudy James

Thlau Goo Yailth Thlee, The First and Oldest Raven
Rudy James
Member, Board of Directors Dated this 16th *day of April 1998*

Figure 26: Invitation issued by IHRAAM, a United Nations NGO, to attend its Tribunal into Canadian Indian Residential schools, Vancouver (June 12-14, 1998)

INTERNATIONAL
HUMAN RIGHTS

ASSOCIATION OF AMERICAN MINORITIES

An International NGO in consultative Status (Roster) with the Economic and Social Council of the United Nations

Press Release

To: All Press and Media
Dateline: Woodinville, WA May 25, 1998
Contact: Diana Wynne James 425-483-9251

Subject: Murder and Atrocities Subject of Tribunal

International Human Rights experts from the International Human Rights Association of American Minorities (IHRAAM) have been asked to investigate murder and atrocities at United States and Canadian Residential Schools.

The International Human Rights Association of American Minorities Northwest Regional Office serves as a Liaison for the Indigenous Peoples of the Americas and is investigating the horrific and shocking allegations by eyewitnesses who have described a legacy of torture and murder at the Canadian Indian residential schools. Following two preliminary interviews with residential school survivors at Port Alberni and Vancouver, B.C., IHRAAM is in possession of approximately seven hours of emotionally charged videotaped testimony, letters of request for help and much written documentation supporting an in-depth investigation.

Invited tribunal jurists will include respected Tribal Elders and leaders from many Indigenous Nations of the Americas and certain others drawn from the non-native community of the United States and Canada. The NorthWest International Tribunal will convene from June 12 - 14, 1998 at the Maritime Labour Centre, 1880 Triumph Street, Vancouver, B.C.

Issues to be discussed are: Forced removal from traditional lands and waters, institutional racism, physical and psychological warfare, ethnocide and murder stemming from the residential school system supported by the government of Canada and the United Church of Canada, the Catholic Church and other churches, organizations and individuals involved with the operation of the residential schools across the United States, Canada and the Northwest Territories.

Figure 27: IHRAAM press release regarding its Tribunal into Genocide in residential schools

Invitations to attend have gone out to representatives of the government of Canada, (the Honorable Prime Minister Jean Chretien), church officials, organizations and individuals involved with the operation of the residential schools across Canada and the Northwest Territories.

Following the Tribunal, IHRAAM is prepared to submit a full report to the Secretary General and High Commissioner of the Human Rights Commission, United Nations, Geneva, Switzerland. Representing IHRAAM will be: ThlauGooYailthThlee (Mr. Rudy James) Member of the Directorate, Native American Division and Diana Wynne James, Public Relations Director. Tribunal Findings and Decision will also be forwarded to the international media.

IHRAAM respectfully requests that any and all persons having personal, family or any kind of knowledge of the abuse, torture and murder of native people at the residential schools and the intergenerational legacy of the residential school system, are invited to attend. We are assured that testimonies can be made to the Judges either in public or in private.

Diana Wynne James

INTERNATIONAL
HUMAN RIGHTS

ASSOCIATION OF AMERICAN MINORITIES

An International NGO in Consultative Status (Roster) with the Economic and Social Council of the United Nation

May 1st, 1998.

Maritine Labour Centre
Suite 10
1880 Triumph St.
Vancouver, B.C. V5L 1K3
Canada

Attn: Murray Drummond

Dear Mr. Drummond:

RE: Rental of a Hall, June, 1998

Enclosed please find IHRAAM cheque in the amount of $1,000.00, which sum has been gifted to Kevin Annett/Circle of Justice for the purpose of holding an event in your facility in the month of June, 1998. This payment in no way forms a contractual relationship between your organization and ourselves with respect to the hall rental.

Any queries in this regard should be addressed to Mr. Annett in Vancouver at 604-254-9550.

Sincerely,

Diana Kly
Director, Communications

DK:lm
Enc.: check payable to Maritime Labour Centre
c.c. Mr. Kevin Annett, 12218 McNutt Rd., Maple Ridge, B.C. V2W 1N6

Ste. 253, 919C Albert Street, Regina, SK. S4R 2P6, Canada
tel/fax: 306-789-0474 • e-mail: ihraam@geocities.com • website: http://www.ihraam.org

Figure 28: Payment of facility for Tribunal by IHRAAM head office

NORTHWEST
INTERNATIONAL-TRIBUNAL COURT
International Tribunal of Original Nations and Invited Tribunal Jurists
Indigenous Holders of Allodial Title

A Convening of the Original Hereditary Forum of Justice

COPY

DIPLOMATIC DISPATCH & SUMMONS

To: Mr. Brian Thorpe, Executive Secretary United Church of Canada, B.C.

Please be advised that you have been listed as a primary witness in an adjudication of a matter before this Court, which is a Tribunal of International and Indigenous Judges. Therefore, your presence is Hereby respectfully requested:

On June 12-14, 1998 at 9:00 AM
At the Maritime Labour Centre
1880 Triumph St., Vancouver, BC

Said Tribunal is convening pursuant to traditional tribal law, the Rule of Natural Law, and the Law of Nations and your attendance is requested to participate in the examination of issues and questions regarding this matter.

Cause No. NWITC-0612-98CCAN

The charges are titled: Forced Removal from Traditional Lands and Waters, Institutional Racism, Physical and Psychological Warfare, Genocide, and Murder, stemming from the Residential School System supported by the Government of Canada and the United Church of Canada, the Catholic Church and other Churches, Organizations and Individuals involved with the operation of Residential Schools across Canada and the Northwest Territories.

You may desire to consult with your attorney in regards to this matter, or have an advocate of your choice attend the hearings with you. You may submit written documents and materials, but be advised that they do not carry the same weight as personal testimony.

Due to the Nation Status of the Original Nations of the North and South American Continents and Hawaii (the Holders of allodial Title) this is a Nation to Nation issue, thereby mandating the presence of representatives from the Government of Canada. Internationally known Human Rights experts from the International Human rights Association of American Minorities, a United Nations NGO with consultative status, will observe the proceedings. Reports will be submitted to the High Commissioner of the Human Rights Commission. .

Filed and Noted:
May 23, 1998
Administrator for the NWITC

Signed this 22nd day of May, 1998 WhatStaw George S. James Jr.
Lead Judge WhatStaw, George Suckinaw James, Jr.

DIPLOMATIC DISPATCH & INVITATION TO TESTIFY
NorthWest International Tribunal • PO Box 1546 • Woodinville, WA 98072
Ph/Fax: 425-483-9251 or 206-362-7725 • Email: wolfhouse48@hotmail.com

Figure 29: Diplomatic Summons issued by IHRAAM Tribunal to thirty two officials of Canadian church and state regarding their complicity in residential school crimes

Probe of Canadian residential schools to be reported at UN

Globe + Mail, June 20, 1998

BY ROBERT MATAS
British Columbia Bureau

VANCOUVER — An international human-rights group investigating allegations of racism at Canada's residential schools for native children expects to deliver its report next month to United Nations Human Rights Commissioner Mary Robinson.

Representatives from the International Human Rights Association of American Minorities were in Vancouver earlier this month to hear from several natives who had been placed in residential schools. The association is formally affiliated with the United Nations.

Charlene Strong Eagle, a member of the tribunal hearing the allegations, criticized the federal government and the United, Anglican and Roman Catholic churches yesterday for not appearing at the tribunal to respond.

Those who spoke during a three-day forum recounted their experiences at the schools and some stated they had witnessed what they described as murder, rape, sexual molestation, routine beatings and electric shock to five-year-old children who misbehaved.

They also said that young native women were involuntarily sterilized, that abortions were induced in pregnant students and that native children were kidnapped and placed forcibly in the residential schools.

Accounts of the offences were given by 27 former students at eight residential schools in B.C., according to a list distributed yesterday by Kevin Annett, a former United Church minister who has done extensive research on the alleged abuses.

A report accompanied by 19 hours of videotaped testimony from former students will be presented to Ms. Robinson on July 31 in London, England, Mr. Annett said in an interview. The human-rights group will ask Ms. Robinson to have the report presented to a UN Human Rights Commission meeting in New York in August, he added.

The human-rights group is also planning to ask the World Council of Churches this summer to start an inquiry into the role of the Anglican and United churches in Canada's residential schools for natives, Mr. Annett said.

"We'd like to see the churches open up their archives to see what information they have about these allegations," he said.

The UN-affiliated group became involved in the issue of residential schools in Canada in response to complaints from former students who felt they have been unable to get justice under Canadian law. The federal government, with the support of the country's leading churches, set up more than 80 residential schools for native children over the past century in almost every province in Canada. Officials estimate that up to 125,000 native children passed through the system before it was closed down in the mid-1980s.

Figure 30: The only media coverage of the IHRAAM Tribunal (June 20, 1998)

Tuesday, October 27, 1998 | The Province • B.C. A13

Church-school victim got no help

MARLON WATTS
mourns brother

Native man's death blamed on stress of abuse by 'monster,' lengthy legal battle

By Suzanne Fournier
Staff Reporter

Marlon Watts wants to know how many more men will die before victims of residential-school sexual abuse see justice.

Marlon's brother Darryl, 40, whose body was found drifting in Nanaimo harbour Saturday, was the second death among 30 plaintiffs who are suing Ottawa and the United Church for abuse they suffered at the Alberni Indian Residential School.

Darryl Watts, who was depressed and drinking, left court Thursday morning, despondent that the United Church had demanded the victims' civil suit be postponed until April.

He never returned to hear the United Church finally ask at the end of the day for a settlement conference, something the church has adamantly refused in the past.

"I'll never see my brother again, because he never got the help he needed to help him cope with the trauma of being raped when he was four, by a monster the church had just rehired," said Marlon Watts, a 42-year-old Vancouver-based counsellor for the Native Courtworkers.

"There were no healing funds for my brother, no matter how many times we applied. No one had money or time for him, not the United Church or the federal government who employed the pedophile who abused Darryl, not the $350-million so-called federal healing fund.

"If any of that money had been made available, my brother would still be alive."

A coroner has ruled the death an accident, but Watts called it "accidental suicide."

Another plaintiff, Simon Danes, committed suicide before the Alberni case came to court.

Now the family wants the church or government to pay for Darryl Watts' body to be returned to the Nisga'a village of Laxgaltsap, said Marlon, "so we can give Darryl a proper burial."

The plaintiffs' lawyer, Allan Early, said the United Church finally agreed Thursday to settlement talks, after new evidence was introduced from the church's own archives. Documents show that in 1960, the church and Ottawa were informed of widespread sexual abuse at the schools but responded with a directive to keep the incidents out of the media.

Arthur Plint was rehired by the school in 1963 and within a year had sexually abused all four Watts brothers.

Between 1948 and 1968, Plint is believed to have molested hundreds of native boys.

The boys' mother, Marie Watts testified that neither she nor her husband, who was illiterate, signed documents produced by the church that surrendered her boys to school.

Marlon noted that when Darryl took the stand last February, he was "raked over the coals" by church lawyer Christopher Hinkson, who accused him of "recovered-memory syndrome."

Figure 31: Admission of a church-state cover up and of the practice of kidnapping Indian children (October 1998)

The New Internationalist, No. 309, Jan-Feb '99

Update

HUMAN RIGHTS

Disturbing revelations

Native Canadian nightmares see the light of day

UNITED Church minister Kevin Annett was puzzled to find no native members of St Andrew's Church when he arrived in Port Alberni, British Columbia, in 1992. Annett started asking local Native people why they had not attended church. Their answer – shocking stories of abuse and murder at the local church-run residential school.

As part of a government program of forced assimilation, Canadian Native children were taken from their homes and placed in residential schools which were operated by most of the major religions. It is estimated that up to 125,000 Native children passed through the system before it was closed down in the 1980s.

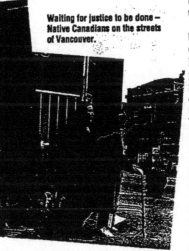

Waiting for justice to be done – Native Canadians on the streets of Vancouver.

KEVIN ANNETT

Now a tribunal has been established in British Columbia to investigate human-rights violations in the province's residential schools for Native children. So far over 30 people have given their eyewitness accounts.

The list of alleged offences is shocking. Eyewitness testimony and other evidence presented to the tribunal recount instances of murder by beating, poisoning, hanging, starvation, strangulation, being thrown from windows and medical experimentation. Other crimes include rape, sexual molestation and admin-

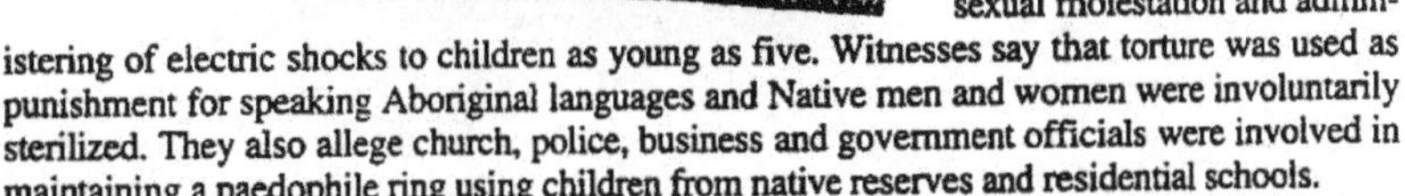

istering of electric shocks to children as young as five. Witnesses say that torture was used as punishment for speaking Aboriginal languages and Native men and women were involuntarily sterilized. They also allege church, police, business and government officials were involved in maintaining a paedophile ring using children from native reserves and residential schools.

Witnesses are regularly threatened and intimidated and Annett himself has received death threats. Annett was also fired from his job at the church. A recent suicide of abuse victim Darryl Watts, who had been badgered by Church lawyers, and the revelation that his parents never signed a release form to send him to the school led the United Church to issue 'apologies' to the survivors. At least 1,400 people are suing the Church and Government.

The tribunal eventually plans to publish its findings and present them to United Nations Human Rights Commissioner, Mary Robinson. Whatever happens at the UN, for the victims of these unimaginable horrors life can never be the same again.

Harriet Nahanee, 60, was the first witness to support the allegations about abuse and killings at the Alberni United Church school. She says she still has nightmares about the time she witnessed the death of a young girl who came from Nitinat Lake. 'I heard her crying. She was looking for her mother. I heard the school administrator yelling at the supervisor for letting the child run around on the stairwell. I heard him kick her and she fell down the stairs. I went to look – her eyes were open, she wasn't moving. I never saw her again.' ■

Alan Hughes

Figure 32: First international media coverage of Indian residential school crimes and Kevin Annett (*The New Internationalist*, January 1999)

THE VANCOUVER SUN, SATURDAY, JUNE 3, 2000 A7

Judge sets new limit on residential school lawsuits

The incidents predate the Charter of Rights and Freedoms, she rules, and therefore are not covered by it.

CANADIAN PRESS

CALGARY — An Alberta judge has eliminated breaches of charter rights as a cause for lawsuits by former residential school students.

Justice Rosemary Nation said the lawsuits claiming cultural genocide involve incidents which occurred before the Charter of Rights and Freedoms came into effect.

"The plaintiffs' claims concern past, discrete events to which the charter has no application," Nation said, in a written judgment released Friday.

More than 2,000 one-time residents of the now-closed, Canadian government-sanctioned schools, are suing the various groups which ran the facilities.

The numerous aboriginal litigants claim, among other things, that they were wrongfully confined and subject to physical and sometimes sexual abuse. The suits also say the purpose of the schools — which ran from the 1920s to 1970s — was to eradicate aboriginal culture in students.

Some of the lawsuits claimed students' constitutional rights, including equality, were violated, but Nation said the alleged breaches pre-dated the 1985 Charter. Nation, in a decision which applies to three of the suits but will be a guideline for all the others, also said the plaintiffs can't seek a declaration cultural genocide was committed.

Along with monetary damages, the plaintiffs had sought recognition the defendants' conduct constituted a breach of the United Nations convention on genocide.

Nation said the UN convention has not been implemented in Canadian law and therefore can't be considered by a court. "The court lacks the jurisdiction to award a declaratory order on the basis of a non-legal, or political code of conduct," she said.

The Queen's Bench judge did rule the lawsuits can proceed on other grounds, including wrongful confinement, religious indoctrination and educational malpractice.

Nation said the allegations the plaintiffs received inadequate schooling could proceed despite authorities which said such claims "aren't generally sustainable as a cause of action in Canada. "The courts have, in most cases, declined to find that educational malpractice constitutes actionable negligence," she noted.

But Nation said the claims the students received improper schooling involved allegations "beyond acceptable community standards.

"The plaintiffs' claims of an inadequate education are also inextricably interwoven with the breach of [trust] duty and breach of treaty claims," Nation added.

Figure 33: Canadian courts restrict the scope of residential school lawsuits to issues not pertaining to human rights violations (June 2000)

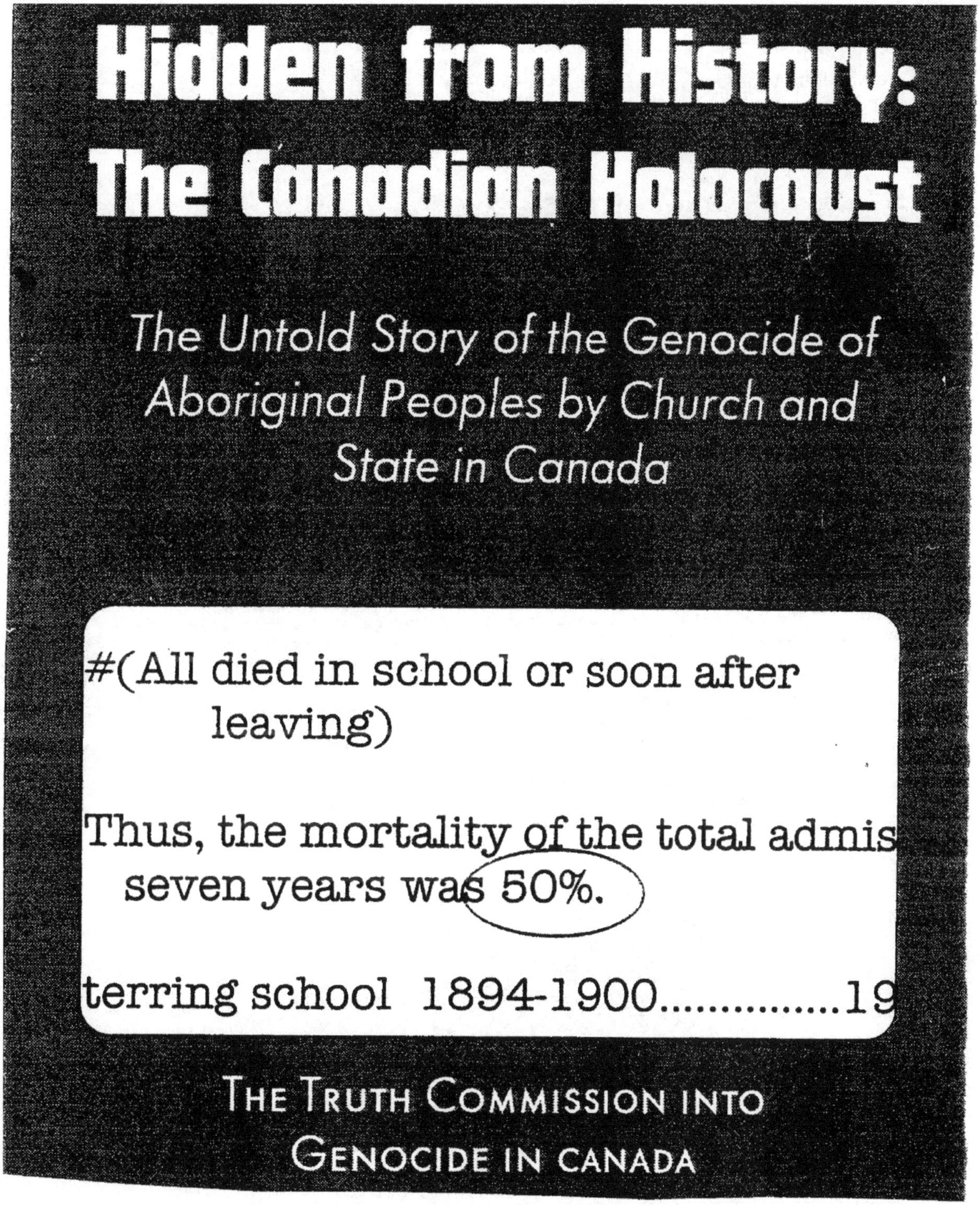

Hidden from History: The Canadian Holocaust

The Untold Story of the Genocide of Aboriginal Peoples by Church and State in Canada

#(All died in school or soon after leaving)

Thus, the mortality of the total admis seven years was 50%.

terring school 1894-1900...............19

THE TRUTH COMMISSION INTO GENOCIDE IN CANADA

Figure 34: First independent report of crimes in Indian Residential Schools, *"Hidden from History: The Canadian Holocaust"* (February 2001)

Mario Dion
Deputy Minister

29 December 2004

c/o Mr. Jeffrey Marder
Deputy Director
Aboriginal and Circumpolar Affairs Division
Foreign Affairs Canada

In response to your declaration of reconciliation apologizing on behalf of your government and the churches of Canada responsible for the physical violation and sexual abuse, the cultural genocide of the indigenous peoples of Canada, we requested three fundamental answers. What was the judicial process to be undertaken to bring all those responsable for the crimes of genocide detailed by us, to justice? What was to be your program of compensation for the victims and their families? And thirdly what legal mechanisms were to be put in place to guarantee that no such crimes may again take place, including our request regarding the ratification of international law on Indigenous Rights?
In your recent response, signed by Mario Dion, Minister, the 18th of December, we wish to state the following:
That you have not taken any responsibility for this ongoing process of impunity. According to The Assembly of First nations, your quasi judicial process has been nothing but an obstacle to a judicial process that is just, adequate and prompt.
Second the compensation package announced by your government is a fraud.
Please describe even one case where the victims of these crimes of genocide have received a fair settlement. This program of compensation appears to be nothing less than a program of support for administrating bureaucrats and social professionals, all non indigenous! This in itself is a clear violation of international indigenous law respecting the rights of consultation, participation and consensus.
And regarding our concern to see legal guarantee of indigenous rights in Canada and ratification of international law, there was no response. We remain preoccupied by this lack of responsibilty of your government. We will continue to maintain our spirit of solidarity with the Indigenous Peoples of Canada, and will not permit this continued impunity for the crimes against humanity and of genocide.

Respectfully,

Figure 35: "Denuncia" (Statement of Protest) issued by Mayan indigenous communities to the Canadian government regarding its genocidal actions (December 2004)

UNREPENTANT
Kevin Annett and Canada's Genocide

(Best Director of an International Documentary Film, New York Independent Film and Video Festival, November, 2006)

UNREPENTANT documents Canada's "dirty secret" - the planned extermination of aboriginal people in church-run Indian Residential Schools - and a clergyman's struggle to document and make public these crimes. First-hand testimonies from residential school survivors are interwoven with Kevin Annett's own story of how he faced firing, "de-frocking", and the loss of his family, reputation and livelihood as a result of his efforts to help survivors and bring out the truth of the residential schools.

This saga continues, as Kevin continues a David and Goliath struggle to hold the government and churches of Canada accountable for crimes against humanity, and the continued theft of aboriginal land.

UNREPENTANT took nineteen months to film, primarily in British Columbia and Alberta, and is based on Kevin Annett's book Hidden from History: The Canadian Holocaust. The entire film was a self-funded, grassroots effort, which is reflected in its earthy and human quality.

Produced & Written by: Kevin Annett, Louie Lawless and Lori O'Rorke
Directed by: Louie Lawless

For more information see:

Figure 36: First documentary film into genocidal crimes in Indian residential schools, *"Unrepentant"* (released January 2007)

Nanaimo Daily News Wednesday, April 18, 2007

Residential school victims remembered at protest

Painful memories recalled at event

The clang of church bells rang through Nanaimo's downtown on Sunday morning, drowning out the voices of protesters, who converged on the steps of the United Church in remembrance of residential school victims.

In seven cities across Canada, people rallied to mark what's been dubbed Aboriginal Holocaust Remembrance Day.

Organizer of the Nanaimo event, Rev. Kevin Annett, likened Canada's former residential school system to a genocide, where he said thousands of children died of abuse and disease.

"We need people responsible for these things brought to justice," said Annett.

Most of the boarding schools, which operated from 1886 to 1984, were run by Catholic, United and Anglican churches, under the auspices of the federal government.

School-aged children were taken from their home and sent to the schools as part of the government's policy.

Annett believes the buried remains of the children who died in the schools are purposely being kept secret from the public.

Last week, church officials said there are no records of any children dying in residential schools.

"That's just an out and out falsehood," said Annett, noting he has found such records at the University of British Columbia.

Bob Seward, 61, and his two brothers were sent to the Alberni residential school, which was run by the United Church, when he was four years old. Though he finds it difficult to discuss what happened during the 11 years he spent at the school, Seward said Sunday's rally was comforting.

"It means a whole lot," he said. "I didn't know there were people out there who cared. I thought everyone wanted to forget."

Some painful memories Seward recalled was the abuse he and his friends went through for speaking their native language.

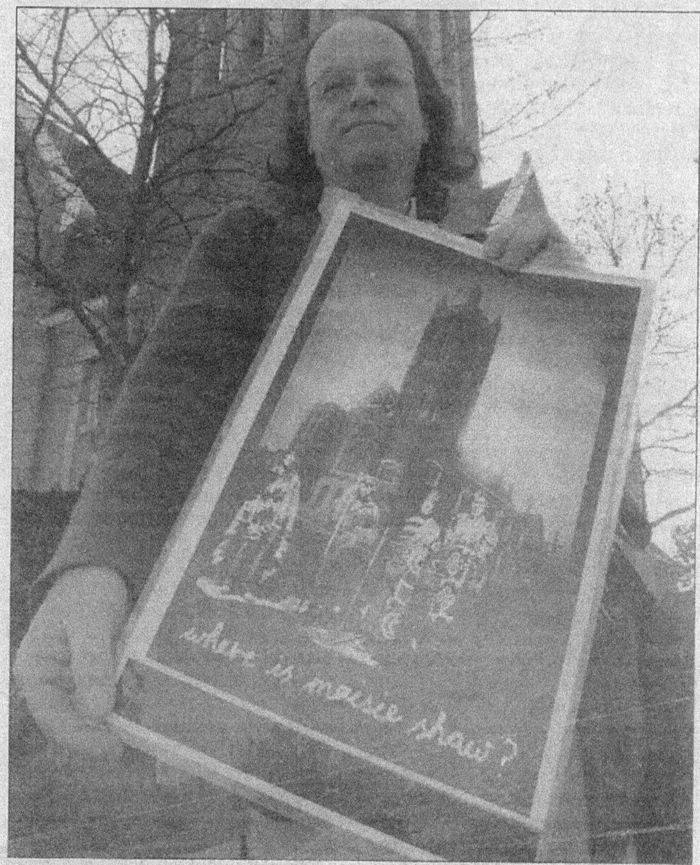

Former United Church Minister Kevin Annett organized the remembrance day gathering at St Andrews church on Sunday. —GLENN OLSEN/THE STAR

Figure 37: Report of one of many actions on Aboriginal Holocaust Memorial Day regarding the missing residential school children, Nanaimo (April 15, 2007)

6 APRIL 25, 2007 • 24 HOURS

Residential school docs pulped: MP

The feds purposely destroyed key Indian residential school documents to erase evidence of crimes committed against First Nations people, a native MP charged yesterday.

Indian Affairs pulped accident reports, inspector reports, principals' diaries and monthly and yearly reports by school and department officials in targeted purges, says a recent study on missing residential school files. The documents could have done much to shed light on the tragic fate of Native children who disappeared while in the care of church and state.

- 24 hours news services

Read more at *24hrs.ca*

May 14, 2007 24 hrs. News

canada

Native group threatens trouble

A native group is threatening an "escalating campaign of civil disobedience" to force the government into identifying and repatriating the bodies of 50,000 native children who the group claims died in residential schools.

Thirty-five members of the group, called The Friends of the Disappeared, occupied the Vancouver offices of Indian Residential Schools Resolution Canada on Friday.

"Until the remains of these children are repatriated [to traditional lands] and their murderers brought to justice, church and government facilities across Canada will be disrupted in an escalating campaign of civil disobedience," said the group in a statement sent to *24 hours news services.*

The group, made up of residential school survivors and their supporters, claims 50,000 children died in the schools.

Prentice

Indian Affairs Minister Jim Prentice has asked the Truth and Reconciliation Commission, created as part of a compensation package for school survivors, to count the dead and find where they are buried.

But naming and finding all the dead may be impossible. Many were buried in unmarked graves and the records are incomplete.

The country's leading scholar on residential schools, Trent University professor John Milloy, was asked 10 years ago by a family to find a child who committed suicide in one school. Milloy, however, said he could find no records to lead him to a body.

However, more records are coming out, including private documents like diaries from school officials, said Bob Watts, interim executive director of the commission.

Native children were buried "two in a grave" in at least one school, according to a document from 1918.

Tuberculosis also killed many children, while others froze to death or died from physical abuse.

- 24 hours news service

Figure 38: Report of the deliberate destruction of residential school records by the government *(top)* and the occupation of government offices by Indian in Vancouver *(below)* (May 2007)

April 24, 2007
Globe + Mail

Natives died in droves as Ottawa ignored warnings

Tuberculosis took the lives of students for at least 40 years

BY BILL CURRY AND KAREN HOWLETT
OTTAWA

As many as half of the aboriginal children who attended the early years of residential schools died of tuberculosis, despite repeated warnings to the federal government that overcrowding, poor sanitation and a lack of medical care were creating a toxic breeding ground for the rapid spread of the disease, documents show.

A Globe and Mail examination of documents in the National Archives reveals that children continued to die from tuberculosis at alarming rates for at least four decades after a senior official at the Department of Indian Affairs initially warned in 1907 that schools were making no effort to separate healthy children from those sick with the highly contagious disease.

Peter Bryce, the department's chief medical officer, visited 15 Western Canadian residential schools and found at least 24 per cent of students had died from tuberculosis over a 14-year period. The report suggested the numbers could be higher, noting that in one school alone, the death toll reached 69 per cent.

With less than four months to go before Ottawa officially settles out of court with most former students, a group calling itself the Friends and Relatives of the Disappeared Residential School Children is urging the government to acknowledge this period in the tragic residential-schools saga - and not just the better-known cases of physical and sexual abuse.

But I think the fact that they're acknowledging there's a criminal element means it's really necessary for there to be an international investigation here, because it's an indication even more so of genocide.

Kevin Annett, a former United Church minister

Kevin Annett, a former United Church minister turned documentary filmmaker, stands in a valley near Port Alberni, B.C., last April. Buried beneath the site, he says, are dead bodies of native children who attended a local residential school. JOHN LEHMANN/THE GLOBE AND MAIL

This has been driven in large part by Kevin Annett, a former United Church minister who had an acrimonious split from the church in 1995. Mr. Annett has spent more than a decade chronicling and videotaping former students telling particularly disturbing stories of their time spent at residential schools.

His work is compiled in a film called *Unrepentant: Kevin Annett and Canada's Genocide* and in an accompanying book.

Figure 39: Media report confirming 50% death rate in Indian residential schools (April 2007)

(The Globe + Mail, April 24, 2007)

Post, 13 Feb, 2008

Native group warns of international court action

Government accused of humanity crimes

By Jorge Barrera

OTTAWA • A group representing a segment of residential school survivors says it is preparing to take the federal government to international criminal court and disinter the bodies of native children.

As part of a growing campaign to seek redress for crimes they claim were committed, the Friends and Relatives of the Disappeared Residential School Children plan to disinter the bodies during a March media event at an unmarked grave site in B.C. where they believe native children who died in a residential school are buried, said Kevin Annett, the group's spokesman.

The group is also planning to file an application against the federal government and the Roman Catholic Church at the International Criminal Court in The Hague. They accuse the federal government of being complicit in crimes against humanity, said Mr. Annett, a former United Church minister who has been campaigning on the issue for more than a decade.

The federal government recently reached a $1.9-billion settlement with residential school survivors and created a $60-million Truth and Reconciliation Commission in addition to the package, but Mr. Annett's group believes the commission lacks the teeth to settle the matter.

The Assembly of First Nations, which was involved in achieving the settlement package, has deliberately kept its distance from Mr. Annett's group.

The group wants criminal sanctions against individuals who staffed the schools and were connected to deaths. They are also looking to the international community for condemnation of the federal government and churches that created and operated the program to assimilate native children into white society.

"We need a genuine inquiry and we need outside groups to monitor this," said Mr. Annett, who would like to see the UN set up a human rights tribunal and launch an investigation. "We need a body that has power to subpoena."

The group has sent letters to the prime minister, the Queen, via Rideau Hall, and the Vatican giving each 30 days to reveal the location of burial sites and causes of death of children who died in residential schools. The group has also staged high-profile demonstrations in Vancouver and Toronto.

Mr. Annett admits it is unlikely there will be a response, but said the deadlines, which all expire by March 8, will trigger the International Criminal Court application. The group also plans to launch civil disobedience, including occupying churches.

The National Post,
Feb. 13, 2008

Figure 40: First threat of international court action against Canada (February 2008)

JACK BOLAND/SUN MEDIA

Members of the Friends and Relatives of the Disappeared stage a protest at the Metropolitan United Church at 56 Queen St. E. yesterday

Show us where dead buried, natives ask

They call it an "Aboriginal Holocaust."

The group Friends and Relatives of the Disappeared claim thousands of native children died or went missing after attending church-run Indian residential schools until they closed in 19[illegible].

Some 15 aboriginal supporters gathered outside the Metropolitan United Church on Queen St. E. yesterday demanding the church disclose to families where their dead are buried.

"We gave the United, Anglican and Catholic churches 30 days to respond and we haven't heard anything," said FRD organizer Kevin Annett.

"Some (native) chiefs across the country think that because the churches are responsible for so many deaths that they're evicting them off their land within 72 hours."

The schools, which opened in 1840, were a hotbed of physical and sexual abuse and disease. The average death rate was 30 to 60% at that time.

"A lot of the deaths happened because the church employees were deliberately putting kids sick with influenza or tuberculosis with healthy children," Annett said.

The students were between 5 to 16 years old.

There are graves behind the schools in British Columbia and Mohawk Residential School in Brantford, claimed Annett. It was that school house 54-year-old Doreen Silversmith's late father survived.

"I remember my dad talking about being beaten for speaking his language," she said. "I remember running away from him in the dark. It's genocide. That violence passed onto his family."

At 11:30 a.m., five women from the FRD were asked by Rev. Malcolm Sinclair to leave the Metropolitan church after they unravelled a banner that claimed 50,000 children died at these schools.

"He said he didn't believe what we're saying happened, but the United Church proper have previously acknowledged that there were deaths by beatings," said Carrie Lester, 48.

Annett said he's written to the prime minister but so far, no response.

But in 1998 the federal government apologized, citing "attitudes of racial and cultural superiority which led to a suppression of aboriginal culture and values."

— Jenny Yuen

For more on this story, go to ... **torontosun.com/video**

One of many protests led by Rev. Annett and Friends and Relatives of the Disappeared, Canada (Toronto, February 2008)

Figure 41: Toronto aboriginals demand to know location of burial sites of residential school children (February 2008)

DEMONSTRATION » VICTIMS OF RESIDENTIAL SCHOOLS

3/24/08 Globe & Mail

Native protesters disrupt Easter services in Vancouver

BY JEREMY HAINSWORTH VANCOUVER

Two dozen native protesters rallied outside Easter services at Vancouver's Roman Catholic cathedral yesterday demanding to know where the bodies of children who died in residential schools are located.

Friends and Relatives of the Disappeared served the church with an eviction notice in a similar protest on March 16. Now, the group says the church is a squatter because the deadline to vacate was last Wednesday.

Spokesman Kevin Annett said yesterday's protest was designed to draw attention to the plight of children who were forced into both Catholic and Protestant residential schools.

"It's time the Catholic church pulled their head out of the sand and responded to the victims and the things people are asking for ... a return of the children who died, their remains, and an identification of who's responsible," Mr. Annett said. "As they would do for anybody."

He claimed there are mass graves of children.

The protest was not without incident. Police had to remove three protesters from the church.

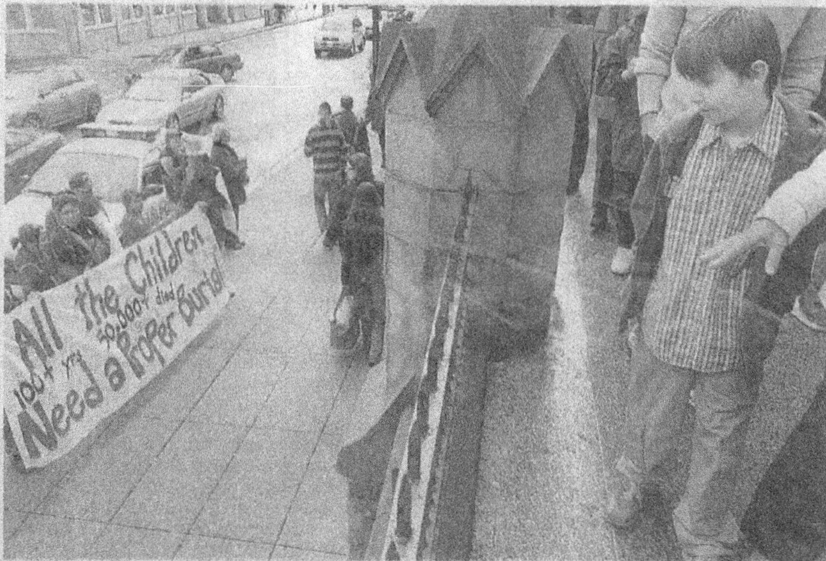

A group protests outside the Holy Rosary Catholic church during Easter services in Vancouver yesterday. Police had to remove three protesters from the church. LYLE STAFFORD FOR THE GLOBE AND MAIL

Similar protests have taken place across the country in the past few weeks against Catholic, Anglican and United churches.

The group's demands include the churches withdrawing from all aboriginal territories and surrendering their buildings to hereditary chiefs.

They also want the churches to identify the burial places of all children who died in residential schools and hospitals.

The schools, which opened in 1840, were a hotbed of physical and sexual abuse and illness.

The students were between seven and 16 years old.

In 1998, the federal government issued an apology, citing "attitudes of racial and cultural superiority which led to a suppression of aboriginal culture and values."

» *The Canadian Press*

The Globe and Mail, Monday, March 10, 2008

RESIDENTIAL SCHOOLS » DEMONSTRATION

Protesters storm church in bid to learn fate of aboriginal children

TORONTO

Demonstrators protested inside a Toronto church yesterday to raise awareness about the aboriginal children that they say disappeared from Canada's residential school system between 1840 and 1940.

The protesters have demanded that the federal government and leaders of several churches reveal the locations of unmarked graves where tens of thousands of children were buried near residential schools.

About two dozen protesters rallied outside the Metropolitan United Church in downtown Toronto, and a few went inside to display a banner at the front of the church.

With police standing by, they left shortly thereafter.

The protesters say they will hold more demonstrations at Anglican, Catholic and United churches across the country until their demands are met and more is known about victims of residential schools.

The federal government estimates as many as 100,000 children attended residential schools, which have long been assailed as hotbeds of physical and sexual abuse and other human rights violations.

The federal government apologized in 1998, saying that "attitudes of racial and cultural superiority led to a suppression of aboriginal culture and values."

Ottawa is in the process of establishing a truth and reconciliation commission, which will investigate ways to identify the number of children who died at residential schools and their causes of death.

In January, Roman Catholic bishops pledged their support for a truth commission on Indian residential schools, saying Catholics will speak publicly at the hearings to "balance" the official history of what happened for decades behind closed doors.

Participation from the Catholic Church, which operated about 70 per cent of the schools jointly with the federal government, had been uncertain until the announcement.

» *The Canadian Press*

Figures 42: Churches in Toronto and Vancouver are occupied by FRD (March 2008)

PROVINCIA DI GENOVA

VICE PRESIDENTE
MARINA DONDERO

ASSESSORA PER LA PACE
MILO' BERTOLOTTO

Prot. n. 41/09-VP

Genova, 1.12.2009

Gent.mo Rev. Kevin ANNETT
Associazione "Amici e Parenti degli Scomparsi del Canada"

Gent.mo Sig. Sergio BUGOLOTTI
Associazione Culturale Hunkapi

LORO INDIRIZZI

In occasione della visita del Rev. Kevin Annet a Genova, il 14 ottobre, abbiamo avuto modo di conoscere attraverso la sua testimonianza e quella del presidente dell'Associazione Hunkapi, Sergio Bugolotti, il forte impegno di quel movimento internazionale che da anni si batte per indagare sui crimini commessi contro le popolazioni native del Canada, sia nel passato che in epoca contemporanea.

In particolare esprimiamo la nostra più ferma condanna per la istituzionalizzazione coatta dei minori nei collegi obbligatori, detti Residential Schools, dalla seconda metà dell'800 al 1996.

Abbiamo appreso con profondo sgomento che in questi istituti vi è stata una mortalità del 50% dei piccoli ospiti che venivano costretti con ogni mezzo – anche tramite vessazioni fisiche – ad abbandonare la propria cultura.

La nostra Amministrazione sostiene convintamente l'azione di quanti sono impegnati a ricostruire la verità e la giustizia sul genocidio perpetrato dallo Stato canadese e ritiene di grande importanza un'indagine 'indipendente' sui tragici fatti avvenuti in Canada ai danni di una minoranza inerme.

Siamo infine interessati a proseguire la conoscenza di quella realtà e vi chiediamo di tenerci aggiornati, inviandoci una documentazione approfondita, in modo da poterla meglio conoscere e individuare insieme a voi i modi più efficaci per rappresentare la nostra solidarietà nei confronti dei Popoli Nativi del Canada.

Con i nostri migliori saluti

ASSESSORA
MILO' BERTOLOTTO
Milò Bertolotto

VICE PRESIDENTE
MARINA DONDERO
Marina Dondero

Figure 43: Letter of endorsement of Kevin Annett and the FRD campaign by Marina Dondero, Vice President of the Province of Liguria, Italy (January 12, 2009)

Lettera di Kevin Annett

traduzione di Camilla Novelli

La Campagna per la Giustizia per gli Indiani Canadesi ottiene nuove vittorie, a Genova e a Roma

Amici e Parenti degli Scomparsi, Canada
www.hiddenfromhistory.org

Nel mese di Ottobre del 2009 ho avuto l'onore e la gioia di visitare Genova, Roma e altre città italiane al fine di diffondere la verità sul genocidio perpetrato per mano dello stato (canadese, n.d.t.) e della chiesa contro le popolazioni native del Canada. In questa occasione è stato anche proiettato il nostro film-documentario "Unrepentant".

Il ricordo del calore e dell'ospitalità con cui sono stato accolto dalla gente di Genova e dai membri dell'Associazione HUNKAPI rimarrà con me per sempre.

Uno degli aspetti più importanti di questo viaggio è stato per me il grande successo che la nostra campagna ha riscontrato a Genova, grazie all'eccellente organizzazione da parte di HUNKAPI: di questo positivo risultato sono parte fondamentale gli incontri con le autorità del Comune e della Provincia di Genova, e il sostegno da loro ricevuto per la nostra campagna sui diritti umani, che sarà nuovamente operativa in Italia nei prossimi mesi di marzo e aprile.

Questi successi sono seguiti al la funzione religiosa da me officiata fuori dal Vaticano, davanti agli occhi del Papa, per commemorare i bambini che sono morti nelle Scuole Residenziali Indiane Cattoliche del Canada. Poco tempo dopo questo evento, sono stato contattato da prelati delle alte gerarchie vaticane che hanno resa nota la loro volontà di incontrarsi con me per parlare di una lettera che lo scorso anno i sopravvissuti delle Scuole Residenziali hanno inviato al Pontefice. Nella lettera gli chiedevano di ammettere i crimini perpetrati dalla sua Chiesa e di restituire i resti dei bambini morti affinché possano avere una degna sepoltura. Una così grande apertura ha dato nuova speranza agli uomini e alle donne aborigeni con cui lavoro nei quartieri più miseri di Vancouver, in Canada. Molti mi hanno detto che il supporto espresso da HUNKAPI alla nostra campagna li incoraggia a continuare a parlare delle sofferenze che sono state loro inflitte. In tal senso una donna ha recentemente dichiarato «...la verità su come i nostri bambini sono stati assassinati è ora nota a tutto il mondo. Ora i criminali non possono più nascondersi, e presto potremo portarli davanti a un tribunale e far sì che i morti possano finalmente trovare giustizia...».

Nella seconda metà di marzo ho in programma di tornare a Genova e in altre città italiane per un mese al fine di continuare la nostra campagna e presentare la proposta di costituire un tribunale internazionale per i crimini di guerra che si occupi della morte di oltre 50.000 bambini causata per mano della Chiesa Cattolica e del Governo canadese.

Se riusciamo a raccogliere fondi sufficienti, porterò con me gli aborigeni sopravvissuti alle Scuole Residenziali, affinché raccontino quanto è successo ai bambini.

Io esorto i lettori e i sostenitori di HUNKAPI ad assisterci in questa campagna affinché possiamo fermare il genocidio che continua a uccidere così tanti nativi nel mio Paese aggiungendo a tutto ciò il fatto che le loro terre e le loro risorse vengono depredate.

Attendo di incontrare di nuovo tutti voi nella prossima primavera.

Desidero ringraziarvi ancora per il vostro costante sostegno, per il vostro amore e per la vostra solidarietà in questa causa così importante.

Insieme potremo sanare le ferite e far si che la giustizia diventi realtà.

Kevin Annett

Figure 44: Kevin Annett meets with Vice President Marina Dondero, Genoa Italy (October 2009)

Rev. Annett conducts the first memorial service for children who died in Catholic Indian Schools, and a public exorcism rite, outside the Vatican, St. Peter's Square, Rome, October 11, 2009

Figure 45: Rev. Kevin Annett conducts a public exorcism at the Vatican in Rome (October 11, 2009)

Rome Suffers Freak Tornado Paralysis

A Public Liturgy of Remembrance and Exorcism performed outside the Vatican Sunday, October 11, 2009 by Kevin Annett

Figure 46: A tornado strikes Rome the day after Rev. Annett's exorcism

Italian State Police Disrupt planned vigil by Rev. Annett and others outside the Vatican, Rome, April 2010

June 15, 2010

Rev Kevin Annatt
260 Kennedy Street
Nanaimo, BC
V9R 2H8

Dear Rev Annatt:

Re: Coroner's Inquiry into the death of:
DAWSON, Johnny Roy: BCCS #09-280-0149

As per your request, I have enclosed a copy of the Coroner's Report and Toxicology Results. I trust these documents will provide you with the information you require.

If I can be of any assistance, please do not hesitate to contact this office.

Sincerely,

for Matt Brown
Coroner

Enclosure
jyd

Ministry of Public Safety and Solicitor General BC Coroners Service Vancouver Metro Region Coroners Office
Suite 800 – 4720 Kingsway
Burnaby, BC V5H 4N2
Phone: 604-660-7708
Facsimile: 604-660-5290
Web: www.pssg.gov.bc.ca/coroners

Figure 48: Coroner's report for Bingo Dawson, refuting cause of death claim of "alcohol poisoning"

Ministry of Public Safety and Solicitor General

Case No.: 2009-0280-0149

CORONER'S REPORT

INTO THE DEATH OF

DAWSON	JOHNNY ROY
SURNAME	GIVEN NAMES

OF

VANCOUVER
MUNICIPALITY OF RESIDENCE

I, Matt Brown, a Coroner in the Province of British Columbia, have investigated the death of the above named, which was reported to me on the 6th day of December, 2009, and as a result of such investigation have determined the following facts and circumstances:

Gender:	☒ MALE ☐ FEMALE		
Age:	51 YEARS		
Death Premise:	HOTEL		
Place/Municipality of Death:	VANCOUVER	Date of Death:	DECEMBER 5, 2009
Municipality of Illness/Injury:	VANCOUVER	Time of Death:	PM HOURS

MEDICAL CAUSE OF DEATH

(1) Immediate Cause of Death: a) Presumed Alcohol Withdrawal - Delirium Tremens

DUE TO OR AS A CONSEQUENCE OF

Antecedent Cause if any: b)

DUE TO OR AS A CONSEQUENCE OF

Giving rise to the immediate cause (a) above, stating underlying cause last. c)

(2) Other Significant Conditions Contributing to Death:

BY WHAT MEANS Natural Disease Process

CLASSIFICATION OF DEATH ☐ ACCIDENTAL ☐ HOMICIDE ☒ NATURAL ☐ SUICIDE ☐ UNDETERMINED

Date Signed: JUNE 4, 2010

Matt Brown, Coroner
Province of British Columbia

Provincial Health
Services Authority
Province-wide solutions.
Better health.

PTC BC's Provincial Toxicology Centre

655 West 12th Avenue, Vancouver B.C., V5Z 4R4 Telephone: (604) 707 2715 Facsimile: (604) 707 2717

RECEIVED
DEC 2 1 2009
MINISTRY OF SOLICITOR GENERAL
B.C. CORONERS SERVICE
VANCOUVER METRO REGION

B.C. CORONERS SERVICE

Coroner BROWN, MATT
6 - 1818 CORNWALL AVE.
VANCOUVER, BC V6J 1C7

TOXICOLOGY REPORT

Dr. WEBBER, DOUGLAS
VANCOUVER GENERAL HOSPITAL

Name of Deceased: **DAWSON, JOHNNY**

PTC No: **2009-1652**

Coroner Case No: **2009-00280-0149** Autopsy No: **09-2463**

The Provincial Toxicology Centre received on 08 December 2009 the following specimens:
.: 1 BILE (RED TOP TUBE): 1 BLOOD (GREY TOP TUBE): 2 BLOOD (RED TOP TUBE): 1 LIVER: 1 STOMACH CONTENTS: 1 VITREOUS (GREY TOP TUBE): 1

The results are as follows: (* indicates new result)

		*** FORENSIC STAT ANALYSIS ***		
BLOOD (GREY TOP TUBE)	HEART	GENERAL DRUG SCREEN		No other Drugs Detected
BLOOD (GREY TOP TUBE)	HEART	ETHYL ALCOHOL		Not Detected
BLOOD (GREY TOP TUBE)	HEART	ACETAMINOPHEN		Detected
BLOOD (GREY TOP TUBE)	HEART	DIPHENHYDRAMINE		Detected
BLOOD (GREY TOP TUBE)	SUBCLAVIAN	ACETAMINOPHEN	0.12 mmol/L	18 mg/L
VITREOUS (GREY TOP TUBE)		ETHYL ALCOHOL		Not Detected
VITREOUS (GREY TOP TUBE)		ACETONE		Not Detected
VITREOUS (GREY TOP TUBE)		BETA-HYDROXYBUTYRATE		0.19 mmol/L

NO ALCOHOL, PRESCRIBED MEDICATIONS OR ILLICIT DRUGS DETECTED.

Acetaminophen and Diphenhydramine are both within the therapeutic range.
Beta-hydroxybutyrate is within the reference range for serum.

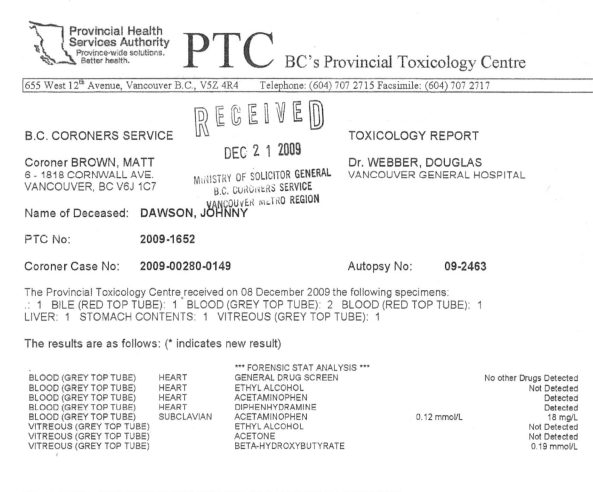

The original report was issued on 15-December-2009 Exhibits will be discarded after 15-March-2010
and was signed by: Dr. Walter Martz, Ph.D., Forensic Toxicologist
his designates

Figure 49: Press conference of Kevin Annett / FRD delegation with politicians in Rome (April 2010)

Rev Kevin Annett, Canadian abuse campaigner (centre) meets Irish clerical abuse survivors before they meet Taoiseach Brian Cowen yesterday. Photograph: PA

Abuse in Canadian residential schools identical to here, says clergyman

The Irish Times

ARIE O'HALLORAN

A CANADIAN clergyman has lescribed the abuse experienced by native children in residential schools in Canada as identical to abuse in Ireland.

"The stories are identical including the extent to which police and government colluded to protect perpetrators" said the Rev Kevin Annett, a former minister of the United Church of Canada.

Mr Annett spoke at a demonstration outside the Dáil yesterday, organised by the Templemore Forgotten Victims group, which has called for a full inquiry into the deaths of children in residential institutions, and a proper burial.

Mr Annett has worked for 20 years with "aboriginal children incarcerated in boarding schools under law by government and churches, both Catholic and Protestant. The parents lost all custody of their children. It went on from 1880 to the 1970s and the last school in Canada only closed down in 1996."

The Canadian clergyman said he was fired from the United Church for highlighting the abuse and allowing victims speak from the pulpit in his church.

Working with survivors in Canada "you hear the same stories all the time. The same crimes, the same murders and unfortunately the same cover-up."

He said abuse was an international problem. "People tend to think they're alone but they're not."

There was a need to "unite across borders to let people know they're not alone".

He had protested outside the Vatican in Rome and said Pope Benedict was "criminally complicit" in abuse, because of the policy not to inform police when cases were reported.

Survivors presented Mr Annett with children's shoes, representing young victims of clerical sex abuse.

Rosaleen Rogers, who established the Templemore Forgotten Victims group with her husband Roy, said she wanted the truth about "the harm that was done to me" and redress.

She spent three years in St Luke's in Clonmel but said psychiatric institutions were excluded from the institutional redress board.

There should be a full inquiry with "evidence given under oath", she said.

She also called for the proper identification of children who died in institutions and were buried in unmarked graves.

That needed to be fully investigated, she said.

Mr Rogers asked why no TD or Minister came out to meet them during their protest.

"Why aren't they listening to what we're saying?"

He said Government and the church had "an awful lot to answer for".

Figure 50: Irish media report of protest by Kevin Annett and survivors of Catholic Church torture in Ireland, Dublin (April 15-16, 2010)

Irish Independent Friday 16 April 2010 NEWS 9

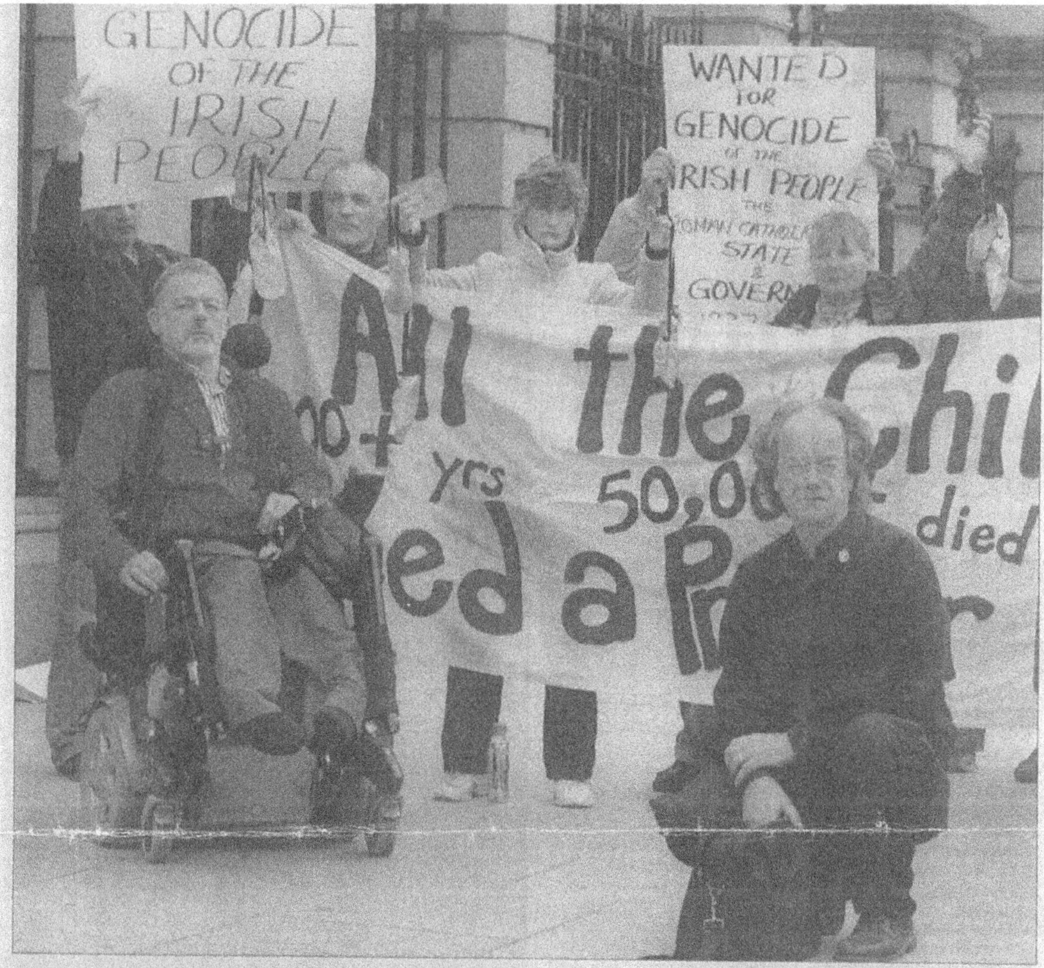

Reverend Kevin Annett, from Vancouver, Canada, along with Irish survivors of institutional abuse at Leinster House yesterday. On the left in a wheelchair is abuse victim Paddy Doyle. TOM BURKE

Survivors demand truth panel to probe claims on care institutions

Fiach Kelly
Political Correspondent

SURVIVORS of abuse at psychiatric institutions yesterday demanded a truth commission be set up to investigate their claims that they were abused while in care.

At a protest outside Leinster House, the Templemore Forgotten Victims group was backed in its call by Reverend Kevin Annett, an international campaigner against clerical and institutional abuse.

The group, founded by Dr Rosaleen Rogers, who comes from the Tipperary town, was also supported by other abuse survivors, such as Paddy Doyle, author of the book 'The God Squad'.

"I was detained as a teenager in Clonmel Mental Hospital," Dr Rogers (65) said.

"At one point I weighed only four stone. I have not been able to keep food down for 40 years. I have not been able to get work because I have had to keep to a liquid diet – it has ruined my life.

"I have lost everything and I want a truth commission to establish the truth of what happened to me and others. I want to know who harmed me.

"I'm here today because I want the truth. I want redress, I want an apology.

"And I want to make sure it doesn't happen to anyone else," she added.

Her husband Roy said it was disgraceful that TDs would not come out and meet them during the protest.

"Why isn't there someone from the Government out here, listening to what we're saying? They're probably hiding. What are they afraid of? The church and the Government have an awful lot to answer for."

Vancouver-based Rev Annett has also campaigned for those who were abused or died in the Indian residential school system in Canada.

Cover-up

"I'm here as a Canadian who has been working with survivors of Catholic institutions to say that the same type of crimes happened in Canada and the same kind of cover-up is going on.

"It's about trying to reach across borders to show that we need to be united in this," he said.

"We're not willing to walk away on this stuff, this is a very deep historical problem and we need more than token remedies."

Rev Annett said he suspected there were thousands of victims in Ireland and said 50,000 aboriginal children died while locked up in Indian schools in Canada from 1880 to 1970.

He also said Pope Benedict XVI should be prosecuted for "concealing" abuse for many years.

Mr Doyle presented him with children's shoes, symbolising the death and suffering of children in care.

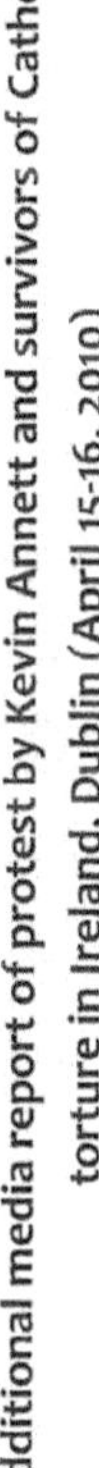

Figure 51: Additional media report of protest by Kevin Annett and survivors of Catholic Church torture in Ireland, Dublin (April 15-16, 2010)

Mohawk Nation of Ouse / Grand River

April 12, 2011

To Whom It May Concern:

We, the Mohawks of the Grand River Territory located at our former settlement in Kanata Village, desire to have forensic investigations conducted on the grounds of the Mohawk Institute Indian residential school and other suspected locations where the children who died in this school may be buried.

We want to know where the children who died in the school are buried and how they died. And to have these spots surveyed so that their remains can be disinterred and brought home for a proper burial according to the customs of our People.

We authorize Kevin Annett aka Eagle Strong Voice to work on this project and on our land with the appropriate technical experts. We grant him our full support and protection and ask that he take the evidence of the deaths of these children at the Mohawk Institute, and other crimes there, to the International Tribunal into Crimes of Church and State (ITCCS) next September in London, England.

We support and officially endorse the ITCCS and we call upon all residential school survivors to support Kevin Annett "Eagle Strong Voice" in his research and work to find justice for our People.

Respectfully Submitted,

Elders of the Mohawk Nation at Kanata Village:

Ilene Johnson, A/Clan Mother, Wolf Clan

Wanda Hess, Turtle Clan

Cheryl Squire, Turtle Clan

Yvonne Hill, A/Clan Mother, Turtle Clan

Lori Monture, Wolf Clan

Annette Beck, Turtle Clan

Edwin Squire
Hereditary Chief, Wolf Clan

Frank Miller, Turtle Clan

Bill Squire, Appointed Speaker
Wolf Clan

Contact: Yvonne Hill 519 445 2478 P.O. Box 16, Ohsweken, Ontario, Canada N0A 1M0

Figure 52: Mohawk traditional elders in Brantford, Ontario invite and authorize Kevin Annett and the ITCCS to conduct a forensic investigation and recovery of buried remains at the former Mohawk Anglican residential school (April 12, 2011)

C78 P6V.

Port Ref: STD/3783561
HO Ref:
United Kingdom Border Agency
Stansted PassengerTerminal
Bassingbourn Road
Stansted
Essex
CM24 1RW
Tel: 01279 680118 Fax: 01279 680 145

REC'D BY	Craig Simons IS 93
SIGNATURE	
DATE	30/5

IMMIGRATION ACT 1971
CHANNEL TUNNEL (INTERNATIONAL ARRANGEMENTS) ORDER 1993
Directions to Remove a Person or Persons

To the owners/agents of **Ryanair**
Leave to enter/remain in the United Kingdom has either been refused to or cancelled in respect of:
Name: **Kevin Daniel Mcnamee Annett**
Date of birth: **10 February 1956** Nationality: **Canada**

ARRIVAL DETAILS
The person named above arrived in the United Kingdom by: **FR9274** *(flight/ship/train)*
t **Stansted Immigration Service Port** *(port)* at **19.45** *(time)* on **29 May 2011** *(date)*
And was either refused leave to enter or had leave to enter/remain cancelled on the **29 May 2011**
You were notified of this decision on 30 May 2011 *(date)*

REMOVAL DIRECTIONS

☒ **I hereby direct you to remove[1]/make arrangements for the removal[2] of the person named above from the United Kingdom to Netherlands by *(flight/ship/train)*:**

FR9271 to Eindhoven at 06:55 on 30/05/2011

☐ **I hereby inform you that I intend to direct you remove[1] or make arrangements for the removal[2] of the person named above from the United Kingdom. You will be informed of such directions as soon as possible.**

If a decision is taken to cancel these directions/this notice of intention to remove, you will be notified immediately. If no directions have been given by **29 August 2011,** the situation will be reviewed. If you contact this office you will be informed of the outcome, and any necessary further review can then be arranged.

The person named above:

☐ holds a current certificate of entitlement
☒ holds NO prior entry clearance
☐ holds a current entry clearance
☐ held continuing leave to enter/remain
☐ is named in a current work permit

Immigration Officer / on behalf of the Secretary of State _Gary K Dawney_ Date **29 May 2011**

To the Captain/Train Manager of flight/train/ship FR9271
In accordance with paragraph 8(1)(b) of Schedule 2 to the Act, as modified by the Channel Tunnel (International Arrangements) Order 1993, I have directed that the person(s) named above be placed aboard your ship/aircraft/train and I require you[3] to prevent the person named above from disembarking in the United Kingdom or before the directions for his removal have been fulfilled. For this purpose you may detain the person above in custody on board.

Figure 53: Deportation Order issued against Kevin Annett by UK Border Agency, Stansted Airport, England (May 29, 2011)

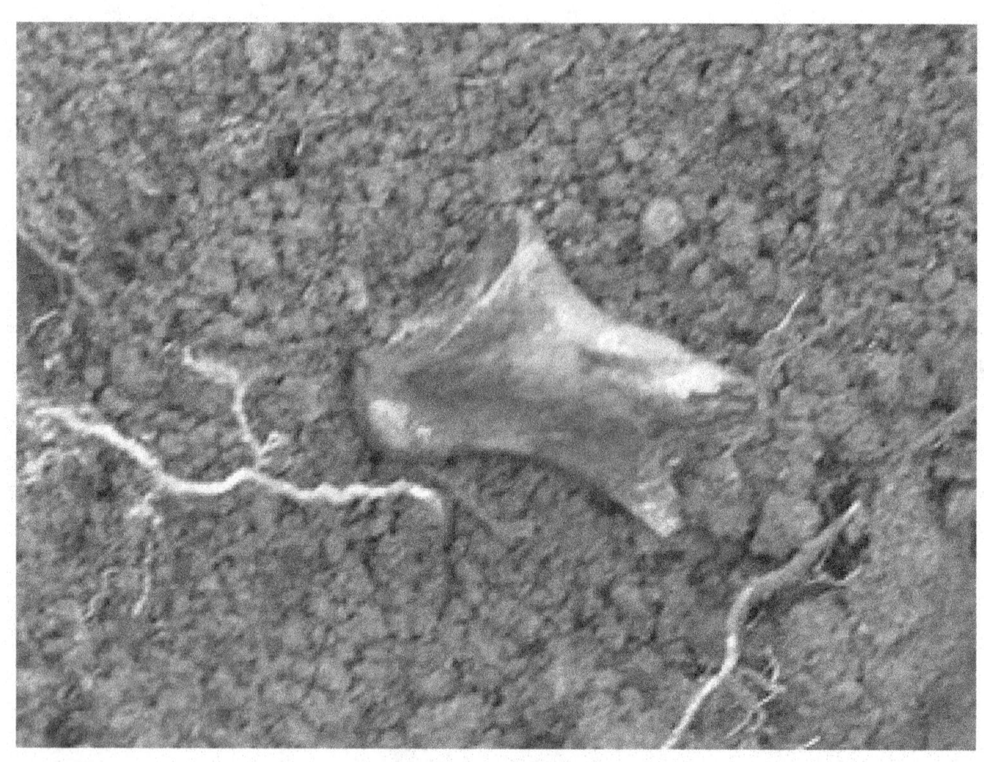

Socket bone from a young girl unearthed at a suspected mass grave site 50' east of the Anglican Mohawk Institute Indian Residential School in Brantford, Ontario

30 November, 2011

www.itccs.org

Figure 54: Confirmed human bone socket of a small female that was excavated in an identified burial site of children on the grounds of the former Mohawk Indian school, Brantford (November 28, 2011)

TEKAWENNAKE

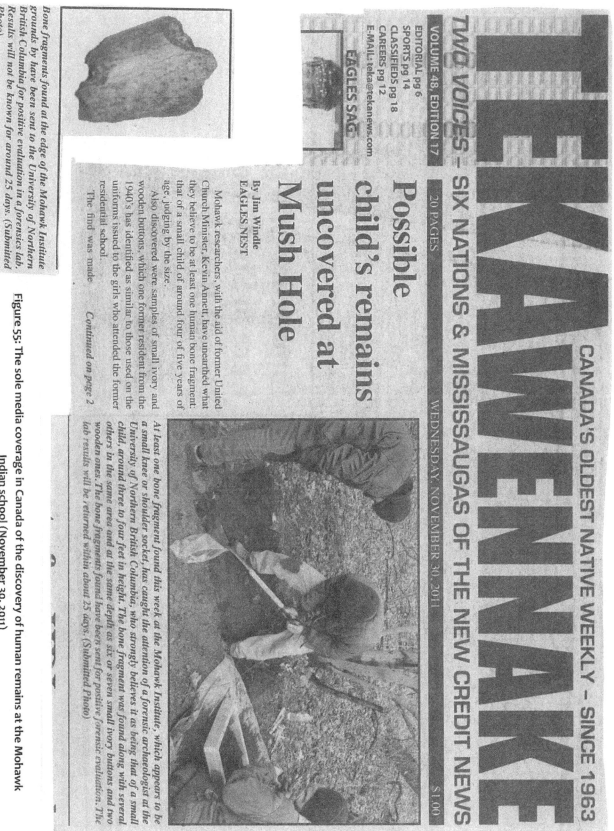

CANADA'S OLDEST NATIVE WEEKLY – SINCE 1963

TWO VOICES – SIX NATIONS & MISSISSAUGAS OF THE NEW CREDIT NEWS

VOLUME 48, EDITION 17 | 20 PAGES | WEDNESDAY, NOVEMBER 30, 2011 | $1.00

EDITORIAL pg 6
SPORTS pg 14
CLASSIFIEDS pg 18
CAREERS pg 12
E-MAIL: teka@tekanews.com

EAGLES SAG

Possible child's remains uncovered at Mush Hole

By Jim Windle
EAGLES NEST

Mohawk researchers, with the aid of former United Church Minister, Kevin Annett, have unearthed what they believe to be at least one human bone fragment: that of a small child of around four of five years of age, judging by the size.

Also discovered were samples of small ivory and wooden buttons, which one former resident from the 1940's has identified as similar to those used on the uniforms issued to the girls who attended the former residential school.

The find was made *Continued on page 2*

At least one bone fragment found this week at the Mohawk Institute, which appears to be a small knee or shoulder socket, has caught the attention of a forensic archaeologist at the University of Northern British Columbia, who strongly believes it as being that of a small child, around three to four feet in height. The bone fragment was found along with several others in the same area and at the same depth as six or seven small ivory buttons and two wooden ones. The bone fragments found have been sent for positive forensic evaluation. The lab results will be returned within about 25 days. (Submitted Photo)

Bone fragments found at the edge of the Mohawk Institute grounds by have been sent to the University of Northern British Columbia for positive evaluation in a forensics lab. Results will not be known for around 25 days. (Submitted Photo)

Figure 55: The sole media coverage in Canada of the discovery of human remains at the Mohawk Indian school (November 30, 2011)

THE INTERNATIONAL COMMON LAW COURT OF JUSTICE
CRIMINAL TRIAL DIVISION - BRUSSELS
FEBRUARY 25, 2013

VERDICT AND SENTENCE OF THE CITIZEN JURY

In the Matter of *The People v. the Government of Canada, the Crown of England, the Vatican, and the Roman Catholic, Anglican and United Church of Canada, and Joseph Ratzinger, Elizabeth Windsor, Stephen Harper and other persons*

We the Jury, consisting of fifty eight sworn men and women, having considered all of the evidence presented to us in this case, do hereby find all of the named defendants guilty as charged on both counts of the indictment, namely, of Crimes against Humanity and of planning and perpetrating a Criminal Conspiracy.

We the Jury therefore sentence all of the named defendants to a prison term of twenty five years without possibility of parole, and to a loss of all of their authority, assets and property.

We swear and acknowledge that this verdict and sentence was decided by we the Jury unanimously and without coercion or influence.

We further affirm that the following men and women are the defendants so tried and sentenced by us:

Jospeh Ratzinger, Bishop of Rome, aka "Pope Benedict"

Adolfo Nicholas Pachon, Superior General, Jesuit Order

Tarcisio Bertone, Vatican Secretary of State

Elizabeth Windsor, aka "Queen of England"

Stephen Harper, Prime Minister of Canada

Angelo Sodano, Vatican College of Cardinals

Angelo Bognasco, Vatican College of Cardinals

Pedro Lopez Quintana, Papal Nuncio to Canada

Rowan Williams, Archbishop of Canterbury

Figure 56: Guilty verdict issued by the International Common Law Court of Justice in Brussels against Joseph Ratzinger, Elizabeth Windsor and 28 other defendants (February 25, 2013)

Fred Hiltz, Anglican Primate in Canada

Bob Bennett, Anglican Bishop, Canada

Murray Sinclair, Chairman, Truth and Reconciliation Commission, Canada

John Milloy, TRC officer

Nora Sanders, General Secretary, United Church of Canada

Gary Paterson, Moderator, United Church of Canada

Jon Jessiman, legal counsel, United Church of Canada

Marion Best, Brian Thorpe, Art Anderson, Foster Freed, Bill Howie and Phil Spencer: Officials and clergy of the United Church of Canada

John Cashore, former government minister, the Province of British Columbia

Robert Paulson, Superintendent of the Royal Canadian Mounted Police

Peter Montague, RCMP Inspector

Daniel Fulton, CEO, Weyerhauser Ltd.

Ron Huinink, Vacouver lawyer

Terry Whyte, former chairman of St. Andrew's United Church, Port Alberni

Sean Atleo, Chairman, Assembly of First Nations

William Montour, Chairman, Six Nations Confederacy, Brantford

Respectfully issued by we, The Jury members
(Jury Chairman: Carl C. Redvers)

Issued 25 ~~September~~ February, 2013 at 4 pm GMT and Duly Registered in the Central Office of the Court by the Court Secretary, George Dufort, LL.B.

G. Dufort

George Dufort, LL.B.
Court Secretary

International Common Law Court of Justice

138550

Cote. Assa.

25th Feb 1898.

Report as to the status of children sent to Industrial Schools and who are not there now. See Circular letter No 0[illegible]26, of 6thFeb,98

	Name.	Married, or single.	Remarks.
			Industrial School, Qu'Appelle.
No I	Alfred Stevenson.	Married.	Supports himself, Works for Settlers, etc.
No 0127	Catherine Que-ewzance.	Single.	At service, Crowstand School.
No 143	Rod'k McLeod.	Single.	Dying, Consumption.
No 142	John McLeod.	Married.	Not strong, useless and lazy, not the fault of the school but himself.
No 0162	Margaret McLeod.	Single.	Living with her Aunt, Mrs Anders Qu'Appelle.
No 0155	Marie Que-ew-zance.	Single	Died.
No 0178	Lily Horne / Angelique Cote.	Single.	Died.
No 178	Louis Cote.	Single.	Died.
No 0171	Marie Josephine Bourassa.	Single.	Died.
No 0165	Marie Louisa Bourassa.	Single.	Died.
No 179	Henry E-qua-nin.	Single.	Died.

Unexplanatory note from the Rev Principal relative to name attached.

Out of a total No of IS sent to this school, 8 have died--I may not live a week, I is very delicate.

[illegible]

Indian Affairs. (RG 10, Volume 3861 File 82,[illegible])

Figure 57: Over 60% of the Indian children at the Catholic Qu'Appelle school are dead or dying in the first year the school was opened – ie: seven of the eleven children listed(1896)

138550

Report as to the status of school children sent to Industrial Schools, and who are not there now.
See Circular No 0128 of 6th Feb 1896.

	Name.	Married or Single.	Remarks.
			Industrial School, Regina.
No 40	Sam'l Ka-ke-we-ass.	Single.	Died.
No 021	Maggie Baldhead.	Single.	Died.
No 024	Jane Fiddler.	Single.	Died.
No 41	Jim Crow.	Single.	Died.
No 90	-- Crow.	Single.	Died.
No 035	Lizzie Severight.	Single.	Died.
No 026	Maggie Torrango.	Single.	Sent home, is dying of consumption
No 69	Joe Cote.	Single.	Sent home, weak lungs.
No 047	Kate Cote.	Single	Sent home weak lungs.
No 60	Alex Shinguish.	Single.	Blind, is recovering.
No 30	John Severight.	Single.	Recovering from effects of fever
No 48	John Cook.	Single.	Died.
			Industrial School, Elkhorn.
No 143	Shannon Coo-pa-pay.	Single.	Died at school.

sgd W.E. Jones.
Indian Agent.

Indian Affairs. (RG 10, Volume 3861, File 82,390)

Figure 58: Two thirds of the students are dead or dying (8 of 12) at the Catholic Regina Indian school in the second year of its operation (1896)

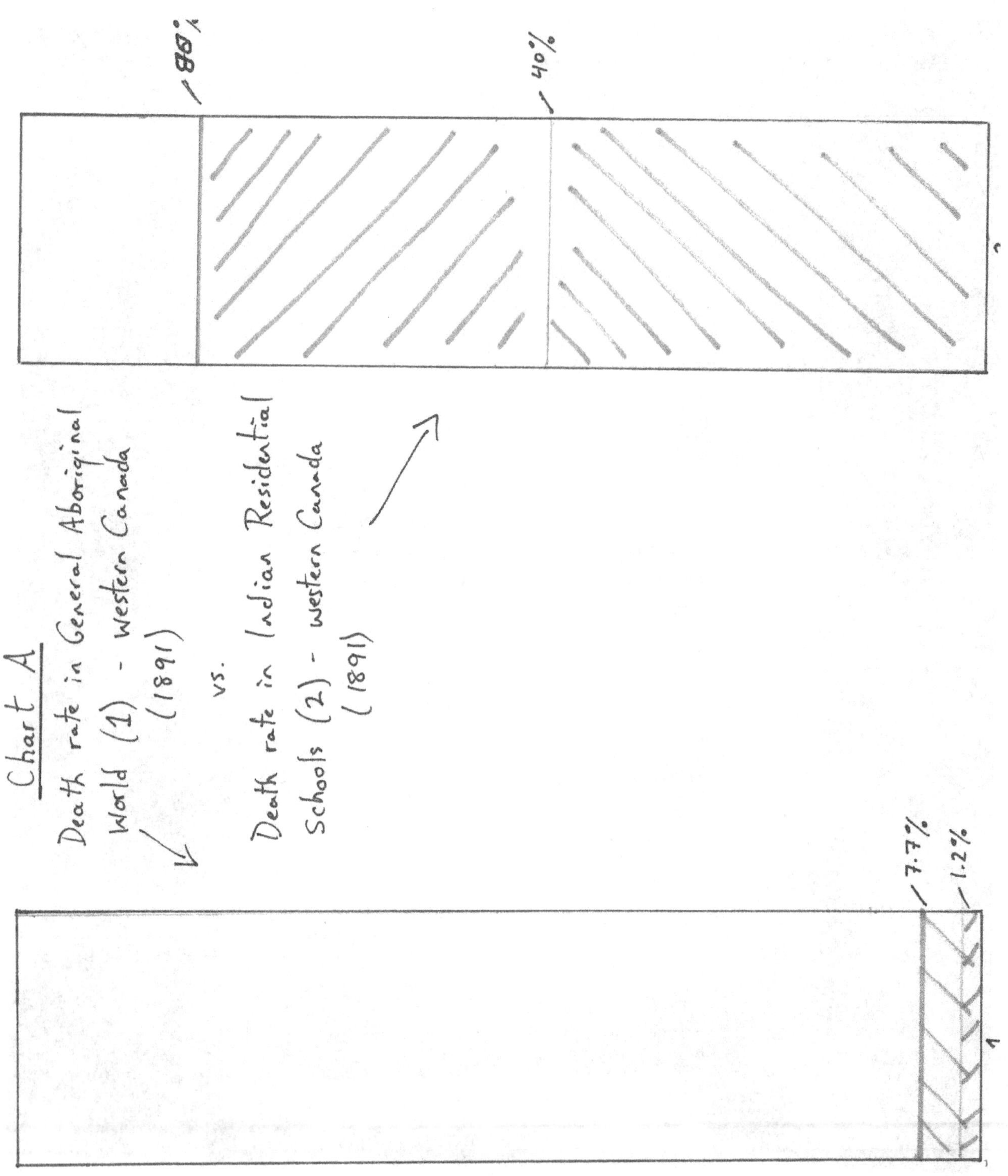

Figure 60: A graphic illustration of this discrepancy between normal Indian death rates and mortality among residential school children (1891)

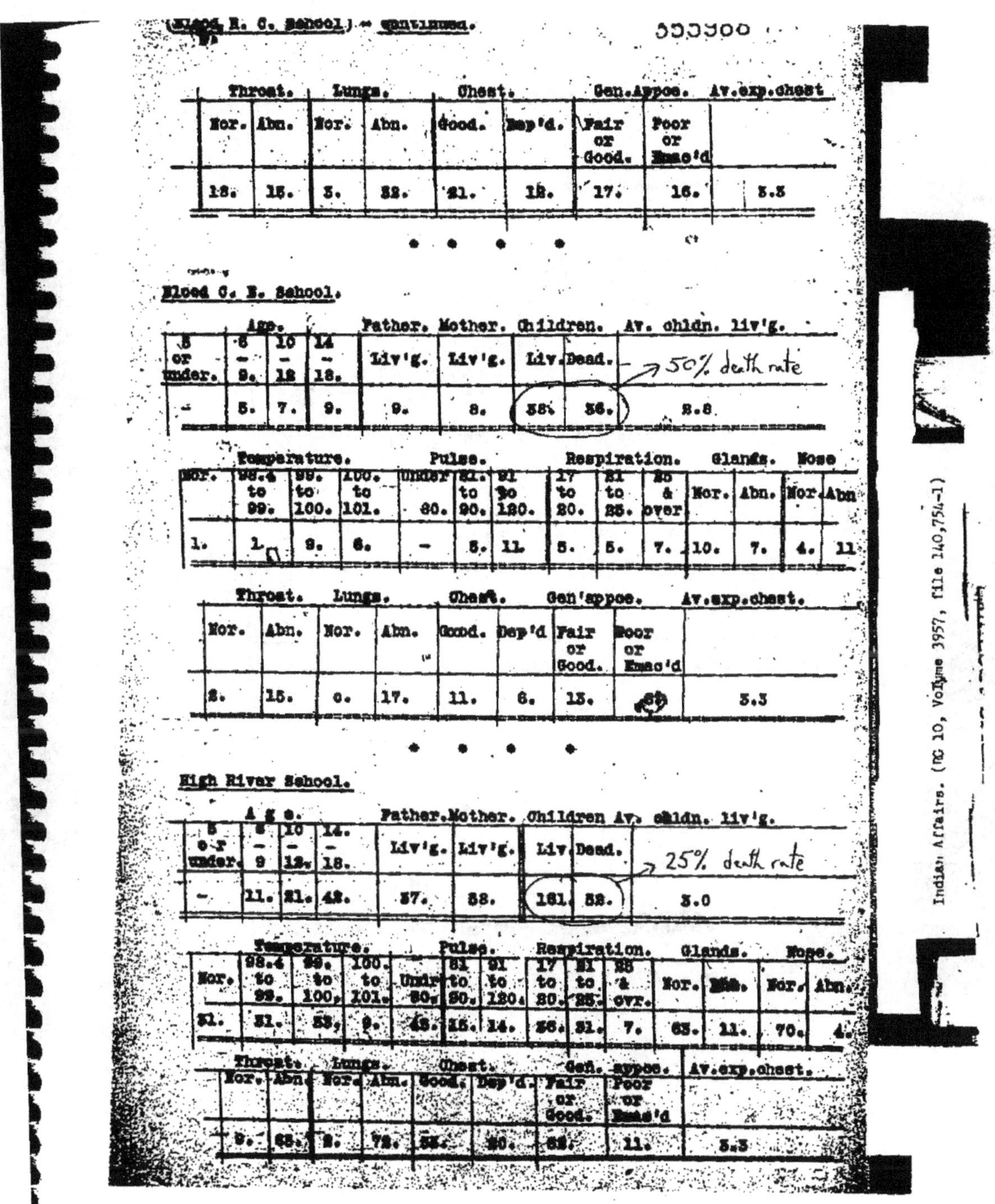

(Blood R. C. School) — continued.

Throat. Nor.	Throat. Abn.	Lungs. Nor.	Lungs. Abn.	Chest. Good.	Chest. Dep'd.	Gen. Appce. Fair or Good.	Gen. Appce. Poor or Emac'd	Av. exp. chest
18.	15.	5.	32.	21.	12.	17.	16.	3.3

• • • •

Blood C. E. School.

Age. 5 or under.	Age. 6 – 9.	Age. 10 – 12	Age. 14 – 18.	Father. Liv'g.	Mother. Liv'g.	Children. Liv.	Children. Dead.	Av. chldn. liv'g.
–	5.	7.	9.	9.	8.	38.	36.	2.8

Temperature. Nor.	Temperature. 98.4 to 99.	Temperature. 99. to 100.	Temperature. 100. to 101.	Pulse. Under 80.	Pulse. 81. to 90.	Pulse. 91 to 120.	Respiration. 17 to 20.	Respiration. 21 to 25.	Respiration. 25 & over	Glands. Nor.	Glands. Abn.	Nose Nor.	Nose Abn
1.	1.	9.	6.	–	5.	11.	5.	5.	7.	10.	7.	4.	11

Throat. Nor.	Throat. Abn.	Lungs. Nor.	Lungs. Abn.	Chest. Good.	Chest. Dep'd	Gen'appce. Fair or Good.	Gen'appce. Poor or Emac'd	Av. exp. chest.
2.	15.	0.	17.	11.	6.	13.	[illegible]	3.3

• • • •

High River School.

Age. 5 or under.	Age. 6 – 9	Age. 10 – 12.	Age. 14. – 18.	Father. Liv'g.	Mother. Liv'g.	Children Liv.	Children Dead.	Av. chldn. liv'g.
–	11.	21.	42.	37.	38.	161.	53.	3.0

Temperature. Nor.	Temperature. 98.4 to 99.	Temperature. 99. to 100.	Temperature. 100. to 101.	Pulse. Undr 80.	Pulse. 81 to 90.	Pulse. 91 to 120.	Respiration. 17 to 20.	Respiration. 21 to 25.	Respiration. 25 & ovr.	Glands. Nor.	Glands. Abn.	Nose. Nor.	Nose. Abn.
31.	31.	53.	9.	48.	15.	14.	56.	31.	7.	65.	11.	70.	4.

Throat. Nor.	Throat. Abn.	Lungs. Nor.	Lungs. Abn.	Chest. Good.	Chest. Dep'd.	Gen. appce. Fair or Good.	Gen. appce. Poor or Emac'd	Av. exp. chest.
9.	65.	2.	72.	53.	20.	63.	11.	3.3

Figure 61: A record of the death rates of between 25% and 50% in western Indian schools, from the report of Dr. Peter Bryce (1907)

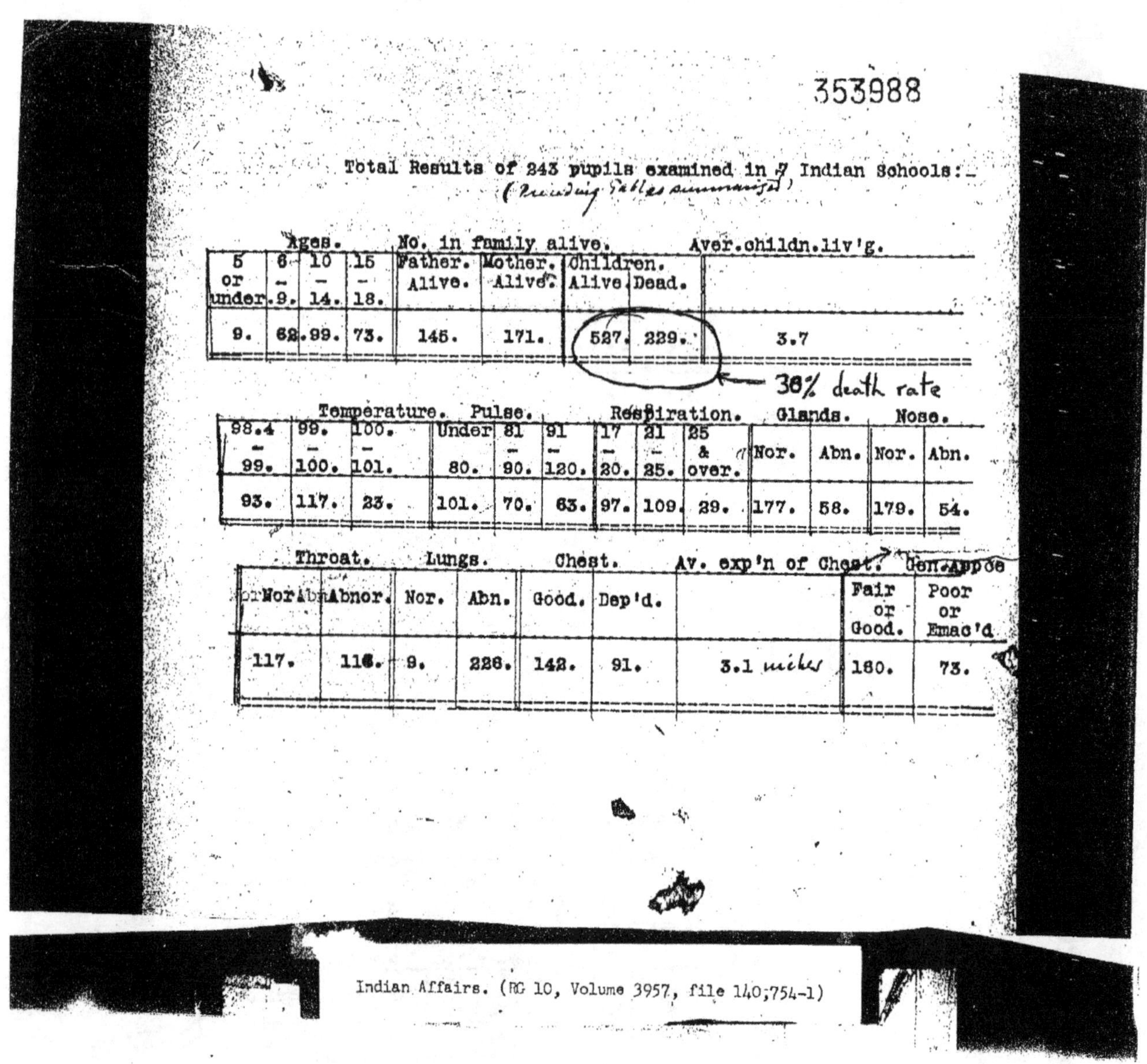

353988

Total Results of 243 pupils examined in 7 Indian Schools:-
(Preceding tables summarized)

Ages.				No. in family alive.				Aver.childn.liv'g.
5 or under.	6 - 9.	10 - 14.	15 - 18.	Father. Alive.	Mother. Alive.	Children. Alive.	Dead.	
9.	62.	99.	73.	145.	171.	527.	229.	3.7

36% death rate

Temperature.			Pulse.			Respiration.			Glands.		Nose.	
98.4 - 99.	99. - 100.	100. - 101.	Under 80.	81 - 90.	91 - 120.	17 - 20.	21 - 25.	25 & over.	Nor.	Abn.	Nor.	Abn.
93.	117.	23.	101.	70.	63.	97.	109.	29.	177.	58.	179.	54.

Throat.		Lungs.		Chest.		Av. exp'n of Chest.	Gen.Appce	
NorAb	Abnor.	Nor.	Abn.	Good.	Dep'd.		Fair or Good.	Poor or Emac'd.
117.	116.	9.	226.	142.	91.	3.1 miles	160.	73.

Indian Affairs. (RG 10, Volume 3957, file 140,754-1)

Figure 62: Dr. Bryce's summary of the total average death rate in all western Indian schools (36%) – from the same report (1907)

April 25, 1910

To – Secretary, Indian Affairs, Ottawa

From – A.W. Neill, Indian Agent, west coast agency

363448

(2)

[pro]perly conducted day school on their reserves.

The number of children of school age among the Ohiats is now about 28, two of whom are in the Alberni Boarding school. Of the 28, experience in similar cases lead one to expect that a local Boarding school would get about 17 or 18 pupils, which is rather a small number for a Boarding school.

The Church have now got two day schools and two teacher's houses on the Ohiat reserves, one each at Dodger's Cove and at Numukamis. If they would pay salaries to induce competent people to undertake the work and stay at it, I think for the present at any rate under all the present conditions, that it would be as well to retain the day school system there and let the teacher try and induce the older children to spend a year or two at Alberni Boarding school.

I may mention here a constant source of trouble in connection with getting Indians to sign in their children into boarding schools.

By the rules of the Dept. a child can be kept in until it is 18 years old. That, in this Agency at least, is too long.

admits R.S. cause fatal illness *

These people have lived for centuries in the open air. A child taken into a school at 8, spends ten years in the school. After that its constitution is so weakened that it has no vitality to withstand disease. These Indians come to maturity so much sooner than whites that it is like keeping white children in a boarding school until they are 22 or 23.

→ It leads to immorality among the children unless they are watched like convicts. It leads to all sorts of concealed bargains between Indian parents and principals who, anxious to get children in, are pressed to promise the parents that they shall get their child out in a specified number of years, often four or five.

Then if the parent has neglected or been unable to make this private arrangement with the principal, he will start when his boy or girl is about 15 years old and perjure himself and suborn all his friends to do the same in an effort to convince me that the child is 18 years old and should therefore be discharged.

Figure 63: Official warning of the murderous effect of conditions in Indian residential schools (1910)

Indian Affairs. (RG 10, Volume 6039, file 159-1AA-1 part 1)

CHAPTER 59.

An Act respecting Sexual Sterilization.

[Assented to 7th April, 1933.]

HIS MAJESTY, by and with the advice and consent of the Legislative Assembly of the Province of British Columbia, enacts as follows:—

1. This Act may be cited as the "Sexual Sterilization Act." Short title.

2. In this Act, unless the context otherwise requires:— Interpretation

"Inmate" means a person who is a patient or in custody or under detention in an institution:

"Institution" means any public hospital for insane as defined in section 2 of the "Mental Hospitals Act," the Industrial Home for Girls maintained under the "Industrial Home for Girls Act," and the Industrial School maintained under the "Industrial School Act":

"Superintendent," in the case of a public hospital for insane, means the Medical Superintendent of that hospital, and, in the case of the Industrial Home for Girls or the Industrial School, means the Superintendent or other head thereof.

3. For the purposes of this Act, the Lieutenant-Governor in Council may from time to time appoint three persons, one of whom shall be a Judge of a Court of Record in the Province, one of whom shall be a psychiatrist, and one of whom shall be a person experienced in social-welfare work, who shall constitute a Board to be known as the "Board of Eugenics." Board of Eug-

4. (1.) Where it appears to the Superintendent of any institution within the scope of this Act that any inmate of that institution, if discharged therefrom without being subjected to an operation for sexual sterilization, would be likely to beget or bear children who Recommenda: Superintendent institution.

199

Figure 64: Sterilization law in British Columbia allowing the legal sterilizing of any inmate in an Indian residential school (1933)

August 1998 WINDSPEAKER Page 5

NEWS

Sterilization victims urged to come forward

By Sabrina Whyatt
Windspeaker Staff Writer

YELLOWKNIFE

The Government of the NorthWest Territories has designed a program to encourage sterilization victims to come forward.

Between 1928 and 1972, 2,800 women were sterilized in Alberta without their permission under the Sexual Sterilization Act. Another 400 women were sterilized in British Columbia under the same law. The act was then repelled.

The procedure was performed if the patients were diagnosed with mental deficiencies. It was ordered by a eugenics board that believed sterilization was the best way to prevent producing defective children.

Many of these patients were sterilized at Edmonton's Charles Camsell Hospital, which was mainly used to treat Aboriginal people. The hospital was operated by the federal government and closed in April 1996.

The NorthWest Territories government is offering support to Aboriginal women in the province through a program where victims can start an inquiry if they believe they've been wrongfully sterilized.

The program regards highly the confidentiality of the victims, and so far there has been one inquiry, said Joan Irwin, executive assistant of Department of Health and Social Services Minister Kelvin Ng.

"We purposely designed it this way where people can call us instead of going out and finding victims. It's out of respect for people's privacy," she said.

Irwin said the territorial government plans to deal with the situation on a case-by-case basis.

"If a woman who suspects she has been wrongfully sterilized comes forward, the government will provide her with help in gathering information about her situation and how her consent should have been given before she was sterilized. The inquiries will be dealt with on the merits of each case," said Irwin.

The probe into the sterilization cases began in the NorthWest Territories last month after Yellowknife North MLA Roy Erasmus disclosed information that some women from the area had been involuntarily sterilized.

"Priest Rene Fumoleau, who's now retired, wrote me a letter indicating some women from Denendeh came to him with concerns of why they weren't having any more children. When it was checked out, they found that since their last child was delivered at the Charles Camsell Hospital, they were sterilized," said Erasmus.

The letter also stated many of the Aboriginal women at the Edmonton hospital were "not sick or retarded, or in any other dangerous situation."

The Alberta government has paid out almost $50 million to 500 people who were wrongfully sterilized under the sterilization law. In 1996, an Alberta woman, Leilani Muir, was compensated near $1 million after a court ruled in her favor that she was wrongly sterilized in a mental institution in Red Deer in 1959. Later tests showed she had no mental defect.

The Alberta government hasn't taken part in the N.W.T. inquiry, but is in the process of forming claims settlement review panel to assist claimants.

Alberta Justice Minister Jon Havelock couldn't be reached for comment, but the department's director of communications, Peter Tadman, said the panel will work with any remaining sterilization victims not included in the $50 package to negotiate a settlement outside the courts.

He said the government anticipates about 300 outstanding claims, and "it is not certain how many of the cases involve Aboriginal women."

Gary McPherson, who will chair the five-member panel, said it is an option for claimants to reach a financial settlement.

"They are not obligated to use the panel, but it will be set up for claimants to get a quicker settlement. My guess is that a lot of people will use it," said McPherson.

If claimants choose not to use the panel, they have the option to resolve their case with a government-appointed mediator, or they can proceed through the courts.

McPherson said he anticipates the panel to be up and running in the fall.

Similar sterilization laws existed in Austria, Norway, Switzerland, Finland, Belgium, Sweden and the United States.

In the U.S. from 1972 to 1978, more than 3,400 Aboriginal women were sterilized without their consent to control population on the reservations. At the same time, rates of induced abortions doubled. Between 1970 and 1980, sterilization rates tripled.

Figure 65: Admission of the sterilizing of thousands of mostly aboriginal women in Alberta between 1928 and 1973, under the same law as in British Columbia

Statement of Pat Taylor, former Psychiatric Social Worker at the Provincial Training School at Red Deer, Alberta in 1956 - Given on Salt Spring Island, B.C., on January 13, 2000 -

Sterilizations were policy in Alberta. This has been reported on the CBC. It went on at the Provincial Training school in Red Deer, and in Saskatchewan, too. Everybody who came to that institution was sterilized. It was the law.

The people who got sterilized were defined as being in one of three categories of so-called "defective" people that came from a 1902 Eugenics Bill from England. It was defeated in England but some people here got ahold of it and used what was in there, which comes from a non-sensical Victorian book that claimed that all crimes in society were the result of mental retardation, and these "defective" people passed on criminality with their genes. So this Bill classed three types of people who were to be stopped from re=producing: moral, intellectual and social "defectives". They didn't define what these terms meant, so they could sterilize anybody they didn't like, or who was different.

It was already the policy back then to segregate people they termed as "ESN", or "Educationally Sub-Normal", into special institutions, either a day school or more often, into psychiatric hospitals. The Provincial Training School was just such a place.

I worked there for six months as a psychiatric social worker, after working in a similar place in Scotland. Any child who was found to have lower intelligence was sent to the PTS. Genuinely sub-normal children like hydrocephalics were mixed together with other, more normal kids on the same ward. But all of the children were sterilized when they reached puberty. A Eugenics Board in Edmonton approved the sterilizations, four times a year.

The children were told they were going to have an appendix operation. They and their parents were lied to. The PTS Superintendent was an absolute crook who claimed to be a psychiatrist when he wasn't. Mr. L.J. LeVan. He was the devil himself. He was very racist, especially towards Indian children and the Chinese. Probably a quarter of the children on the wards were Indians. They were all sterilized, like the others, right when they reached puberty, because they were considered defective.

I got out of there as soon as I could. I tried not to go onto the wards, they smelled so badly. This has been documented in court cases. But the Sterilization laws were still on the books in Alberta in the 1980's.

The PTS even had young girls who were picked off the streets and accused of prostitution. The law gave the police that power, and they were brought to PTS. Often they'd be put into isolation rooms until they went mad, and then they'd be sent off to the Ponoka mental hospital. A friend of mine who worked in that mental hospital told me that inmates there were told that they couldn't be discharged unless they agreed to be sterilized. So the same practice was going on in the mental hospitals.

Figure 66: Testimony of Pat Taylor, former social worker at the Provincial Training Center, Red Deer, Alberta, where children and Indians were routinely sterilized

Another fellow and I tried to get the records of PTS, we were going to take them to Macleans magazine, but we couldn't get the lock open. Those were records of the children who were put in isolation, the kids who shouldn't even have been there. A whole villa of girls were at PTS who had IQ's well above normal but were there because they were considered morally defective or something. And they were all sterilized. Everybody! You couldn't be there and not go for sterilizing. There was absolutely no consent involved.

The children were put in the isolation rooms for misbehaving, and it drove them mad of course. There was absolutely nothing in these rooms, and the children were left in them until they behaved. There was no psychological assessment done of these children at all.

I told people about these things but nobody believed me. And it wasn't just the sterilizations; they were beating kids and assaulting kids and they were doing medical experiments on them. Even lawyers can't find out the details now. Nobody wants to know these things or talk about what they know. For the same reason as in Nazi Germany. Nobody wants to confront the shadow, the cultural shadow that has to be looked at.

Pat Taylor

Witnessed by:

(Rev.) Kevin Annett

Pamela Holm

January 13, 2000
Salt Spring Island, B.C.

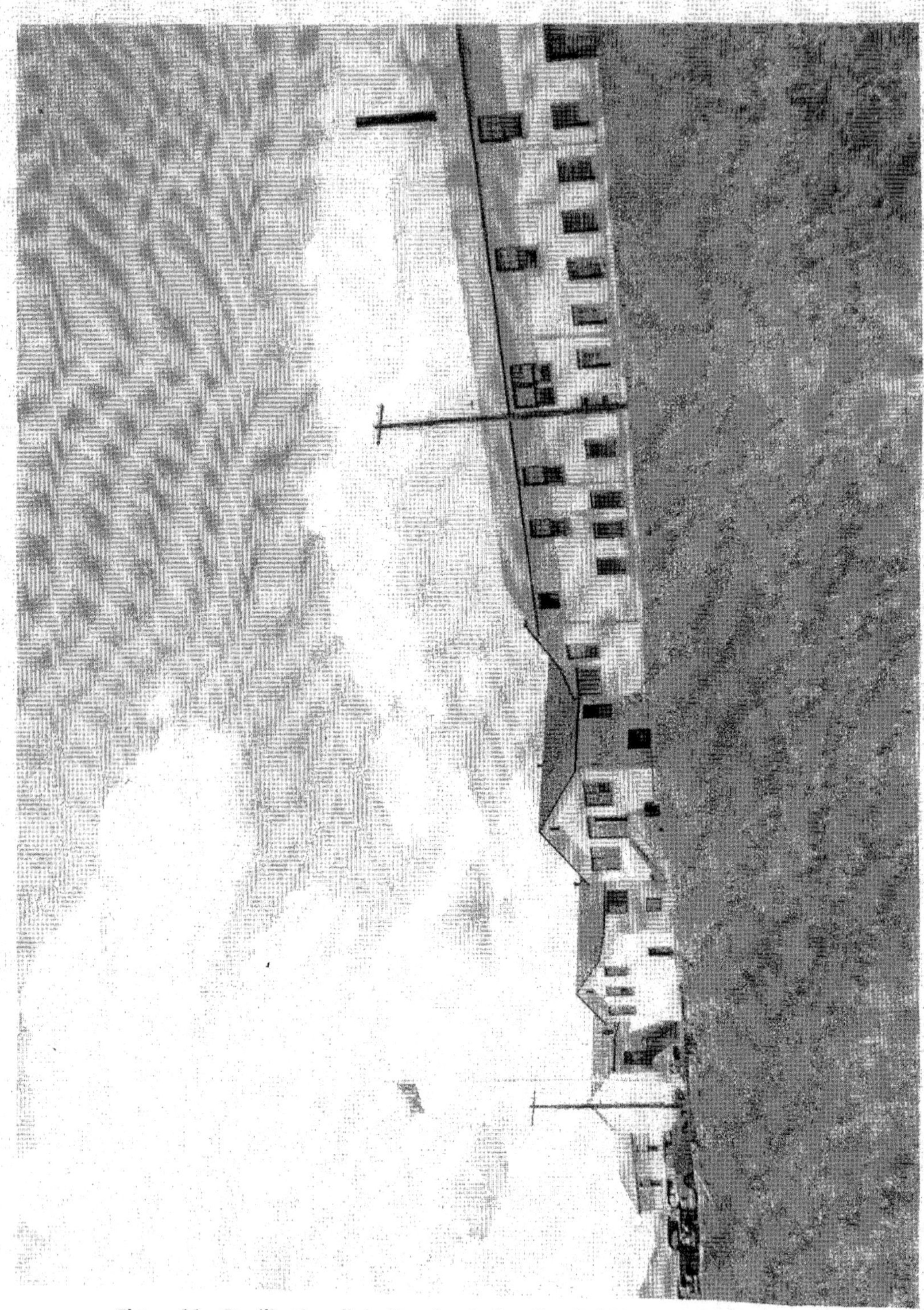

Figure 66a: Sterilization clinic, Nanaimo Indian Hospital, Vancouver Island

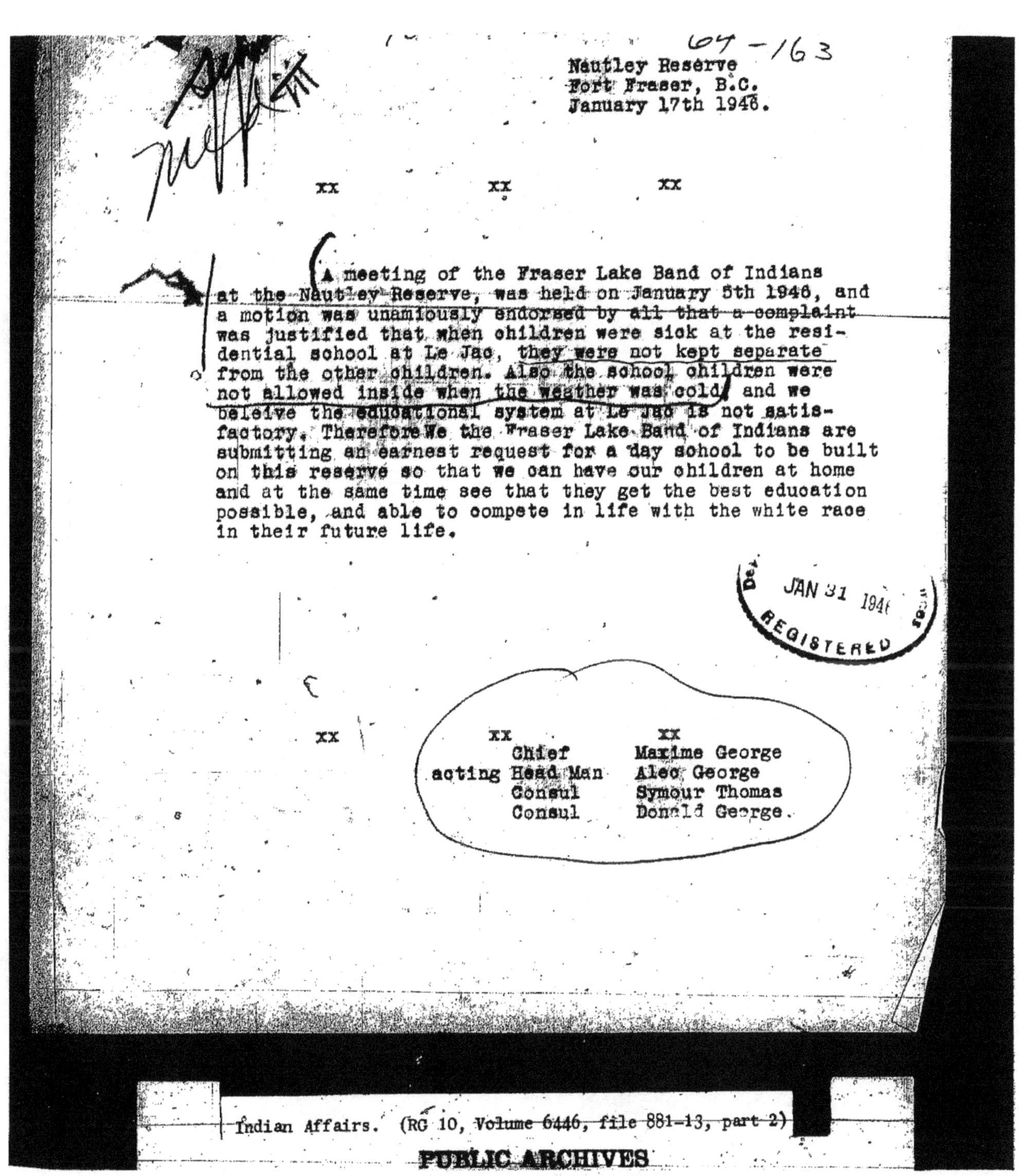

64-163

Nautley Reserve
Fort Fraser, B.C.
January 17th 1946.

xx xx xx

A meeting of the Fraser Lake Band of Indians at the Nautley Reserve, was held on January 5th 1946, and a motion was unamiously endorsed by all that a complaint was justified that when children were sick at the residential school at Le Jac, they were not kept separate from the other children. Also the school children were not allowed inside when the weather was cold, and we beleive the educational system at Le Jac is not satisfactory. Therefore We the Fraser Lake Band of Indians are submitting an earnest request for a day school to be built on this reserve so that we can have our children at home and at the same time see that they get the best education possible, and able to compete in life with the white race in their future life.

JAN 31 1946
REGISTERED

xx xx xx

Chief	Maxime George
acting Head Man	Alec George
Consul	Symour Thomas
Consul	Donald George.

Indian Affairs. (RG 10, Volume 6446, file 881-13, part 2)

PUBLIC ARCHIVES

Figure 67: Petition of complaint from native chiefs stating that children at the Le Jac Catholic school are never separated when they become sick (1946)

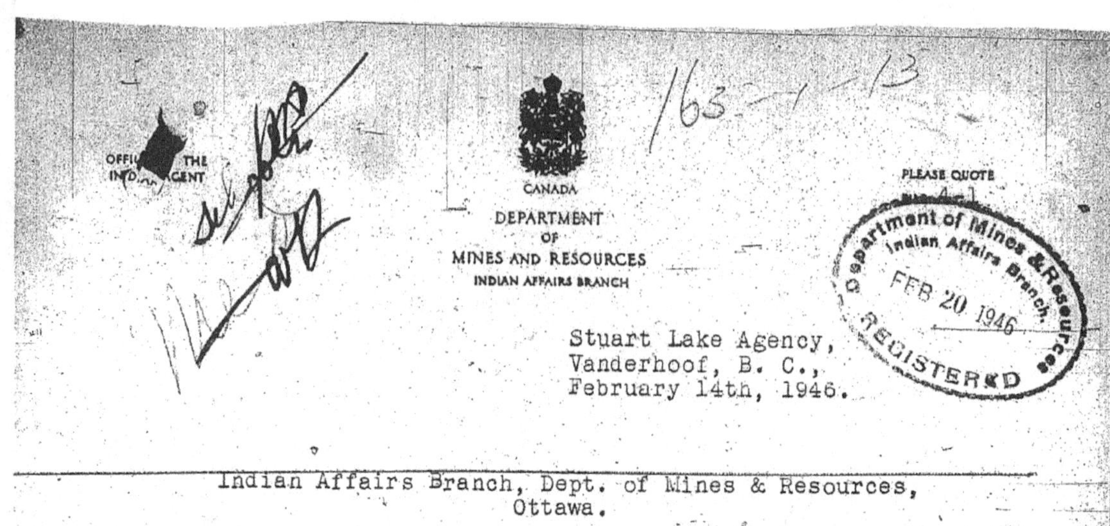

Stuart Lake Agency,
Vanderhoof, B. C.,
February 14th, 1946.

Indian Affairs Branch, Dept. of Mines & Resources,
Ottawa.

Your file 163-1-13

I have your letter of February 4, with regard to a letter received by the Department from Chief Maxine George and Headmen of the Fraser Lake Band, Fort Fraser, B. C., complaining about conditions at Lejac School.

I discussed the complaints with the Reverend A.R. Simpson yesterday and wish to assure the Department that they are unfounded. Sick pupils are placed in the infirmary and when justified on the advice of Dr. Findlay, they are immediately admitted to hospital. Eleven pupils, T.B. suspects were admitted to hospital recently for x-ray and observation by the authority of Dr. Barclay. Of course, when there is an epidemic of colds it is impossible to segregate the pupils.

I believe these complaints are promoted by the desire of the Indians for day schools on the Reserves.

R. Howe,
Indian Agent.

RH/S

Figure 68: The Indian Agent for the same area acknowledges that sick pupils are not kept separate from the healthy ones (1946)

2/

Admission of Pupils at Squamish Residential **School during** Sept **Quarter, 192**4

No.	NAME	Date of Admission 192	Age on Admission	No. of Ticket under which Child's Annuity is paid	BAND	Name of Parents and Living or Dead (Insert L. for living, D. for dead, after name): Father	Mother	Religion of Parents	State of Education upon entering the School	Place and period of Previous Education
0163	Annie Williams	Aug. 1934	8		Squamish	Billie Williams, L.	Suzan Williams L.	R.C.	Nil	Nil
0164	Elsie Gonzales	" "	5		" "	Arthur Gonzales L.	Bernadette Christopher L.	R.C.	Nil	Nil

DISCHARGE OF PUPILS

No.	NAME	Date of Discharge	Age on Discharge	Periods in the School: Years	Months	Days	State of Education: On Admission	On Discharge	Trade or Industry Taught and Proficiency in it	Remarks upon Discharge Reasons for Same
0132	Rose Timothy	Aug. 1934	17	5	10	15	Grade I	Grade V	Domestic Science	
0156	Muriel Peters	" "	10	5	9	14	Nil	Nil		Had T.B. germs when admitted

Sister Mary Amy, Principal

NOTE—One or more of these forms should be forwarded with each quarterly return and full particulars should be given regarding all pupils either admitted or discharged during the quarter.

Figure 69: Admission record for the Squamish Catholic Indian School indicates that children sick with tuberculosis are brought into the school (1924)

COPY.

Fraser Lake, B.C.,

Jan. 5th. 1937.

R.H.Moore, Esq.,
Indian Agent,
Vanderhoof, B.C.

Dear Sir:-

Re. Paul Shorty:- This boy, a pupil at the Indian School, you may remember was sent to the School from Harper Reed's agency, some time ago. I protested his admission to the school at the time but, being an orphan, there seemed to be no place to send him. He did very well at school for a time and nothing more was done about discharging him although he has never been cured of the tubercular infection with which he was admitted.

During the past fall he has gone down hill again. Is now affected with discharging glands and a continual cough. He has again become a source of infection to the other children and I should very much like to have him discharged if any arrangements can be made for his care elsewhere. Would be obliged if you could take this up with the Department.

Yours sincerely,

Signed:- C. Pitts, M.D.

Figure 70: Medical Inspector Dr. C. Pitts acknowledges the admission of tuberculosis-sick children into the Le Jac Catholic Indian school (1937)

March 7, 1910 - 2 - D. C. Scott, DIA Deputy Superint.

Dr. Lafferty does not join with Dr. Bryce in these recommendations and finds himself at a loss to offer any suggestions unless he is aware of the views of the Department.

Suggestions by the Department.

It will be obvious at once that Dr. Bryce's recommendations while they may be scientific are quite inapplicable to the system under which these schools are conducted. Even were the Department prepared to take the schools over from the Churches, it is self evident that the Churches would not be willing to give up their share of the joint control. These preliminary examinations by Dr. Lafferty and Dr. Bryce have already caused considerable irritation and brought protests from the Roman Catholic authorities who have the larger number of pupils under their charge. Dr. Lafferty's caution in not committing himself to sweeping changes seems to show that he has some idea of the impossibility of carrying out such innovations as are prescribed by Dr. Bryce.

If the schools are to be conducted at all we must face the fact that a large number of the pupils will suffer from tuberculosis in some of its various forms. The admission indiscriminately of such pupils into the schools in the past, and the failure to recognize any special treatment which could be accorded to them has no doubt led to the high death rate which has rendered ineffectual to a large degree the past expenditure on Indian education in Boarding and Industrial schools. More stringent regulations as to the admi...

Figure 71: Legitimating Genocide: Indian Affairs Superintendent Duncan Campbell Scott claims that "a large number" of children with tuberculosis will inevitably be present in residential schools (1910)

OFFICE OF THE DEPUTY SUPERINTENDENT GENERAL,
OTTAWA.

April 11, 1911.

Mr. Scott,-

With reference to the first rule of your memorandum of March 7, 1910, marked herewith, the tuberculosis must be advanced far enough to make the child a danger to the rest of the pupils or by confining him to the school-room the danger to himself will be much aggravated. It will be almost impossible to get pupils who have not some taint of tuberculosis. Judgment should be exercised in excluding or admitting pupils on tuberculous grounds.

With reference to the third rule, a dietary may be employed very easily in certain localities where a variety of food is easily obtainable, but in some of the remote, and particularly in northern districts, the food is mostly of one kind, as, for instance, fish or game, and it will be pretty difficult to establish a dietary in cases of this kind, as that word is generally understood.

D. S. G. I. A.

Indian Affairs. (RG 10, Volume 3957, file 140,754-1)

Figure 72: Another Indian Affairs official voices the same "inevitability of tuberculosis" statement of Superintendent Scott (1911)

Fraser Lake, B.C.,

October 22nd. 1935.

R.H.Moore, Esq.,
Indian Agent,
Vanderhoof, B.C.

Dear Sir:-

Your letter of October the 10th. received with complaints of attention I am giving the Indians. These complaints have been so frequent lately and so unjustified that I begin to believe they are promoted by personal feeling against me rather than an interest in the welfare of the Indians. This may be on your part but I prefer to think it comes from Rivet, for whom I have little use and who probably guesses that I feel so toward him.

F. Pitts, Port Alberni

Since my father is principal of an Indian School and I have had opportunity to meet the principals and medical attendants of other schools, I happen to know that the attention I am giving the Lejac School is as good or better than in any other place in the province. As for the general medical examination you speak of, this is not done in any other school that I have any knowledge of. This would bear no weight with me if I thought that any purpose would be served by doing so, but I do not think so. Where is the point of this, when I know that, were I to apply the standards of health to them that is applied to children of the white schools, that I should have to discharge 90% of them and there would be no school left; and when I know that they are under the constant observation of a staff who have the opportunity of reporting any ill health to me either on my weekly visit to the school or by phone. If the department makes this a regulation applying to all schools I have nothing to say, otherwise I shall use my own judgement. ←*

As for dental work, anyone knows that there is always dental work in such an institution. I have asked for a dentist on two previous occasions and am surprised that the department does not arrange for an annual attednance of a dentist, rather than wait for the doctor to examine the whole school and tell them a dentist is required (which everyone knows). I am only too pleased to facilitate his work, when I know he is coming, by going over the children and picking out the ones who require work done.

In conclusion, I feel that I am doing everything that experience and commonsense dictates for the welfare of the children. If any more complaints emanate from the school through you I shall put it up to the department at Ottawa, giving them a statement of just how I am carrying on the work and let them decide whether it should be satisfactory or not.

Yours,

Signed:- C. Pitts, M.D.

Figure 73: Medical Inspector Dr. C. Pitts confirms the existence of a lower standard of health care for Indian residential school children (1935)

The Vancouver Sun, MONDAY, DECEMBER 18, 1995

Claim of murder goes back to '40s

A report that a girl was killed by a residential-school official has sparked an investigation.

KAREN GRAM

RCMP are launching an investigation today into an allegation that a young girl was murdered at a United Church residential school for Indians on Vancouver Island 50 years ago.

Art Anderson, an official with the United Church, said Sunday that police were notified of the allegation as soon as the church learned of it.

Rev. Kevin McNamee-Annett, a former United Church minister for the Alberni area, reported the allegation to the current minister Thursday. On Friday, both McNamee-Annett and the church lawyer reported it to the police.

"We are uncertain what this means, but we have to treat it seriously," Anderson said. "As of tomorrow, the police will be beginning an investigation."

The investigation was triggered by a statement from a North Vancouver woman who told McNamee-Annett she was nearby when a six-year-old girl was kicked down some stairs and died.

Harriet Nahanee, 60, is the first witness to come forward to support recent allegations about killings at residential schools on the island.

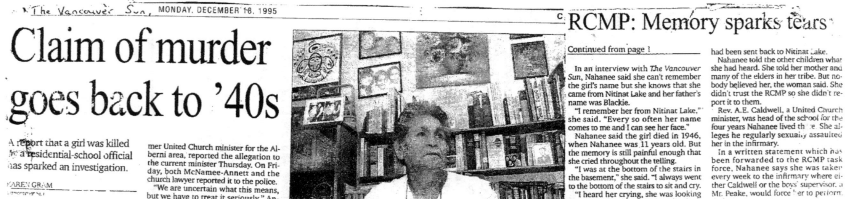

PETER BATTISTONI / Vancouver Sun

DEADLY NIGHTMARES: Harriet Nahanee, 60, says she is haunted by a murder she witnessed at a United Church residential school in Port Alberni 50 years ago.

In another case, a boy is said to have bled to death after he was beaten as punishment for breaking a jar at the school in Ahousaht in the 1940s.

Reports of sexual and physical assaults at the Port Alberni area school sparked a province-wide investigation of residential schools by an RCMP task force. It has been gathering evidence for about one year.

Please see RCMP, B3

RCMP: Memory sparks tears

Continued from page 1

In an interview with *The Vancouver Sun*, Nahanee said she can't remember the girl's name but she knows that she came from Nitinat Lake and her father's name was Blackie.

"I remember her from Nitinat Lake," she said. "Every so often her name comes to me and I can see her face."

Nahanee said the girl died in 1946, when Nahanee was 11 years old. But the memory is still painful enough that she cried throughout the telling.

"I was at the bottom of the stairs in the basement," she said. "I always went to the bottom of the stairs to sit and cry.

"I heard her crying, she was looking for her mother. I heard [the school administrator] yelling at the supervisor for letting the child run around on the stairwell.

"I heard him kick her and she fell down the stairs. I went to look — her eyes were open, she wasn't moving. They didn't even come down the stairs.

"They were arguing at the top of the stairs.

"I never saw her again."

Nahanee said other students later told her the girl had died and her body had been sent back to Nitinat Lake.

Nahanee told the other children what she had heard. She told her mother and many of the elders in her tribe. But nobody believed her, the woman said. She didn't trust the RCMP so she didn't report it to them.

Rev. A.E. Caldwell, a United Church minister, was head of the school for the four years Nahanee lived there. She alleges he regularly sexually assaulted her in the infirmary.

In a written statement which has been forwarded to the RCMP task force, Nahanee says she was taken every week to the infirmary where either Caldwell or the boys' supervisor, a Mr. Peake, would force her to perform oral sex.

Nahanee said she believes other deaths, which at the time the church said were the result of exposure when students tried to run away, were really caused by beatings in the school barn.

The woman still has nightmares about the killing and lives with rage and shame resulting from her treatment.

"I would love to be free of the shame — to leave all that behind me and have some pride in myself."

Figure 74: First report of a residential school killing: the death of Maisie Shaw, Vancouver (December 1995)

Principal A.E. Caldwell stands before the Alberni Indian Residential School on Vancouver Island in the 1950s. Residential schools were run by the mainstream churches: the United, Anglican and Catholic churches. The churches now face litigation over the harm done to children. — *File photo*

Figure 74a: Principal Alfred Caldwell, The Murderer of Albert Gray (1938) and Maisie Shaw (1946)

PORT ALBERNI

Form 2

DOMINION OF CANADA -21

REGISTRATION OF DEATH OF AN INDIAN

(Within the meaning of the "Indian Act" of Canada)

Registered No. 095610
For use of Provincial Office only

Province British Columbia   Agency to which deceased belonged West Coast

1. PLACE OF DEATH:
If on a Reserve .... (Give name and location)
or If in a Rural Municipality .... (Give name or number)
or If in a City, Town or Village Port Alberni (Give name) Street .... House No. ....
and If in a hospital or institution (give name instead of street and number) West Coast Hospital

2. PRINT FULL NAME OF DECEASED   Surname or last name SHAW
Given or Christian names MAISIE

3. Band or tribe to which deceased belonged Nitinaht
4. Residence of deceased Alberni Residential School, Alberni, B. C. 56 (If on a Reserve give name and location)

5. Sex Female   6. Single, married, widowed or divorced (write the word) single   7. Birthplace (Province or country) British Columbia

8. DATE OF BIRTH August (Month by name) 26 (Day) 1932 (Year)   9. AGE Years 14 Months 4 Days ...... If less than one day ...... hrs. or ...... min.

OCCUPATION 10. (a) Trade, profession or kind of work as teamster, trapper, canner, etc. School pupil
(b) Kind of industry or business as lumbering, fur trading, fish canning, etc. ....

11. Name of father Shaw (Surname or last name) Walter (Given or Christian names)
12. Name of mother Williams (Surname or last name) Ella (Given or Christian names)
13. Birthplace: Father British Columbia (Province or country) Mother British Columbia (Province or country)

14. I certify the foregoing to be true and correct to the best of my knowledge and belief.
Given under my hand at Alberni, B. C. this 7 day of January 1947
Signature of informant R.W. Garrard   Relationship to deceased: Indian Agent
Address Alberni, B. C.

15. Burial, Cremation or Removal Burial (Write the word)   Date December 27 (Month by name) (Day) 1946 (Year)
Place .... (Municipality) Cemetery Sheshaht

16. Undertaker's Name Steven's Funeral Home   Address Port Alberni, B. C.

17. Marginal Notations (Office use only)

IN CASE OF STILLBIRTH CONSULT INSTRUCTIONS ON REVERSE SIDE BEFORE MAKING OUT CERTIFICATE.
WRITE PLAINLY WITH UNFADING INK. THIS IS A PERMANENT RECORD.
Every item of information should be carefully supplied.

MEDICAL CERTIFICATE OF DEATH

18. DATE OF DEATH DECEMBER (Month by name) 26 (Day) 1946 (Year)

19. I HEREBY CERTIFY that I attended deceased from December 18 1946 to December 26 1946, and last saw her alive on December 26 1946

CAUSE OF DEATH		DURATION Yrs.	Mos.	Dys.
I. Immediate cause. Give disease, injury or complication which caused death, not the mode of dying, such as heart failure, asphyxia, asthenia, etc.	(a) Acute Rheumatic Carditis			3
Morbid conditions, if any, giving rise to immediate cause (stated in order proceeding backwards from immediate cause).	due to (b)			
	due to (c)			
II. Other morbid conditions (if important) contributing to death but not causally related to immediate cause.				

20. If a woman, was the death associated with pregnancy? No
21. Was there a surgical operation? No   Date of operation .... 19....
State findings .... Was there an autopsy? No
22. If death was due to external causes (violence) fill in also the following:—
Accident, suicide or homicide? .... (State which) Date of injury .... 19....
Manner of injury .... (How sustained)
Nature of injury ....
Specify whether injury occurred in industry, in home or in public place ....

Signed by W.H. Jones   Designation M. D. M.D., Coroner, etc.
Address Port Alberni, B. C.   Date January 6 1947

23. I hereby certify that the above return was made by me at Alberni, B. C.
Dated January 7 1947   R.W. Garrard Indian Agent actg.
Indian Agency No. 3

(SEE REVERSE SIDE FOR INSTRUCTIONS)

GR-2951 BRITISH COLUMBIA. BRITISH COLUMBIA VITAL STATISTICS AGENCY.
Volume 095B Indian death registrations 095501 to 095693
1946

Figure 75: Fabricated death certificate for murdered residential school student Maisie Shaw

Beaten to death for theft of a prune

Indian elder recalls strapping of 15-year-old boy at Island residential school in 1938 by United Church minister.

MARK HUME
Vancouver Sun

A 15-year-old boy who stole a prune from a jar in the kitchen of a United Church residential school was strapped so relentlessly his kidneys failed him and he later died in bed, says a native Indian elder who was there at the time.

Archie Frank, now 68, was just 11 years old when his school mate, Albert Gray, was caught stealing in the Ahousat Residential School kitchen one night in 1938.

Frank, a retired commercial fisher, says he's never forgotten what happened to Gray, a husky youngster from the remote Vancouver Island community of Nitinat.

"He got strapped to death," said Frank in an interview on Tuesday.

"Just for stealing one prune, [Rev. A.E.] Caldwell strapped him to death.

"Beat the s— right out of him."

Frank's story, told after a 57-year silence, crystallizes much of what the furore over residential schools is all about.

For the past year the RCMP has been probing a series of alleged abuses at church-run residential schools. So far they have found evidence that 54 people were victims of abuse at the hands of 94 offenders. The investigation is concerned with 14 residential schools operated by the Anglican, United and Roman Catholic churches from the late 1800s to 1984.

The First United Church has come under scrutiny by the RCMP this week because of new allegations that two children were killed while at the residential school in the Port Alberni area in the 1940s and '50s.

Frank said Caldwell left Ahousat after the residential school burned down in 1940 and went on to be principal of the United Church school in Port Alberni.

Please see SCHOOL, A2

SCHOOL: Beaten to death for theft of a prune

Continued from page 1

Frank said Gray was caught with his hand in the prune jar by the night watchman at the Ahousat school.

"The day after he got strapped so badly he couldn't get out of bed. The strap wore through a half inch of his skin.

"His kidneys gave out. He couldn't hold his water anymore," said Frank, who has never told his story to the police.

He said Gray lay in his bed for several weeks after the beating, while he and another boy at the school cared for him, bringing him meals, and changing the urine-soaked sheets on his bed.

"They wouldn't bring him to a doctor.

"I don't think they wanted to reveal the extent of his injuries," said Frank, who still lives in the tiny village of Ahousat, just outside Tofino on the west coast of Vancouver Island.

Frank said he spent several years attending the First United Church residential school in Ahousat, and for the most part found it to be a good place.

"I had a very good experience in that school.

"That was the only one [bad incident] I experienced," said Frank of the death of his friend.

He said he never thought of reporting the death at the time because he was only 11 years old and because the principal of the school was seen as the ultimate authority.

When he grew older he sometimes remembered Gray, he said, but didn't go to the police because his philosophy was: "Keep out of harm's way — and learn to forgive."

Frank was asked why he thought a boy would be beaten so severely for such a minor offence.

"I don't know how you guys operate. That's not the Indian way," he replied.

Frank said he's aware of a province-wide inquiry into residential schools by the RCMP, but it's not something he wants to get caught up in.

"I don't want to get involved for something that happened so long ago."

Frank also said there seems little point because Caldwell is now dead.

"There's no use having hard feelings for a dead man. If he was alive, I'd still be angry," he said.

Rev. Bruce Gunn, the United Church minister in Ahousat, said Frank's attitude of forgiveness is typical of the older generation of Indian people.

"Their tradition was to get along because they lived in survival cultures. They knew how important it was to forgive," he said.

But Gunn said younger Indian people feel it's important to get to the bottom of what happened, and they are pressing for inquiries into crimes that may have happened more than 50 years ago.

Gunn said he has been talking to elders in Ahousat, trying to confirm some of the stories that have been going around.

He hadn't talked to Frank, but said he would.

Attention was drawn to the United Church residential school system on Vancouver Island earlier this month when Jack McDonald, a candidate for the New Democratic Party leadership, called for a public inquiry into alleged deaths at schools in the Port Alberni area.

McDonald said he'd heard of at least two deaths, one of which was in Ahousat.

Sgt. Paul Willms, who is heading the RCMP investigation into abuse at B.C. residential schools, said he hadn't heard any allegations about deaths in the Port Alberni area until McDonald brought them up.

The police in Port Alberni this week began questioning witnesses and promised a thorough investigation.

Meanwhile, Kevin McNamee-Annett, a former United Church minister, issued a statement Monday saying he's going on a fast to protest against the church's handling of the issue.

McNamee-Annett was fired by the Port Alberni presbytery last January. He claims he was dismissed for trying to unearth the truth about the residential schools

But United Church representative Rev. Art Anderson said McNamee-Annett was let go because he wasn't doing a good job.

McNamee-Annett said that by undertaking his fast he hopes "to bring greater public and moral attention to the wrongs and negligence at work within the United Church. In this way the community as a whole can call th church back to its true spirit: that of truthful, just and loving people who the servants of the poor."

Vancouver Sun, December 20, 1995

Figure 76: Report of a second murder of a residential school child by Principal Alfred Caldwell

Statement of Harry Wilson, former pupil at Alberni Residential School (1961-1970), given on September 17, 1997 in Vancouver, B.C. to (Rev.) Kevin Annett

I was born in Bella Bella in 1953 and lived there until I was sent with a bunch of other kids to the Alberni Residential School in 1961. I was just seven years old.

The Principal there, Mr. J. Andrews, he was a real alcoholic. He always came into the school drunk. When I told him that Mr. Plint, the boys' supervisor, had molested me, Mr. Andrews said he'd strap me if I told anybody else about what Mr. Plint had done. So I never said anything to anyone.

Mr. Plint used to grab me by the hair and drag me off into his bedroom, where he'd molest me. He'd hit me over the head when I yelled for help, so I kept quiet. He threatened to beat me up bad if I told anyone what he'd done.

Plint was the one who drove kids to Vancouver and Nanaimo for medical appointments. He drove us in what he called the "bunny van". He'd molest us in there, too.

Other kids were beaten really bad. Victor Robinson got hit forty times with a hockey stick by Mr. Mike Flint, another boys' supervisor. Victor was 15. Flint was from Campbell River. He beat Victor and two other kids with the hockey stick because they'd accidentally broken a window playing ball. That was in June, 1963.

In 1967, I discovered a dead body behind the Caldwell Hall at the school. Two kids from the Tseshaht reserve and me found a young girl, she was about 16, lying dead, completely naked and covered in blood. There was blood everywhere. I ran and told Mr. Andrews, and he said he was calling the RCMP. But I never saw them show up, and the girl's body disappeared. They just took her away and that was it. And the RCMP never questioned me or the other kids who found her.

I can't remember the dead girl's name, but she was from far away, up north somewhere. She was a new girl who didn't have any family nearby. There was never any investigation into her death.

Less than two months later, after I had told Andrews about finding her body, I was shipped out to Nanaimo and put in the hospital there for three months.

Figure 77: Testimony of Alberni school survivor Harry Wilson regarding his discovery of a dead girl's at the school in 1967

By 1970, I tried to kill myself twice. I was expelled from the school in 1970. I was sent to the Bella Bella hospital then, after the RCMP talked to my family. The Mounties had me committed and I was strapped down in bed. I was in there like that for months.

That year the girl was killed, in 1967, another kid died at the school. Frank Williams was found hanged in the lunchroom. He was a nice kid. He was from Vancouver Island.

Plint and Principal Andrews always carried straps on their belts. Andrew's strap looked like a whip. At six different times, he strapped me in front of all the girls. He made me strip naked and made them all watch me get whipped, after I had skipped school.

The food at the school was terrible. Kids were always getting sick from it. I got really sick twice.

I remember Mr. Caldwell and Mr. Peake, too. They were mean to everyone.

I also remember Reverend McKenzie. He worked in a church in Port Alberni, but he was always hanging around the school. He used to have kids stay over at his house. I stayed there once, along with Debra Clark from Prince Rupert. There were three bedrooms, one downstairs, where I slept, and the girls and Reverend McKenzie were upstairs. The house was on River Road.

A lot of other bad things happened in the school that no-one will talk about.

Harry Wilson

Harry Wilson

September 17, 1997
Vancouver, B.C.

Witnessed by:

Kevin D. Annett

(Rev.) Kevin D. Annett

Addendum - Jan. 2, 1998

Whenever we got caught doing something bad, we got stripped naked and had to crawl like a dog on our hands and knees in front of the Principal and some teachers. They'd whip us and beat us as we crawled past in front of them. Andrews (the Principal) and the others did this to me a lot, sometimes once a week.

Harry Wilson

Statement of Harry Wilson, 45, of Burnaby, B.C., given to (Rev.) Kevin Annett on March 31, 1998

I went to the Circle of Justice forum in Port Alberni on March 28, 1998, so that I could give my testimony about finding the dead body of a young girl at the Alberni Indian Residential School in May, 1967.

Just before I was to give my testimony to the United Nations Human Rights Commissioner, Rudy James, a man called Ron Hamilton came to talk to me. He is closely connected to the Nuu-Chah-Nulth Tribal Council and has worked with the RCMP on their residential school Task Force.

Ron Hamilton came to me just before I was to speak and he said to me,

"Are you going to talk about that dead girl you found?"

I told him that I was.

He then said to me,

"I wouldn't talk about her if I was you. If you say anything about it, you'll be sorry."

His words scared me, and so I didn't say anything that day about what I knew. I felt that I was in danger from Ron Hamilton.

It was the RCMP who put me in the hospital against my will after I talked about finding the dead girl. I think Ron Hamilton was trying to protect the RCMP, who he works with, by scaring me into not talking. I think the RCMP and the United Church were involved in that girl's death, and maybe even other natives too.

As Nuu-Chah-Nulth Tribal Council official Charlie Thompson left our Circle, he walked by me and said to me,

"You have half a brain and no-one will miss you if you're found floating face down in the water."

I feel my life was being threatened by these members of the Nuu-Chah-Nulth Tribal Council.

Harry Wilson

Witnessed by:

(Rev.) Kevin Annett

March 31, 1998

Figure 78: Testimony of Harry Wilson concerning his attempted silencing by tribal council officials (March 1998)

Statement of Dennis Tallio, student at Alberni Residential School, 1962-1967, given to (Rev.) Kevin Annett in Vancouver, B.C., October 13, 1997

I went to the Alberni school between 1962 and 1967. I'll never forget that time, because of all the constant punishment. Mr. Flint was a really bad man. When he found any of us smoking, he'd make us smoke a whole cigar in front of everybody, even if it choked us. Once, when he caught a kid taking his tube of toothpaste, he made that kid eat four or five tubes of toothpaste.

* We even found a dead body at the school. It was in the fall of 1965. We were playing soccer in the back field behind the school, where it was really covered in weeds. The ball got kicked among the weeds, and in those weeds I came across the remains of a body, maybe three feet long. It was decomposed and you could see a lot of skeleton. It must have been there for awhile.

I ran to the school, and then we had to call the RCMP from a house nearby, on the reserve. They came and took away the remains. I heard it was the body of a girl, seven to nine years old. The autopsy showed that she had been sexually assaulted by four or five guys, or at least that's what the cops said.

After that, the RCMP came to us and told us not to say anything about what we had discovered in the field. I thought this was strange. Why would they want us to keep quiet?

The previous year, in 1964, a seven year old boy named Joseph had also died at the Alberni school. He got strangled in a towel roll. It appeared to be an accident, but there was negligence involved. That towel roll was dangerous, and no-one told us to be careful about it. Harry Wilson knew this boy, too.

Principal Andrews used to beat me with a horse harness strap, a really thick strap. He did it every weekend, like clockwork, usually on Saturday. All I'd do was take a walk with some other kids and I'd get this beating from Andrews for it.

I still can hear the screams coming from the other dorm, girls yelling "Don't do it!", and then screaming and screaming afterwards. I couldn't do anything to help those girls; all I could do was lie there. I can't ever get those screams out of my head.

Figure 79: Testimony of Alberni school survivor Dennis Tallio concerning his discovery of a dead body at the school in 1965

p. 2

It's true that the dentist never gave us painkillers when he worked on our teeth. He'd even drill us, right on the nerve. He liked to jab my gums all the time, prick me badly if I moved at all while he was working on me..

The judo intructor at the school was another sexual abuser. I can't remember his name, but he used to take kids into his cabin all the time.

I remember the name of Clifford Tate (another child claimed to have been killed by Principal A.E. Caldwell). But Clifford Tate was one of those names no-one wants to talk about.

Dennis Tallio

October 13, 1997
Vancouver, B.C.

Witnessed by:

(Rev.) Kevin D. Annett

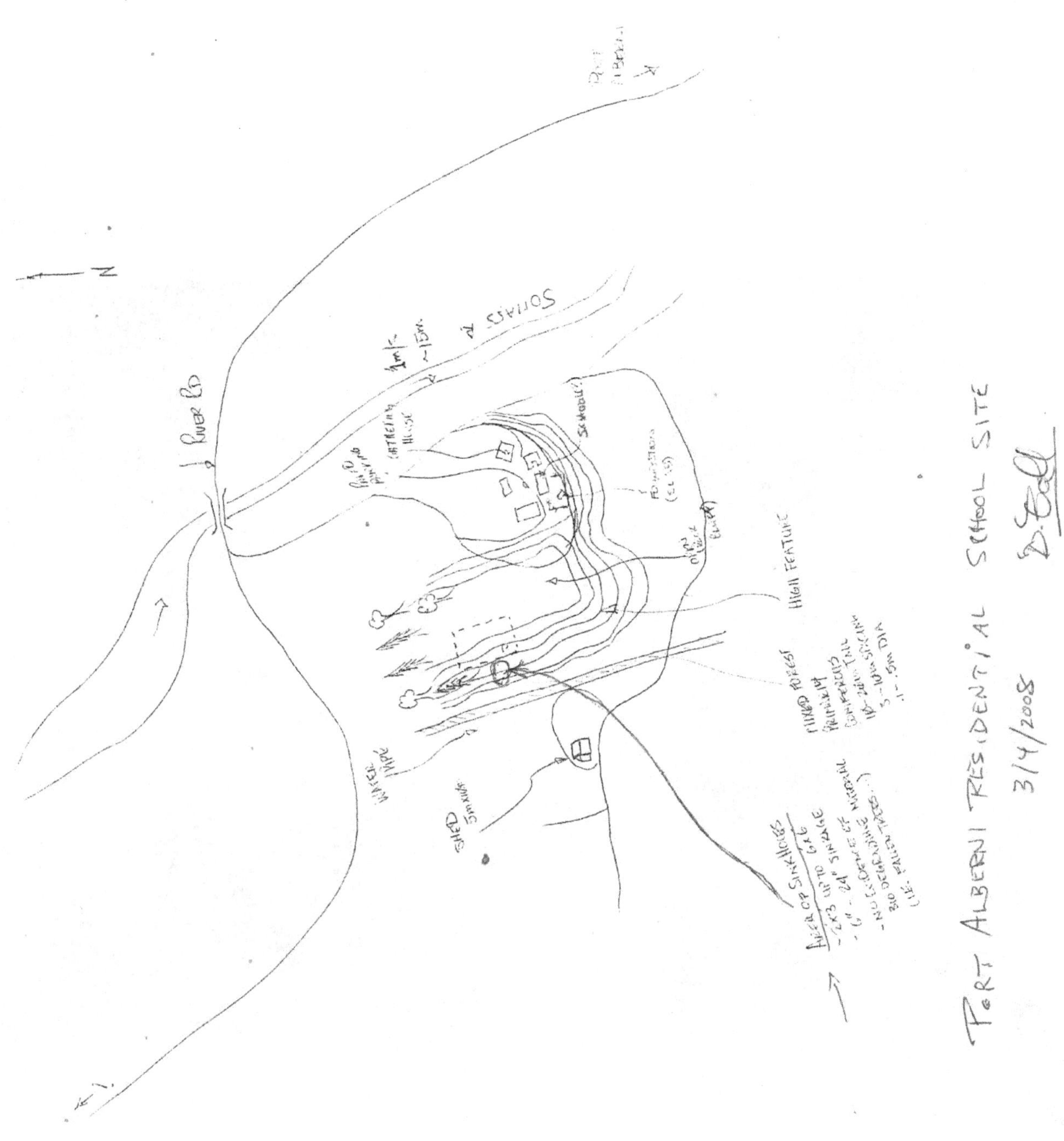

Figure 80: Forensic survey of the reported mass grave site of children at the former United Church Alberni residential school, made April 3, 2008. Sinkholes are noted, indicating probably graves.

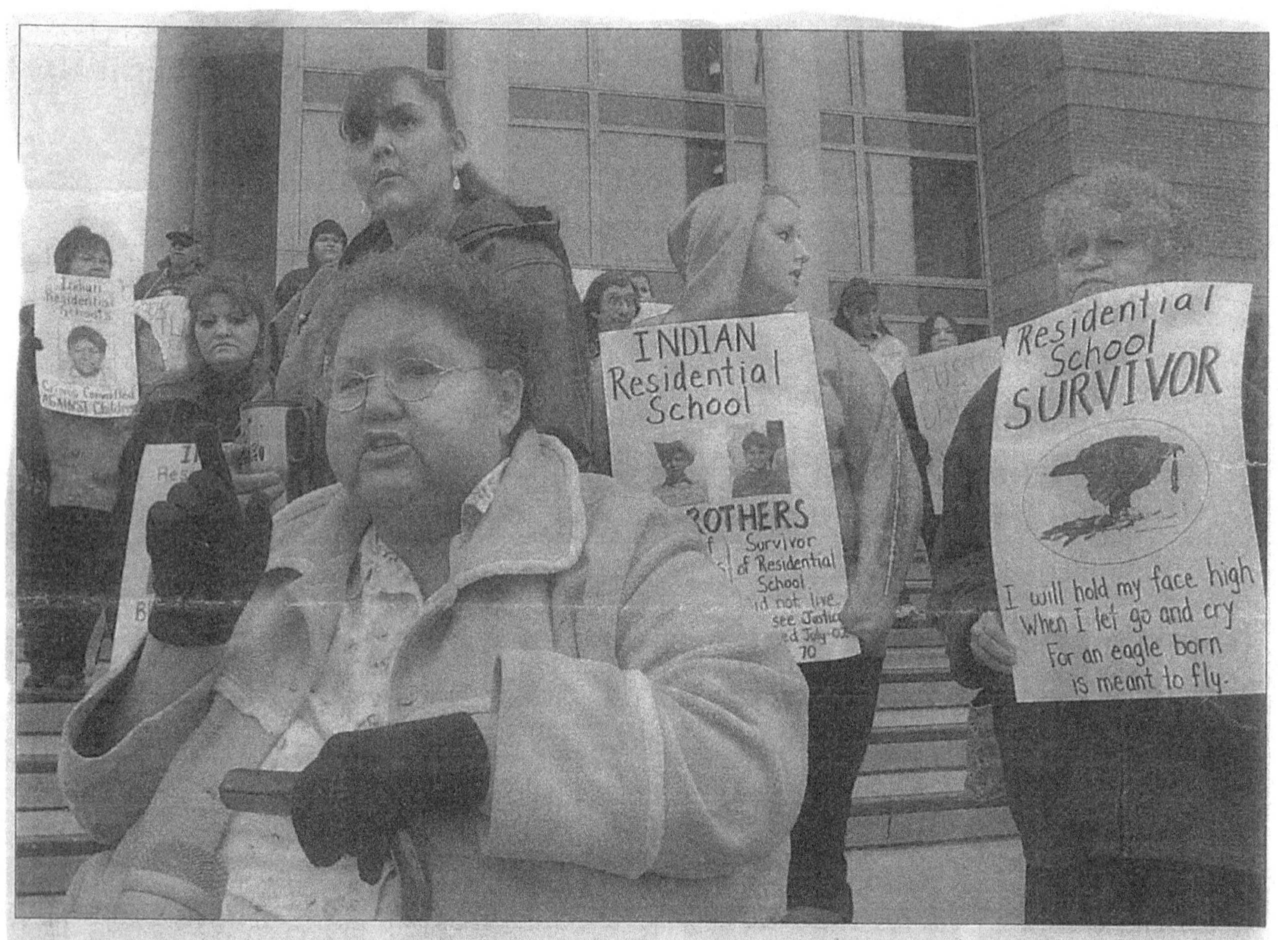

VIRGINIA BAPTISTE tells her story of life in a residential school during a protest at the court house on Wednesday.

Figure 81: The late Virginia Baptiste, survivor of Catholic St. Eugene residential school, Cranbrook

My name is Inez Beryl Spencer and I just want people to know what happened to my sister, Victoria Kathleen Stewart, in Edmonton, in 1958. She died there at the age of nine because of a beating that happened. She was hit over the head with a two by four by one of the supervisors and shortly after that she started getting sick, and she ended up going to the Camsell Hospital. This was very late in the evening. Then by next morning they told us she had died. Miss Knizky was the one who hit her on the head with that two by four. We were running in from the yard and just because we were running that's why she hit her. First she got me in the back with the two by four and then she got Vicky over the head. At the United Church Edmonton Residential School.

Inez Beryl Spencer, Terrace, B.C., May 27, 2009

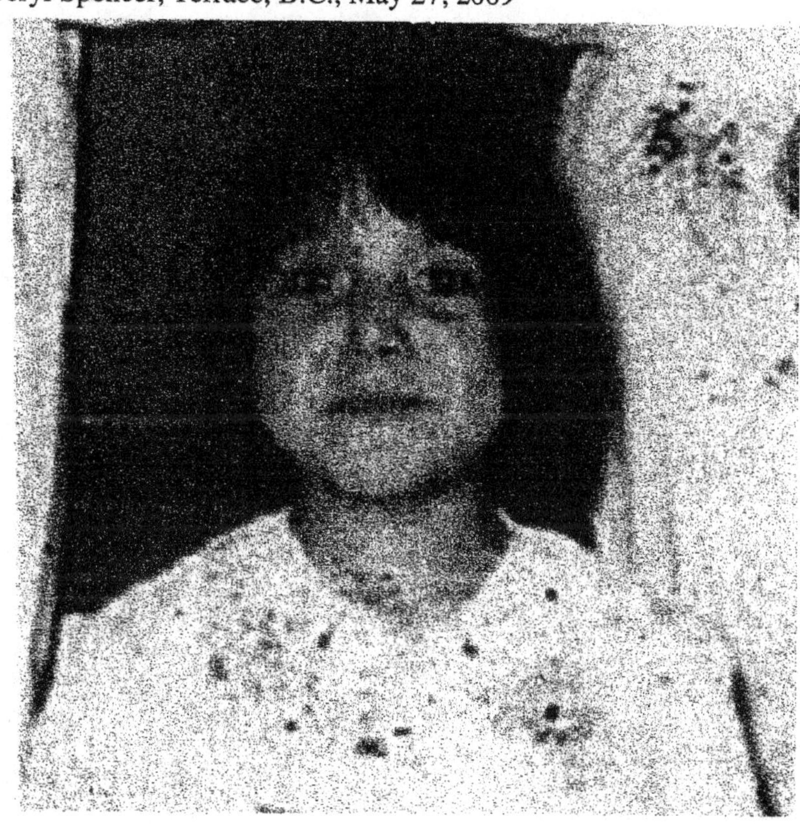

Victoria Stewart, 1949-1958
Murdered April 9, 1958 by Ann Knizky, Supervisor, United Church residential school in Edmonton, Alberta

Figure 82: *Murdered* - Nine year old Vicky Stewart, killed by United Church employee Ann Knizky, Edmonton residential school (1958)

THURSDAY, MAY 28, 2009 THEPROVINCE.COM | NEWS | A13

Family says school staffer killed 9-year-old girl sister

50-YEAR-OLD LIE? Death not from 'TB meningitis,' siblings say

BY SAM COOPER
STAFF REPORTER

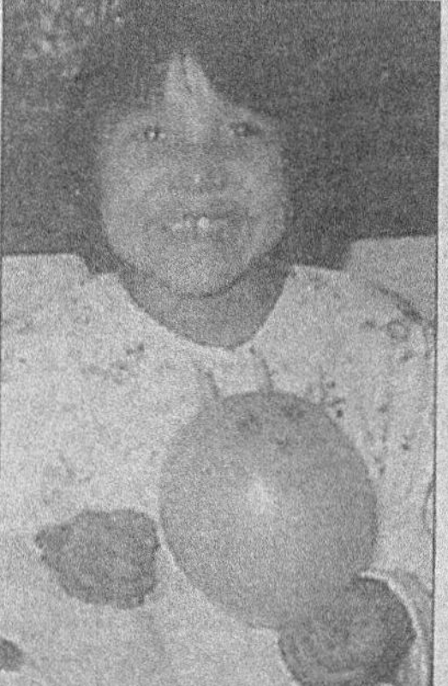

Vicky Stewart (left) was brought home in 1958 'in a box,' age 9. Her sister, Eliza Stewart (right), wants her death properly investigated. WAYNE LEIDENFROST — THE PROVINCE

Eliza and Moses Stewart remember being propped up on kitchen chairs to see their nine-year-old sister, Vicky, who was brought home from Edmonton's Indian Residential school in 1958.

She was dead.

That image, 51 years later, still haunts them.

Official burial records said Vicky died of "TB meningitis," but the Stewarts believe their sister was hit over the head with a two-by-four by a school staff member.

At a press conference yesterday in Vancouver, the siblings — who now live in the Lower Mainland — said Ann Knizky "murdered" Vicky and also struck their sister Beryl with the same piece of wood.

They said Vicky and Beryl were taken from their parents and sent to Edmonton in the 1950s.

They played a tape recording by Beryl [Spencer], now 61 and living in Terrace.

"We were running in from the yard and, just because we were running, that's why [Knizky] hit Vicky," Beryl said.

"First she got me in the back with the two-by-four and then she got Vicky over the head." Beryl said Vicky was sent to hospital. "Then by next morning they told us she had died."

The Stewarts didn't have the confidence to report the allegation to police.

"Nobody in the family really knew what to do — they didn't have money for a lawyer," said Eliza.

Last year, she contacted Kevin Annett, a former United Church minister who now advocates from Vancouver's Downtown Eastside, and "started getting answers."

Annett and the Stewarts are demanding the church admit responsibility and work with Alberta RCMP to bring Knizky "to justice."

The family also wants compensation and a "proper burial" and memorial for Vicky.

"Those memories of them putting me up in a chair to see my sister in a box, they stick with you," Moses said.

The Province located an Edmonton man, Jim Kniazky, who said his aunt had worked as a caregiver at an Edmonton residential school and died three years ago, aged 92. The two spell their names differently.

Told of the murder allegation, Kniazky said: "I don't think she could have been [involved in killing] . . . She was very kind."

Alberta RCMP spokesman Cpl. Wayne Oakes said there is no statute of limitation on murder and, even if an accused killer dies, an investigation could continue.

Dan Chambers, president of the B.C. Conference of the United Church of Canada, said he could not comment on the allegations.

In June 2008, Prime Minister Stephen Harper made an official apology to First Nations for the century-long policy that forced 150,000 aboriginal children to live in schools where their language and culture were banned and where many were abused.

scooper@theprovince.com

Figure 83: Media report of Vicky Stewart's murder, Vancouver Province, May 28, 2009

DEPARTMENT OF CITIZENSHIP AND IMMIGRATION
INDIAN AFFAIRS BRANCH

PAYLIST - RESIDENTIAL SCHOOL

Name of School: EDMONTON RESIDENTIAL.
CERTIFIED CORRECT

Month of: JANUARY, 19 (1962)

BOX 2 File 73 pl

Name of Employee	Gross Pay	Room	Board	Income Tax		U.I.	Misc.	Total Deduct.	Net Pay	Cheque No.
				Federal	Provincial					
CALDWELL, A.E.	391.66		30.00	43.75				73.75	317.91	12.
KNIZKY, Miss Ann	250.00	20.00	30.00	24.40		3.38		77.78	172.22	13
GADD, Miss A.V.	241.66	20.00	30.00	22.70		3.12		75.82	165.84	14
JARVIS, W.A.	266.66	35.00				3.38		38.38	228.28	15
DESMOND, Mrs. E.M.	250.00	20.00	30.00	24.40		3.38		77.78	172.22	16
MARTIN, Mrs. Grace	225.00	20.00	30.00	20.15		3.12		73.27	151.73	17
MARTIN, Mrs. Vera	200.00	20.00	30.00	15.90		2.64		68.54	131.46	18
SCHUBERT, Emil	266.67	20.00	30.00	27.15		3.38		80.53	186.14	19
HARRIS, Dianne	100.00	20.00	30.00					50.00	50.00	20
FREGIN, Mrs. Julie	225.00	20.00	30.00	20.15		3.12		73.27	151.73	21.
SWARE, Mrs. E.M.	225.00	20.00	30.00	20.15		3.12		73.27	151.73	22
PAULSON, Mrs. Ida	200.00	20.00	30.00	15.90		2.64		68.54	131.46	23
LOWNEY, E.C.	175.00	20.00	30.00			2.64		52.64	122.36	24
LUCIEN, A.L.	233.33	20.00	30.00	4.80		3.12		57.92	175.41	25
LUCIEN, Mrs. E.M.	92.50	5.00	15.00			1.32		21.32	71.18	26
GRIFFITH, Donald	233.33	20.00	30.00	21.00		3.12		74.12	159.21	27.
ROYCE, F.J.	266.66	20.00	30.00	27.15		3.38		80.53	186.13	28.
MOSTROM, Mrs. A.R.	91.66	10.00	15.00	6.25		2.64		33.89	57.77	29
TOTALS	3934.13	330.00	480.	293.85		47.50		1151.35	2782.78	

Figure 84: Edmonton residential school record indicating that accused killer Alfred Caldwell was Principal at the same time as Vicky Stewart's killer Ann Knizky (1962)

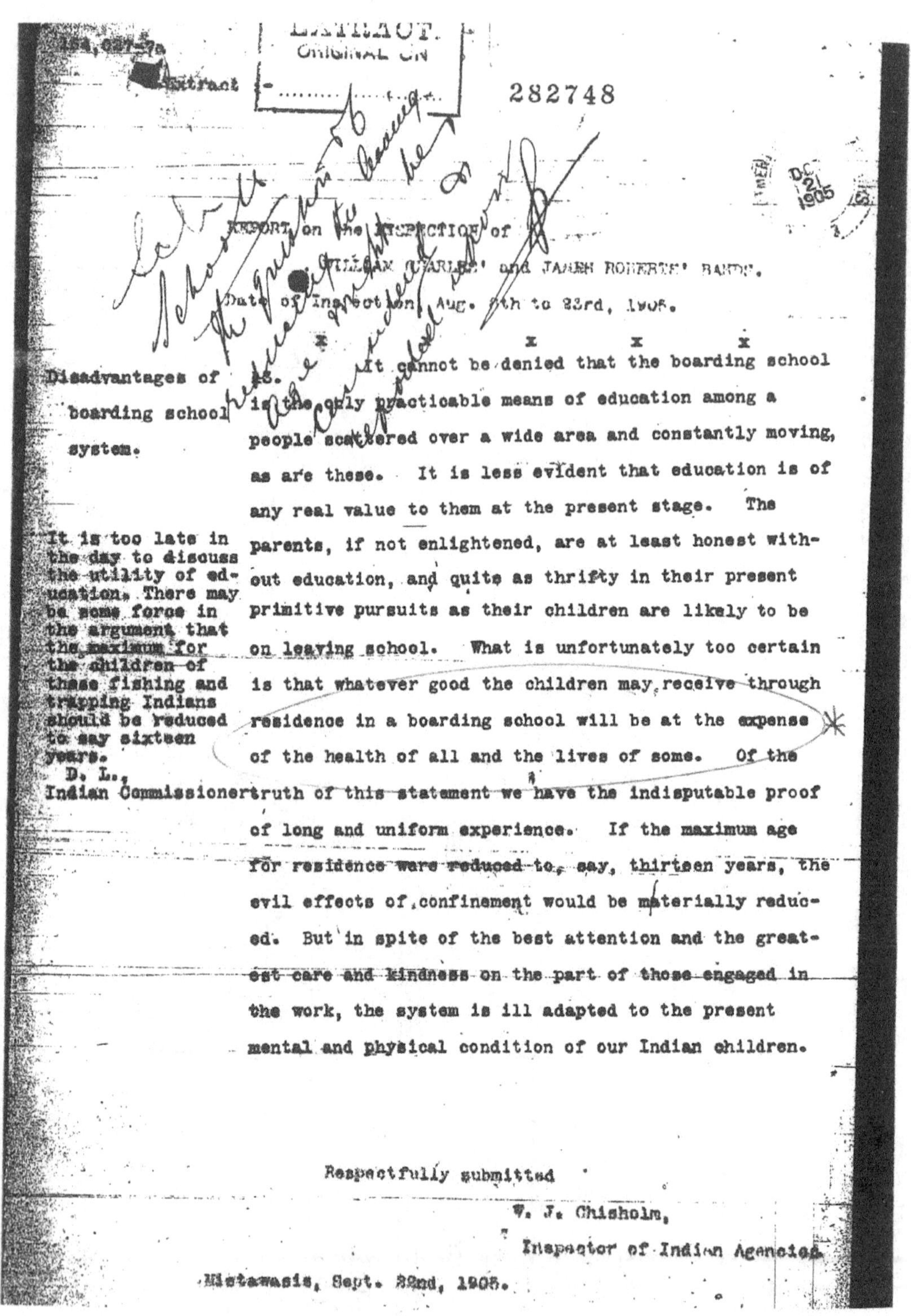

EXTRACT. ORIGINAL ON

Extract

282748

DEC 21 1905

REPORT on the INSPECTION of

WILLIAM CHARLES' and JAMES ROBERTS' BANDS.

Date of Inspection, Aug. 8th to 23rd, 1905.

x x x x

Disadvantages of boarding school system.

13. It cannot be denied that the boarding school is the only practicable means of education among a people scattered over a wide area and constantly moving, as are these. It is less evident that education is of any real value to them at the present stage. The parents, if not enlightened, are at least honest without education, and quite as thrifty in their present primitive pursuits as their children are likely to be on leaving school. What is unfortunately too certain is that whatever good the children may receive through residence in a boarding school will be at the expense of the health of all and the lives of some. Of the truth of this statement we have the indisputable proof of long and uniform experience. If the maximum age for residence were reduced to, say, thirteen years, the evil effects of confinement would be materially reduced. But in spite of the best attention and the greatest care and kindness on the part of those engaged in the work, the system is ill adapted to the present mental and physical condition of our Indian children.

It is too late in the day to discuss the utility of education. There may be some force in the argument that the maximum for the children of these fishing and trapping Indians should be reduced to say sixteen years.
D. L.,
Indian Commissioner

Respectfully submitted

W. J. Chisholm,

Inspector of Indian Agencies

Mistawasis, Sept. 22nd, 1905.

Figure 85: Reference to the universally unhealthy conditions in Indian residential schools by school Inspector W. Chisholm (1905)

Figure 86: *Proof of genocidal intent* – Native children with open tubercular sores (bandaged) sitting among healthy students at the Anglican Indian school, Sarcee reservation, Alberta (1912)

Bella Bella Hospital

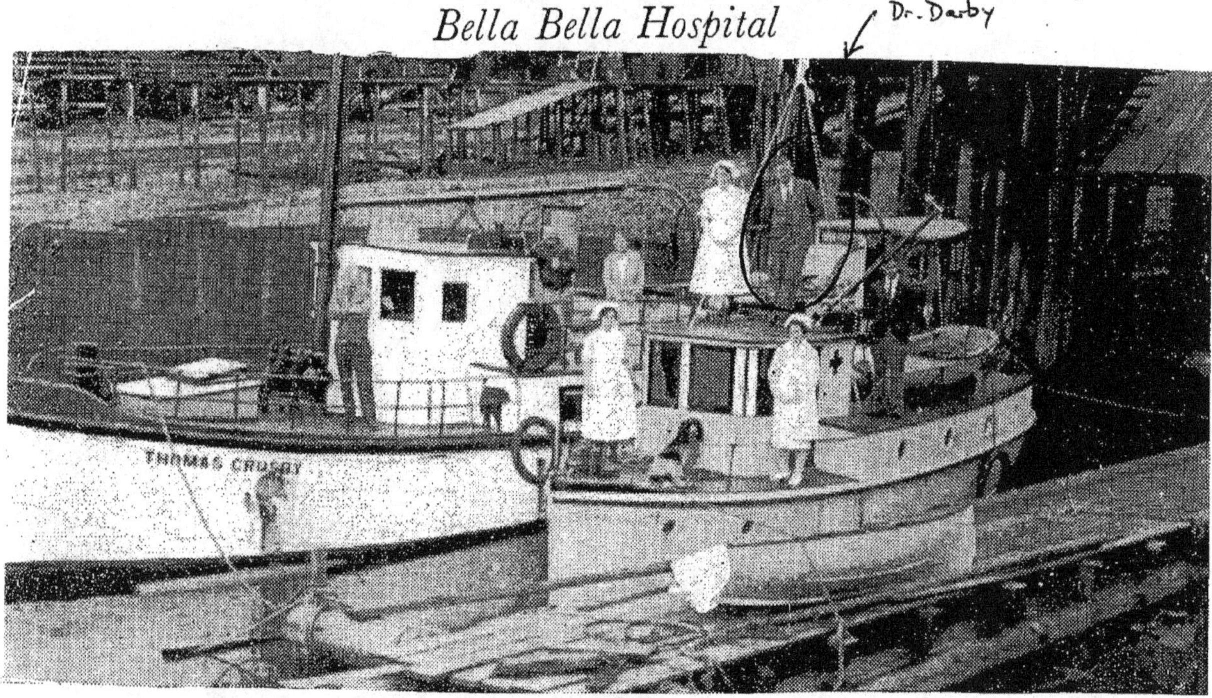

Dr. Darby with staff on "Edward White" at Bella Bella dock

Figure 87: *Sterilization clinic* – The R.W. Large Hospital in Bella Bella, British Columbia operated by United Church missionary doctor George Darby sr. (in photo)

Practical policy sought for North

Native women told birth-control pills vitamins: nurse

OTTAWA (CP) — Birth control in the North is such a sensitive and confusing issue that the Roman Catholic Church there is not sure its anti-contraception dogma makes sense for Eskimos.

About a quarter of the Eskimos are Catholics. The native birth rate is triple that of Canada as a whole.

Bishop Omer Robidoux of Churchill, Man., has called about 10 of his missionary priests together to work out a practical policy with northern doctors and health department officials. The eight-day conference starts in Churchill on Monday at the mission of the Oblates of Mary Immaculate.

The meeting has not been publicly announced but its purpose was learned in an interview with one of the priests involved.

The problem is greater than the ordinary issue of religious ethic because when whites gather alone to determine the future of another people, they are vulnerable to charges of racism.

James Arvaluk, a Keewatin District Eskimo working here with Inuit Tapirisat, the Eskimo Brotherhood, said yesterday that the native association had not even been told of the meeting.

"This is just another example that there is no participation of the Eskimo people in controlling their own lives.

"Who are these people? They think they have control like they did in the past just because they are priests."

Some whites who have worked in Northern settlements made more direct accusations against Health Department personnel.

Loretta Gamble, a nurse who has served in native communities, said she has seen another nurse prescribe birth-control pills "just because she didn't like Indians and didn't want to see any more of them running around."

Mrs. Gamble said native women are sometimes told the pills are vitamins and do not realize they are preventing pregnancy.

A former official of the Indian Affairs Department who spent two years in Eskimo communities charged that there is an unofficial policy of recommending sterilization of Eskimo women after their fifth child.

The man refused to allow his name to be used.

In a telephone interview from the department's northern headquarters in Edmonton, Dr. F. J. Covill confirmed that Eskimo women sometimes undergo sterilization after the fifth delivery.

He said the number of such sterilizations "is not readily available" but he said the rate was above the national average. "It may happen more frequently because that's the way the consumer wants it."

There is no undue pressure on the women, Dr. Covill said, but there is a continuous program of "counselling."

The Pill had disadvantages over other methods: "You realize that the Pill demands a certain amount of literacy. Therefore the intrauterine device is more practical. Some of the native peoples are not quite so highly educated in counting and the Pill demands that you be able to count at least a little."

He said sterilization was suggested as a means of birth control but denied that the poorly educated women are deceived in any way about its permanency: "Right from the beginning they are told that you can limit your family and that it may be a good idea. And then it would be put to them that this is a method and it could be conveniently carried out."

The doctor said there is no apparent conflict of government and church birth-control policy.

He said the Northern priests do not aggressively try to undermine the birth-control program.

One of the Oblate priests attending next week's conference said in a telephone interview from Churchill that the Church is, in effect, without a birth-control policy for Eskimos.

Rev. Roland Courtemanche, an experienced missionary, said the purpose of the meeting is to come up with one.

Education, he suggested, would be a major subject of the discussions.

"You see, they need education—that's what they are missing. With more education we will be able to control the population."

Asked directly if Catholic policy is in any way different in the North and the South, Father Courtemanche answered: "We are not too much in contact with the South—we should know better next week."

Figure 88: Sterilizing methods used against Inuit and Dene families, northern Canada (1979)

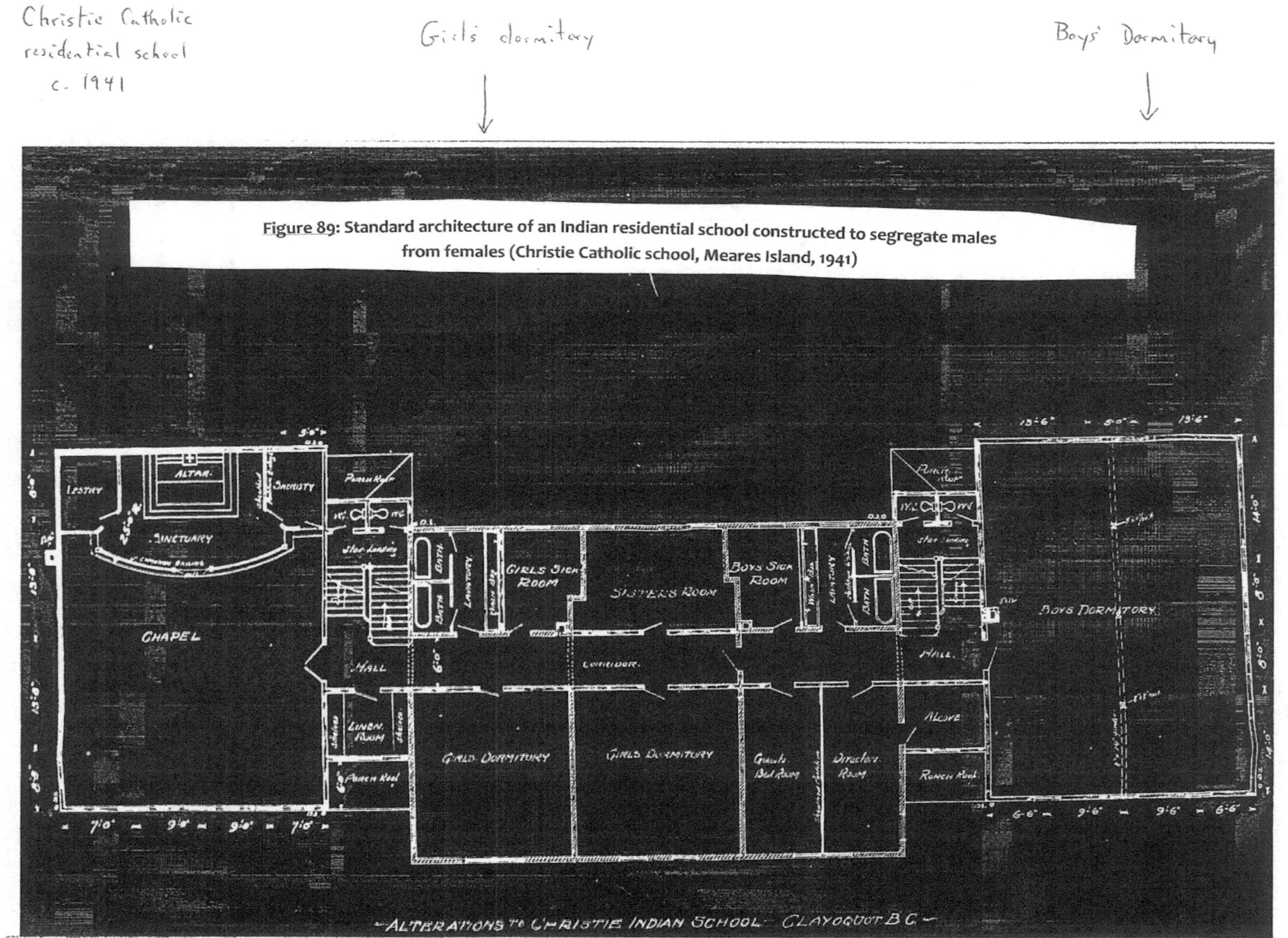

Figure 89: Standard architecture of an Indian residential school constructed to segregate males from females (Christie Catholic school, Meares Island, 1941)

Methodist Mission Rooms,
TORONTO, 1st March, 1888.

The Hon. the Superintendent General
of Indian Affairs,
Ottawa.

Dear Sir,-

As you have kindly intimated your willingness to meet Senator Macdonald and the undersigned to confer in regard to matters affecting Indian Schools, &c, I beg to submit for your information the following memorandum of points that we would like to have considered:

I. INDIAN SCHOOLS AND MISSION PREMISES IN ONTARIO.

On the 2nd April, 1883, I sent a communication in reply to two letters received from the Department in which I set forth our views in regard to the Industrial Institution at Muncey, and also in regard to our ordinary Indian Schools. If the Superintendent General will kindly refer to that communication he will be in possession of the points we wish to present, so far as schools in Ontario are concerned.

In regard to sites for Mission premises on the different Reserves, we have frequently a good deal of trouble with the Indians, growing out of the fact that we have no legal or formal claim to any particular quantity of land. Sooner or later some grievance is sure to crop up, and some Indian will complain that we are occupying more ground than we are entitled to. We desire very much that this unsatisfactory condition of affairs should be ended, and we ask, therefore, that on all Reserves on which we have established missions there should be a distinct understanding reached between the Missionary Society, the resident Indian Agent and the Indian Department, in which the amount of land to be occupied for mission purpose should be clearly defined. Secondly, that the Department should give us a title of occupation (so long as we continue our mission work), protecting us alike from complaints of individual Indians, and also from trespass either by individuals or by the Band. This last request is owing to the fact that in some cases,- Cape Croker, for example,- the Indians have erected some of their own buildings upon land that was set apart for the use of the mission. Thirdly, if for any reason we should deem it expedient to withdraw from any particular Reserve, we desire either that the Department will take our buildings at a price to be fixed by arbitration, or else that we shall have a right to sell the buildings to any other purchaser who may offer to buy them.

II. SCHOOLS, &C, IN THE NORTHWEST TERRITORIES.

In regard to ordinary Indian Schools in the Northwest I beg to refer the Superintendent General to a communication of mine dated July 30th, 1883, in which the various points are presented in detail.

For the efficient carrying out of educational work among the Indians, we think it most important that provision should be made for Boarding Schools, and also for Industrial Institutions, where the children can be kept for a series of years away from the influences which surround them on the Reserves, and we call especial attention to the needs of the Indians in the following locations:

Indian Affairs. (RG 10, Volume 6040, file 160-3A, part 1)

Figure 90: Early church pressure to establish full time residential schools and thereby facilitate control over native children (1888)

1st, Lake Winnipeg. For more than forty years we have been carrying on educational and missionary work among the Bands around this lake, and to the north and east; but nothing has yet been done toward supplying either a boarding school or an industrial institution. We think that the work we have done among the Indians of that region entitles us to the consideration of the Government. 2ndly, Battle River. At the last session of Parliament the sum of $10,000 was voted for an Industrial Institution at Battle River, but so far as we are informed nothing futher has been done. The amount voted is entirely inadequate for an efficient institution, and is in suggestive contrast with the amounts expended on the institutions placed in charge of other religious bodies. 3rdly, the Morley Reserve. The Superintendent General is doubtless aware that an Orphanage and Training School have been established by the Missionary Society. Repeated applications have been made to the Government for buildings and a grant towards maintenance. Hitherto the first part of the request has been refused, while in regard to the second an annual grant of $700 has been made for the past two years, and recently a communication from the Department stated that Parliament would be asked during the present session to grant an amount equal to $60 for each pupil in the Institution. There are very strong reasons why this institution should be enlarged in its scope, and made similar to those at Battleford, High River, Indian Head and Qu'Appelle, and the reasons which have led the Government to give such liberal support to these latter institutions apply with equal if not greater force in the case of Morley.

In regard to sites for mission premises our request is that in all cases they be excluded from the Reserves, so that we may obtain an absolute title to the property.

III. SCHOOLS IN BRITISH COLUMBIA.

What has been said about schools in the Northwest territories will apply, to some extent at least, to schools in British Columbia; but in regard to Industrial or Boarding Schools I would say that we regard an institution of the kind, located in the neighborhood of Chilliwhack in the valley of the Fraser, an urgent necessity. It has been rumored that the Government have in contemplation the establishment of two institutions, one on Vancouver Island and the other on the mainland, but that the latter is not to be located in the valley of the Fraser. I sincerely hope that this will not be the final decision of the Department, and that in the establishment and management of these schools, the work which has been done among the Indians by our Missionary Society will receive practical recognition. In this connection we beg to call attention to the needs of the Indians in the northern part of the province, where nothing has been done by the Government in the way of education, except in certain small grants made to particular mission schools. It is of great importance that some more advanced work be done in that region, especially on the line of industrial pursuits. In this connection I beg to mention the case of the Indian Girls' Home at Port Simpson, which has hitherto been supported exclusively by the voluntary gifts of Christian people. I think this institution is fairly entitled to consideration by the Government, and I hope that when the nature of the enterprise is understood, a grant will be made towards its maintenance.

Any further information I can give touching any of the foregoing points will be cheerfully furnished in a personal interview.

Yours Faithfully,

A. Sutherland

? $400 per annum given by Dept $300 to Mrs [illegible] 100 " [illegible] Underwood

Indian Affairs. (RG 10, Volume 6040, file 160-3A, part 1)

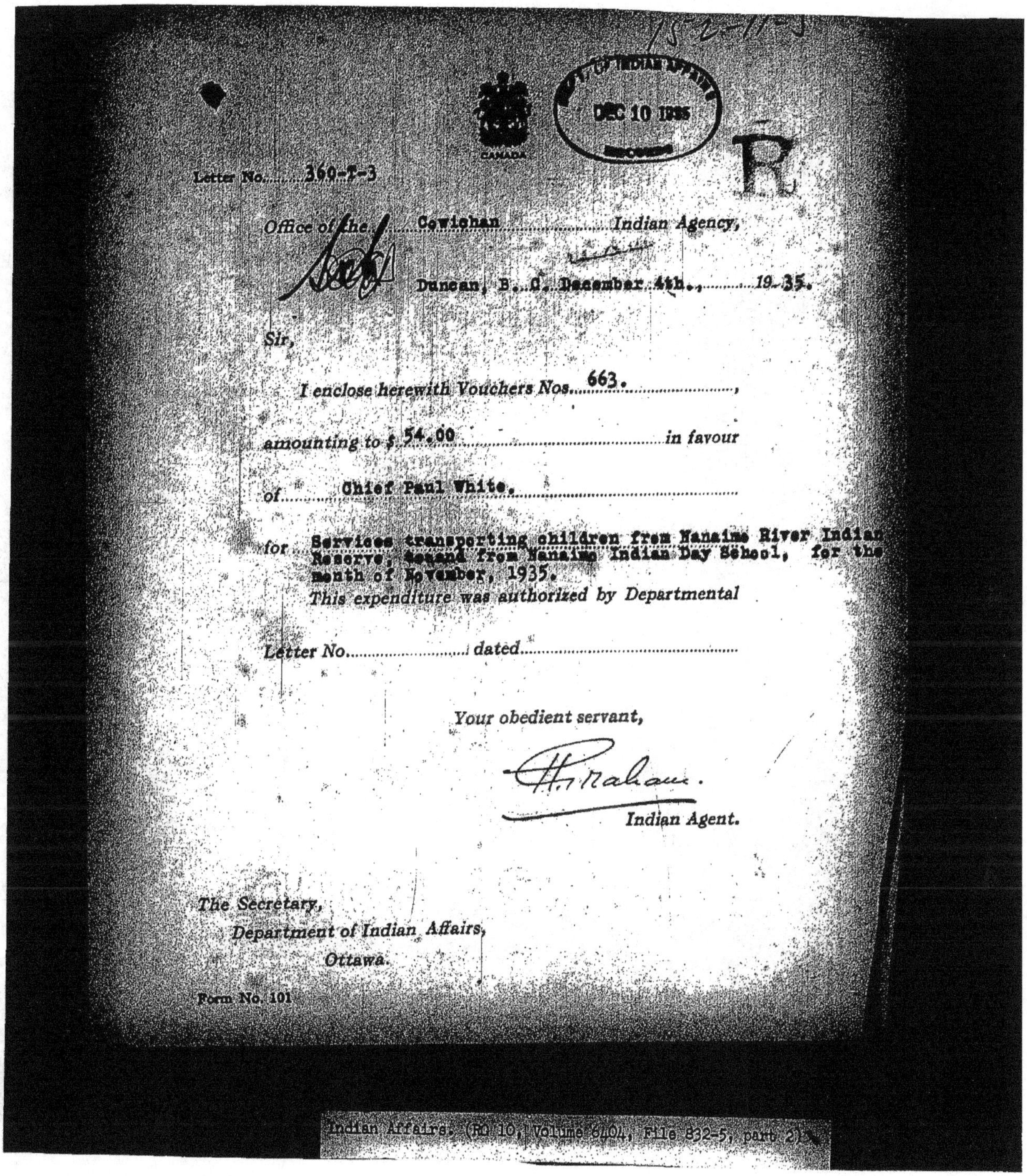

Letter No. 360-T-3

Office of the Cowichan Indian Agency,

Duncan, B. C. December 4th., 19 35.

Sir,

I enclose herewith Vouchers Nos. 663.,

amounting to $ 54.00 in favour

of Chief Paul White.

for Services transporting children from Nanaimo River Indian Reserve, to and from Nanaimo Indian Day School, for the month of November, 1935.

This expenditure was authorized by Departmental

Letter No. dated

Your obedient servant,

Indian Agent.

The Secretary,
Department of Indian Affairs,
Ottawa.

Form No. 101

Indian Affairs. (RG 10, Volume 6404, File 832-5, part 2)

Figure 91: *Aboriginal accomplice* – Payment from government to Vancouver Island tribal "chief" Paul White to transport children from his reservation to the local residential school (1935)

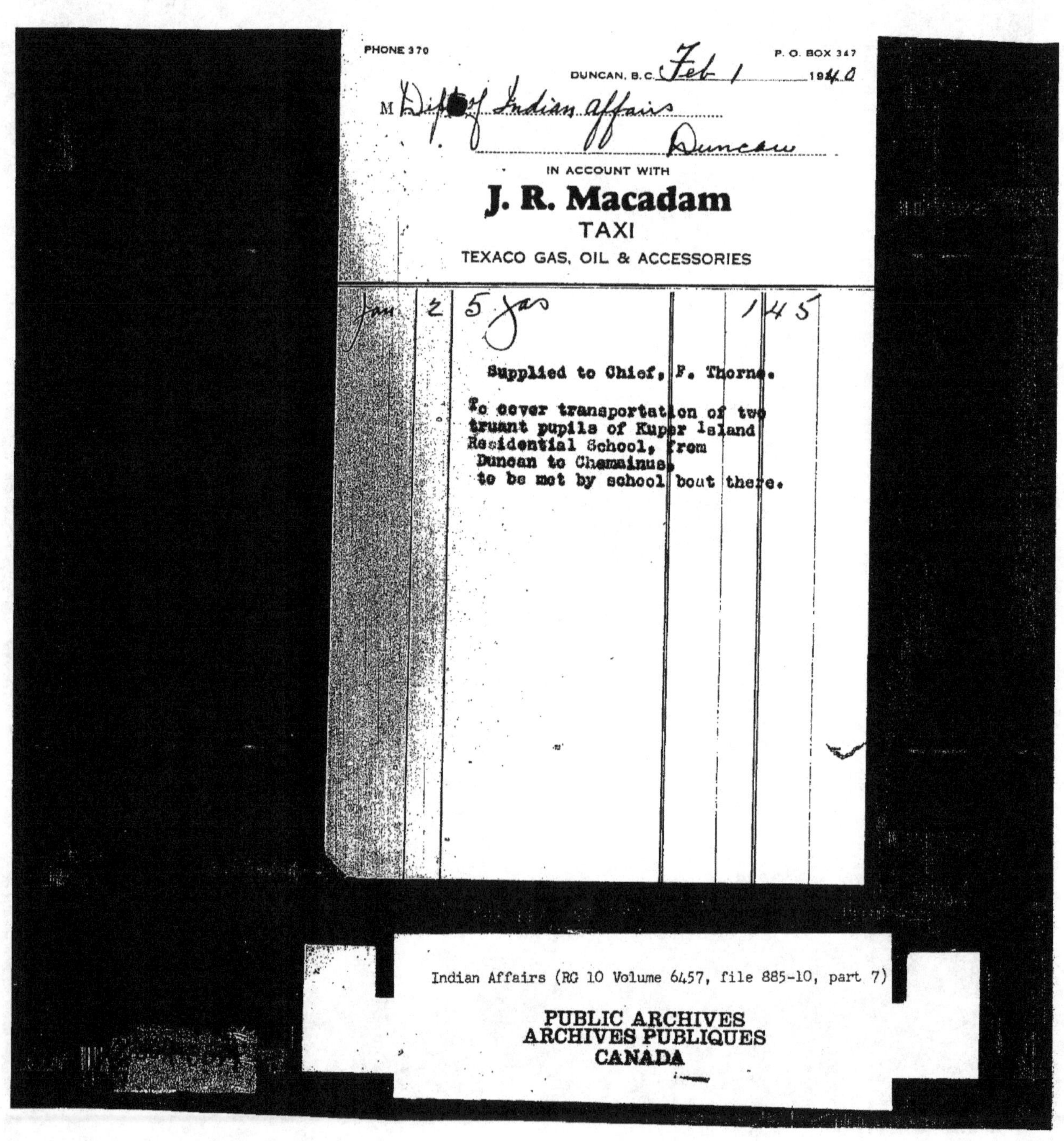

PHONE 370

P. O. BOX 347

DUNCAN, B.C. Feb 1 1940

M Dept of Indian Affairs
Duncan

IN ACCOUNT WITH

J. R. Macadam

TAXI

TEXACO GAS, OIL & ACCESSORIES

Jan	2	5 Jas		1	45

Supplied to Chief, F. Thorne.

To cover transportation of two truant pupils of Kuper Island Residential School, from Duncan to Chemainus, to be met by school boat there.

Indian Affairs (RG 10 Volume 6457, file 885-10, part 7)

PUBLIC ARCHIVES
ARCHIVES PUBLIQUES
CANADA

<u>Figure 92:</u> *Another aboriginal accomplice* – Payment from government to Vancouver Island tribal "chief" F. Thorne to transport children from his reservation to the local residential school (1940)

APPLICATION FOR ADMISSION

To the
Director of Indian Affairs,
Ottawa, Canada

April 15th 1939

Sir,—

I hereby make application for admission of the undermentioned child into the Kuper Island *Residential School; to remain therein under the guardianship of the Principal for such term as the Minister of Mines and Resources may deem proper:*

0432

Indian name of child: Clara Jack
English name: Same
Age: 15
Name of Band: Cowichan (Clemclemaluts)
No. of ticket under which child's annuity is paid:
Father's full name and No.: Joseph Jack
Mother's full name and No.: Justine Edwards
Parents living or dead: Living (seperated)
State of child's health: apparently good
Religion: R.C.
Does applicant speak English?: Yes
Previously attended: Yes school for 2 years

*R. H. Moore for father who is not responsible, child illegitimate
(Signature of father)

NOTE—If mother or guardian signs, agent must forward full explanatory note.

I hereby certify that the above application for admission has been read over and interpreted to the parent or guardian and that the contents were understood by him or her and that I witnessed his or her signature to this document.

Signature of Missionary or other Witness

I recommend the admission of the above child, who is of good moral character and is eligible to be admitted as a grant-earning pupil.

R. H. Moore
Agent

*Principal or other official of the school must not sign as witness.

NOTE—All the above particulars must be fully given, especially the "Name of Band," "No. of ticket under which child's annuity is paid" and "Religion." The minimum age for admission is seven (7) years, except in the case of an orphan, destitute or neglected child. When application is made for the admission of such cases, full particulars should accompany the application.

FORM No. 1-A 406
R 7724

(OVER)

*(note the Indian Agent has signed for the father)

Indian Affairs ... volume 6457, file 885-10, part 6)

ARCHIVES
PUBLIQUES

Figure 93: **The Application for Admission Form making the church-appointed Principal the legal guardian of all residential school children (1939) – *Note that the Indian Agent has signed on behalf of the child's father***

Figure 94: Indian Agent refers to unstated policy of denying higher education to Indian children (1934)

159-1-22

DEPARTMENT OF INDIAN AFFAIRS
CANADA

250/34/S.1.

OFFICE OF
INDIAN AGENT

West Coast Agency,
Port Alberni, B. C.
Aug. 18, 1934.

Sir:-

I have the honour to advise the Department that the Rev. F. E. Pitts, Principal of the Alberni Indian Residential School, today brought to this office a copy of a letter written by him to the Department of Indian Affairs, Ottawa, on the 13th. instant, direct, asking for the Department's authority for pupils Nos. 160 Charlie Watts, 161 Oscar Tom, 191 Eddie Clutesi, 188 Warren Rush and 171 Willie Tatoosh, to attend the Alberni District High School for tuition, and requesting the Department's sanction of an expenditure of $ 50.00 each, school fees, and $ 10.00 each for school books. The pupils to remain on the register of the Alberni Residential School and live and board there. The total cost entailed is $ 300.00.

The ages of the pupils in question are as under:

# 160 Charlie Watts	- 18-	admitted to school.	7. 9.26.
# 161 Oscar Tom	- 18-	" " "	15.10.26.
# 171 Willie Tatoosh	- 16-	" " "	17. 9.27.
# 188 Warren Rush	- 17-	" " "	4. 9.28.
# 191 Eddie Clutesi	- 17-	" " "	20. 9.28.

I have to state that these pupils appear to be above the ordinary run of intelligence, but unless technical training can be given them during the High School training, such as instruction in repairs and operation of internal combustion engines, carpentry and navigation, I fail to see where a High School training is going to benefit them, as all classes of employment are now over stocked with white students, and yearly becoming more so, waiting for opportunities for employment, and it is an indisputable fact that whites always get the preference in employment. I fail to see where a High School training can benefit them other than in the fact that they are better educated than their fellows usually are, or to fit them for enfranchisement. I have to point out that these pupils will be about 22 years old, should they decide to finish their High School training, and will be too old to study further to advantage, even if their financial circumstances were such as to admit them to do so.

I am not making these remarks as pertaining to the above mentioned pupils only, but I consider they apply generally to Indian pupils, at least in this Agency, that being the only one with which I am perfectly familiar.

Your obedient servant,

Ed. E. Frost

EEF/N.

Ed. E. Frost,
Indian Agent.

The Secretary,
Department of Indian Affairs,
Ottawa.

(enlargement)

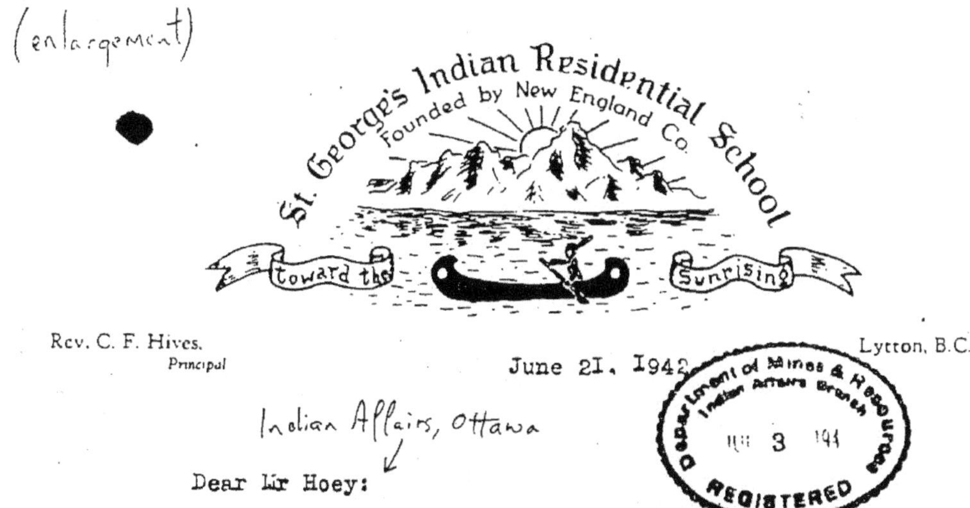

St. George's Indian Residential School
Founded by New England Co.
toward the
Sunrising

Rev. C. F. Hives,
Principal

Lytton, B.C.

June 21, 1942

Department of Mines & Resources
Indian Affairs Branch
3
REGISTERED

Indian Affairs, Ottawa

Dear Mr Hoey:

Many thanks for your letter received today. (manacles) → The little present enclosed with this letter will surprise you, wont it? But it a relic of the past administration of St. George's. Lytton. Not during the administration of Mr Lett, I am happy to say, but not so many years ago. I was talking to a man the day before yesterday, who was a pupil of the school, when they were in use. And although he assured me he has never been a victim, yet he had seen them used on boys and girls. He said two girls ran away, and they were chained together and driven home in front of the Principal. They used the shackles to chain runnaways to the bed. They also had stocks in the playgrounds. And they were used.

I am telling you this, because I want you to know how very much has to be irradicated from the memories of these people, before they will develope confidence in the administration of this school. And until that confidence is developed, very little will be done in the matter of autonomy and pupil organization. It will come. I know it will come, by God's help. After I came here. I looked into the matter of forming groupes and placing captains and their respective assistants at the head of each groupe of 12 boys. The Sr. Teacher said it could never work. He ridiculed the idea, and gave no support or encouragement to the movement. He has gone, and rightly so. I have kept the idea alive, and the Captains have been recognised. Recognised by the payment to them of one dollar a month, and I know it will succeed. During the last six months, I have tried to teach my boys just one thing: A sense of Honour. Toward the end of the term, they were just beginning to realize a little of the glory of it. And next term they will realize more.

After years and years of mal-administration, please dont look for definite results too quickly from St.

Figure 95: Reference to the use of shackles and public stocks at the St. George Anglican residential school in Lytton, British Columbia (1942)

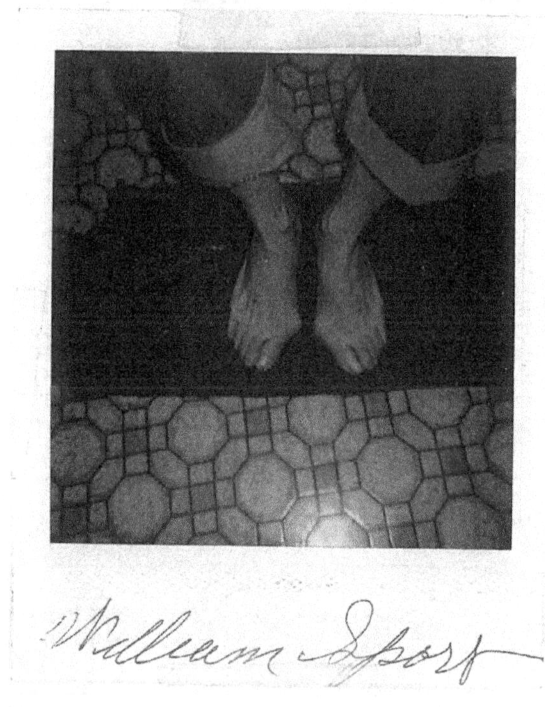

Figure 96: Feet of Alberni school survivor Willie Sport, deliberately deformed to prevent his escaping (1998)

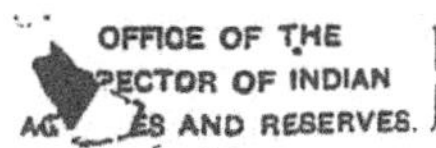

OFFICE OF THE INSPECTOR OF INDIAN AGENCIES AND RESERVES.

Department of Indian Affairs,

ADDRESS REPLY TO
Inspector of Indian Agencies
OTTAWA.

Ottawa, 6th February, 1903.

Sir,

I have just completed my annual examination of such vital and mortal statistics relating to the Indians of my Inspectorate as are available and it becomes my duty to direct your attention to the conclusions arrived at. In doing this please allow me to refer you to former communications of mine in respect to disease, and to the reports furnished me by Doctors Mitchell and Constantine in regard to tuberculosis. These are on file.

I have before pointed out that the Indian death-rate is terribly high; that our medical advisers attribute the frightful mortality largely to tuberculous affections; that such advisers as Doctors Montizambert, Bryce, Gorrell and many others whom I have consulted, entertain a firm belief that the mortality might be largely reduced without any great expense; that our medical, vital and mortal returns are most imperfect; that in my opinion, we are taking no effective steps to reduce the death-rate; and that skilled supervision and proper organization of our medical service is very much needed.

Submitted herewith are some statements con-

structed

The Deputy Superintendent General
of Indian Affairs,

from Dr. T. McRae Indian Affairs medical inspector

Figure 97: Medical Inspector's claim that no steps are being taken by government to reduce the Indian school death rate (1903)

C. J. FAGAN, M. D.,
SECRETARY.

PROVINCIAL BOARD OF HEALTH,

VICTORIA, B. C., July 7th, 1909.

Dr. J. H. Bryce,
Chief Medical Officer,
Department of the Interior,
OTTAWA.

Dear Sir,

I am in receipt of many complaints regarding Kuper Island Indian School.

The complaints are that the Institution is not properly constructed and that the location in which the school is placed is unhealthy.

I have had many statements sent to me that healthy children have contracted Consumption in this place and I certainly think it is someone's duty to look into the conditions existing at Kuper Island.

What is being done regarding the checking of Tuberculosis among the Indians? That the disease is rapidly increasing there is no doubt. You know better than I do the habits and customs of the Indians and if matters are allowed to proceed, as they are proceeding to-day, it will be be but a short time before the Indians are wiped out of existence by this disease.

The question of the health of the Indians is, of course, not within my province to deal with, but their intercourse with the white population is one that concerns me intimately and I, therefore, appeal tp you to have some action taken, so that the spread of Consumption from the Indian population to the white people will be checked.

Figure 98: Similar warning by a Vancouver Island doctor that Indians may be wiped out by tuberculosis (1909)

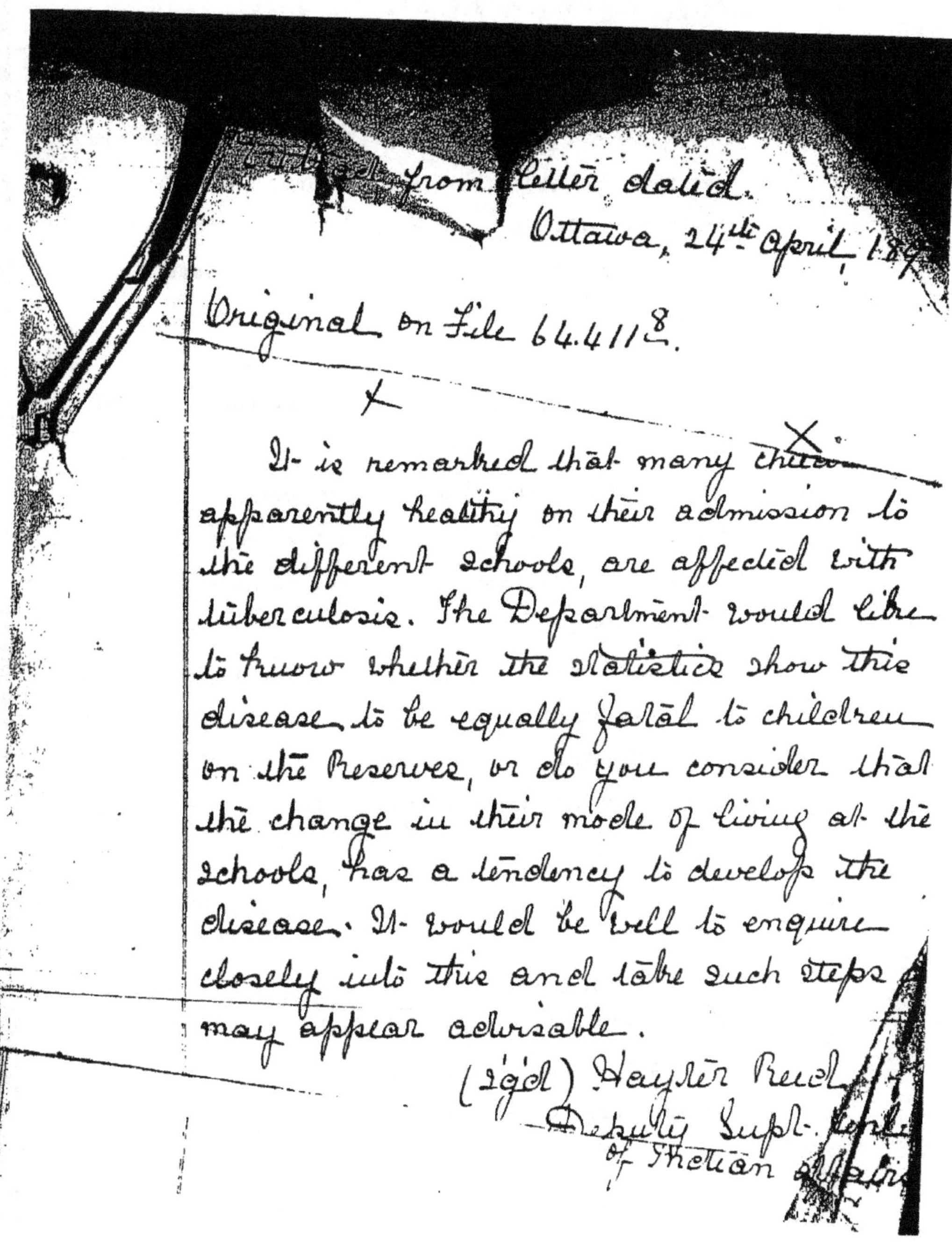

Extract from letter dated.
Ottawa, 24th April, 189

Original on File 64.411 8.

It is remarked that many children apparently healthy on their admission to the different schools, are affected with tuberculosis. The Department would like to know whether the statistics show this disease to be equally fatal to children on the Reserves, or do you consider that the change in their mode of living at the schools, has a tendency to develop the disease. It would be well to enquire closely into this and take such steps may appear advisable.

(sgd) Hayter Reed
Deputy Supt. Genl.
of Indian Affairs

Figure 99: Indian Affairs official observes that healthy Indian children become sick with tuberculosis after entering residential schools (1896)

2.

Corpl. Clearwater, R.C.M.P.

June 13, (1922)

Cpl. Clearwater to RCMP Command, Prince Rupert

We arrived at Kitimat June 4th. and found only five pupils in the Boarding School.

The next day a meeting was held with the natives, at which also were present: Miss Ida Clarke, the principal, Miss S.E.Alton, field matron, Rev. E.Couldray, missionary, constables Clearwater and Sutherland, besides the Indian agent.

Several Indians spoke and complained that the school was injurious to the health of the pupils, that there was not proper medical service, and that the children were not properly fed or clothed. One made the statement that of all the girls who had attended the school 49 have died, and 50 are alive.

Miss Clarke, the principal, and Miss Alton, the field matron replied to the charges of the Indians. Corpl. Clearwater, and the Indian agent also spoke to the meeting of the rights of the Indians to make complaints, if they had cause for it; but they should not take the matter in their own hands: that both the Indians and the school had rights that must be respected. On behalf of the Department I promised the natives that a physician would visit the school after the fishing season, and examine the children, and sanitary conditions in the school.

The Indians at last agreed to return the children to the school, if the principal would sign a paper that the children would be properly fed.

Figure 100: Reference to a fifty percent death rate among children at a west coast Indian school from a report issued by RCMP Constable Clearwater (1922)

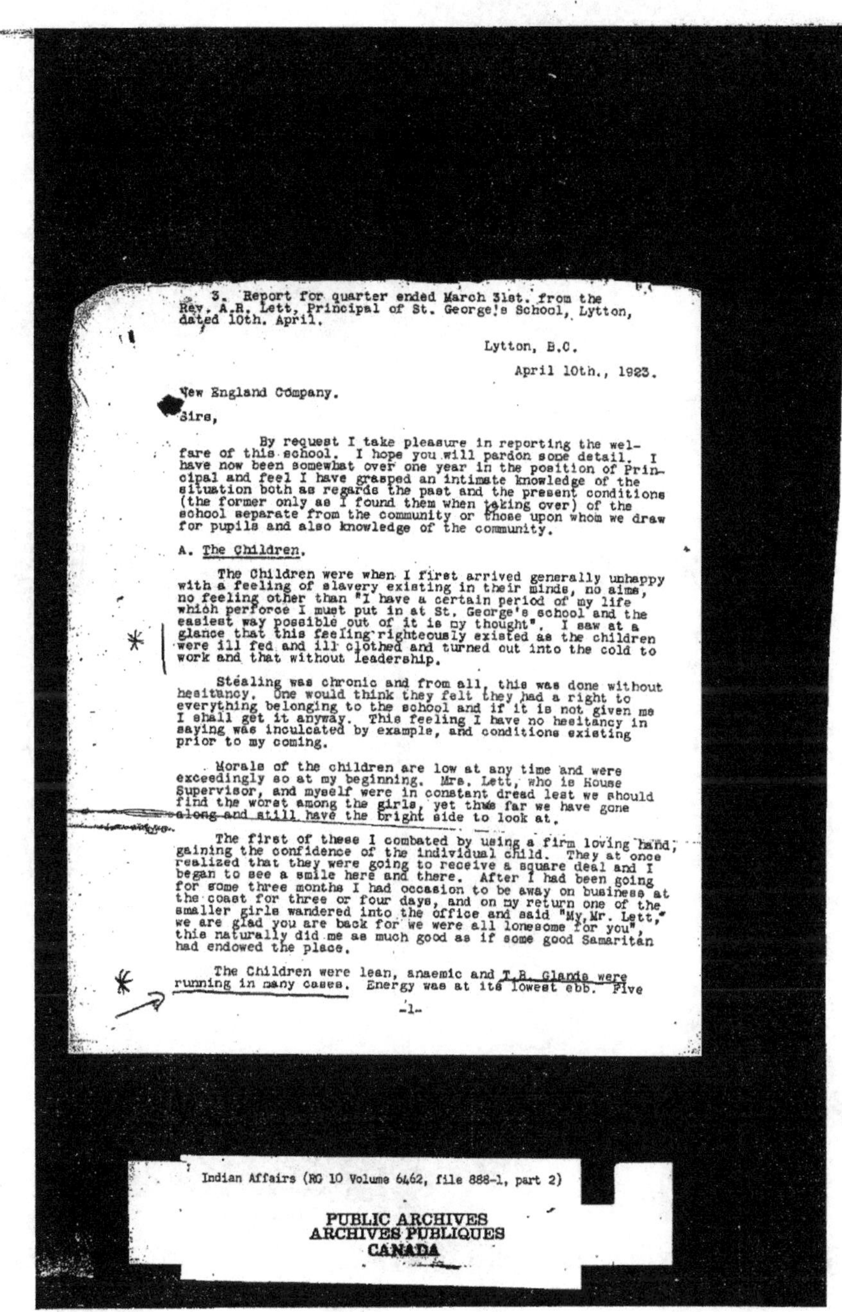

3. Report for quarter ended March 31st. from the Rev. A.R. Lett, Principal of St. George's School, Lytton, dated 10th. April.

Lytton, B.C.

April 10th., 1923.

New England Company.

Sirs,

By request I take pleasure in reporting the welfare of this school. I hope you will pardon some detail. I have now been somewhat over one year in the position of Principal and feel I have grasped an intimate knowledge of the situation both as regards the past and the present conditions (the former only as I found them when taking over) of the school separate from the community or those upon whom we draw for pupils and also knowledge of the community.

A. The Children.

The Children were when I first arrived generally unhappy with a feeling of slavery existing in their minds, no aims, no feeling other than "I have a certain period of my life which perforce I must put in at St. George's school and the easiest way possible out of it is my thought". I saw at a glance that this feeling righteously existed as the children were ill fed and ill clothed and turned out into the cold to work and that without leadership.

Stealing was chronic and from all, this was done without hesitancy. One would think they felt they had a right to everything belonging to the school and if it is not given me I shall get it anyway. This feeling I have no hesitancy in saying was inculcated by example, and conditions existing prior to my coming.

Morals of the children are low at any time and were exceedingly so at my beginning. Mrs. Lett, who is House Supervisor, and myself were in constant dread lest we should find the worst among the girls, yet thus far we have gone along and still have the bright side to look at.

The first of these I combated by using a firm loving hand, gaining the confidence of the individual child. They at once realized that they were going to receive a square deal and I began to see a smile here and there. After I had been going for some three months I had occasion to be away on business at the coast for three or four days, and on my return one of the smaller girls wandered into the office and said "My, Mr. Lett, we are glad you are back for we were all lonesome for you", this naturally did me as much good as if some good Samaritan had endowed the place.

The Children were lean, anaemic and T.B. Glands were running in many cases. Energy was at its lowest ebb. Five

-1-

Indian Affairs (RG 10 Volume 6462, file 888-1, part 2)

Figure 101: Admission by Principal of St. George Anglican Indian school that children had open tubercular sores (1923)

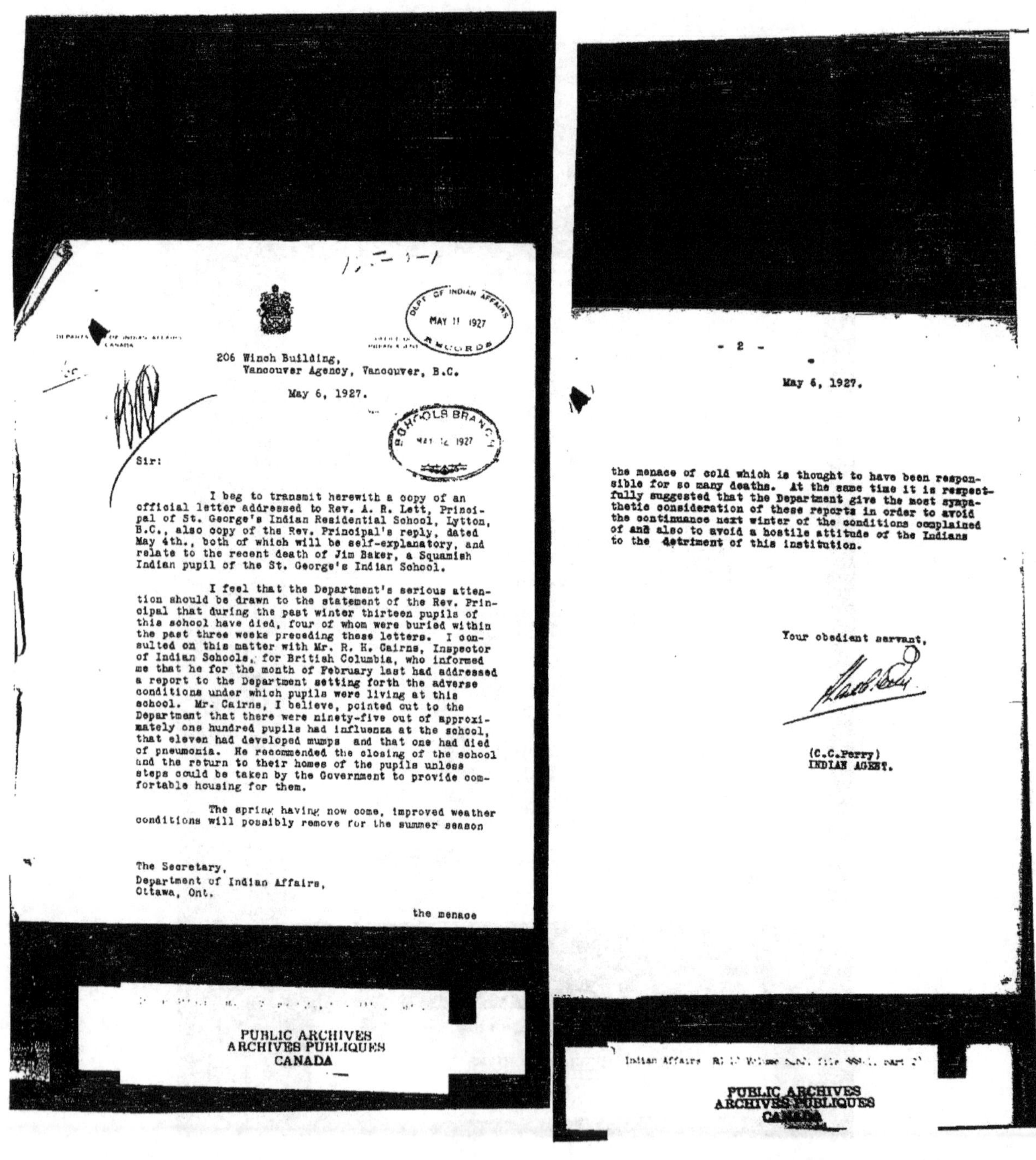

206 Winch Building,
Vancouver Agency, Vancouver, B.C.

May 6, 1927.

Sir:

I beg to transmit herewith a copy of an official letter addressed to Rev. A. R. Lett, Principal of St. George's Indian Residential School, Lytton, B.C., also copy of the Rev. Principal's reply, dated May 4th., both of which will be self-explanatory, and relate to the recent death of Jim Baker, a Squamish Indian pupil of the St. George's Indian School.

I feel that the Department's serious attention should be drawn to the statement of the Rev. Principal that during the past winter thirteen pupils of this school have died, four of whom were buried within the past three weeks preceding these letters. I consulted on this matter with Mr. R. H. Cairns, Inspector of Indian Schools, for British Columbia, who informed me that he for the month of February last had addressed a report to the Department setting forth the adverse conditions under which pupils were living at this school. Mr. Cairns, I believe, pointed out to the Department that there were ninety-five out of approximately one hundred pupils had influenza at the school, that eleven had developed mumps and that one had died of pneumonia. He recommended the closing of the school and the return to their homes of the pupils unless steps could be taken by the Government to provide comfortable housing for them.

The spring having now come, improved weather conditions will possibly remove for the summer season

The Secretary,
Department of Indian Affairs,
Ottawa, Ont.

the menace

\- 2 -

May 6, 1927.

the menace of cold which is thought to have been responsible for so many deaths. At the same time it is respectfully suggested that the Department give the most sympathetic consideration of these reports in order to avoid the continuance next winter of the conditions complained of and also to avoid a hostile attitude of the Indians to the detriment of this institution.

Your obedient servant,

(C.C.Perry)
INDIAN AGENT.

Figure 102: Report on the death of thirteen children during the winter, St. George school (1927)

COPY

Ahousaht, January 30th, 1929.

RECEIVED
FEB 8 1929
INDIAN AGENT'S OFFICE
Port Alberni, B.C.

E.E.Frost, Esqr,
Indian Agent,
Port Alberni.B.C.

Dear Mr, Frost,

Following your recent visit to and inspection of the Ahousaht Indian School premises, I am enclosing a copy of the statement then drawn up, setting out conditions and needs as they appear et this time, and proposing certain solutions.

May I say that I have conferred with the School Staff, all of whom have longer acquaintanse than I with these conditions, and they are agreed that the statement is a fair, and accurate representation of conditions now obtaining, and that such reforms as are proposed are vitally and urgently necessary, if results are to be expected in the training of children here.

In facing the solution of these problems I recognize the factor of dual control;- a church organization on the one hand and the Indian Department on the other. I may tell you that I am putting before the Women,s Missionary Society and the Home Mission Board with which they are associated, the necessity of their undertaking a substancial share of the cost. To be specific, I am urging them to become responsible for the cost of the well, the engine and engine house- the most immediately urgent of our needs,-and if possible also the kitchen range, which roughly might perhaps be estimated at $ 750.00.

If they can- and I am somewhat hopeful they may, undertake this, then I think it reasonable to hope that the Indian Department will undertake the instalation of the water system, including toilets, and a heating plant for the building.

Recognizing, as I am sure you do, that the school cannot do effective work until these basic conditions, not of luxury, but of elementary decency and comfort are met, I hope you will press upon the Department the urgency of the need. It is not only that a measure of discomfort results to both Staff and children, which is a handicap to efficiency, the matter is far more cerious than that, The nature of the present water supply and the so called toilet system is a positive menace to health, To house forty children in a damp building where they are often chilled and shivering is to make them fertile ground for disease. And it is not to be wondered at that there has been in recent years a very unusual number of deaths and discharges from school due to physical ailments, nor that at the present time the proportion of thoroughly healthy children in the school is alarmingly low. I am convinced that if we can give them pure water, claen toilets and housing in which the chill and dampness are removed we can change the health situation for the better in a single season.

I am communicating also with the Commissioner and the Department, and ernestly hope that some action may be secured in the near future, With very cordial appreciation of your interest in the well being of the school.

I am yours truly,
(sd) Wm. R. Wood,
Principal.

Figure 103: Damning report of conditions at Ahousaht United Church Indian school (1929)

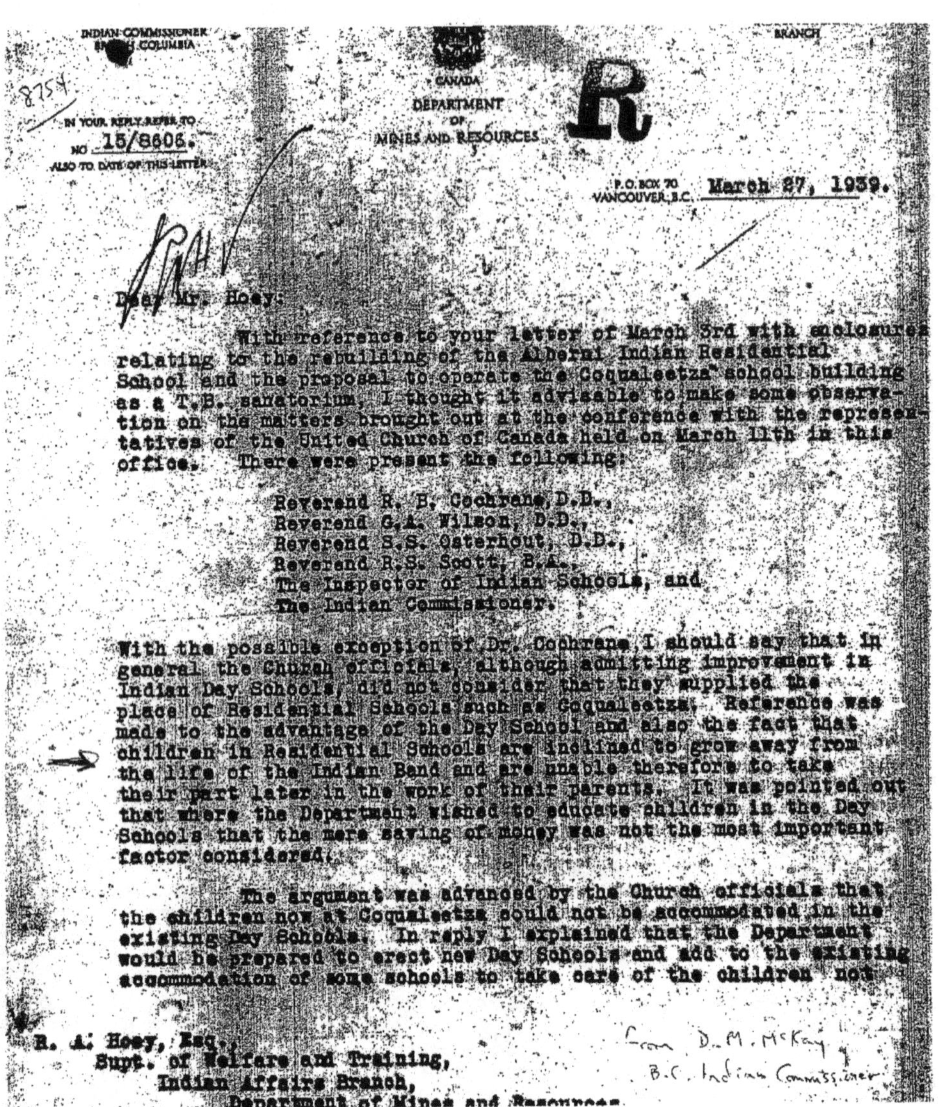

INDIAN COMMISSIONER BRITISH COLUMBIA

CANADA
DEPARTMENT OF MINES AND RESOURCES

BRANCH

IN YOUR REPLY REFER TO
NO. 15/8606.
ALSO TO DATE OF THIS LETTER

P.O. BOX 70
VANCOUVER, B.C. March 27, 1939.

Dear Mr. Hoey:

With reference to your letter of March 3rd with enclosures relating to the rebuilding of the Alberni Indian Residential School and the proposal to operate the Coqualeetza school building as a T.B. sanatorium, I thought it advisable to make some observation on the matters brought out at the conference with the representatives of the United Church of Canada held on March 11th in this office. There were present the following:

Reverend R. B. Cochrane, D.D.,
Reverend G.A. Wilson, D.D.,
Reverend S.S. Osterhout, D.D.,
Reverend R.S. Scott, B.A.
The Inspector of Indian Schools, and
The Indian Commissioner.

With the possible exception of Dr. Cochrane I should say that in general the Church officials, although admitting improvement in Indian Day Schools, did not consider that they supplied the place of Residential Schools such as Coqualeetza. Reference was made to the advantage of the Day School and also the fact that children in Residential Schools are inclined to grow away from the life of the Indian Band and are unable therefore to take their part later in the work of their parents. It was pointed out that where the Department wished to educate children in the Day Schools that the mere saving of money was not the most important factor considered.

The argument was advanced by the Church officials that the children now at Coqualeetza could not be accommodated in the existing Day Schools. In reply I explained that the Department would be prepared to erect new Day Schools and add to the existing accommodation of some schools to take care of the children not

R. A. Hoey, Esq.,
Supt. of Welfare and Training,
Indian Affairs Branch,
Department of Mines and Resources.

From D. M. McKay
B.C. Indian Commissioner

Figure 104: Admission at a conference of United Church officials of the destructive long term effects of residential schools on aboriginal families (1939)

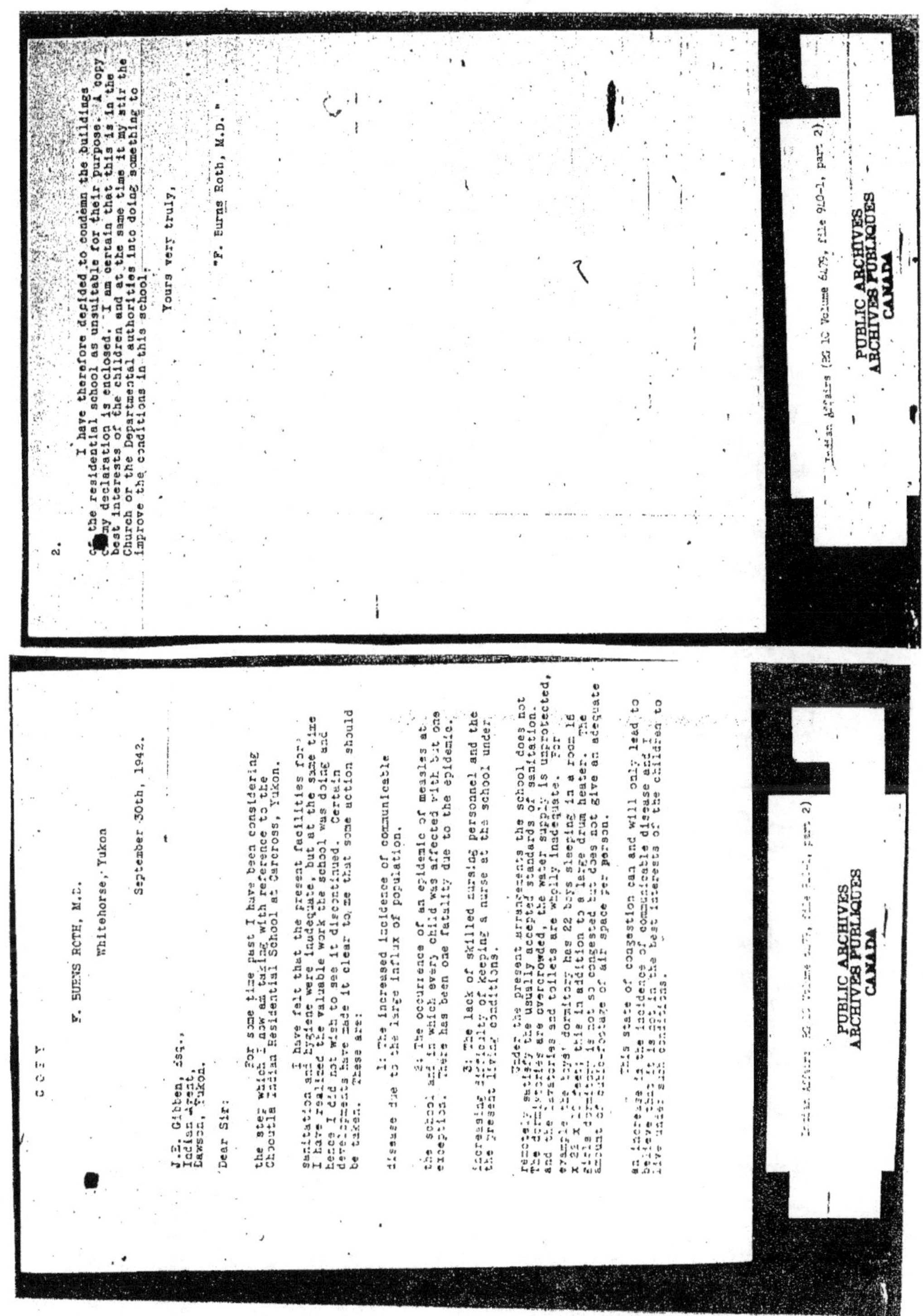

COPY

F. BURNS ROTH, M.D.

Whitehorse, Yukon

September 30th, 1942.

J.E. Gibben, Esq.,
Indian Agent,
Dawson, Yukon.

Dear Sir:

For some time past I have been considering the step which I now am taking with reference to the Chooutla Indian Residential School at Carcross, Yukon.

I have felt that the present facilities for sanitation and hygiene were inadequate, but at the same time I have realized the valuable work the school was doing and hence I did not wish to see it discontinued. Certain developments have made it clear to me that some action should be taken. These are:

1: The increased incidence of communicable disease due to the large influx of population.

2: The occurrence of an epidemic of measles at the school and in which every child was affected with but one exception. There has been one fatality due to the epidemic.

3: The lack of skilled nursing personnel and the increasing difficulty of keeping a nurse at the school under the present living conditions.

Under the present arrangements the school does not remotely satisfy the usually accepted standards of sanitation. The dormitories are overcrowded, the water supply is unprotected, and the lavatories and toilets are wholly inadequate. For example the boys' dormitory has 22 boys sleeping in a room 16 x 22 x [illegible] feet; this in addition to a large drum heater. The girls dormitory is not so congested but does not give an adequate amount of cubic-footage of air space per person.

This state of congestion can and will only lead to an increase in the incidence of communicable disease and I believe that it is not in the best interests of the children to live under such conditions.

Indian Affairs (RG 10 Volume 6479, file 940-1, part 2)

PUBLIC ARCHIVES
ARCHIVES PUBLIQUES
CANADA

2.

I have therefore decided to condemn the buildings of the residential school as unsuitable for their purpose. A copy of my declaration is enclosed. I am certain that this is in the best interests of the children and at the same time it my stir the Church or the Departmental authorities into doing something to improve the conditions in this school.

Yours very truly,

"F. Burns Roth, M.D."

Indian Affairs (RG 10 Volume 6479, file 940-1, part 2)

PUBLIC ARCHIVES
ARCHIVES PUBLIQUES
CANADA

Figure 105: Condemning of Carcross Anglican school by health official for sanitation reasons (1942)

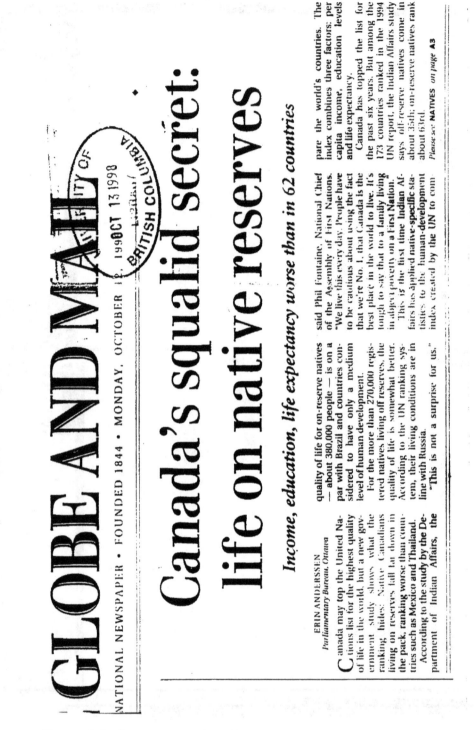

GLOBE AND MAIL

NATIONAL NEWSPAPER • FOUNDED 1844 • MONDAY, OCTOBER 12, 1998

Canada's squalid secret: life on native reserves

Income, education, life expectancy worse than in 62 countries

ERIN ANDERSSEN
Parliamentary Bureau, Ottawa

Canada may top the United Nations list for the highest quality of life in the world, but a new government study shows what the ranking hides: Native Canadians living on reserves fall far down in the pack, ranking worse than countries such as Mexico and Thailand.

According to the study by the Department of Indian Affairs, the quality of life for on-reserve natives — about 380,000 people — is on a par with Brazil and countries considered to have only a medium level of human development.

For the more than 270,000 registered natives living off reserves, the quality of life is somewhat better. According to the UN ranking system, their living conditions are in line with Russia.

"This is not a surprise for us," said Phil Fontaine, National Chief of the Assembly of First Nations. "We live this every day. People have to be cautious about using the fact that we're No. 1, that Canada is the best place in the world to live. It's tough to say that to a family living in abject poverty on a First Nation."

This is the first time Indian Affairs has applied native-specific statistics to the human-development index created by the UN to compare the world's countries. The index combines three factors: per capita income, education levels and life expectancy.

Canada has topped the list for the past six years. But among the 173 countries ranked in the 1994 UN report, the Indian Affairs study says off-reserve natives come in about 35th; on-reserve natives rank about 63rd.

Please see NATIVES *on page* A3

Figure 106: Media report on third world conditions facing Canadian aboriginals (1998)

ada Communicable Disease Report CCDR

able of Contents]

Volume: 24S2 - June 1998

Proceedings of the National Consensus Conference on Tuberculosis
December 3-5, 1997

Figure 4: Crude Rates of Reported Tuberculosis Cases in Canada by Population Subgroup, 1985

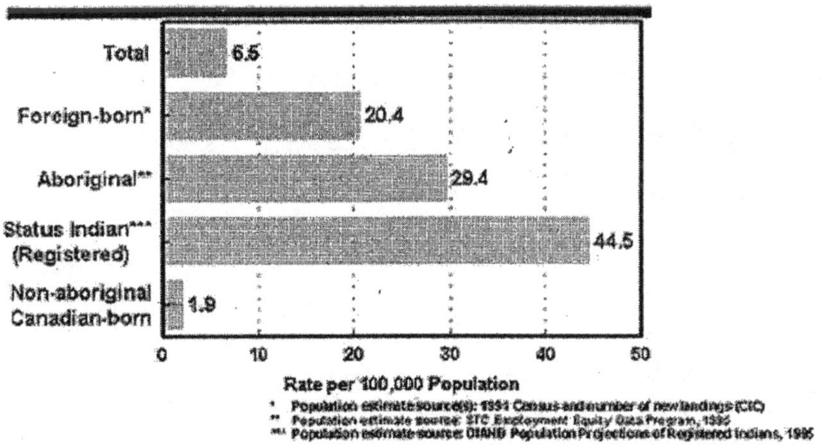

Total 6.5
Foreign-born* 20.4
Aboriginal** 29.4
Status Indian*** (Registered) 44.5
Non-aboriginal Canadian-born 1.9

0 10 20 30 40 50
Rate per 100,000 Population

* Population estimate source(s): 1991 Census and number of new landings (CIC)
** Population estimate source: STC Employment Equity Data Program, 1991
*** Population estimate source: DIAND Population Projections of Registered Indians, 1985

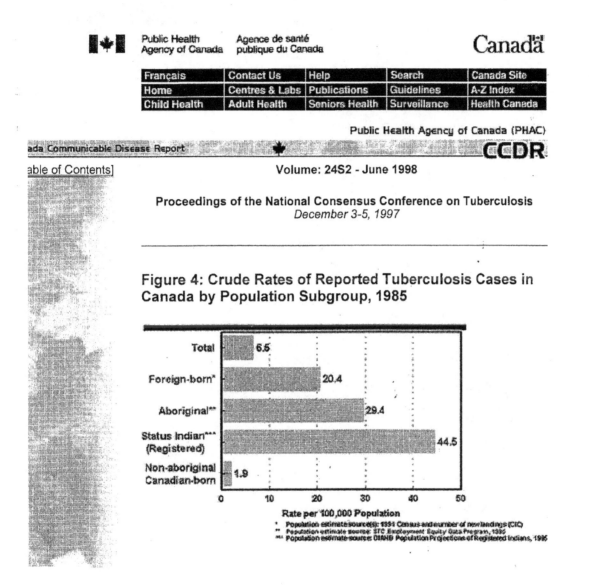

Figure 107: Statistics on the ongoing high rate of tuberculosis among Indians in Canada (1998)

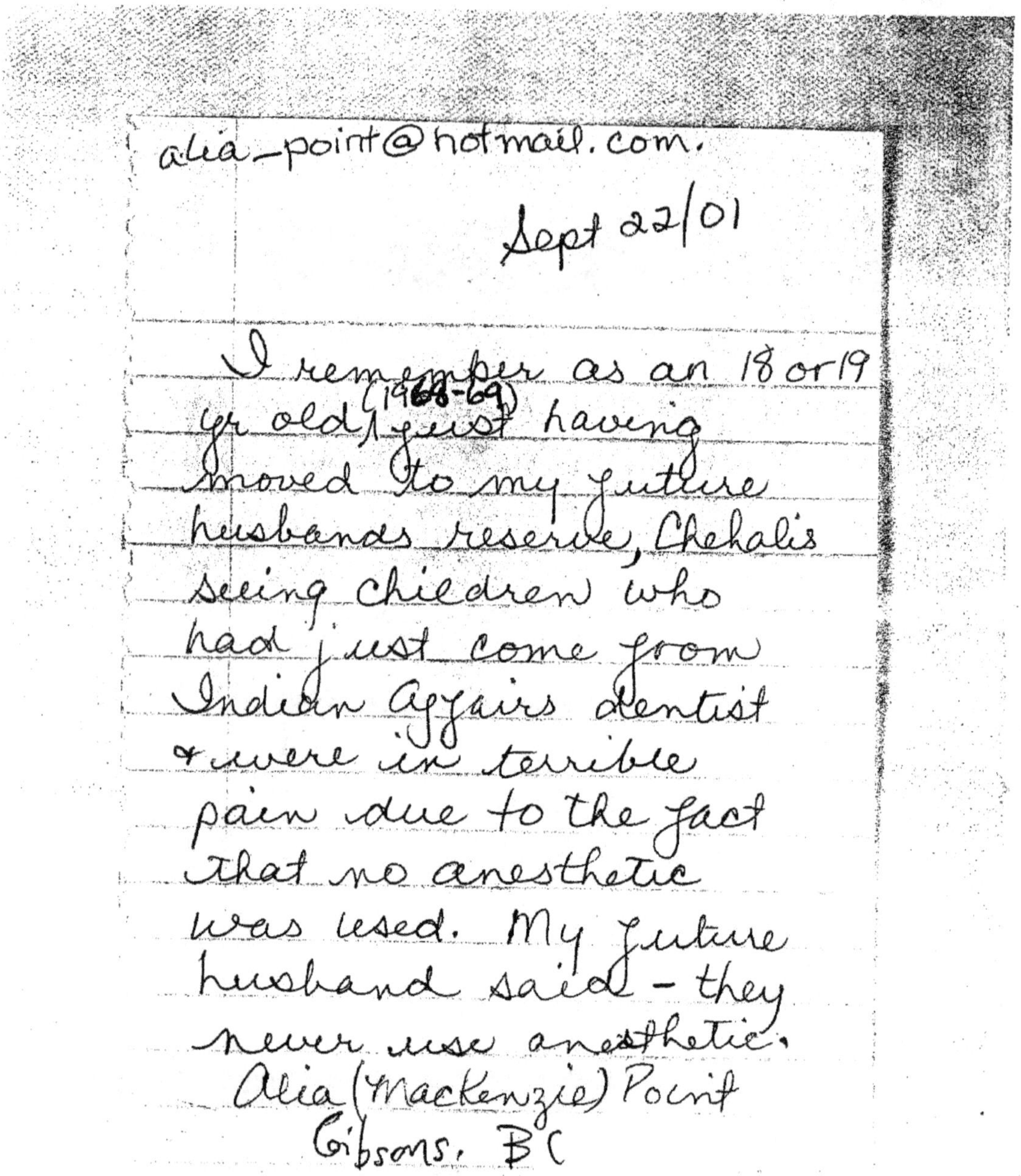

alia_point@hotmail.com.

Sept 22/01

I remember as an 18 or 19 yr old (1968-69) just having moved to my future husbands reserve, Chehalis seeing children who had just come from Indian Affairs dentist & were in terrible pain due to the fact that no anesthetic was used. My future husband said - they never use anesthetic.

Alia (MacKenzie) Point
Gibsons, BC

Figure 108: Testimony of Alia Point concerning the non-use of anesthesia by dentists on reservations (2001)

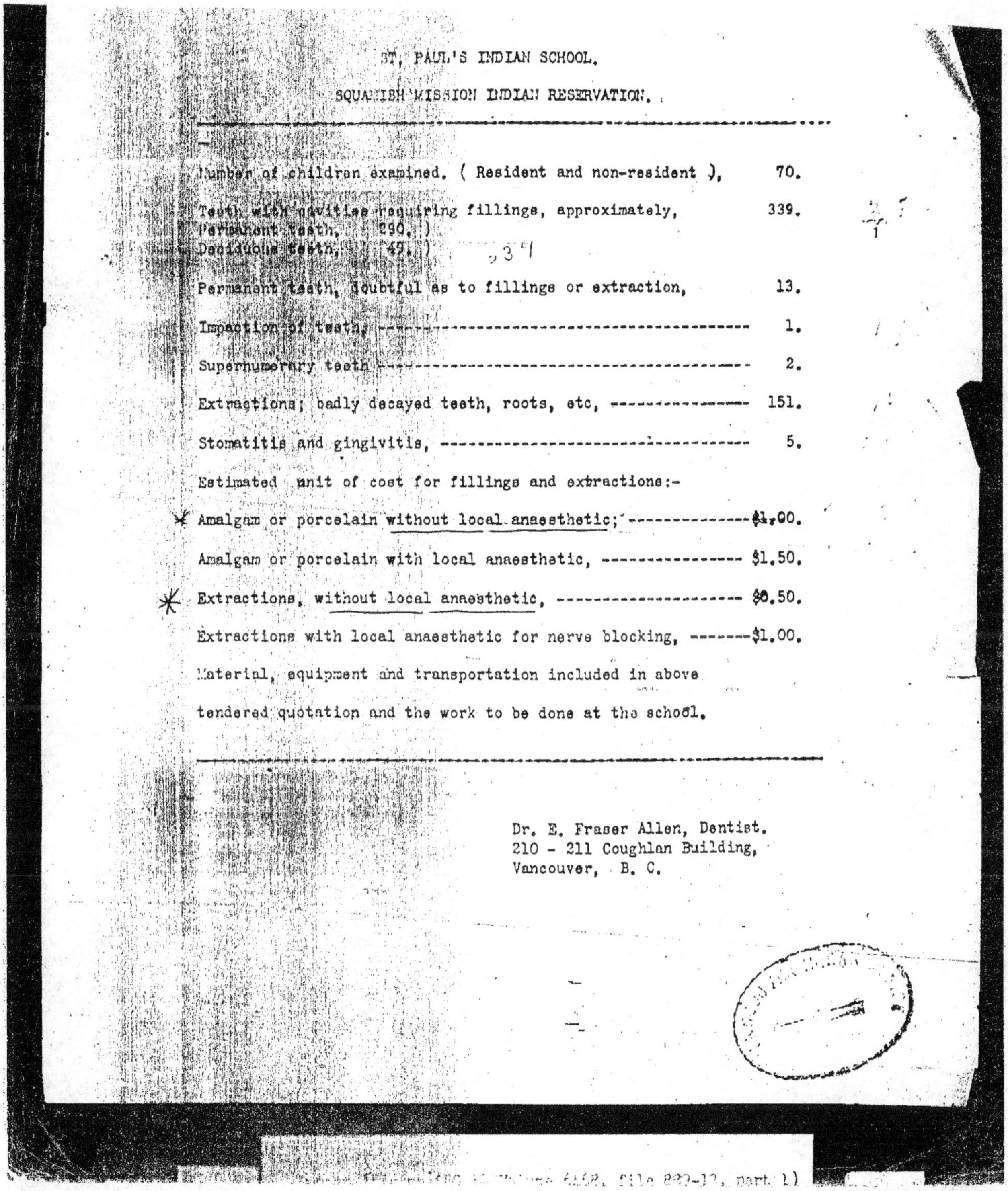

ST. PAUL'S INDIAN SCHOOL.

SQUAMISH MISSION INDIAN RESERVATION.

Number of children examined. (Resident and non-resident),	70.
Teeth with cavities requiring fillings, approximately, Permanent teeth, 290.) Deciduous teeth, 49.) 339	339.
Permanent teeth, doubtful as to fillings or extraction,	13.
Impaction of teeth, --	1.
Supernumerary teeth --	2.
Extractions; badly decayed teeth, roots, etc, -----------------	151.
Stomatitis and gingivitis, -----------------------------------	5.

Estimated unit of cost for fillings and extractions:-

* Amalgam or porcelain without local anaesthetic; --------------	$1.00.
Amalgam or porcelain with local anaesthetic, ----------------	$1.50.
* Extractions, without local anaesthetic, --------------------	$0.50.
Extractions with local anaesthetic for nerve blocking, -------	$1.00.

Material, equipment and transportation included in above tendered quotation and the work to be done at the school.

Dr. E. Fraser Allen, Dentist.
210 - 211 Coughlan Building,
Vancouver, B. C.

[illegible] 6468, file [illegible], part 1)

Figure 109: Annotated record of dentist who used anesthesia only selectively on aboriginal children at St. Paul's reservation, Vancouver (1924)

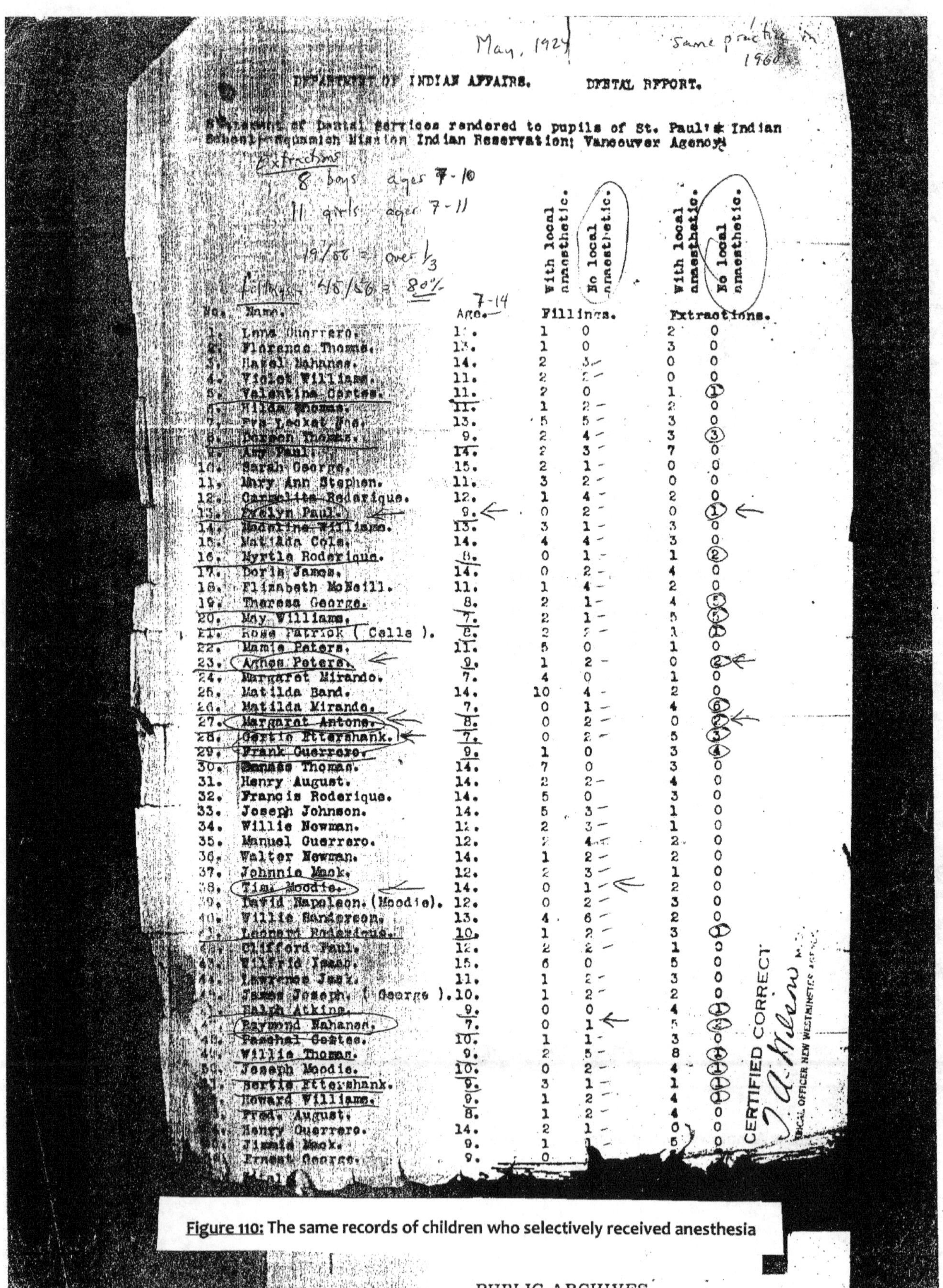

May, 1924 — same practice in 1960s

DEPARTMENT OF INDIAN AFFAIRS. DENTAL REPORT.

Statement of Dental services rendered to pupils of St. Paul's Indian School, Squamish Mission Indian Reservation; Vancouver Agency.

Extractions
8 boys ages 7-10
11 girls ages 7-11
19/56 = over 1/3
Fillings 45/56 = 80%

No.	Name.	Age. (7-14)	Fillings. With local anaesthetic.	Fillings. No local anaesthetic.	Extractions. With local anaesthetic.	Extractions. No local anaesthetic.
1.	Lena Guerrero.	1[illegible].	1	0	2	0
2.	Florence Thomas.	1[illegible].	1	0	3	0
3.	Hazel Nahanee.	14.	2	3	0	0
4.	Violet Williams.	11.	2	2	0	0
5.	Valentina Cortes.	11.	2	0	1	1
6.	Hilda Thomas.	11.	1	2	2	0
7.	Eva Lockat Joe.	13.	5	5	3	0
8.	Doreen Thomas.	9.	2	4	3	3
9.	Amy Paul.	14.	2	3	7	0
10.	Sarah George.	15.	2	1	0	0
11.	Mary Ann Stephen.	11.	3	2	0	0
12.	Carmelita Roderique.	12.	1	4	2	0
13.	Evelyn Paul.	9.	0	2	0	1
14.	Madeline Williams.	13.	3	1	3	0
15.	Matilda Cole.	14.	4	4	3	0
16.	Myrtle Roderique.	8.	0	1	1	2
17.	Doris James.	14.	0	2	4	0
18.	Elizabeth McNeill.	11.	1	4	2	0
19.	Theresa George.	8.	2	1	4	5
20.	May Williams.	7.	2	1	5	5
21.	Rose Patrick (Celia).	8.	2	2	1	1
22.	Mamie Peters.	11.	5	0	1	0
23.	Agnes Peters.	9.	1	2	0	2
24.	Margaret Mirando.	7.	4	0	1	0
25.	Matilda Band.	14.	10	4	2	0
26.	Matilda Mirando.	7.	0	1	4	6
27.	Margaret Antone.	8.	0	2	0	2
28.	Gertie Ettershank.	7.	0	2	5	3
29.	Frank Guerrero.	9.	1	0	3	4
30.	Dennis Thomas.	14.	7	0	3	0
31.	Henry August.	14.	2	2	4	0
32.	Francis Roderique.	14.	5	0	3	0
33.	Joseph Johnson.	14.	5	3	1	0
34.	Willie Newman.	1[illegible].	2	3	1	0
35.	Manuel Guerrero.	12.	[illegible]	4	2	0
36.	Walter Newman.	14.	1	2	2	0
37.	Johnnie Mack.	12.	2	3	1	0
38.	Tim Moodie.	14.	0	1	2	0
39.	David Napoleon. (Moodie).	12.	0	2	3	0
40.	Willie Sanderson.	13.	4	6	2	0
41.	Leonard Roderique.	10.	1	2	3	1
42.	Clifford Paul.	12.	2	2	1	0
43.	Wilfrid Isaac.	15.	6	0	5	0
44.	Lawrence Jack.	11.	1	2	3	0
45.	James Joseph. (George).	10.	1	2	2	0
[illegible]	Ralph Atkins.	9.	0	0	4	1
4[illegible]	Raymond Nahanee.	7.	0	1	5	[illegible]
48.	Paschal Cortes.	10.	1	1	3	0
49.	Willie Thomas.	9.	2	5	8	1
50.	Joseph Moodie.	10.	0	2	4	1
[illegible]	Bertie Ettershank.	9.	3	1	1	1
[illegible]	Howard Williams.	9.	1	2	4	1
[illegible]	Fred. August.	8.	1	2	4	0
[illegible]	Henry Guerrero.	14.	2	1	0	0
[illegible]	Jimmie Mack.	9.	1	[illegible]	5	0
[illegible]	Ernest George.	9.	0	[illegible]	[illegible]	[illegible]

CERTIFIED CORRECT
J. A. Mclean M.D.
MEDICAL OFFICER NEW WESTMINSTER AGENCY

PUBLIC ARCHIVES

Figure 110: The same records of children who selectively received anesthesia

The Grey Nuns, a Roman Catholic order, helped in the operation of St. Anne's Residential School, above. Former band chief Edmund Metatawabin, left, remembers being forced to sit in a homemade electric chair at the school and then being given painful jolts to entertain visiting dignitaries.

(PETER MOON/The Globe and Mail)

School's electric chair haunts natives

Oct 21/96

BY PETER MOON
The Globe and Mail
Fort Albany First Nation, Ont.

First it was used for entertainment, then for punishment for aboriginal children.

THE homemade electric chair that was used for years to punish aboriginal children at St. Anne's Residential School has disappeared, but its memory endures.

Hundreds of children who survived the horrors of the school have bitter memories of the chair that was used first for entertainment but eventually as a means of forcing them to bend to the will of the Roman Catholic missionaries who ran the school.

"People were put in the electric chair as a form of punishment," Mary Anne Nakogee-Davis, 41, who attended St. Anne's between Grades 1 and 8, said in an interview. "They would put children in it if they were bad. The nuns used it as a weapon.

"It was done to me on more than one occasion. They would strap your arms to the metal arm rests, and it would jolt you and go through your system. I don't know what I did that was bad enough to have that done to me."

Edmund Metatawabin, 49, a former chief of the Fort Albany First Nation, said he remembers he and his class being forced to take turns sitting in the chair and receiving painful jolts of electricity to entertain visiting dignitaries.

"I was six years old," he said. "There was no sense of volunteering or anything. We were just told by the brother to do it and there was never any question of not doing it.

"Once the thing was cranked up, I could feel the current going through me, mainly through my arms. Your legs are jumping up, and everyone was laughing."

St. Anne's operated as a residential school from 1904 to 1973 in this isolated Cree community of 1,400 people on the west coast of James Bay, 1,000 kilometres north of Toronto.

The federal government forced Cree and Ojibwa children to leave their families and live at the school for 10 months of the year.

Please see Electric / A4

Figure 111: Media report of the use of an electric chair to punish students and "entertain dignitaries" at St. Anne's Catholic residential school, Fort Albany Ontario (1996)

116620-1

File

May 27th. 1919

Dear Mr. Edmison,

I have received a protest from Alberni as to the location of the proposed new Indian boarding school there, where it is stated, there are very few Indians, and a suggestion that it be located at Ucluelet where the native population is more numerous. It is asserted that the proximity of the Indian reserves is detrimental to the town, and that the presence of the school will attract the Indians to the reserve in the vicinity of Alberni, thus tending to perpetuate the Indian holdings which the town people hope will soon be opened up for settlement. They wish to know whether the Department has definitely decided upon locating the school at Alberni.

I should be glad if you would let me have your opinion on these questions at the earliest possible moment.

Yours sincerely,

Duncan C Scott.

Deputy Superintendent General.

Rev. J. H. Edmison,
Secretary,
Board of Home Missions,
Presbyterian Church in Canada,
Confederation Life Building,
Toronto, Ont.

DCS

Figure 112: Locating of residential schools to benefit local Caucasian settlers

REV. A. LLOYD SMITH, D.D.
CHAIRMAN

Board of Home Missions

The United Church of Canada

299 QUEEN ST. WEST
TORONTO 2 B, ONTARIO

REV. GEORGE DOREY, D.D.
SECRETARY

REV. MALCOLM C. MACDONALD, B.A.
ASSOCIATE SECRETARY

REV. JOHN R. LENG, B.A., B.D.
ASSISTANT SECRETARY

Department of Mines & Resources
Indian Affairs Branch
FEB 13 1948
P.M.
REGISTERED

Mr. R.A. Hoey,
Director,
Indian Affairs Branch,
Department of Mines & Resources,
O t t a w a, Ontario.

~~November~~ February 11th,
1 9 4 8.

Dear Mr. Hoey: Re: Alberni Residential School

I enclose copy of a letter which I am sending to the Minister to-day.

I want to say to you that I mean exactly what I say when I suggest that the Secretaries will recommend to the Board the closing of the Alberni School, if it means having to carry on at the expense of Home Mission money. There is no reason in the world why the Churches should have to find money to perform in part the functions which are in whole the responsibility of the Government.

With kindest regards,

Yours sincerely,

Geo. Dorey

GD.MLT

Encls.

Figure 113: Threats against federal government from the United Church of Canada regarding funding of residential schools

Feb. 3, 1940.

Jan. 26, 1940. 6:30 p.m. - school burned down

- 4 -

Agent's Report on fire at Ahousaht Residential School. (cont.)

School Nurse. The school nurse, Mrs. M.B. Griffin, is remaining, pending instructions, and I would recommend that she be retained at Ahousaht until the end of March, as she is doing valuable work in the village and can be of great assistance with the day school, if such is approved.

Remarks. As this school was the property of, and conducted by, the Church, care was taken to avoid too close inquiry.

Too much credence was not placed upon comments and theories advanced by different people, as all were more or less laboring under excitement and strain.

It is however my opinion that faulty wiring was the cause. It will be noted from my reports on this school that, due to its condition, I have at all times stressed the importance of fire drills and the upkeep of escapes.
Thanks to the discipline of the children, no one was lost or hurt.
Great credit is due to Mrs. Preece, Kitchen Matron, Mrs. Griffin, Nurse, and Mrs. Sainsbury, Sewing Matron, whom I am informed were instrumental in giving the alarm, evacuating the school, and mustering the pupils in a place of safety.

In conclusion I would respectfully request that authority be granted to expend up to the amount of $200.00, for the purpose of supplying clothing, bedding, etc. at discretion, in cases where hardship is being experienced due to influx of children in homes unprepared for them, and where parents are not in a position to supply necessities.

Respectfully submitted,

Your obedient servant,

P. B. Ashbridge,
Indian Agent.

PBA/AM

Figure 114: Indian Agent P. Ashbridge covers for the United Church during his "investigation" of deaths of children following a fire at the Ahousaht residential school (1940)

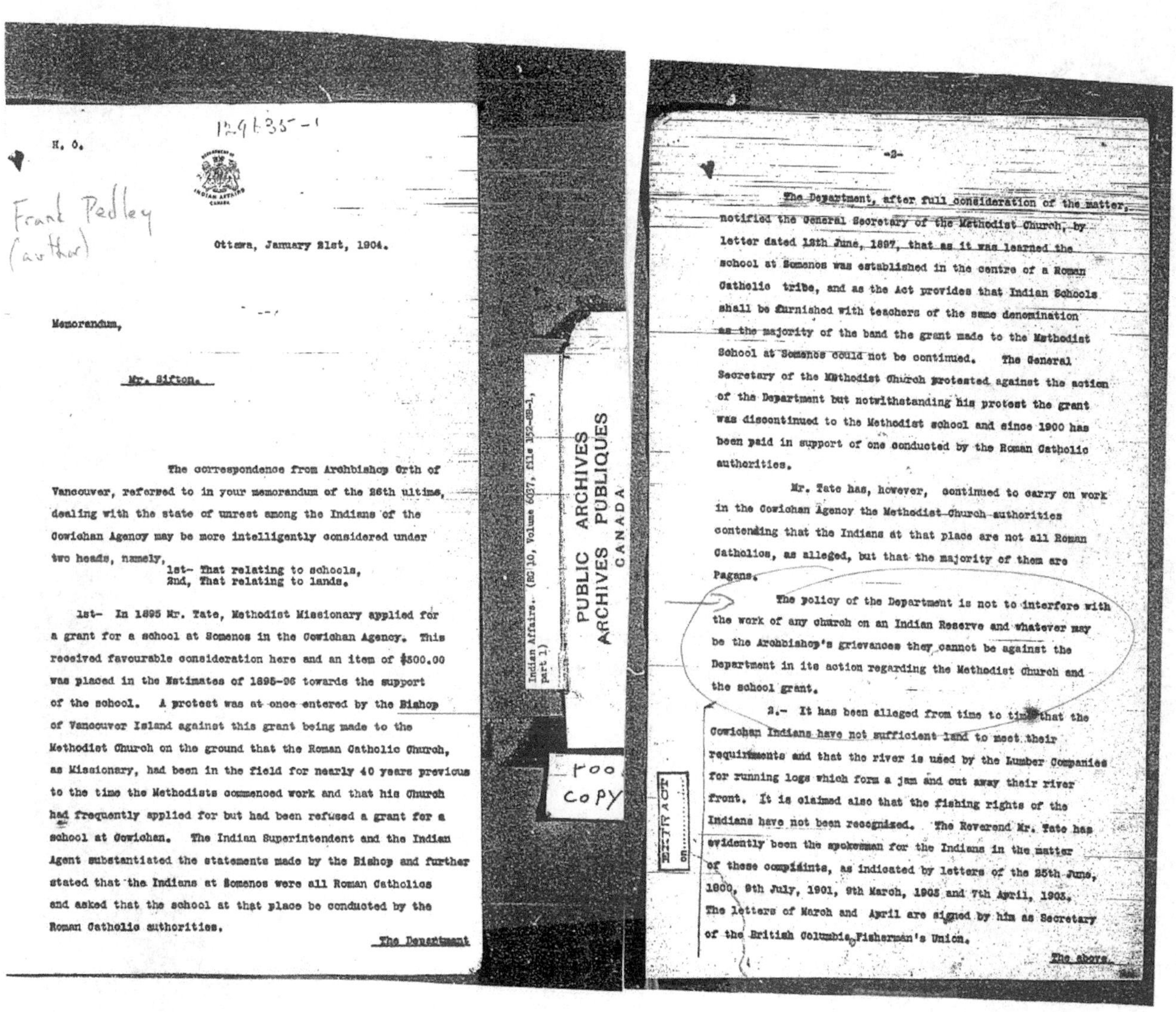

129635-1

H. O.

Frank Pedley (author)

Ottawa, January 21st, 1904.

Memorandum,

Mr. Sifton.

The correspondence from Archbishop Orth of Vancouver, referred to in your memorandum of the 26th ultimo, dealing with the state of unrest among the Indians of the Cowichan Agency may be more intelligently considered under two heads, namely,

1st- That relating to schools,
2nd, That relating to lands.

1st- In 1895 Mr. Tate, Methodist Missionary applied for a grant for a school at Somenos in the Cowichan Agency. This received favourable consideration here and an item of $500.00 was placed in the Estimates of 1895-96 towards the support of the school. A protest was at once entered by the Bishop of Vancouver Island against this grant being made to the Methodist Church on the ground that the Roman Catholic Church, as Missionary, had been in the field for nearly 40 years previous to the time the Methodists commenced work and that his Church had frequently applied for but had been refused a grant for a school at Cowichan. The Indian Superintendent and the Indian Agent substantiated the statements made by the Bishop and further stated that the Indians at Somenos were all Roman Catholics and asked that the school at that place be conducted by the Roman Catholic authorities.

The Department

TOO COPY

-2-

The Department, after full consideration of the matter, notified the General Secretary of the Methodist Church, by letter dated 12th June, 1897, that as it was learned the school at Somenos was established in the centre of a Roman Catholic tribe, and as the Act provides that Indian Schools shall be furnished with teachers of the same denomination as the majority of the band the grant made to the Methodist School at Somenos could not be continued. The General Secretary of the Methodist Church protested against the action of the Department but notwithstanding his protest the grant was discontinued to the Methodist school and since 1900 has been paid in support of one conducted by the Roman Catholic authorities.

Mr. Tate has, however, continued to carry on work in the Cowichan Agency the Methodist Church authorities contending that the Indians at that place are not all Roman Catholics, as alleged, but that the majority of them are Pagans.

The policy of the Department is not to interfere with the work of any church on an Indian Reserve and whatever may be the Archbishop's grievances they cannot be against the Department in its action regarding the Methodist Church and the school grant.

2.- It has been alleged from time to time that the Cowichan Indians have not sufficient land to meet their requirements and that the river is used by the Lumber Companies for running logs which form a jam and cut away their river front. It is claimed also that the fishing rights of the Indians have not been recognized. The Reverend Mr. Tate has evidently been the spokesman for the Indians in the matter of these complaints, as indicated by letters of the 25th June, 1900, 9th July, 1901, 9th March, 1903 and 7th April, 1903. The letters of March and April are signed by him as Secretary of the British Columbia Fisherman's Union.

EXTRACT on.........

The above

Figure 115: Government policy "not to interfere with the work of any church"

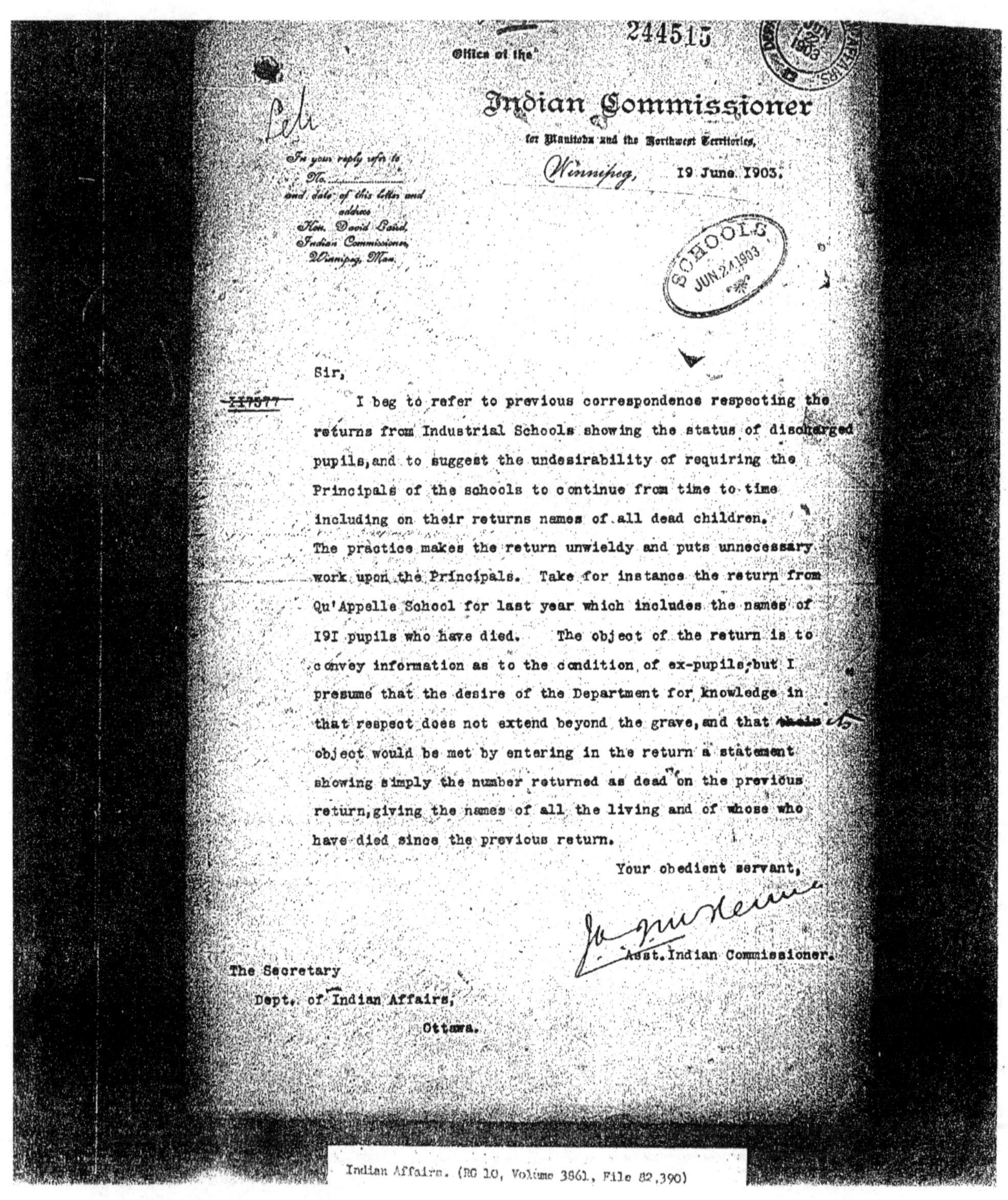

244515

Office of the

Indian Commissioner

for Manitoba and the Northwest Territories,

Winnipeg, 19 June 1903.

In your reply refer to No. .... and date of this letter and address Hon. David Laird, Indian Commissioner, Winnipeg, Man.

SCHOOLS JUN 24 1903

Sir,

I beg to refer to previous correspondence respecting the returns from Industrial Schools showing the status of discharged pupils, and to suggest the undesirability of requiring the Principals of the schools to continue from time to time including on their returns names of all dead children. The practice makes the return unwieldy and puts unnecessary work upon the Principals. Take for instance the return from Qu'Appelle School for last year which includes the names of 191 pupils who have died. The object of the return is to convey information as to the condition of ex-pupils, but I presume that the desire of the Department for knowledge in that respect does not extend beyond the grave, and that its object would be met by entering in the return a statement showing simply the number returned as dead on the previous return, giving the names of all the living and of those who have died since the previous return.

Your obedient servant,

J. A. McKenna

Asst. Indian Commissioner.

The Secretary

Dept. of Indian Affairs,

Ottawa.

Indian Affairs. (RG 10, Volume 3861, File 82,390)

Figure 116: Indian Affairs official requests permission to delete from reports the names of children who have died in residential schools (and admitting the deaths of 191 students at one school) (1903)

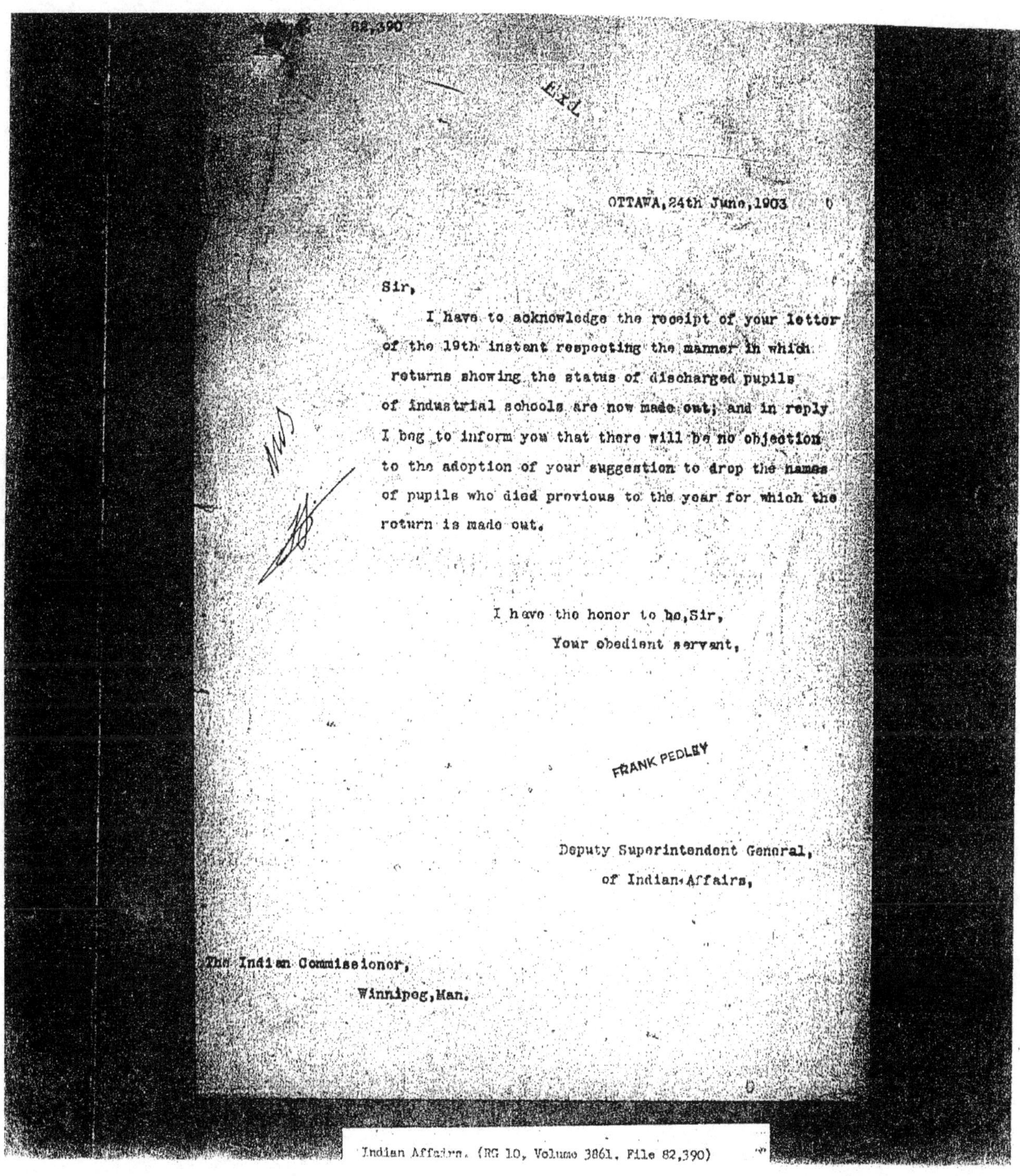

82,390

OTTAWA, 24th June, 1903

Sir,

I have to acknowledge the receipt of your letter of the 19th instant respecting the manner in which returns showing the status of discharged pupils of industrial schools are now made out; and in reply I beg to inform you that there will be no objection to the adoption of your suggestion to drop the names of pupils who died previous to the year for which the return is made out.

I have the honor to be, Sir,
Your obedient servant,

FRANK PEDLEY

Deputy Superintendent General,
of Indian Affairs,

The Indian Commissioner,
Winnipeg, Man.

Indian Affairs. (RG 10, Volume 3861, File 82,390)

Figure 117: Official approval for Cover up: Deputy Superintendent Pedley grants permission to "drop the names of pupils who died"

Mr. BUREAU: A question was asked by the hon. member for Last Mountain (Mr. Johnston) as to the appropriation for a particular school, and the letter which he read showed a pitiful condition of things in that school. Now, the amount we are asked to vote is $1,064,415 for 34,000 people.

Mr. MEIGHEN: Over 100,000.

Mr. BUREAU: The total population of the Indians?

Mr. MEIGHEN: Yes.

Mr. BUREAU: Are these schools built on the reserves? I had the impression the schools were on the reserves?

Mr. MEIGHEN: Boarding schools usually are on the reserves but not always. There is an Indian boarding school at Portage la Prairie and that is not on a reserve, but they usually are on reserves.

Mr. BUREAU: The policy, as I understand the minister, of improving the condition of the Indian is to take him away from the habits and environment he has on the reserve would not seem to help to improve the Indian very fast, if the idea is to take him away from his environment. Suppose a white child were to go amongst Indians and to live with them. Although he is supposed to be superior to the Indians he would have a hard time of it if

11 p.m. he were not allowed to go back among white people again. It seems hard—I will not say cruel—to take an Indian child away from his people and to mix him up with white people in one of these schools. If it is necessary, in order to improve the condition of the Indian, to take him away from his environment and to place him in one of these schools, it would be well that the school should be outside of the reserve. But on the other hand, from a purely humanitarian point of view it would be cruel to take that child from the reserve and put him among white people without giving him a chance to go back to his people and choose the life he would like to live. Does this amount of over a million dollars that we are asked to vote include buildings, or the improvement of the schools? Or is it just for the purpose of carrying on the schools and paying the teachers and the various staffs? If so it seems to be rather a large amount for the number of schools under the control of the department.

Mr. MEIGHEN: It is exactly the same as last year, and certainly it is none too much; we would like to be able to afford more. There ought to be more Indian boarding schools built and we would like to build the one in Last Mountain if we could afford to undertake it with the money in hand, as well as others equally urgent.

[Mr. Meighen.]

Mr. BUREAU: How many are there? Take Manitoba where the population is the largest.

Mr. MEIGHEN: In Manitoba there are 39 day schools and 8 boarding schools; in Quebec 28 day schools and no boarding schools. Day schools seem to be a success in Eastern Canada at all events.

Mr. BELAND: Is the school at Qu-Appelle a boarding school?

Mr. MEIGHEN: It is an industrial school. It really is a boarding school.

Mr. BELAND: Is not that one of the best Indian schools you have now?

Mr. MEIGHEN: It is out of the Qu'Appelle school that the File Hills colony has come. The File Hills colony is undoubtedly a phenomenal success. The number of day schools in the Dominion is 248, boarding schools 58, industrial schools 16, total 322. This is a vote for the maintenance of these schools.

69% mortality

Mr. BUREAU: It is not too much.

Mr. MEIGHEN: And for the construction of such school buildings as are contemplated for next year.

Mr. BUREAU: And the maintenance of the old schools?

Mr. MEIGHEN: The maintenance of the whole of them.

Mr. BUREAU: Is it not possible to comply with the request of the hon. member for Last Mountain (Mr. Johnston) under the conditions existing there? It seems a pitiable state of things if the letter contains the truth.

Mr. MEIGHEN: It was not altogether right; it was not up to date in some respects.

Mr. BUREAU: Out of this amount will there be any money which can be used to improve the condition there?

Mr. MEIGHEN: No.

Mr. BUREAU: Is there any other amount which will be used for that purpose?

Mr. MEIGHEN: No.

Mr. COCKSHUTT: Before passing from the question of the education of the Indians, I would like to make a few remarks in regard to the Indians in the county of Brant. We have there the largest number

of Indians to be found
in Canada, or in Nor
about 4,500. The hon
Cape Breton (Mr. McK
tion about them bein
their education. I ha
touch with a good mar
I think that does not
The Six Nation India
most intelligent, if not
on the North America
are capable of a very
have the opportunity.
eral instances they ha
ant positions almost i
have passed out of t
heard of one last we
commercial course ar
school, received a sala
her services. That go
Indian has a fair ch
very substantial adv
like to know if the
whether there can b
for those Indian boy
to push on beyond th
take a high school co
few in our city who
school course at the
has been a contention
the county as to who
these children comin
institution and from
pleting their course
the city. The city ke
and it is customar
pupils for the educa
appears to me that if
to advance the edu
dren there should be
might be drawn upo
boys and girls who h
can in the common
opportunity of prosec
ther in the high sch
ticularly. I am not
that kind exists; I
But I know that re
quite a sharp contro
Brant on that very p
minister to say whe
opportunity for thos
higher branches that
schools and collegia
parents are not abl
whether the departm
which it can pay a
expenses of those st
sue the higher bra
feel certain that if
tended and if such

House of Commons, Ottawa 6/8/20

Figure 118: Prime Minister lauds the "phenomenal success" of the File Hills residential school during the same period that its mortality rate was 69% (1920)

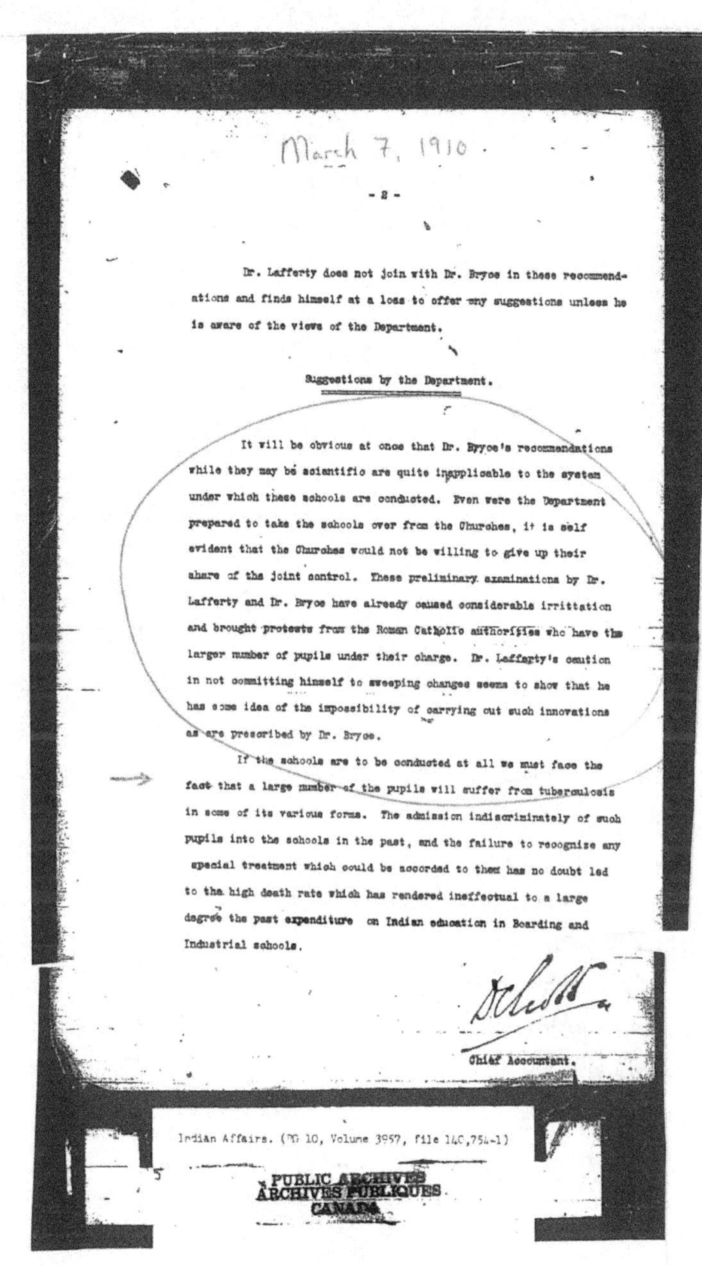

March 7, 1910.

- 2 -

Dr. Lafferty does not join with Dr. Bryce in these recommendations and finds himself at a loss to offer any suggestions unless he is aware of the views of the Department.

Suggestions by the Department.

It will be obvious at once that Dr. Bryce's recommendations while they may be scientific are quite inapplicable to the system under which these schools are conducted. Even were the Department prepared to take the schools over from the Churches, it is self evident that the Churches would not be willing to give up their share of the joint control. These preliminary examinations by Dr. Lafferty and Dr. Bryce have already caused considerable irritation and brought protests from the Roman Catholic authorities who have the larger number of pupils under their charge. Dr. Lafferty's caution in not committing himself to sweeping changes seems to show that he has some idea of the impossibility of carrying out such innovations as are prescribed by Dr. Bryce.

If the schools are to be conducted at all we must face the fact that a large number of the pupils will suffer from tuberculosis in some of its various forms. The admission indiscriminately of such pupils into the schools in the past, and the failure to recognize any special treatment which could be accorded to them has no doubt led to the high death rate which has rendered ineffectual to a large degree the past expenditure on Indian education in Boarding and Industrial schools.

DCScott

Chief Accountant.

Indian Affairs. (RG 10, Volume 3957, file 140,754-1)

Figure 119: Top Indian Affairs official Duncan Campbell Scott rationalizes tuberculosis conditions in the residential schools (1910)

Ottawa, 6th November, 1919.

Sir:-

I beg to point out that under the terms of your appointment as salaried medical officer to Indians, you are required to attend not only Indians of certain reserves (Nicomen, Matsqui, Whonocka, Skweahin) but also the pupils of the St. Mary's Mission Boarding School, which is in the New Westminster Agency.

A serious epidemic of small-pox occurred recently. The disease was prevalent in the New Westminster Agency and other Indian Agencies, and it is understood that the outbreak of the disease was due, to a large extent, to pupils from St. Mary's Mission School who had contracted small-pox, being sent to their homes before their recovery. It has been stated that one child was taken off the train with an eruption visible. In view of the fact that you are the salaried medical officer for the School, it is not understood why you did not take necessary precaution to stamp out the disease while it was confined to the School. Owing to the lack of precaution being observed the disease became widespread and a serious state of affairs resul[ted] which has entailed much expense upon the Department. Under the circumstances, I beg to say that the Department will be glad to receive an explanation from you. Be good enough to state whether your attention was drawn by the Principal of the School to illness amongst the pupi[ls]. You should also state whether you have visited the Institution once a month or more frequently during the past six months, and whether you gave special attendance in small-pox cases. I may say that the Department has not received reports from you with regard to your work since the fall of 1918. A report with regard to the performance of your duty, should be submitted to the Department at the close of eac[h] month, and the said reports should reach the Department through the office of the local Indian Agent, Mr. Bryne.

Your obedient servant,

A.J.Stuart Esq., M.D.,
Mission City, B.C.

Asst. Deputy and Secretary

Figure 120: Reprimand of a local doctor for allowing the spread of smallpox among Indians (1919)

December 12th, 1919.

Dear Dr. Stuart,

My attention has been drawn to your letter of November 13th. and to previous correspondence on the subject of a small-pox epidemic in your district.

To my mind the letter of November 6th. should never have been written to you, and no imputation of neglect should have been made. I regret exceedingly that you have been annoyed by this letter and I would like to cancel it entirely.

It seems clear from your letter that you did everything in your power to control the situation which was to be expected, as your service in the past has left nothing to be desired.

With kind regards, I am,

Yours sincerely,

D.C. Scott

Deputy Superintendent General.

Alex. J. Stuart, Esq., M.D.,

Mission City, B. C.

exoneration of germ warfare practitioner

Principal V. Rohr resigns July 29, 1920

Indian Affairs (RG 10 Volume 6468, file 890-1, part 1)

Figure 121: The exoneration of the same doctor by top Indian Affairs official Duncan Campbell Scott

Fraser Lake, B.C.,

October 22nd. 1935.

R.H.Moore, Esq.,
Indian Agent,
Vanderhoof, B.C.

Dear Sir:-

Your letter of October the 18th. received with complaints of attention I am giving the Indians. These complaints have been so frequent lately and so unjustified that I begin to believe they are promoted by personal feeling against me rather than an interest in the welfare of the Indians. This may be on your part but I prefer to think it comes from Rivet, for whom I have little use and who probably guesses that I feel so toward him.

Since my father is principal of an Indian School and I have had opportunity to meet the principals and medical attendants of other schools, I happen to know that the attention I am giving the Lejac School is as good or better than in any other place in the province. As for the general medical examination you speak of, this is not done in any other school that I have any knowledge of. This would bear no weight with me if I thought that any purpose would be served by doing so, but I do not think so. Where is the point of this, when I know that, were I to apply the standards of health to them that is applied to children of the white schools, that I should have to discharge 90% of them and there would be no school left; and when I know that they are under the constant observation of a staff who have the opportunity of reporting any ill health to me either on my weekly visit to the school or by phone. If the department makes this a regulation applying to all schools I have nothing to say, otherwise I shall use my own judgement.

As for dental work, anyone knows that there is always dental work in such an institution. I have asked for a dentist on two previous occasions and am surprised that the department does not arrange for an annual attednance of a dentist, rather than wait for the doctor to examine the whole school and tell them a dentist is required (which everyone knows). I am only too pleased to facilitate his work, when I know he is coming, by going over the children and picking out the ones who require work done.

In conclusion, I feel that I am doing everything that experience and commonsense dictates for the welfare of the children. If any more complaints emanate from the school through you I shall put it up to the department at Ottawa, giving them a statement of just how I am carrying on the work and let them decide whether it should be satisfactory or not.

Yours,

Signed:- C. Pitts, M.D.

Figure 122: The "two standards of health care" genocidal practice

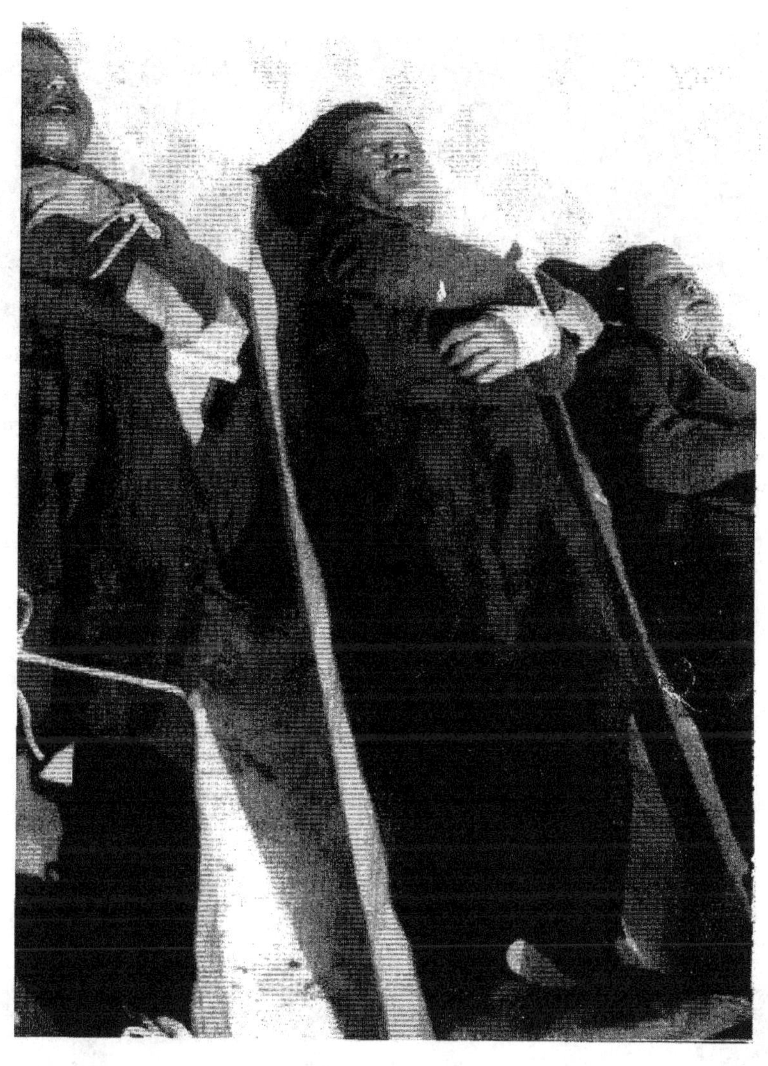

<u>Figure 123:</u> *More cover up* - Staged photo of three of the four boys from the Le Jac Catholic school who ran away in light clothing in mid winter and froze to death (1937)

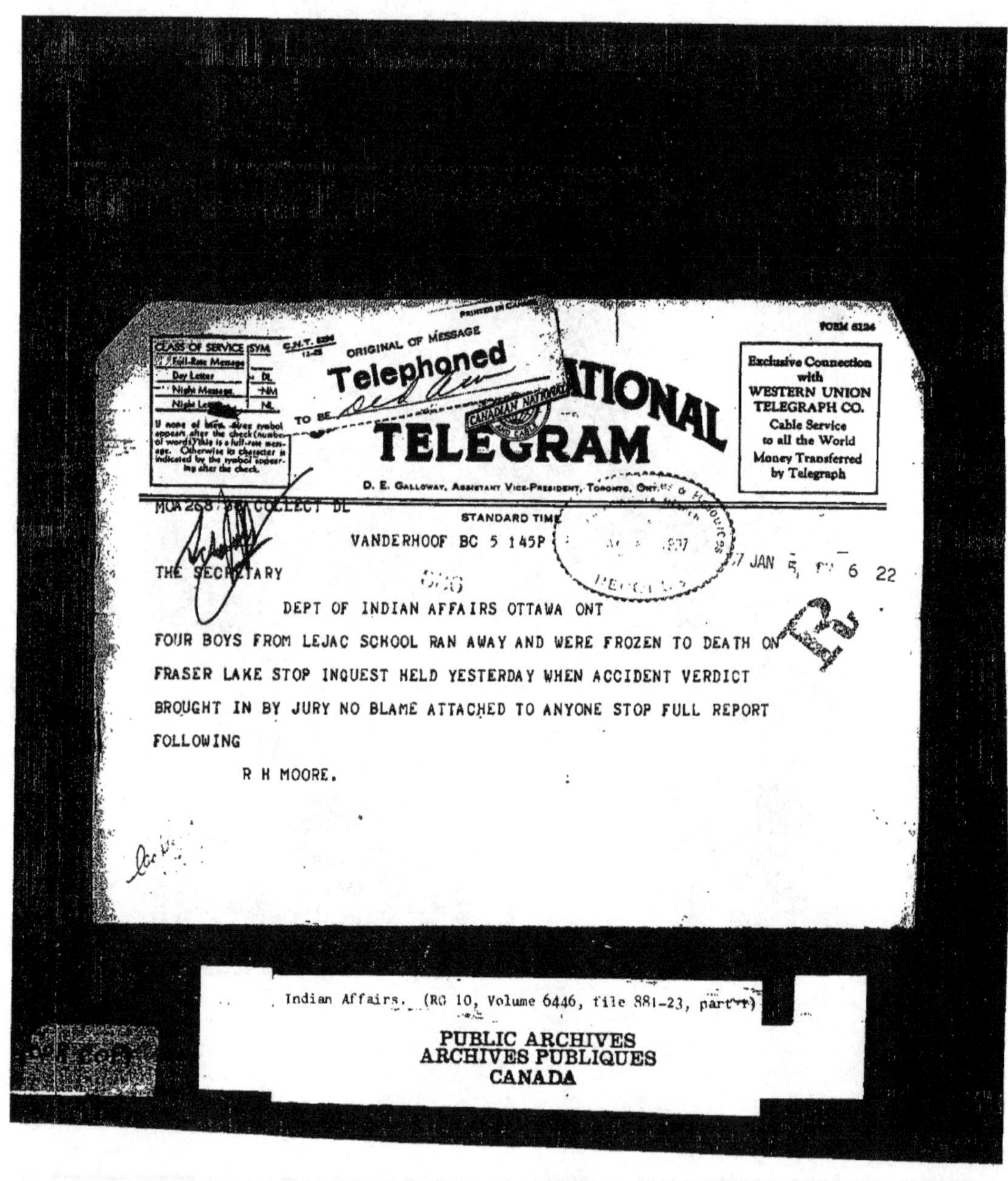
FORM 6124

CLASS OF SERVICE | SYM
Full-Rate Message
Day Letter | DL
Night Message | NM
Night Letter | NL

ORIGINAL OF MESSAGE

Telephoned

CANADIAN NATIONAL TELEGRAM

D. E. GALLOWAY, ASSISTANT VICE-PRESIDENT, TORONTO, ONT.

Exclusive Connection with WESTERN UNION TELEGRAPH CO.
Cable Service to all the World
Money Transferred by Telegraph

STANDARD TIME

VANDERHOOF BC 5 145P

JAN 5 6 22

THE SECRETARY

DEPT OF INDIAN AFFAIRS OTTAWA ONT

FOUR BOYS FROM LEJAC SCHOOL RAN AWAY AND WERE FROZEN TO DEATH ON FRASER LAKE STOP INQUEST HELD YESTERDAY WHEN ACCIDENT VERDICT BROUGHT IN BY JURY NO BLAME ATTACHED TO ANYONE STOP FULL REPORT FOLLOWING

R H MOORE.

Indian Affairs. (RG 10, Volume 6446, file 881-23, part 1)

PUBLIC ARCHIVES
ARCHIVES PUBLIQUES
CANADA

Figure 124: Local Indian agent exonerates the Lejac school officials for complicity in the boys' death

Winnipeg Tribune 5-1-37.

JURY HEARS HOW 4 INDIAN BOYS FROZE TO DEATH

(By The Canadian Press)

VANDERHOOF, B.C., Jan. 5—Recommendation that "excessive corporal discipline in practice" at the Indian school at Lejac, B.C., should be limited, was written today into the findings of a coroner's jury which investigated the deaths of four Indian boys during a trek from the school to the Nautley reservation.

The jury, sitting at Nautley last night, found the boys died in the slush ice over Fraser lake on the night of Jan. 1 from exhaustion and freezing. They found that "such circumstance was unavoidable in view of the evidence in this case."

The verdict said, however, "that more definite action by school authorities might or should have been taken the night on which the disappearance (of the boys from the school) took place."

The boys, all under 10 years old, were found huddled together on the ice Saturday night. They were lightly clad for the bitterly-cold trek they undertook. All were without caps, and one had only one shoe.

Fraser Lake is 20 miles east of Vanderhoof and 50 miles west of Prince George.

THE VANCOUVER SUN—*Vancouver's Own Newspaper*—WEDNESDAY, JANUARY 6, 1937

Indian School Authorities Absolved in Lake Tragedy

Special to The Vancouver Sun

VICTORIA, Jan. 6.—There is no blame attached to anyone in connection with the death of four Indian boys who ran away on New Year's Day from the Tejac Indian School and were later found frozen to death on Fraser Lake, according to a message received by the Indian Office here from Vanderhoof today.

The message was a reply to a query sent from the local office yesterday which followed word that the jury had recommended limiting of corporal punishment at the school.

R. H. Moore, Indian agent at Vanderhoof, reported the deaths in his wire and added a note that no blame attached to anyone. A full report is being forwarded by mail to the agent here.

NO EVIDENCE OF CRUELTY AT SCHOOL

FRASER LAKE, B.C., Jan. 6.—Coroner C. Pitts said today that an Indian witness' testimony prompted an inquest jury, investigating the deaths of four boys found frozen on the ice of Fraser Lake Saturday, to recommend in their verdict that corporal punishment, if practised at the Lejac Indian School, should be curtailed.

The coroner, who did not give the witness' name, said he testified that corporal punishment resulted in runaways from Indian schools.

However, Pitts said, there was no evidence to show that cruelty at the Lejac School prompted the four boys in question to attempt a fatal trek from the institution to Nautley Reservation New Year's Eve.

Other testimony at the inquest showed the boys left the school only so that they could spend a holiday at the reserve seven miles away across the lake, Pitts said.

The school principal said boys often left on such expeditions and as they had access to proper clothing, no alarm was felt for their safety immediately. A search was started the next day.

The school principal further testified that runaways occurred more frequently lately due to the fact corporal punishment was being discouraged by higher authorities.

The four boys, all under 10 years old, covered more than six miles of their trek before falling from cold and exhaustion. They were hatless and lightly clad for the bitter cold.

Indian Affairs." (RG 10, Volume 6446, file 881-23, part 1)

Figure 125: Media report of the deaths and cover up (1937)

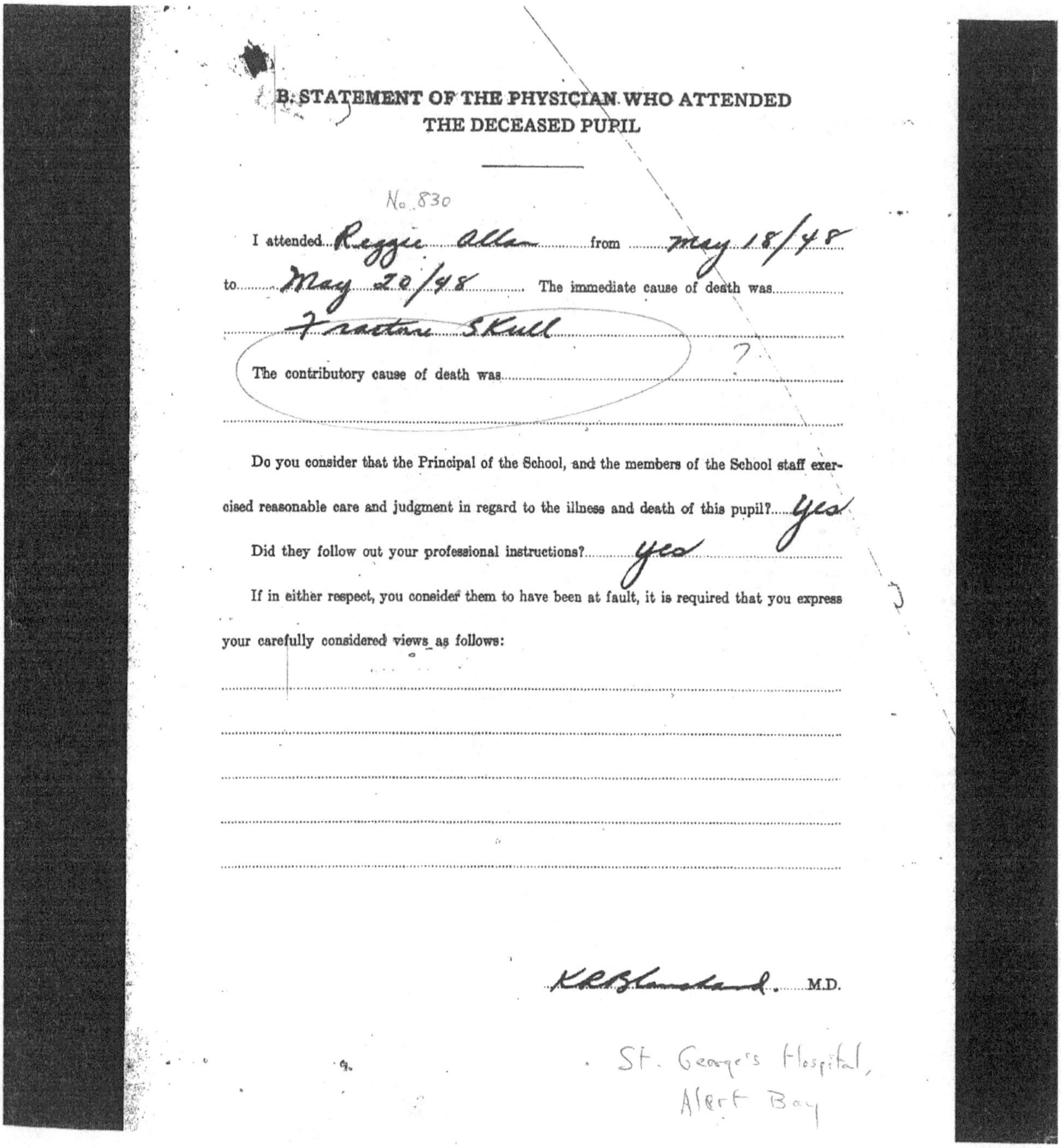

B. STATEMENT OF THE PHYSICIAN WHO ATTENDED THE DECEASED PUPIL

No. 830

I attended Reggie Allan from May 18/48 to May 20/48. The immediate cause of death was Fracture Skull

The contributory cause of death was ?

Do you consider that the Principal of the School, and the members of the School staff exercised reasonable care and judgment in regard to the illness and death of this pupil? Yes

Did they follow out your professional instructions? Yes

If in either respect, you consider them to have been at fault, it is required that you express your carefully considered views as follows:

K.R. Blanchard M.D.

St. George's Hospital, Alert Bay

Figure 126: No cause of death listed - 1948

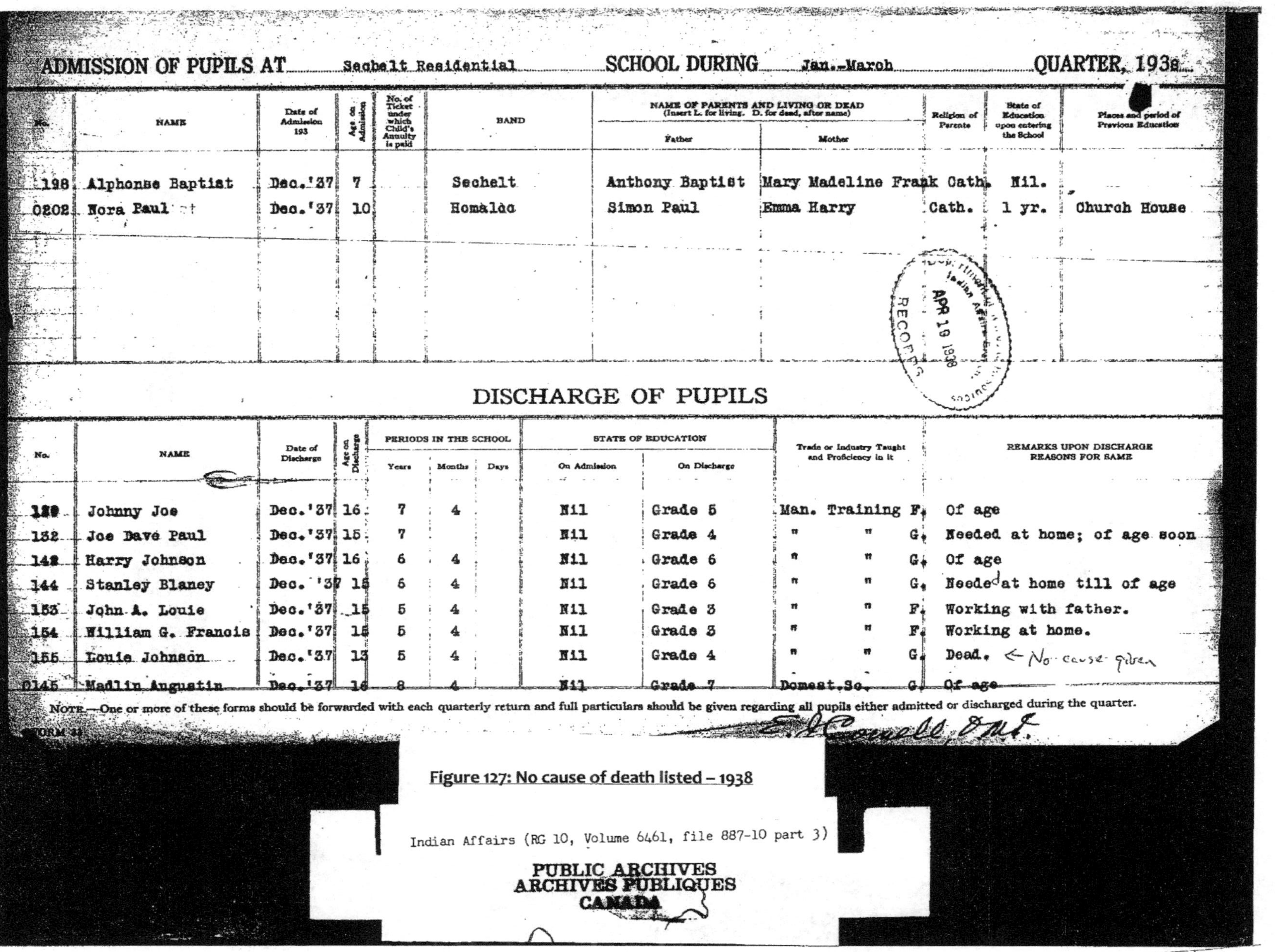

ADMISSION OF PUPILS AT Sechelt Residential SCHOOL DURING Jan.-March QUARTER, 1938

No.	NAME	Date of Admission 193	Age on Admission	No. of Ticket under which Child's Annuity is paid	BAND	NAME OF PARENTS AND LIVING OR DEAD (Insert L. for living. D. for dead, after name)		Religion of Parents	State of Education upon entering the School	Places and period of Previous Education
						Father	Mother			
198	Alphonse Baptist	Dec.'37	7		Sechelt	Anthony Baptist	Mary Madeline Frank	Cath.	Nil.	
0202	Nora Paul	Dec.'37	10		Homalco	Simon Paul	Emma Harry	Cath.	1 yr.	Church House

DISCHARGE OF PUPILS

No.	NAME	Date of Discharge	Age on Discharge	PERIODS IN THE SCHOOL			STATE OF EDUCATION		Trade or Industry Taught and Proficiency in it	REMARKS UPON DISCHARGE REASONS FOR SAME
				Years	Months	Days	On Admission	On Discharge		
1[illegible]	Johnny Joe	Dec.'37	16	7	4		Nil	Grade 5	Man. Training F.	Of age
132	Joe Dave Paul	Dec.'37	15	7			Nil	Grade 4	" " G.	Needed at home; of age soon
14[illegible]	Harry Johnson	Dec.'37	16	6	4		Nil	Grade 6	" " G.	Of age
144	Stanley Blaney	Dec. '37	15	6	4		Nil	Grade 6	" " G.	Needed at home till of age
153	John A. Louie	Dec.'37	15	5	4		Nil	Grade 3	" " F.	Working with father.
154	William G. Francis	Dec.'37	15	5	4		Nil	Grade 3	" " F.	Working at home.
155	Louie Johnson	Dec.'37	13	5	4		Nil	Grade 4	" " G.	Dead. ← No cause given
0145	Madlin Augustin	Dec.'37	16	8	4		Nil	Grade 7	Domest.Sc. G.	Of age

NOTE.—One or more of these forms should be forwarded with each quarterly return and full particulars should be given regarding all pupils either admitted or discharged during the quarter.

FORM 34

E. J. Conell O.M.I.

Figure 127: No cause of death listed – 1938

Indian Affairs (RG 10, Volume 6461, file 887-10 part 3)

PUBLIC ARCHIVES
ARCHIVES PUBLIQUES
CANADA

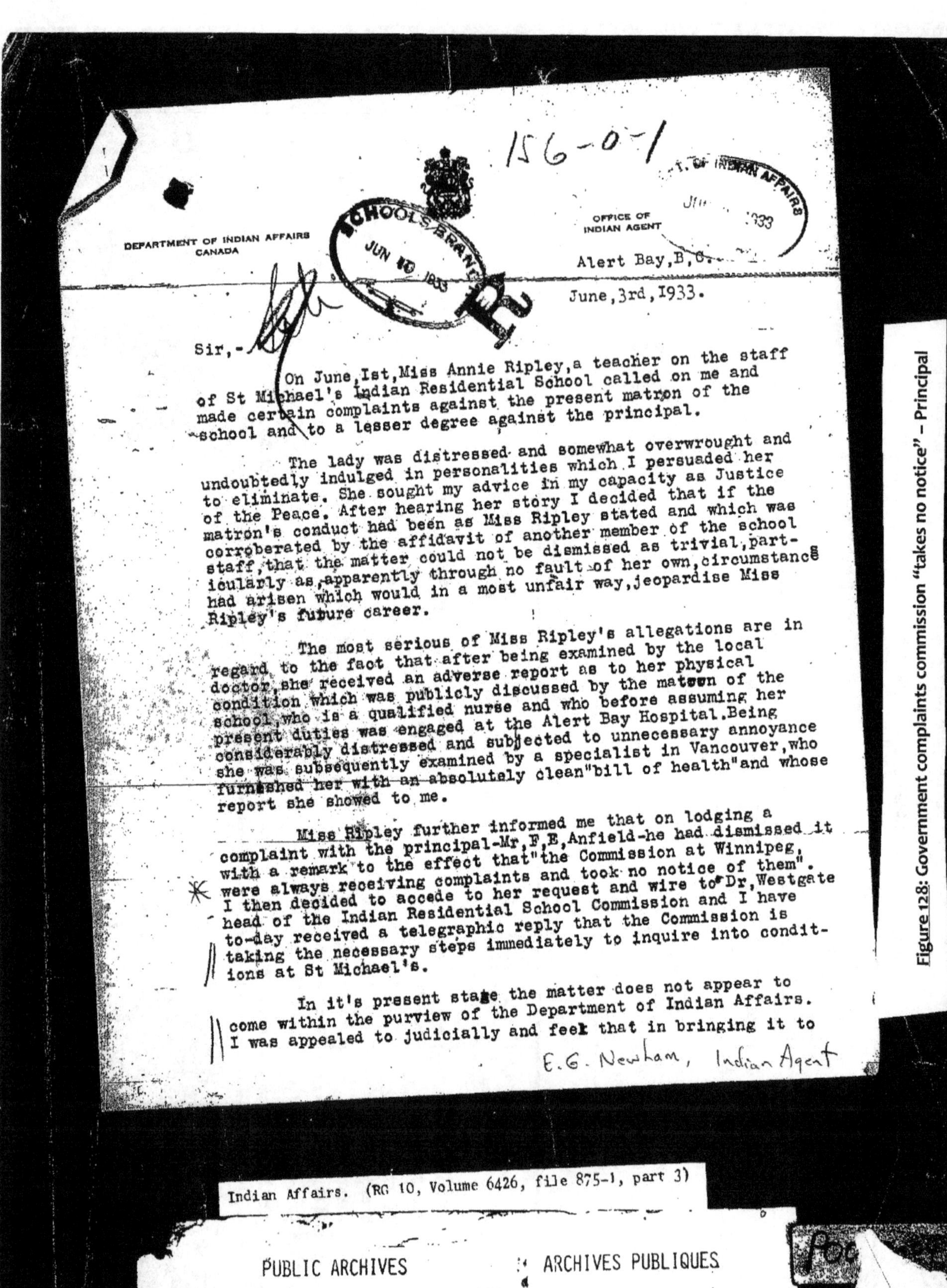

156-0-1

DEPARTMENT OF INDIAN AFFAIRS
CANADA

SCHOOLS BRANCH
JUN 16 1933

OFFICE OF
INDIAN AGENT

DEPT. OF INDIAN AFFAIRS
JUN ... 1933

Alert Bay, B, C. ...

June, 3rd, 1933.

Sir,-

On June, Ist, Miss Annie Ripley, a teacher on the staff of St Michael's Indian Residential School called on me and made certain complaints against the present matron of the school and to a lesser degree against the principal.

The lady was distressed and somewhat overwrought and undoubtedly indulged in personalities which I persuaded her to eliminate. She sought my advice in my capacity as Justice of the Peace. After hearing her story I decided that if the matron's conduct had been as Miss Ripley stated and which was corroberated by the affidavit of another member of the school staff, that the matter could not be dismissed as trivial, particularly as, apparently through no fault of her own, circumstances had arisen which would in a most unfair way, jeopardise Miss Ripley's future career.

The most serious of Miss Ripley's allegations are in regard to the fact that after being examined by the local doctor, she received an adverse report as to her physical condition which was publicly discussed by the matron of the school, who is a qualified nurse and who before assuming her present duties was engaged at the Alert Bay Hospital. Being considerably distressed and subjected to unnecessary annoyance she was subsequently examined by a specialist in Vancouver, who furnished her with an absolutely clean "bill of health" and whose report she showed to me.

Miss Ripley further informed me that on lodging a complaint with the principal-Mr, F, E, Anfield-he had dismissed it with a remark to the effect that "the Commission at Winnipeg, were always receiving complaints and took no notice of them". I then decided to accede to her request and wire to Dr, Westgate head of the Indian Residential School Commission and I have to-day received a telegraphic reply that the Commission is taking the necessary steps immediately to inquire into conditions at St Michael's.

In it's present stage the matter does not appear to come within the purview of the Department of Indian Affairs. I was appealed to judicially and feel that in bringing it to

E. G. Newnham, Indian Agent

Indian Affairs. (RG 10, Volume 6426, file 875-1, part 3)

Figure 128: Government complaints commission "takes no notice" – Principal

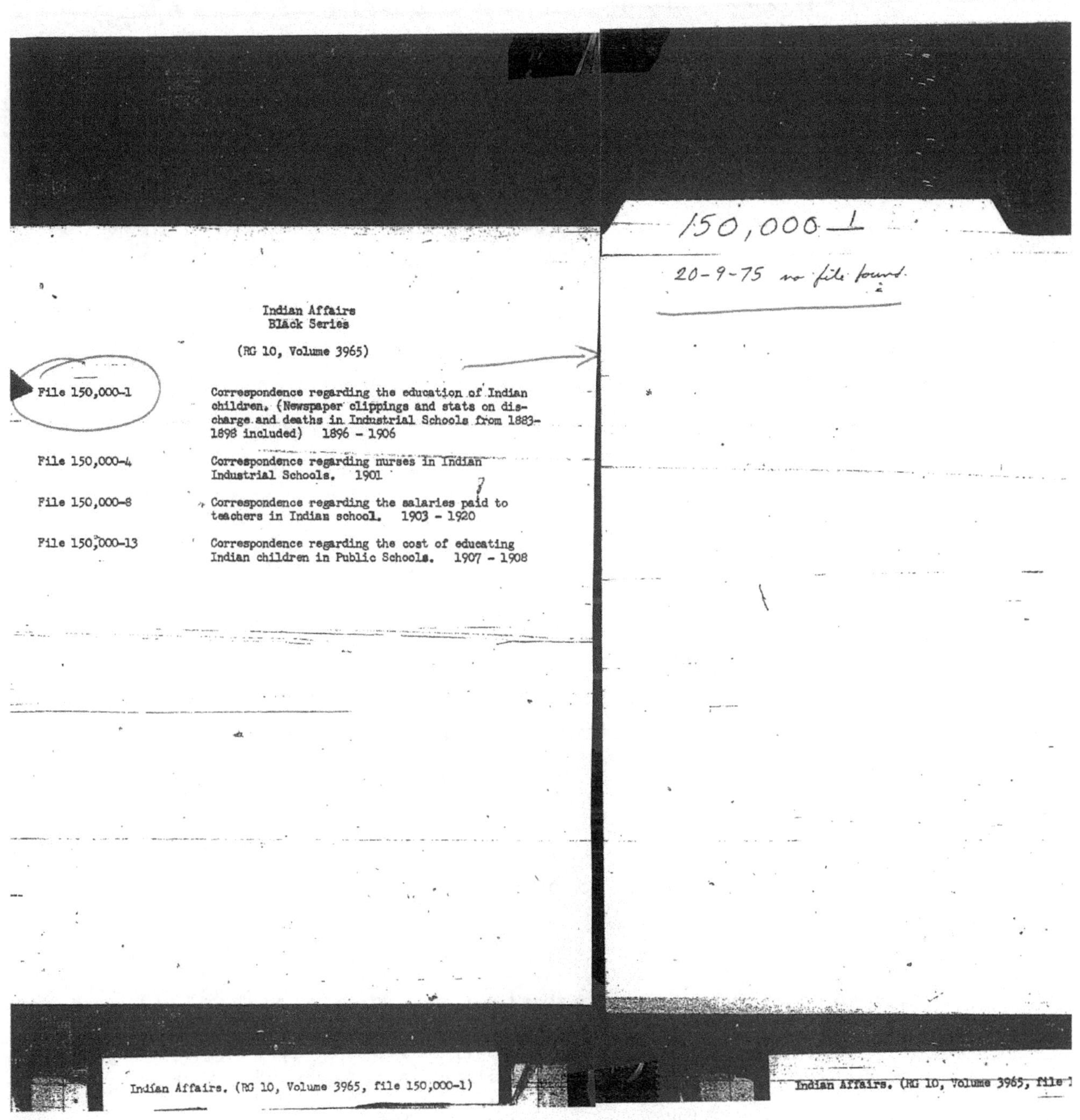
Indian Affairs
Black Series

(RG 10, Volume 3965)

File 150,000-1	Correspondence regarding the education of Indian children. (Newspaper clippings and stats on discharge and deaths in Industrial Schools from 1883-1898 included) 1896 - 1906
File 150,000-4	Correspondence regarding nurses in Indian Industrial Schools. 1901
File 150,000-8	Correspondence regarding the salaries paid to teachers in Indian school. 1903 - 1920
File 150,000-13	Correspondence regarding the cost of educating Indian children in Public Schools. 1907 - 1908

Indian Affairs. (RG 10, Volume 3965, file 150,000-1)

150,000-1

20-9-75 no file found.

Indian Affairs. (RG 10, Volume 3965, file 1

Figure 129: Censored residential school death records

F.J. SCOTT HALL LAW CORPORATION

#300 – 848 Courtney Street
Victoria, BC V8W 1C4
Email: scotthall@pacificcoast.net

Telephone: (250) 384-6600
Call Toll Free: 1-800-435-6625
Facsimile: (250) 388-9406

March 3, 2008

Private & Confidential

TRUDY SMITH
4051 BARKLAY ROAD
CAMPBELL RIVER, BC V9W 4Y5

Via Courier

287-5863

Dear Ms. Smith:

RE: ***Your Residential School Claim***

I confirm that, on your instructions, I have advised Canada that you have accepted the compensation of $160,000, arrived at in the decision by the Adjudicator, Susan Ross.

I further confirm that we had talked about your waiting for the new government program (called the IAP). However, in order to move your case into the new plan and wait until all of the evidence is heard again and wait until a Decision-Maker hears your case again, you might have to wait for a year or a year and a half or even longer before the Decision-Maker decides how much money to award you. You would probably get more money under that program but you have decided to accept this offer because the money will be paid to you quicker.

Please recollect that my fees to you are 15% of the total amount. The Government pays me the other 15%.

I enclose **three** copies of an Acceptance Letter to be signed by you where indicated by a sticky bit of paper and ask that you be kind enough to sign them in the presence of a witness, who will first sign his or her signature and then print his or her name. This witness can be anyone you choose.

Figure 130: The legal indemnification of churches and government for any liability for crimes in Indian residential schools (2008)

In addition, I enclose a Direction to Pay to be signed by you where indicated by a sticky bit of paper.

Once you have signed and had witnessed the **three** Acceptance Letters and Direction to Pay please give me a call and I will arrange to have them picked up.

For your information, by signing the Acceptance Letter you release Canada and the Church for responsibility for the pain and suffering caused to you by the conduct of their employees or agents while you were at the Residential School in return for paying you $160,000. This is final and means that you cannot bring a claim in the future against Canada and the Church for damages you suffered at the Residential School.

Please telephone me if you have any questions at all. The terms are acceptable to me provided that you have not promised to pay monies from the proceeds of the settlement amount to any other person or corporation, and provided that you feel that it is better to have this money rather than going on with your claim.

Best wishes,

SCOTT HALL
FJSH/ew
Enc.

April 24, 2007
Globe + Mail

Natives died in droves as Ottawa ignored warnings

Tuberculosis took the lives of students for at least 40 years

BY BILL CURRY AND KAREN HOWLETT
OTTAWA

As many as half of the aboriginal children who attended the early years of residential schools died of tuberculosis, despite repeated warnings to the federal government that overcrowding, poor sanitation and a lack of medical care were creating a toxic breeding ground for the rapid spread of the disease, documents show.

A Globe and Mail examination of documents in the National Archives reveals that children continued to die from tuberculosis at alarming rates for at least four decades after a senior official at the Department of Indian Affairs initially warned in 1907 that schools were making no effort to separate healthy children from those sick with the highly contagious disease.

Peter Bryce, the department's chief medical officer, visited 15 Western Canadian residential schools and found at least 24 per cent of students had died from tuberculosis over a 14-year period. The report suggested the numbers could be higher, noting that in one school alone, the death toll reached 69 per cent.

With less than four months to go before Ottawa officially settles out of court with most former students, a group calling itself the Friends and Relatives of the Disappeared Residential School Children is urging the government to acknowledge this period in the tragic residential-schools saga – and not just the better-known cases of physical and sexual abuse.

Figure 131: *Globe and Mail* headline before censoring : "Natives died in droves ..." (compare with Figure 132)

Globe and Mail investigation

Natives died as Ottawa ignored warnings

Tuberculosis took the lives of students at residential schools for at least 40 years

BILL CURRY AND KAREN HOWLETT
FROM TUESDAY'S GLOBE AND MAIL
APRIL 24, 2007 AT 1:30 AM EST

OTTAWA — As many as half of the aboriginal children who attended the early years of residential schools died of tuberculosis, despite repeated warnings to the federal government that overcrowding, poor sanitation and a lack of medical care were creating a toxic breeding ground for the rapid spread of the disease, documents show.

A Globe and Mail examination of documents in the National Archives reveals that children continued to die from tuberculosis at alarming rates for at least four decades after a senior official at the Department of Indian Affairs initially warned in 1907 that schools were making no effort to separate healthy children from those sick with the highly contagious disease.

Peter Bryce, the department's chief medical officer, visited 15 Western Canadian residential schools and found at least 24 per cent of students had died from tuberculosis over a 14-year period. The report suggested the numbers could be higher, noting that in one school alone, the death toll reached 69 per cent.

With less than four months to go before Ottawa officially settles out of court with most former students, a group calling itself the Friends and Relatives of the Disappeared Residential School Children is urging the government to acknowledge this period in the tragic residential-schools saga – and not just the better-known cases of physical and sexual abuse.

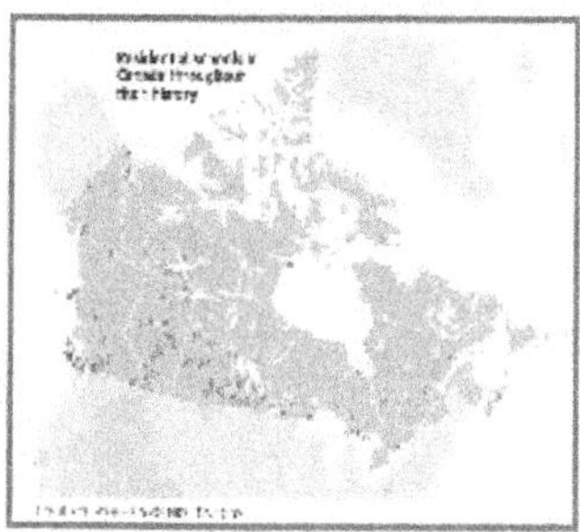

Figure 132: *Globe and Mail* headline after post-TRC censoring: "Natives died ..."

Appendices

Appendix One: A Comprehensive List of Offences committed within Indian Residential Schools and Indian Hospitals (1889-1996), with a List of these Facilities

Appendix Two: Supplemental Testimonies of Eyewitnesses to these Offences

Appendix Three: A National Crime - The Report of Dr. Peter Bryce concerning Genocidal Practices in Indian Residential Schools (1922)

Appendix Four: A Blueprint for Criminal Conspiracy: *Crimen Sollicitationas*, the Vatican policy regarding the concealment of child rape and trafficking within the Roman Catholic Church

Appendix Five: Mass Graves in Canada – A List of Twenty Eight Burial Sites at former Indian residential schools

Appendix Six: The Mush Hole Inquiry – The first survey and excavation of a mass burial site near a former Indian residential school (The Anglican Mohawk Institute in Brantford, Ontario)

Appendix Seven: Missing People - A Memorandum on the Organized Disappearance and Murder of Women and Children on Canada's West Coast – A Summary from Eyewitnesses (2006)

Appendix Eight: A Joint Plan for Genocide – The 1910 Contract to operate the Indian residential schools established between the government of Canada and mainline churches

Appendix Nine: Rules and Regulations governing an Indian residential school - the United Church facility in Port Alberni in 1962

Appendix Ten: Germ Warfare in British Columbia – The Case of John Sheepshanks and the Extermination of the Chilcotin People

<u>Appendix One:</u> Documented Offences committed within Indian Residential Schools and Indian Hospitals (1889-1996), with a List of these Facilities

<u>Preamble</u>

The following offences were perpetrated at Indian Residential Schools and Hospitals across Canada during the 107 year tenure of these facilities, from 1889 to 1996. The victims were aboriginal and Metis people between the ages of three and nineteen. The perpetrators were clergy, school and hospital staff, government and military agents, doctors, police and aboriginal accomplices.

These offences are attested by the testimonies of 358 survivors of forty three separate facilities listed in Part B of this Appendix. These testimonies are recorded and stored in trust in the archives of the International Tribunal into Crimes of Church and State (ITCCS). The offences have been verified independently by other persons, archival documents, forensic evidence and other material. At least 66,000 children and youths died as a direct result of these offences, and an indeterminably greater number in the wake of these crimes.

The institutions directly and legally responsible for these offences are the Crown of England and the Vatican, the federal government of Canada, various provincial governments, the RCMP, and the Roman Catholic, Anglican and United Church of Canada.

<u>Part A:</u> List of Offences (*This is not a complete list but one based on existing evidence*)

1. Homicide and premeditated murder, by beatings, starvation, rape, imprisonment, germ warfare, poisoning, medical experimentation, incineration, electric shocks and other tortures, and institutionalized terror
2. Routine sexual assault by individuals and groups.
3. Routine physical assault by individuals and groups.
4. Daily, unprovoked beatings and floggings using prescribed, standardized devices including whips, belts, sticks, leather harnesses, metal bars and bare fists
5. Deliberate denial of food and water for days at a time.

6. Deliberate denial of clothing, bedding and warm and healthy living conditions.

7. Deliberate denial of medical and dental care and treatment.

8. Deliberate exposure to communicable diseases, including smallpox, influenza and tuberculosis, accompanied by forced confinement and a denial of all medical care

9. Public floggings as punishment followed by confinement in restraining stocks and manacles, including outside in the midst of winter.

10. Routine physical, emotional and mental torture, administered as discipline, punishment and entertainment, including but not restricted to:

a) Electric shocks administered to the genitals, head, tongues and ears, and through specially designed electric chairs

b) Sticking needles through tongues, ears and penises

c) Tightening fish twine and wire around penises

d) Forcing victims to eat excrement, vomit and animal remains

e) Holding victims over open graves or burying them alive

f) Publicly degrading victims in front of others

g) Ripping hair from victims' heads and smashing their heads against hard surfaces

h) Forcing victims to stand for hours outside in the snow or in tubs of ice water

i) Forcible confinement in closets and basement prisons for days without food or water

j) Forcing victims to beat and rape others, and strangle or beat small animals to death

k) Making victims "run the gauntlet" and be beaten by others

l) Telling victims their parents were dead and isolating them from all outside contact

m) Employing victims in forced slave labour regimens and as unpaid workers

n) Removing teeth, tonsils and other organs without painkillers

o) Forcing victims to eat soiled or regurgitated food

11. Involuntary sexual sterilization of victims through vasectomies, tubal ligations, castration and prolonged exposure to X rays, these methods targeted specifically at non-Christian peoples

12. Involuntary medical experimentation on victims including but not restricted to:

a) Drug testing

b) Intrusive surgery

c) Removal of organs

d) Skin grafting and eye color altering surgery

e) Prolonged exposure to radiation and communicable diseases
f) Ice water immersion and exposure to sub-zero conditions while naked
g) Injection with experimental drugs and cancer-inducing substances
h) Behavior modification and mind altering methods including through electric shocks, sensory and sleep deprivation, prolonged isolation and rape
i) Prolonged confinement in a restricted physical position or in tiny compartments
j) Pain threshold experiments resulting in death

13. Trafficking victims for sexual and experimental purposes to pedocides and unknown parties
14. Trafficking victims to the government corporations and the military for experimental purposes
15. Inducing abortions in victims made pregnant by staff, clergy and others, or killing their new born babies
16. Conducting medical and dental procedures without anaesthesia, including fillings, tooth extractions and appendectomies
17. Imprisoning victims for years on end to extort money or compliance from their parents
18. Forcibly kidnapping victims from their communities, including through the use of vigilante groups and private mercenaries
19. Falsifying school and hospital records and disinterring graves to conceal these offences, and generally obstructing justice and police investigations
20. Blackmailing, threatening and killing witnesses to these and other crimes
21. Displacing victims' families from their homes and traditional lands to acquire their wealth and resources, including by deliberately spreading communicable diseases in those communities
22. Secretly disposing of the remains of victims through burials, incinerations and oceanic disposal
23. Systematically concealing these and other offences from the public through criminal acts

Part B: List of Facilities (This does not include an equal number of Indian Day schools)

1. Indian residential schools

Roman Catholic:

Christie – Meares Island, British Columbia (BC)

Kuper Island (BC)

Sechelt – North Vancouver (BC)

St. Paul's – Vancouver (BC)

St. Mary's – Mission (BC)

Kamloops (BC)

St. Eugene – Cranbrook (BC)

Lejac (BC)

Ermineskin – Hobbema, Alberta

Blue Quills – Saddle Lake, Alberta

Muscowequan – Saskatchewan

Norwood House – Manitoba

Sandy Bay – Manitoba

Spanish – Fort Albany, Ontario

Shubanacadie – Nova Scotia

United Church of Canada:

Ahousaht (Flores Island, BC)

Alberni (Port Alberni, BC)

Coqualeetza (Sardis, BC)

Kitimat (BC)

Edmonton – Alberta

File Hills – Saskatchewan

Birtle – Manitoba

Brandon – Manitoba

Portage la Prairie – Manitoba

Norway House – Manitoba

Cecilia Jeffrey – Fort Frances, Ontario

Anglican – Church of England

Carcross – Yukon

St. Michael's – Alert Bay, BC

St. George's – Lytton, BC

Pelican Lake – Ontario

Shingwauk – Sault Ste. Marie, Ontario

Mohawk Institute – Brantford, Ontario

2. Indian Hospitals - Church facilities operated with federal government funding. (* Indicates the site of sexual sterilization and military research programs)

*Nanaimo Indian Hospital, BC – United Church

*King's Daughter's Clinic, Duncan, BC – Anglican Church

*R.W. Large Hospital, Bella Bella, BC – United Church

*St. Paul's Hospital, Vancouver BC – Roman Catholic Church

Coqualeetza Tuberculosis Sanitarium, Sardis, BC – United Church

*Charles Camsell Hospital, Edmonton, Alberta – United Church

*Provincial Training School, Red Deer, Alberta – Federal government

*Lincoln Park Air Force Base, Edmonton, Alberta – Federal government

*Ponoka Mental Hospital, Alberta – Federal government

*Lake Head Psychiatric Hospital, Thunder Bay, Ontario – Federal government

*McGill University Hospital, Montreal Quebec – Roman Catholic Church

Appendix Two: Supplemental Testimonies of Eyewitnesses to these Offences

I'm Irene Favel. I'm seventy five. I went to residential school in Muscowequan from 1944 to 1949, and I had a rough life. I was mistreated in every way.

There was a young girl, and she was pregnant from a priest there. And what they did, she had her baby, and they took the baby, and wrapped it up in a nice pink outfit, and they took it downstairs where I was cooking dinner with the nun. And they took the baby into the furnace room, and they threw that little baby in there and burned it alive. All you could hear was this little cry, like "Uuh!", and that was it. You could smell that flesh cooking.

CBC Town Hall Forum, Regina, July 3, 2008

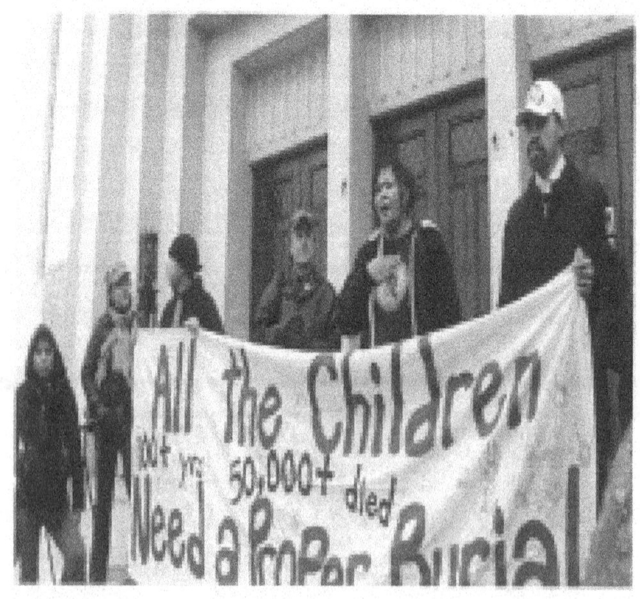

Testimony of Willie Sport, 75, given to (Rev.) Kevin Annett on March 28, 1998

I was born in Sarita in 1923. I was eight when I was sent to the Alberni Residential School. My father refused to send me to that school, so they put him in a small prison in the north end of Port Alberni.

I remember the first day there. I was lined up and told to eat this strange food. I hated it. They wouldn't let me leave until I finished it. I was speaking to this other boy named William Dennis in our own language, and this teacher named Miss Torkelson came up and slapped me hard on my cheek. I asked the boy in our language why she hit me, and she slapped me even harder. That was the beginning of me getting beaten up a lot.

My feet have been permanently deformed by the shoes they forced me to wear at the school. (see picture) They were much too small for me, but I had to wear them until they wore out, for years. When I passed 50 years old, my toe joints started pointing in the wrong direction. It's been terrible, and painful every time I take a step. I'm always so embarrassed to take my shoes off.

This happened to many kids. Some of them would damage their shoes on purpose to get a new pair, that fit, but they got whipped badly for that - for wanting decent shoes!

Another time, I spoke Indian in front of Reverend Pitts, the Principal of the Alberni school. He said, "Were you speaking Indian?". Before I could answer, he pulled down my pants and whipped my behind until he got tired. When I moved, he put my head between his knees and hit me harder. He used a thick conveyor belt, from a machine, to whip me.

That Principal Pitts was trying to kill us. **He wouldn't tell parents about their kids being sick and those kids would die, right there in the school. The plan was to kill all the Indians they could, so Pitts never told the families that their kids had tuberculosis.**

I got sick with TB and Pitts never told anyone. I was getting weaker each day, and I would have died there with all those others but my Dad found out and took me away from that school. I would be dead today if he hadn't come.

My Dad took me to his Dad, my grandfather, who was an Indian doctor. I told him I was hurting in the chest; it hurt most in the left bottom lung. Grandfather kept his finger there on my chest and he chanted, then he sucked on my chest where it hurt the most. He spat out three times, into a bowl, and each time it was pitch black stuff he spat.

p. 2

I remember so well watching him: three times, pitch black stuff into that bowl, a mouth-full each time. Then he said, "You're going to live, son." Over the next few days I got hungry again, I started playing, and I got well.

I was the only kid who survived from a bunch of us who were given TB by Pitts. He fed us this poisoned food to kill us. *That Principal wanted me to die. He had his orders to feed us this food that was contaminated with TB, and sure enough I was the only one of that group to survive,* thanks to my Grandfather. That poisoned food was strange, a canned food I'd never seen before. After eating it I got sick with TB.

This happened to tribes up north a lot. They were given this poisoned ham, and whole villages would die off. I couldn't even sit up, I was so weak after eating that canned food.

I somehow survived for three years at the Alberni school. But when I got back from being cured by my grandfather, Principal Pitts saw me, and said quickly, "Did you know you can't come back to school?". I asked why, and he said, "TB is contagious." That was the only reason they gave for not letting me back, even though I had been cured by then.

That proved to me that Pitts knew I had TB, and he didn't want me around because I knew the truth of his plan to kill kids. Two of my best friends were in the group he infected: James Thomas' son from Nitinaht and a boy from Port Renfrew. They were dead within a week of eating that food. Only when they were about to die were their families told.

We were never allowed in certain parts of the Alberni school building, like the basement, and the second floor. It was a death sentence to be sent there.

William Sport

Witnessed by:

(Rev.) Kevin Annett

March 28, 1998
Port Alberni, B.C.

Testimony of Mabel Sport, 70, of Nanaimo, B.C., given to (Rev.) Kevin Annett on March 28, 1998

I was born in 1928 in Hesquait, and I went to the Christie Residential School from 1935 to 1944. It was run by the Roman Catholics.

I can't even stand to look at nuns, even if they're on TV. They beat us all so badly. They put my sister in the hospital for a long time after beating her on the neck with a ruler, and it got badly infected.

I think they were trying to deliberately infect us with tuberculosis, because they always made me sleep in the same bed with girls who had TB. One on each side of me. I was very scared, so I slept turned away from them, even under the bed sometimes. I'd always open the windows, too. The school officials put us like that on purpose so we'd all get TB and die.

This one girl named Rose Johnson, from Friendly Cove, she was eight years old and she died after they didn't treat her for an appendicitis. She was vomiting black blood, but the nuns wouldn't take her to the hospital. Her eyes were rolling back, and she was in real trouble, but those two nuns - Sister Justine and Sister Loretta - they just pulled her hair and strapped her, even when she was so sick!

She died soon after that. They killed her, just beat her silly while she was dying from that appendicitis. That was in the early 1940's. She was Sam Johnson's daughter.

I once overheard the nuns and priests talking. One of the priests said, ***"Those poor Indian kids: they're so smart but they're not supposed to go to highschool."*** They never intended to educate us - just beat and kill us.

For example, they'd often put men in the same prison cell as people with tuberculosis. Then the entire families of those men would come down with TB and be wiped out. That's how they dealt with us. Anything was okay if it killed Indians.

Mabel C. Sport
Mrs. Mabel Sport

Witnessed by:

Kevin Annett
(Rev.) Kevin Annett

March 28, 1998
Port Alberni, B.C.

Testimony of Vera Hunt, 50, given to (Rev.) Kevin Annett on March 3, 1998

I was born in 1948 in Bella Bella. I was sent to St. Michael's residential school in Alert Bay when I was nine, then when I was thirteen I was sent to Alberni school. That would have been in 1961. I stayed at Alberni until 1967.

I stood up for other kids, so I was beaten a lot, and locked up in the infirmary at St. Mike's. The staff there would provoke the kids to be bad so they'd have a reason to beat them. For example, the dorm supervisors would steal from the kids and say "That's my stuff now." Miss Roffel was one: she would steal our wristwatches and combs, and then hit us and threaten us. Mrs. Dalton was also a bad one: I felt the cold in her.

Once, my cousin Emily Humpchit (she's Marilyn Campbell now) was dragged by her hair around a table by some other kids, some bullies. But Miss Roffel ignored it, and let them do that to her.

A lot of us were whipped with skipping ropes by Miss Elliott. The staff there called me bad because I hid kids from the supervisors and protected them. They locked me up in the infirmary for three months after that, and I screamed for help.

Scary things were happening in the boys' dorm at St. Mike's. Once, these three male supervisors dragged a little eight year old boy out of the dorm, and then he disappeared for good. No-one ever saw him again.

A lot of boys became gay after being molested by the male staff there. George Whonnock was one. Poor Toby Willey's back was so scarred after what they did to him. They spread-eagled him against a wall in front of all the boys and whipped him. Then they made him clean up his urine totally naked in front of everyone.

Mr. Dalton molested a lot of girls at St. Mike's, like Gloria Nelson and Ruby Williams. Ruby was killed just recently.

I heard a lot of stories about babies' bodies being found buried at St. Michael's Residential School in Alert Bay. Barbara Hanuse in Campbell River knows more about that. Girls at the school tried to teach me how to use a knife when I was ten years old, to protect me from the supervisors, who were all rapists.

In 1961, when I was thirteen, I went to the Alberni school. Two male supervisors tried to attack me as soon as I got there. Then I was beaten by Mrs. Sack and Miss Wiebe after they found me with a radio. Mrs. Sack went crazy, and said, "Give me that radio, you slut, you bitch!". She dragged me by the hair into the hall, enraged like she was crazy, and she kicked me and punched me. Then she threw me into the staff house, and kept me out of school, bringing me food.

Mr. Alcock, the bus driver, tried to fondle me. I told Mr. Andrews, the Principal, what had happened, and he refused to do anything about Mrs. Sack or Mr. Alcock. At the same time, Mr. Plint was molesting Victor Jackson, who was just nine.

The police found out about what happened to me, and they were coming to the school to investigate. My cousin, Margaret Thompson, knew about how I had been mistreated. So Mr. Andrews, that Principal, said to her *"If you know what's good for you, you won't tell the truth to the police. Say what I tell you to if you want to graduate from here."*

So Andrews made Margaret lie in her testimony, and made her say that I hadn't been attacked by Mrs. Sack and Mr. Alcock. After that, Mrs. Sack and Miss Wiebe tried to push me down the stairs.

A young girl who went to the Alberni Residential School named Violet, who was fourteen, was found strangled in Nanaimo in 1963. Her body was found right on the railway tracks. She was pregnant. The police never investigated her death. Violet Joseph knew about this, but she's dead now.

The girls who got pregnant were expelled immediately. Some of them were even found dead on the grounds of the Alberni school. None of us could ever leave the school grounds, and we couldn't mix with the boys - we couldn't even hold hands with them - so the staff had to be the ones who fathered those kids.

Vera Hunt
Vera Hunt

Witnessed by:

Kevin Annett
(Rev.) Kevin Annett

March 3, 1998
Vancouver, B.C.

Statement of Ethel Wilson, age 81, given to (Rev.) Kevin Annett on 25 August, 1998 in Vancouver, B.C.

I was born in Bella Bella in 1916. My brothers and sisters and I, we all went to the residential school in Alert Bay (*St. Michael's, Anglican - KA*). I never got to go to school when I was there. They just had me work in the kitchen. But when I was young, maybe nine years old, I caught tuberculosis in that school, like a lot of kids, and I had to stay in the Bella Bella hospital as I grew up. I had the TB in my knee, and I still can't walk right.

It was in that hospital that I was molested by Dr. Darby, the United Church minister and doctor in Bella Bella. He was an awful man. He was the local minister, doing all the marriages and burials. He was in Bella Bella a long time, maybe forty years. He died up there and is buried in the village.

Dr. Darby molested me when I was helpless. Later, in the hospital, he operated on me to stop me from having babies. I was 23 then. I felt his big hand on my private area. Then he got out of that room fast, and he always avoided me after that, he was so guilty.

Dr. Darby was always doing the wrong thing. He wrecked my leg, deformed it, by putting a cast on it after I got TB. He didn't even ask me. A lot of young girls were sterilized by Dr. Darby. Today, many women in Bella Bella can't have babies because they were sterilized, lots by him.

Another thing Dr. Darby did was remove all the gold teeth from peoples' mouths. Gold was cheap back then, and many of our people had gold linings or whole gold teeth. Without telling me why or asking me for permission, Dr. Darby pulled all my teeth that had gold in them. My uncle had all his teeth pulled by Darby, since they were all gold.

Dr. Darby's son, George Darby, he also molested young girls in the hospital there. That would have been in the 1950's. He was a doctor, too, and he visited Bella Bella one summer to help out in the clinic. That's when he molested my daughter. She was having her tonsils out and he molested her when she was helpless. George Darby's still alive, I think.

Lots of children came back from the Alert Bay residential school in coffins. It was often from tuberculosis. Those poor kids were deliberately killed. My late sister, Nora Gladstone, got TB at that school. She died quickly from it. She got it in the throat, and they sent her home, where she died. She was 14 when it happened, in 1934.

They were dying like flies, even at the TB hospitals, like the Coqualeetza one. My aunt Addy White, and my two cousins Hazel Housty and the Jackson girl, whose name I can't remember, they all died from TB at the Coqualeetza hospital.

The strange thing was how those deaths never stopped. They were supposed to be treating us, making us better, and they never did. It didn't make any difference when the Coqualeetza place went from being a residential school *(United Church - KA)* to a hospital. Kids kept coming home in coffins.

They found bones between the walls of the Coqualeetza residential school when they rebuilt it, around 1940. Those bones were of teenagers, almost full-sized skeletons. They must have been graves, since the bones were all together. Why would they have buried kids between walls, unless they wanted to hide something?

Ethel Wilson
Ethel Wilson

Witnesed by:

Kevin Annett
(Rev.) Kevin Annett

25 August, 1998

Testimony of Harriett Nahanee, age 60, concerning abuses at the United Church Native Residential School, Port Alberni (1945-50) ... given to (Rev.) Kevin McNamee-Annett in North Vancouver, December 14, 1995

When I was five years old, all my brothers and sisters were taken to the Ahousaht residential school. But it burned down, and so they were sent home. My mother hid me at that time (1940), and I stayed hidden with relatives for five years, at places like Neah Bay and Zeballos, so that I wouldn't be taken to the residential school.

She hid me so that one of us would keep our culture, which is that we are keepers of the land. The whites had to change us from being keepers so they could have the land.

My mother was sent a letter saying she'd go to jail unless I went to residential school, so when I was ten I went to the Port Alberni school.

I looked forward to going to this school, because I didn't speak much English, being hidden for so long. But I was trained to speak the truth from age five on, since we don't have a written language and have to speak the truth to pass it on from person to person.

My enthusiasm changed quickly when I got to the school, since we were given immediate humiliation. They expected me to speak English only, immediately. We were deloused, DDT put in our hair, then it was shaved off. Cod liver oil was forced down our throats with an oil can. We weren't allowed to laugh, and were beaten a lot, especially for laughing.

They used to beat us with a conveyor belt strap three inches wide and three feet long. There was one hung on the cubicle wall of every floor in the school. The dorms were all locked each night, so we couldn't escape. It was a jail. We would have died if a fire broke out.

There were 300 kids there with me, and we were always lining up and praying before everything. They were trying to control us all the time. I was in a family of a chief, so the other kids looked to me when the whites gave them orders. This made the whites punish me because they didn't want their authority challenged by a ten year old.

They punished me by sexually abusing me at nights. They would take me into the infirmary when it was dark, and a man would be in there, waiting for me. There were only two men in the school then, Mr. Peake, the supervisor, and Reverend Caldwell, the minister.

I ran away a lot, but they always caught me. Mr. Caldwell would put me over his desk, take down my panties, and beat me in a way that, looking back, makes me think he was jerking himself off while he was doing it. If I tried to look around he would scream at me and hit me on the back of my head with the strap. He was one of the men who raped me in the infirmary at night, I know it. I had his penis in my mouth at least once a week.

He was always drinking and screaming, and I was terrified of him. So whenever I heard him coming, I would run away and hide somewhere. He was always strapping and humiliating me.

One day in 1946, I was eleven, and I went to the place under the stairs where I would go and sit and cry. I heard Mr. Caldwell at the top of the stairs with another little girl, a few years younger than me. Her father's last name was "Blackie", and they were from Nitinat. Mr. Caldwell was screaming at her, and then I heard this sound, like a kick, and I heard her falling down the stairs. I looked out and saw her facing me, with her eyes open, not moving or breathing. I never saw her again after that.

All my life I've had nightmares about that sound, like a kick.

I told other people about what happened to that little girl, but no-one believed me, not even my own mother.

We used to resent Mr. Caldwell's daughter because she would pick through all the clothes that came to us from churches, and take what she wanted first.

Mr. Peake, the Boys' Supervisor, used to make kids take off their clothes in the infirmary and he would take pictures of them naked. He was always wandering around everywhere.

He once had a girl friend of mine in his room. She was a few years younger than me. I heard her in there giggling, and she had no clothes on, so I ran upstairs with her to Dorm 5, and we took somebody else's clothes so she could get dressed. She was strapped later for taking those clothes. Mrs. Stevenson was another supervisor who used to slap us all the time.

The only other kids I remember from that time were Edna Robinson and Clara Joseph. And later, Arlena Jones, my niece, was one of the girls Mr. Peake made undress and took pictures of.

Another thing I was punished for was not bowing my head at prayer time. We were taught in our own culture not to look down and be ashamed, but to always be proud. Everytime I wouldn't bow my head I was taken into the infirmary. They told me I couldn't go home on holidays if I didn't bow my head.

At Christmas in 1945, Miss Lawrence, the Grade one teacher, said to me, "Your mother has come and taken your brothers and sisters home already, but you have to stay here because you wouldn't bow your head." So I bowed my head right away, and she let me go. I saw that it was a lie, they hadn't left yet.

I've always hated Christmas because that's the day I had to bow my head. That's the day they stole my soul, those Christians.

A lot of kids got tuberculosis at the residential school from all the cows they kept there. Hundreds of us were in the hospital for TB, the one in Nanaimo. My niece was in bed there for five years, some kids for ten or eleven years, just lying in bed, doing nothing. They had no muscles left after, and were completely helpless. They were used like guinea pigs, in experiments. Then they were told never to have any children.

We would dance and sing our native songs in a corner somewhere in the school, but another kid would tell on us, usually a half-breed, and they would get a reward for informing. The half-breeds were treated much better than we were because they looked more white, and they didn't have any culture of their own.

The school dentist used to work on our teeth without any pain-killer, because he would sell half the novocaine given him by the government and use the rest in his own practice in Port Alberni. Many of us today never look after our teeth, or go to a dentist.

2

That experience made us hate dentists, doctors, teachers. Why send our kids to them to have them go through what we did?

We had no love, no mothers to cuddle us, no elders to teach us. I never showed my children affection, never hugged them, because I grew up without affection. I was just programmed to be a servant.

We didn't learn anything; we just learned to labour. They only gave us two hours of school each day. The rest of the time we were the labourers in the school, washing walls and windows, doing all the chores. I was groomed for servitude. We were completely powerless, just brainwashed to forget our own culture.

The supervisors used to put rocks in our mouths if we spoke our own language. My counsellor told me to go back and take the rock out of my mouth, and then I realized it wasn't a rock, but Mr. Peake's penis in my mouth.

When I was fifteen, I ran away and spent my last pennies on a phonecall to my brother Ray, and he came and got me. I never went back to that school.

My daughter Annie killed herself when she was eighteen. She was thrown out of her schools, she didn't care about school or working. She grew up without hope. I survived because I have a culture. But I didn't pass it on to Annie because I was ashamed of being an Indian.

Harriett Nahanee
Harriett Nahanee
December 15, 1995

Witnessed by:

Kevin McNamee-Annett
Kevin McNamee-Annett
(Rev.)

Kevin Annett
November 1, 1996

Statement of Irene Starr (nee Wilson), student at Alberni Residential School, given to (Rev.) Kevin Annett on October 24, 1997, in Vancouver, B.C.

I was born in Bella Bella in 1945, and lived there until the Indian Agent told my mother "If your children don't go to the residential school, they'll all be put up for adoption." So they scared her into sending me away when I was seven or eight. My heart was broken. It ruined my entire way of thinking and living.

The Alberni school was a terrible, awful place. I wet my bed constantly, I was so lonely and afraid. Whenever I wet my sheets, the staff made me stomp on the sheets in a tub of cold water, up to my waist. I stood in ice water for an hour often, and three women on staff laughed at me as I froze. They'd bang me with a mop whenever I stopped, and tell me to hurry up. Then, I'd have to go to school, frozen, ice cold. I had permanent bladder problems because of that.

I was just a little girl of seven, and I wanted to kill myself. What makes a child want to committ suicide? I was so mistreated. All I heard from the teachers was "You dumb Indian", "You'll never amount to anything". They were constantly smacking me on the head. So I grew up thinking I was ugly and stupid. I was ashamed of myself, and my people, and I wished I was white.

I was always freezing. All I had each night was one little blanket over my cot. I was never warm. All of us were hungry. The food was rotten, the oatmeal and milk was bad. Kids were always getting sick from the food, and many of them refused to eat it. They starved. That's why I thought of killing myself, I was starving there.

A lot of girls got pregnant after they got to the Alberni school. The fathers were the men who worked there. We never knew what happened to the babies. The pregnant girls would be taken to the Alberni Hospital and then come back without their babies. I'd hear them crying all the time: "Where's my baby? What have they done with my baby?".

The staff at the school probably killed most of those babies because they were the fathers. They were not only sadists but murderers. And they got paid to be so.

I've been a loner ever since that school. It still hurts so bad to think of that place. Like the big lady in black, who was always beating me and my sister Donna with a wooden brush, and dragging Donna into a closet to sexually abuse her.

p. 2

I was hit either with a wooden scrubbing brush or a mop, always on the head. I also got strapped with a leather strap in class, whenever I dozed off, from staying awake all night taking care of the babies. The strap was two inches thick. I had welts on my arms, up to my shoulders.

So many of our people are dying, every day, because of the residential schools. I only got to grade eight. Eventually, beer calmed my nerves. I became an alcoholic, and eventually, a heroin addict.

The church spokesmen, the officials, they don't mean what they say when they speak. I can't understand how those people in the school learned to be so cruel.

Irene C. Starr
Irene Starr

October 24, 1997
Vancouver, B.C.

Witnessed by:

Kevin Annett
(Rev.) Kevin Annett

Bill Seward

Nanoose, BC.

Born 1920

Attended Kuper Island RS 1930-35

I was put into Kuper Island school by force by terrorists in uniform. They punished by denying me food for three or four days, just for speaking my language.

My sister Maggie was thrown from a three-story window by a nun at the school, and she died. Everything was swept under the rug. No investigation was ever done. Maggie was killed by the Roman Catholic Church. She was just a teenager. *We couldn't hire a lawyer at that time, being Indians, so nothing was done.* They wouldn't even let us ride upstairs on the ferry with everyone else. We were stuck down with the freight.

It was like being black in the States. We couldn't go into theaters or bars. They could do anything they wanted to us. They stuck my hands into freezing water for hours on end to punish me. I'd be forced to kneel in the corner all night without food.

I was given injections, too, but not in the chest, in the arms, but they made me very sick, with the same symptoms as the later ones: dizzy, sick, fainting. I was given the shots regularly around 1935.

A lot of kids came home in coffins from Kuper Island school. We tried floating away on logs, anything, just to escape. Many drowned.

The residential schools were set up because the whites knew we were sitting on gold, coal, and good land. The churches were worshipping the devil, not us. They helped the other whites squat on our land, burning our masks, killing our elders. Nothing's changed.

Belvy Breber

Halalt Nation, Vancouver Island, BC.

Born 1947

Attended Kuper Island RS (Catholic) 1961-63.

My brother, Richard Thomas, was murdered at the Kuper Island school. We got a call that he was found hanging in the gym by a Father Lamond. He said that Richard had killed himself. But Richard was happy that week, because he was about to graduate after seven years at that "hell-hole" as he called it. He had phoned me the day before and said, "When I get out of here I'm going to tell all." The phone he was using was right next to the priests' office, and they could hear everything that Richard said. The day he died kids had looked for him for four hours, including in the gym, and they couldn't find him. But then his body turned up there. Father Dunlop said he found the body. His was the office closest to the phone Richard used. The coroner told us he didn't think Richard died by suicide.

They used to stick my head in the toilet, those nuns, to punish me. Sister Mary Peters sexually abused boys and girls at the school. Father Dunlop, the principal, knew about this and did nothing.

I think Father Dunlop and Father Terry MacNamara both killed Richard. I wrote to MacNamara and told him so, and two days later he was transferred by the Oblates to the Holy Land. Now he's living up in Prince Rupert. We've asked the RCMP to exhume Richard's remains and do an investigation but they've refused.

Addendum:

The police report into Richard's death was totally different than all the information we had. It said that Richard's body was always in the gym, when eyewitnesses said it wasn't there just before the priests "discovered" it. The coroner at McColl's funeral home in Duncan said that Richard's body was not like those of suicide victims; "he was too easy to dress." My nephew, Gerry Thomas, was present when Richard died. He said that they were coached in their testimonies by the Mounties. In 1997, Constable Tugood said, "It is illegal for you to see their testimonies, since it happened so long ago. You're not allowed to speak to them."

Maureen Maquire, another student, claims that she saw Father Dunlop carrying Richard's body into the gym in a vision, since she is a trained psychic used regularly by the police. She says she sees a man with a "crooked face" carrying Richard; Dunlop's face was deformed.

Delmer Johnny

Penelakut Nation, BC.

Born 1945

Attended Kuper Island RS 1961-68.

I was a friend of Richard Thomas, who was found hanging. It was impossible for him to hang himself the way they said he did. He couldn't have got up there, it was too high. One of the priests killed him, probably Father Dunlop. After Richard's death, we were all silenced. Philip George saw everything but was threatened into silence. A priest, Thomas Furlong, was sleeping with a nun, Mary Lucille, and Sister Mary was having sex with Father Dunlop, and that caused an investigation by Bishop de Roo out of Victoria, in the 1960's. But de Roo whitewashed Richard's death. We weren't even interviewed as part of the Bishop's "investigation." We were told to stay quiet about this murder, by the church and the cops. That Constable Tugood did a completely bogus report on the death. We were even told not to speak to other witnesses who found Richard hanging in the gym. Valerie Thomas of the Coal Bay reserve and Michel Horn of Saanich told Belvy Breber that her brother was killed by Terry MacNamara.

Denise Joseph (nee Toochie)

Opitchesaht Nation, Port Alberni, BC.

Born 1943

Attended Alberni RS (United Church) 1955-57.

Three of my brothers were killed at the Alberni school. They were in the unprotected group, so they were fair game. A twelve-year-old friend of mine from Ahousat killed herself by jumping into a burning building, back in the village, rather than be sent back to the Alberni School. She'd rather burn up ~~and~~ than go back. Why not? I was raped so often I can't remember. Mrs. Brown, a teacher, did so after strapping me for going to the bathroom. I was seven.

Michael David

Chemainus Nation, Vancouver Island, BC

Born 1955

Attended Kuper Island RS (Catholic) 1962-70.

My mother told me last week that when I was little, the Department of Indian Affairs came to see her and said, "If you have any children who are sick you're to send them to the Kuper Island school." This was strange, since all the kids were dying at that school from all the tuberculosis.

We knew that they were doing experiments on the kids at the school. Injections of some kind. Everyone talked about it but we were too scared to tell anyone.

Glen Doughty, a priest, was charged with raping kids at the school. He only got three months in jail.

When Richard Thomas was found hanging in the gym, the priests kept us away, like they were hiding something. My friend, Gerry Thomas, said he saw the priests string up the body.

I was forced to wear a diaper whenever I wet my bed. I was thirteen. Sister Angela made us sing a song, "We wet our beds and we're proud of it." It was all designed to break our spirits and humiliate us.

After Richard Thomas died, the RCMP told us boys who were in the gym not to talk about what we saw. They didn't even take our testimonies. Even when a friend of mine who was raped by Glen Doughty killed himself, the RCMP wouldn't even investigate his death.

Dennis Charlie

Penelakut Nation, Vancouver Island, BC

Born 1929

Attended Kuper Island RS (Catholic) 1939-45

When I was ten, fifty boys and myself were made to line up in the infirmary and some German speaking doctors gave us injections in our chests. Two needles, near each nipple. We started falling down right away, it made us sick, dizzy, and some of us passed out. We carried each other to our dorm, but two boys were sent home, they were so ill. One of them was my friend, Sandy Mitchell, who died soon after. They didn't tell us what the needles were for, and we never saw those German doctors again. Father Thibeault took notes and watched us after we got the shots.

It was torture. They were experimenting on us, and we couldn't do a thing to stop it. We were continually told not to talk to anyone about the injections. It was the Montfort Brothers who were running the school then. But one day in 1940 we woke up and the Montforts were gone, including Father Gertz, the Principal. Gone in the night, and replaced by the Oblates. That was soon after word got out about Sandy Mitchell's death.

South of the school there were four or five unmarked graves. Those were kids who had been killed at the school, away from the graveyard. In 1972, just before the school was closed, the priests dug up those graves one night. We [i.e., the people of the Island as well as the students] were told to stay away and not watch what they were doing.

My brother John was hit in the head with a metal chain by a priest. They refused to take him to hospital because they were afraid of the priest getting into trouble. So John died there when he could have been saved by local doctors. They deliberately killed him and let him die there unattended, those priests. Our parents were never told anything about this, and we were told that we'd be hurt or killed if we said anything. They always beat me with a horse harness.

Addendum:

After Sandy Mitchell got sick from the injections, they sent him to the TB sanitorium in Coqualeetza. A friend of mine saw him there. He was put in an isolation ward where no one could see him. His whole body was swelled up, big and smelly. My friend said you could smell Sandy way down the hall. They were experimenting on him, because those aren't the symptoms of tuberculosis. It was Fathers Gertz, Neway and Thibeault who were responsible for that, the same ones who beat kids with pool cues and raped kids in front of others.

Sandy's body was rotting away in that sanitorium. And he wasn't the only one. Ed Seymour was sent to the same place after getting the shots, along with Raymond Recalma. Another boy, a friend of Raymond's, died after one of the needles broke off in his chest during one of the experiments.

The Germans started those shots, but other doctors were in on it, local people from Chemainus, three of them in white coats. The Principal, Gertz, he spoke German. He used to take five girls at a time into his bedroom and made them fondle his penis. The priests regularly slept with the girls, and they got pregnant and were shipped out right away. Some were even killed, and I think they're the bodies that were dug up so quickly by the priests in 1972. We weren't allowed to talk about this.

Arnold Sylvester

Penelakut Nation, BC

Born 1932

Attended Kuper Island RS (Catholic) 1939-44

I got those shots in my chest, too. I still have the scars. A lot of us got sick and some of us died after the Germans injected us. You couldn't walk straight; the pain was so bad from the shots. It made you vomit, dizzy, and double over. You hurt all over, it was terrible. We were never told what the needles were for. The year later, though, they gave us some more shots, still in the chest, but local nuns gave them to me. Like before, they made me sick and drowsy.

Sandy Mitchell was one of the boys who died after getting the shots. Other tried swimming away, they were so scared, and they drowned.

Sister Marie, the school nurse, gave me the second round of shots. She and Sister Mary Elaine, a teacher. They said we'd get punished if we talked about the needles. Principal Cameron said, "Never tell anyone about the shots," even though we were all getting sick from them. They canceled school for three days because we were all sick from the shots. The shots left permanent scars on your body. The scars were round, like warts, and made your skin thicker.

The same Principal, Cameron, used to beat me up with another priest, Brother Michael. I was only eleven and these two grown men were punching me out, taking turns.

George Harris

Chemainus Nation, Vancouver Island, BC, (Halkomelem Treaty Group).

Born 1947

Attended Kuper Island RS (Catholic), 1954-57

We were expendable. Our lives had no value. Whenever we got sick in that school we were completely ignored. My mother was even forced to sleep in the same bed with kids who were dying of tuberculosis. This was common. The church officials were trying to kill us off. Tuberculosis spread like wildfire among us because of this policy of deliberately infecting us. So many of us died from that, and from the food they made us eat, which was rancid and filled with bugs. I suspect that we were operated on, used like guinea pigs, when we got sick. They used our illness as a justification to experiment on us. That happened to my mother. They kept her in hospital for two years, and did an operation on her that left a wide scar on her from the top of her left shoulder to her lower back. She was told by the church people never to talk about the operation.

I also remember Rick Thomas, a young friend of mine who was found dead hanging in the school gym. The priest, Terry MacNamara, he made us walk by the body of Rick and he said, "That will happen to you to if you run away." We all knew what he meant, that we'd be murdered too. We all knew that MacNamara killed Rick because he was about to graduate and tell what he knew about the other killings at the school.

Kathy Brown

Hesquait Nation, Bella Bella, BC.

Born 1952

Mother, Elsie Robinson, (born 1920) attended Ahousat day school (United Church) 1931-37

My mother's hair turned white before she was twenty because she was used as a guinea pig in penicillin experiments around 1935, while going to the Ahousat Day school. The church staff were in on it, and some local doctors. They used the native kids in a lot of experiments, like skin grafting. It was common practice. The same thing that happened to my mother happened to Alice Humpchit. The experiments were going on in the day school.

Even war criminals go to church

A deacon of the Anglican Church confesses crimes to Reverend Kevin D Annett

"The Christian Churches in Nazi Germany were filled every Sunday, even during the worst persecutions. It was always business as usual for the church."

—Wolf-Dieter Zimmerman, German Resistance Leader and Pastor of the anti-Nazi "Confessing Church," 1982.

For a religion with so much blood on its hands, European Christianity is unashamedly bold. Even now, after the Anglican, United, and Catholic churches in Canada have been proven to have killed off more than 50,000 kids in their "residential schools," they continue to speak of themselves and that poor carpenter in the same breath, as if sterilized and murdered native children were part of Jesus's plan.

One doesn't realize the enormity of this historical deception until confronted by one of the practitioners of religious genocide, face to face. It happened to me in June of 1998, during a UN "tribunal held into Indian residential schools" in Vancouver.

Perhaps he was trying to get rid of some of his own demons, like war criminals are prone to do. Or maybe he wanted to do the right thing, finally. But the old man who spoke to me over coffee in an eastside diner had the haunted look of someone who has spilled innocent blood.

"We used to flog them until they died," he began to mutter, in hushed, sad tones.

"Who?" I asked.

"The runaways. Five-, six-year-old kids, even. They were brought back by the Mounties, in chains. Leg irons and manacles. Then we'd put them in the stocks."

"You mean, wooden stocks, like out of the Middle Ages?"

"Yes," the old man replied, not looking at me. "They were set up right in the middle of the school yard. The runaways would be put in there and left for a few days, rain or shine. They wouldn't be fed or anything. Then we'd flog them with a whip until it was over."

"Over?" I asked. "You mean, the child was deliberately killed?"

The man nodded, avoiding my stare.

"Was that a regular practice?"

"Of course. It happened all the time. The kids were given one warning, and if they ran away a second time, they'd get the flogging."

"And the government knew about this murder?" I asked.

"Everybody knew. How else could we have gotten away with it for decades? The Indian Agent, the Mounties, local doctors and coroners, and of course the church officials—they were all in on it."

"And what did you do with all the bodies?"

The old man looked at me for the first time.

"Every residential school had a furnace. Ours was kept going all the time. Just like the one in Port Alberni."

"And like the one at Auschwitz," I said to him.

He nodded.

"The only difference is that this is Canada, and the victims were Indians," he continued. "That made it perfectly legal. And that's why I never have to worry about going to jail, either, which is why I'm telling you all this."

"Come again?" I replied, feeling my blood boil.

"Look, son, you seem to think the winners have to answer for their crimes. We're the Anglican Church of Canada, for god's sake. Who's ever going to think we murdered children?"

"Me," I answered.

He smiled for the first time.

"And who's going to believe you?" the criminal said, still smiling.

"I have your testimony. And documents which prove that manacles were used on children at the St. George's Anglican school in Lytton, BC, in 1952."

"And a lot later than that," he added. "The kids were dying like flies there until it closed in the '70s. But who cared then? And who really cares now?"

I stared out the window, not knowing whether to slug the bastard or turn off the tape recorder I had going in my pocket.

Instead, I asked him, "Are you still active in the Anglican church?"

"Of course. I'm a deacon."

"And you go before God every Sunday knowing that you and your church have all this innocent blood on your hands?"

The criminal stared at me for a long time, and finally said, "We believe that God forgives us."

His answer actually seemed to satisfy him.

That night I didn't think too much about a shivering and terrified child, awaiting death at the end of a whip. It was too difficult, even for me.

What I kept realizing, over and over, was that my Uncle Bob had died for nothing during World War II. Along with fifty million others.

By Rev Kevin D Annett

Appendix Three: A National Crime - The Report of Dr. Peter Bryce concerning Genocidal Practices in Indian Residential Schools (1922)

Appendix 3: An Early Whistle Blower: Dr. Peter Bryce's 1922 work "A National Crime" and its description of massive mortality rates in Indian residential schools *(pages are not numbered)*

THE STORY OF A NATIONAL CRIME

BEING A

Record of the Health Conditions of the Indians of Canada from 1904 to 1921

—BY—

DR. P. H. BRYCE, M. A., M. D.

Chief Medical Officer of the Indian Department.

110 - 7

I. By Order in Council dated ~~Jan. 22nd,~~ Feb 23rd 1904, the writer was appointed Medical Inspector to the Department of the Interior and of Indian Affairs, and was entrusted with the health interests of the Indians of Canada. The Order in Council recites : —

"The undersigned has the honour to report that there is urgent necessity for the appointment of a medical inspector to represent the Department of the Interior and Department of Indian Affairs. The undersigned believes that the qualifications for the position above mentioned are possessed in an eminent degree by Mr. Peter Henderson Bryce, M. D., at present and for a number of years past Secretary for the Provincial Board of Health of Ontario, and who has had large experience in connection with the public health of the province."

(Signed) CLIFFORD SIFTON,

Minister of the Interior and
Superintendent General of Indian Affairs.

For the first months after the writer's appointment he was much engaged in organizing the medical inspection of immigrants at the sea ports ; but he early began the systematic collection of health statistics of the several hundred Indian Bands scattered over Canada. For each year up to 1914 he wrote an annual report on the health of the Indians, published in the Departmental report, and on instructions from the minister made in 1907 a special inspection of thirty-five Indian schools in the three prairie provinces. This report was published separately ; but the recom-

3

246

[...]ndations contained in the report were never published and the [p]ublic knows nothing of them. It contained a brief history of [th]e origin of the Indian Schools, of the sanitary condition of the schools and statistics of the health of the pupils, during the 15 years of their existence. Regarding the health of the pupils, the report states that 24 per cent. of all the pupils which had been in the schools were known to be dead, while of one school on the File Hills reserve, which gave a complete return to date, 75 per cent. were dead at the end of the 16 years since the school opened.

Recommendations of school report 1907.

Briefly the recommendations urged, (1) Greater school facilities, since only 30 per cent. of the children of school age were in attendance; (2) That boarding schools with farms attached be established near the home reserves of the pupils; (3) That the government undertake the complete maintenance and control of the schools, since it had promised by treaty to insure such; and further it was recommended that as the Indians grow in wealth and intelligence they should pay at least part of the cost from their own funds; (4) That the school studies be those of the curricula of the several Provinces in which the schools are situated, since it was assumed that as the bands would soon become enfranchised and become citizens of the Province they would enter into the common life and duties of a Canadian community; (5) That in view of the historical and sentimental relations between the Indian schools and the Christian churches the report recommended that the Department provide for the management of the schools, through a Board of Trustees, one appointed from each church and approved by the minister of the Department. Such a board would have its secretary in the Department but would hold regular meetings, establish qualifications for teachers, and oversee the appointments as well as the control of the schools; (6) That Continuation schools be arranged for on the school farms and that instruction methods similar to those on the File Hills farm colony be developed; (7) That the health interests of the pupils be guarded by a proper medical inspection and that the local physicians be encouraged through the provision at each school of fresh air methods in the care and treatment of cases of tuberculosis.

II. The annual medical reports from year to year made reference to the unsatisfactory health of the pupils, while different local medical officers urged greater action in view of the results of their experience from year to year. As the result of one such report the Minister instructed the writer in 1909 to investigate the health of the children in the schools of the Calgary district in a letter containing the following:—

"As it is necessary that these residential schools should be filled with a healthy class of pupils in order that the expenditure on Indian education may not be rendered entirely nugatory, it seems desirable that you should go over the same ground as Dr. Lafferty and check his inspection."

Recommendations based upon examination of 243 school children.

These instructions were encouraging and the writer gladly undertook the work of examining with Dr. J. D. Lafferty the 243 children of 8 schools in Alberta, with the following results:—

(a) Tuberculosis was present equally in children at every age; (b) In no instance was a child awaiting admission to school found free from tuberculosis; hence it was plain that infection was got in the home primarily; (c) The disease showed an excessive mortality in the pupils between five and ten years of age; (d) The 10,000 children of school age demanded the same attention as the thousand children coming up each year and entering the schools annually.

Recommendations, made in this report, on much the same lines as those made in the report of 1907, followed the examination of the 243 children; but owing to the active opposition of Mr. D. C. Scott, and his advice to the then Deputy Minister, no action was taken by the Department to give effect to the recommendations made. This too was in spite of the opinion of Prof. George Adami, Pathologist of McGill University, in reply to a letter of the Deputy Minister asking his opinion regarding the management and conduct of the Indian schools. Prof. Adami had with the writer examined the children in one of the largest schools and was fully informed as to the actual situation. He stated that it was only after the earnest solicitation of Mr. D. C. Scott that the whole matter of Dr. Bryce's report was prevented from becoming a matter of critical discussion at the annual meeting of the National Tuberculosis Association in 1910, of which he was then president, and this was only due to Mr. Scott's distinct promise that the Department would take adequate action along the lines of the report. Prof. Adami stated in his letter to the Deputy Minister :—

"It was a revelation to me to find tuberculosis prevailing to such an extent amongst these children, and as many of them were only suffering from the early incipient form of the disease, though practically everyone was affected, when under care it may be arrested, I was greatly impressed with the responsibility of the government in dealing with these children .... I can assure you my only motive is a great sympathy for these children, who are the wards of the government and cannot protect themselves from the ravages of this disease."

III. In reviewing his correspondence the writer finds a personal letter, written by him to the Minister dated March 16th, 1911, following an official letter regarding the inaction of the Department with regard to the recommendations of the report. This letter refers to the most positive promises of Mr. D. C. Scott that the Department would at once take steps to put the suggestions contained in the report into effect. The letter further says :—

"It is now over 9 months since these occurrences and I have not received a single communication with reference to carrying out the suggestions of our report. Am I wrong in assuming that the vanity of Mr. D. C. Scott, growing out of his success at manipulating the mental activities of Mr. Pedley, has led him to the fatal deception of supposing that his cleverness will be equal to that of Prospero in calming any storm that may blow up from a Tuberculosis Association or any where else, since he knows that should he fail he has through memoranda on file placed the responsibility on Mr. Pedley and yourself. In this particular matter, he is counting upon the ignorance and indifference of the public to the fate of the Indians; but with the awakening of the health conscience of the people, we are now seeing on every hand, I feel certain that serious trouble will come out of departmental inertia, and I am not personally disposed to have any blame fall upon me."

It will then be understood with what pleasure the writer hailed the appointment of Dr. W. A. Roche as Superintendent General of Indian Affairs after the year's term of the Hon. R. Rogers, whose chief activity was the investigation of the Deputy Minister, which led up to his retirement. Now at last he said, "A medical minister exists who would understand the situation as relates to the health of the Indians." So an early opportunity was taken to set forth in a memorandum to Dr. Roche, dated Dec. 9th, 1912, data and statistics relating to the several hundred scat-

tered bands on whose health the total expenditure was but little more than $2 per capita, while the death rate in many of the bands was as high as forty per thousand. The reply acknowledging receipt of this memorandum contained the following :—

Dr. Roche is urged to act.

"There is certainly something in your suggestion that should meet with every consideration, and some time when I can find an opportunity and it is convenient for you, I shall be pleased to discuss this matter with you." As Dr. Roche became ill and was absent for some months nothing further was done; but on his return the writer in a personal interview urged that this serious medical Indian problem be taken up in earnest. It was stated that medical science now knows just what to do and what was necessary was to put our knowledge into practice. Dr. Roche stated that on his return from the West he would certainly take the matter up. Since that moment however, to the present, the matter has awaited the promised action.

The writer had done no regular inspection work since Mr. D. C. Scott was made Deputy minister in 1913, but had in each year up to 1914 prepared his medical report, printed in the annual report of the Department. About this time the following letter was received :—

P. H. Bryce, M. D.
Medical Inspector,
Immigration Branch.

Ottawa,
June 17, 1914.

Dear Sir,

In reply to your letter of the first instant, asking that the files of the Department, containing our medical officers' reports be placed at your disposal, so that you may peruse them to enable you to furnish a report for publication, I desire to point out, that by the organization of this Department, under the Civil Service Act of 1908 you were not included therein and since that time your whole salary has been a charge against the Department of the Interior. It is true that since then we have availed ourselves of your services on a few occasions; but during the past year, so far as I am aware, you have not been called upon to do any duty for the Department. I may say also that Dr. Grain of Winnipeg, has lately been appointed to oversee the Western schools and reserves and his time is fully occupied in the work. Under these circumstances, I do not think that you should be asked to furnish a report on the medical work in connection with Indians during the fiscal year.

Not on file here.

File 110-7

must thank you cordially for the offer to again prepare a report for publication.

Yours sincerely,

DUNCAN C. SCOTT,

D. S. G. I. A.

The transparent hypocrisy contained in this remarkable communication sent, not by the Minister Dr. W. A. Roche, but by his deputy, will be seen in the fact that from 1908, five annual reports had been prepared by the writer, while the special report on the eight schools of the Calgary district with the recommendations already referred to had been made on the instructions of the Department in 1909. The other reason given, to the effect that a certain physician, since retired for good cause, quite inexperienced in dealing with Indian disease problems, had been appointed as Medical Inspector for the Western Provinces, showed how little the Minister cared for the solution of the tuberculosis problem. As a matter of fact the Order in Council appointing the writer had neither been changed nor rescinded, while the transfer to the Interior Department of the payment of the total salary was made in 1908 in order that his regular increase of pay under the new classification of the Civil Service Act of that year might be made.

Mr. Scott's malign influence.

IV. As the war broke out in 1914 and immigration was largely suspended, an unexpected opportunity occurred through the greater time at his disposal for the writer's special knowledge and experience to be utilised in improving the health of the Indians; but in no single instance, thereafter, were the services of the writer utilised by this medical Minister, who in 1917 was transferred to preside over the Civil Service Commission, and who must be held responsible for the neglect of what proved to be a very serious situation. In 1917, the writer prepared, at the request of the Conservation Commission, a pamphlet on "The Conservation of the Man Power of Canada," which dealt with the broad problems of health which so vitally affect the man power of a nation. The large demand for this pamphlet led to the preparation of a similar study on "The Conservation of the Man Power of the Indian Population of Canada," which had already supplied over 2000 volunteer soldiers for the Empire. For obvious reasons this memorandum was not published, but was

Dr. Roche's culpable apathy.

8

placed in the hands of a minister of the Crown in 1918, in order that all the facts might be made known to the Government. This memorandum began by pointing out that in 1916 4,862,303 acres were included in the Indian reserves and that 73,716 acres were then under cultivation, that while the total per capita income for farm crops in that year in all Canada was $110, that from the Indian reserves was $69, while it was only $40 for Nova Scotia. It is thus obvious that from the lowest standard of wealth producers the Indian population of Canada was already a matter of much importance to the State. From the statistics given in the "Man Power" pamphlet it was made plain that instead of the normal increase in the Indian population being 1.5 per cent. per annum as given for the white population, there had been between 1904 and 1917 an actual decrease in the Indian population in the age period over twenty years of 1,639 persons whereas a normal increase would have added 20,000 population in the 13 years. The comparisons showed that the loss was almost wholly due to a high death rate since, though incomplete, the Indian birth rate was 27 per thousand or higher than the average for the whole white population.

Value of man power of Indians.

The memorandum states, "As the Indian people are an unusually strong native race, their children at birth are large and sturdy, and under good sanitary conditions have a low mortality. Thus of the 134 children born in the File Hills Farm Colony in 17 years only 34 died, while of 15 births in 1916 only 1 died, giving the unusually low rate of 77 per thousand within the year."

As it was further desirable to obtain the latest returns of deaths by age periods and causes the writer communicated with the Secretary of the Indian Department asking for such returns. In reply he received the following letter.

Dear Dr. Bryce, Ottawa, May 7, 1918.

I have your letter of the third instant asking for certain vital statistics. I am unable to give you the figures you ask as we are not receiving any vital statistics now, and last year we obtained only the total number of births and deaths from each Agency. These were not printed and are not therefore available for distribution. The causes of deaths have never been noted in our reports and we have no information.

Your obedient servant,

(Signed) J. D. McLean,

Asst. Deputy and Secretary.

9

[illegible]ence of [illegible]auses of deaths.

Thus after more than a hundred years of an organized De[illegible]ent of Indian Affairs in Canada, though the writer had at once begun in 1904 on his appointment the regular collection of statistics of diseases and deaths from the several Indian bands, he was officially informed that in a Department with 287 paid medical officers, due to the direct reactionary influence of the former Accountant and present Deputy Minister no means exists, such as is looked upon as elementary in any Health Department today, by which the public or the Indians themselves can learn anything definite as to the actual vital conditions amongst these wards of the nation.

A study of the 1916-17 statistics shows that in the wage earning period of life, from 21 to 65 years, the Indians of Alberta had 161 less population, of British Columbia 901 less, of Ontario 991 less and of Nova Scotia 399 less. In order however to show how an Indian population may increase, the writer obtained from Mr. W. M. Graham, at that time Superintendent of the File Hills colony from 1901 to 1917, the complete record for this period. In all there were 53 colonists from the neighbouring Indian schools, starting with five in 1901, who had taken up homesteads in the colony. Most of them married although 15 either left or had died previous to marriage. In June 1917 there were resident 38 men, 26 women and 106 children, or 170 colonists in all. Thus we have the picture of a young Indian population of 49 males who remained in the colony, of whom 10 died of tuberculosis after an average sickness there of 2.7 years and of 29 females of whom 3 died and to whom had been born in all 134 children.

The famous File Hills Farm colony.

In 1916 the colony had 3,991 acres under cultivation or over a hundred acres per farmer. This was one nineteenth of the total area cultivated by 105,000 persons in all the Indian bands in Canada, while 87,498 bushels of grain were grown, and 33,052 head of live stock were kept. That this variation from the normal is viewed as an anomaly may be judged from the following extract from the Deputy Minister's Annual Report for 1917; "The Indian population does not vary much from year to year." How misleading this statement is may be judged from the fact that between 1906 and 1917 in the age periods over 20 years in every Province but two the Indians had decreased in population by a total of 2,632 deaths.

10

Naturally it is asked; Why this decrease should have taken place? In 1906 the report of the Chief Medical Officer shows that statistics collected from 99 local medical officers having the care of a population of 70,000 gave a total of 3,169 cases of tuberculosis or 1 case for every seven in a total of 23,109 diseases reported, and the death rates in several large bands were 81.8, 82.6, and in a third 86.4 per thousand; while the ordinary death rate for 115,000 in the city of Hamilton was 10.6 in 1921. What these figures disclose has been made more plain year by year, namely that tuberculosis, contracted in infancy, creates diseases of the brain, joints, bones, and to a less degree of the lungs and also that if not fatal till adolescence it then usually progresses rapidly to a fatal termination in consumption of the lungs.

Extraordinary mortality from tuberculosis.

The amazing reduction of tuberculosis in Hamilton.

The memorandum prepared by the writer in 1918 further showed that the city of Hamilton with a population greater than the total Indian population had reduced the death rate from tuberculosis in the same period, from 1904 to 1917, by nearly 75 per cent. having in 1916 actually only 68 deaths. The memorandum further states, "If a similar method had been introduced amongst the bands on the health-giving uplands of Alberta, much might have been done to prevent such a splendid race of warriors as the Blackfeet from decreasing from 842 in 1904 to 726 in 1916, or, allowing for natural increase, an actual loss of 40 per cent. since they should have numbered at least 1,011."

V. Such then is the situation made known to the Hon. N. W. Rowell, who applied to the writer in 1918 to supply him with such facts and arguments as would support the Bill he proposed to introduce into Parliament for the creation of a Federal Department of Health.

It was with pleasure that the memorandum dealing with Indian health matters was given him, along with a proposed Bill for a Department of Health, which contained amongst its provisions one for including the Indian Medical Service along with the other Medical Federal services in the new Department. In the special medical committee called by Mr. Rowell to discuss the

11

[illegible] was of course approved of and the clause appeared in the [illegible] Reading in Parliament. But something then happened: What special 'occult influences came into action may be imagined, when the Second Reading of the Bill took place with this clause regarding the Indian Medical Service omitted. It has been noted that from 1913 up to the time when Dr. W. A. Roche was eliminated from the government in 1917 to make room for a more hardy and subtle representative of Unionism the activities of the Chief Medical Inspector of the Indian Department, had in practice ceased; yet now he was to see as the outcome of all this health legislation for which he had been struggling for years, the failure of one of his special health dreams, which he has hoped to see realized.

If the writer had been much disturbed by the incapacity or inertia of a medical Minister in the matter of the Indian health situation, he now saw that it was hopeless to expect any improvement in it when the new Minister of Health, who had posed as the Bayard of Social Uplift, the Protagonist of Prohibition, the Champion of Oppressed Labour, the Sir Galahad of Women's rights, and the *preux Chevalier* of Canadian Nationalism, could with all the accumulated facts and statistics before him condemn to further indefinite suffering and neglect these Wards of the Canadian people, whom one Government after another had made treaties with and whom deputies and officials had sworn to assist and protect.

One who failed them in their agony.

A side light however, may serve to illumine the beclouded situation. With the formation of the Unionist Government the usual shuffle of portfolios was made and the then dominating Solicitor General, grown callous and hardened over a franchise Bill, which disfranchised many thousands of his fellow native-born citizens, had now become Minister of the Interior. That the desire for power and for the control appointments should override any higher consideration such as saving the lives of the Indians must be inferred from the following statement of the Hon. A. Meighen, Minister of the Interior and now Prime Minister. On June 8th, 1920, the estimates of the Indian Department were under consideration in Parliament. Page 3275 of Hansard has the following:—

Mr. D. D. McKenzie, "I understand that frightful ravages are being made amongst them (Indians) by tuberculosis and the conditions of life are certainly not such as to preserve them from the ravages of that dread disease. I should be pleased to know at the earliest possible moment if that branch of the Department was going to be transferred to the Department of Health."

Mr. Meighen, "The Health Department has no power to take over the matter of the health of the Indians. That is not included in the Act establishing the department. It was purposely left out of the Act. I did not then think and do not think yet that it would be practicable for the Health Department to do that work, because they would require to duplicate the organization away in the remote regions, where Indian reserves are, and there would be established a sort of divided control and authority over the Indians."

Mr. Beland, "Is tuberculosis increasing or decreasing amongst the Indians?"

Mr. Meighen, "I am afraid I cannot give a very encouraging answer to the question. We are not convinced that it is increasing, but it is not decreasing.

In this reply of the Minister we see fully illustrated the dominating influence, stimulated by the reactionary Deputy Minister, which prevents even the simplest effective efforts to deal with the health problem of the Indians along modern scientific lines. To say that confusion would arise is the equivalent of saying that co-operation between persons toward a desired social end is impracticable; whereas co-operation between Provincial and Federal Health Departments is the basis upon which real progress is being made, while further a world peace is being made possible in a league of once discordant nations. The Premier has frankly said he can give no encouraging answer to Dr. Beland's question, while at the same moment he condemns the Indians to their fate by a pitiable confession of utter official helplessness and lack of initiative, based upon a cynical "*non possumus*."

Red tape condemns the Indians because of a pitiable inertia

Thus we find a sum of only $10,000 has been annually placed in the estimates to control tuberculosis amongst 105,000 Indians scattered over Canada in over 300 bands, while the City of Ottawa, with about the same population and having three general hospitals spent thereon $342,860.54 in 1919 of which $33,364.70 is devoted to tuberculous patients alone. The many difficulties of our pro-

[illegible] have been frequently pointed out, but [illegible] these have also been made plain. It can [illegible] cruder or weaker arguments by a Prime [illegible] the position of responsibility to these treaty [illegible] Canada could hardly be conceived, and such recall the [illegible] of Voltaire, regarding the Treaty of Shackmaxon between Wm. Penn and the Indians, which he describes as "the only known treaty between savages and Christians that was never sworn to and never broken."

The degree and extent of this criminal disregard for the treaty pledges to guard the welfare of the Indian wards of the nation may be guaged from the facts once more brought out at the meeting of the National Tuberculosis Association at its annual meeting held in Ottawa on March 17th, 1922. The superintendent of the Qu'Appelle Sanatorium, Sask., gave there the results of a special study of 1575 children of school age in which advantage was taken of the most modern scientific methods. Of these 175 were Indian children, and it is very remarkable that the fact given that some 93 per cent. of these showed evidence of tuberculous infection coincides completely with the work done by Dr. Lafferty and the writer in the Alberta Indian schools in 1909.

It is indeed pitiable that during the thirteen years since then this trail of disease and death has gone on almost unchecked by any serious efforts on the part of the Department of Indian Affairs, placed by the B. N. A. Act especially in charge of our Indian population, and that a Provincial Tuberculosis Commission now considers it to be its duty to publish the facts regarding these children living within its own Province.

EPILOGUE.

This story should have been written years ago and then given to the public; but in my oath of office as a Civil Servant swore that "without authority on that behalf, I shall not disclose or make known any matter or thing which comes to my knowledge by reason of my employment as Chief Medical Inspector of Indian Affairs." Today I am free to speak, having been retired from the Civil Service and so am in a position to write the sequel to the story. It has already been stated that in 1918 and 1919 I had supplied to my then Minister of Immigration, the Hon. J. A. Calder and to the then President of the Council, the Hon. N. W. Rowell various memoranda regarding the establishment of a Federal Department of Health, amongst these being a draft of the Bill which later became the Act establishing the Department of Health. To my disappointment the position of Deputy Minister of Health to which I had a right to aspire after twenty-two years as Chief Medical Officer of Onatrio, and fifteen years as Chief Medical Officer of Immigration and Indian Affairs was given to another, wholly outside the Federal Civil Service and in violation of the principle of promotion which was supposed to prevail when the patronage system was to be done away with. The excuse was on the ground of my advancing years, although at that moment the position of Auditor General was being filled by the promotion of one who had reached sixty-five years, while a Historian to the Militia Department was appointed at a salary of $7,000 per year, who likewise had reached just then this age.

Naturally I felt that it would be impossible to carry on and retain my self respect as a subordinate, while performing the duties, which I had been engaged in for fifteen years as Chief Medical Officer and so asked that I be given other congenial work. That my claims to the position were deemed reasonable may be judged from the following letter addressed to my brother the Rev. Professor Bryce, D.D., of Winnipeg. Writing from Victoria, B. C., on March 9th, 1920, to myself he said, quoting from a letter received from the Hon. Mr. Calder in reply to one of his own :—

[illegible] your brother in reference to his [illegible] ld be only too glad to do anything I [illegible] lic Health Department was created, your [illegible] to the appointment as Deputy Minister. [illegible] however, Council finally concluded that a [illegible] man [illegible] ceive the appointment. The government has on [illegible] occasions [illegible] sidered the question of placing your brother in some other branch of the Service, and I have no doubt that this will be arranged in some way or other shortly. He is now an official of the Public Health Department. He could of course remain there but this apparently is not agreeable to him. As a consequence some other arrangement, if possible must be made.

Signed, J. A. Calder.

My indignation at subsequent treatment may be imagined when the same Mr. Calder introduced the Act in 1920, commonly known as the Calder Act, providing for the "Retirement of Certain Members of the Civil Service." This Act states that anyone retired thereunder shall receive 1/60 of his salary for each year of service. So it came about that on the 17th Sept. 1920, I received notice that I was recommended for retirement under this Act. The clause of the Act quoted for my information states :—

"Section 2 (3). When it is decided to retire anyone under the provisions of this Act, notice in writing giving the reasons for such retirement shall be sent to such person, and he shall have the right to appeal to the Civil Service Commission, and the Commission, after giving such person an opportunity to be heard, shall make full report to the Governor in Council and the decision of the Council thereon shall be final."

I appealed and in my appeal stated that no reason was assigned as provided in the Act, and further that I was still Chief Medical Officer in the Department of Indian Affairs as set out in the Order in Council of 1904.

As bearing on this point made in my appeal I find the following in Hansard of June 8th, 1921. The matter being dealt with is the amendment to the Calder Act :

Mr. Fielding : But cases have been brought to my attention of men in advanced years—some may think them old, I do not—being notified of their retirement, although they are blessed with good health and strength, both mental and physical, and are well able to discharge their duties. How is such a man dealt with?

Mr. Calder : No man will be notified unless a proper official has advised that his condition of life is such that in the public interest he should be retired...........

Mr. Calder : That in the main has been the practice in the past and that is what the law contemplated last year. The question of age alone was not taken into consideration.

But it was hardly to be supposed that Dr. W. A. Roche, now Chairman of the Civil Service Commission, who during the years 1913-17 referred to had failed to utilise my services when he was Superintendent of Indian Affairs would now consider my services as necessary in that Department. So my protest was of no avail ; my elimination from the Service had been decreed and I received the following Order in Council :

Ottawa, 14th Feb., 1721.

The Committee have had before them a report, dated Feb. 1st, 1921, from the acting Secretary of State, from the Civil Service Commission :

In accordance with the provisions of Cap. 67, 10-11 George V. "An Act to provide for the Retirement of Certain Members of the Public Service" the Civil Service has to report that Dr. P. H. Bryce of the Department of Health at Ottawa was recommended by the Deputy Minister of Health for retirement ; that under Section 2 (3) of the said Act he was given a personal hearing, which has resulted in the Civil Service Commission now recommending that his appeal be not allowed, but that his retirement be made effective from the 1st of March, 1921. Dr. Bryce was born on August 17th, 1853, and is consequently sixty-seven years of age. He was appointed temporarily to the Service on Feb. 1st, 1904, and was made permanent on September 1st, 1908, and therefore will have been in the Service seventeen years and one month on the 1st March, 1921, the date upon which his retirement is proposed to be effective."

So it came about that I was retired in March. 1921, without any years being added to my term of Federal service, though I had been brought to Ottawa as an expert after 22 years in the Ontario Health Service, as is provided for in the Superannuation Act of 1870. Neither did I get any gratuity on leaving the Ontario Service after twenty-two years, the excuse being then given that I was improving my position.

The irony and injustice of this Order in Council will be seen when it is stated that a similar Order was passed on May 18th, 1921, retiring 231 persons from the Customs Department as being over sixty-five years of age ; but which was recalled when the protests of the many friends of men who were faithfully performing their duties were made. These and hundreds of other Civil

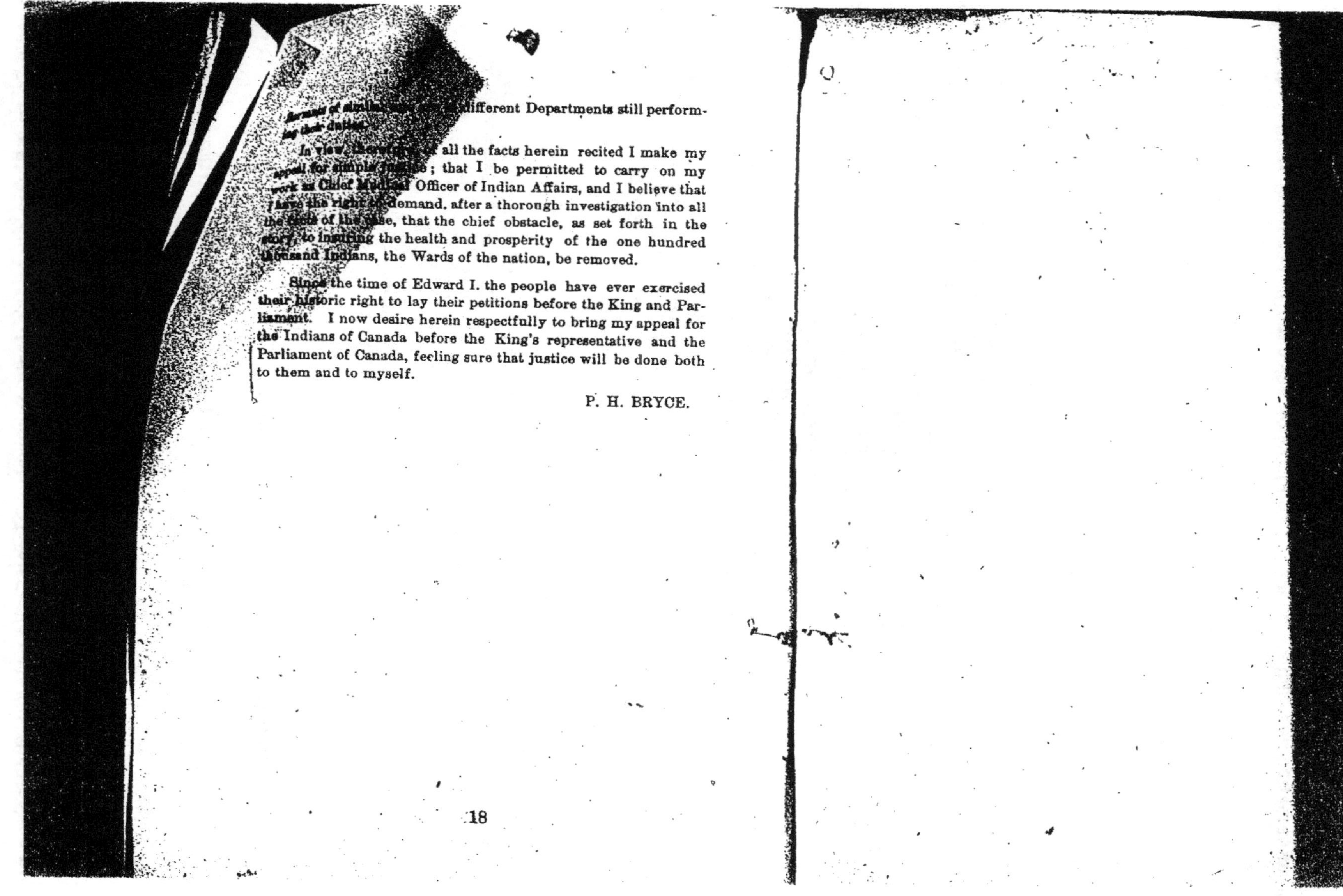

servants of similar [illegible] different Departments still performing their duties.

In view, therefore, of all the facts herein recited I make my appeal for simple justice; that I be permitted to carry on my work as Chief Medical Officer of Indian Affairs, and I believe that I have the right to demand, after a thorough investigation into all the facts of the case, that the chief obstacle, as set forth in the story, to insuring the health and prosperity of the one hundred thousand Indians, the Wards of the nation, be removed.

Since the time of Edward I. the people have ever exercised their historic right to lay their petitions before the King and Parliament. I now desire herein respectfully to bring my appeal for the Indians of Canada before the King's representative and the Parliament of Canada, feeling sure that justice will be done both to them and to myself.

P. H. BRYCE.

18

<u>Appendix Four</u>: A Blueprint for Criminal Conspiracy: *Crimen Sollicitationas*, the Vatican policy regarding the concealment of child rape and trafficking within the Roman Catholic Church.

FROM THE SUPREME AND HOLY CONGREGATION OF THE HOLY OFFICE

[TO] ALL PATRIARCHS, ARCHBISHOPS, BISHOPS AND OTHER DIOCESAN ORDINARIES "EVEN OF THE ORIENTAL RITE"

INSTRUCTION

CONFIDENTIAL

ON THE MANNER OF PROCEEDING IN CASES OF SOLICITATION

The Vatican Press, 1962

++5++

INSTRUCTION

On the manner of proceeding in cases of the crime of solicitation

[This text is] to be diligently stored in the secret archives of the Curia as strictly confidential. Nor is it to be published nor added to with any commentaries.

PRELIMINARIES

1. The crime of solicitation takes place when a priest tempts a penitent, whoever that person is, either in the act of sacramental confession, whether before or immediately afterwards, whether on the occasion or the pretext of confession, whether even outside the times for confession in the confessional or [in a place] other than that [usually] designated for the hearing of confessions or [in a place] chosen for the simulated purpose of hearing a confession. [The object of this temptation] is to solicit or provoke [the penitent] toward impure and obscene matters, whether by words or signs or nods of the head, whether by touch or by writing whether then or after [the note has been read] or whether he has had with [that penitent] prohibited and improper speech or activity with reckless daring (Constitution <u>Sacrum Poenitentiae</u>, § 1).

2. [The right or duty of addressing] this unspeakable crime in the first instance pertains to the Ordinaries of the place in whose territory the accused has residence (V. below, numbers 30 and 31), and this not to mention through proper law but also from a special delegation of the Apostolic See; <u>It is enjoined upon these aforementioned persons to the fullest extent possible, [in addition to their being] gravely encumbered by their own consciences, that, after the occurrence of cases of this type, that they, as soon as possible, take care to introduce, discuss and terminate [these cases] with their proper tribunal</u>. However, because of particular and serious reasons, according to the norm of <u>Canon 247, § 2</u>, these cases can be directly deferred to the Holy Congregation of the Holy Office or be so ordered. Yet [the right of] the accused respondents ++6++ remains intact in any instance of judgment to have recourse to the Holy Office. However, recourse thus interposed does not suspend, excluding the case of an appeal, the exercise of the jurisdiction of the judge who has already begun to accept the case; and he can therefore be able to pursue the judgment up to the definitive decision, unless it has been established that the Apostolic See has summoned the case to itself (Cfr. <u>Canon 1569</u>).

Extracts from the Vatican Document "Criminales Solicitations", silencing victims and perpetrators of rape and other abuse within the Roman Catholic church, 1962 – See paragraphs #11 and 13 – <u>This policy is still in effect.</u>

he has been legitimately cited and is not present at some [parts of the] Acts, the Acts indeed are valid, but afterwards [those Acts] will be totally subject to his examination so that he is able to comment upon all of them either in words or in writing and to propose what he has judged to be necessary or opportune" (Canon 1587).

9. It is fitting that the notary, on the other hand, be present at all the Acts under pain of nullity and to note down with his own hand or at least to affix his signature [to the aforesaid Acts] (Canon 1585, § 1). Because of the special character of these procedures, however, it is necessary for the Ordinary to dispense from the presence of the notary, though because of a reasonable excuse in the acceptance, as will be noted in its own place, of the denunciations and also in the expenditure of the degrees of attention or care expected of a notary in a given situation, as they say, in pursuing and in examining the witnesses inducted [into the case].

10. Minor helpers are to be used for nothing unless it is absolutely necessary; and these are to be chosen, in so far as possible, from the priestly order; always, however, they are to be of proved faithfulness and mature without exception. But it must be noted that, if, when necessity demands it, they can be nominated to accept certain acts, even if they are non-subjects living in another territory or the Ordinary of that territory [can] be interrogated (Can. 1570, § 2), observing, of course, all of the cautions treated as above and in Canon 1613.

11. Because, however, what is treated in these cases has to have a greater degree of care and observance so that those same matters be pursued in a most secretive way, and, after they have been defined and given over to execution, they are to be restrained by a perpetual silence (Instruction of the Holy Office, February 20, 1867, n. 14), each and everyone pertaining to the tribunal in any way or admitted to knowledge of the matters because of their office, is to observe the strictest ++7++ secret, which is commonly regarded as a secret of the Holy Office, in all matters and with all persons, under the penalty of excommunication latae sententiae, ipso facto and without any declaration [of such a penalty] having been incurred and reserved to the sole person of the Supreme Pontiff, even to the exclusion of the Sacred Penitentiary, are bound to observe [this secrecy] inviolably. Indeed by this law the Ordinaries are bound ipso jure or by the force of their own proper duty. The other helpers from the power of their oath which they they must always take before they undertake their duties. And these, then, are delegated, are interpolated, and are informed in their absence by means of the precept in the letters of delegation, interpellation, [or of] information, imposing upon them with express mention of the secret of the Holy Office and of the aforementioned censure.

12. The aforesaid oath, the formula for which is to be found in the appendix of this instruction (Form A), must be used (by those, obviously, who will use it habitually, once for all; by those, however, who are deputed only for some determined piece of business or case, as often as required (toties quoties), in the presence of the ordinary or his delegate done upon the Gospels of God (also by priests) and not otherwise and with the added promise of fulfilling faithfullly their duty, to which, howver, the excommunication, mentioned above, is not extended. There must be an

308

he has been legitimately cited and is not present at some [parts of the] Acts, the Acts indeed are valid, but afterwards [those Acts] will be totally subject to his examination so that he is able to comment upon all of them either in words or in writing and to propose what he has judged to be necessary or opportune" (Canon 1587).

9. It is fitting that the notary, on the other hand, be present at all the Acts under pain of nullity and to note down with his own hand or at least to affix his signature [to the aforesaid Acts] (Canon 1585, § 1). Because of the special character of these procedures, however, it is necessary for the Ordinary to dispense from the presence of the notary, though because of a reasonable excuse in the acceptance, as will be noted in its own place, of the denunciations and also in the expenditure of the degrees of attention or care expected of a notary in a given situation, as they say, in pursuing and in examining the witnesses inducted [into the case].

10. Minor helpers are to be used for nothing unless it is absolutely necessary; and these are to be chosen, in so far as possible, from the priestly order; always, however, they are to be of proved faithfulness and mature without exception. But it must be noted that, if, when necessity demands it, they can be nominated to accept certain acts, even if they are non-subjects living in another territory or the Ordinary of that territory [can] be interrogated (Can. 1570, § 2), observing, of course, all of the cautions treated as above and in Canon 1613.

11. Because, however, what is treated in these cases has to have a greater degree of care and observance so that those same matters be pursued in a most secretive way, and, after they have been defined and given over to execution, they are to be restrained by a perpetual silence (Instruction of the Holy Office, February 20, 1867, n. 14), each and everyone pertaining to the tribunal in any way or admitted to knowledge of the matters because of their office, is to observe the strictest ++7++ secret, which is commonly regarded as a secret of the Holy Office, in all matters and with all persons, under the penalty of excommunication latae sententiae, ipso facto and without any declaration [of such a penalty] having been incurred and reserved to the sole person of the Supreme Pontiff, even to the exclusion of the Sacred Penitentiary, are bound to observe [this secrecy] inviolably. Indeed by this law the Ordinaries are bound ipso jure or by the force of their own proper duty. The other helpers from the power of their oath which they they must always take before they undertake their duties. And these, then, are delegated, are interpolated, and are informed in their absence by means of the precept in the letters of delegation, interpellation, [or of] information, imposing upon them with express mention of the secret of the Holy Office and of the aforementioned censure.

12. The aforesaid oath, the formula for which is to be found in the appendix of this instruction (Form A), must be used (by those, obviously, who will use it habitually, once for all; by those, however, who are deputed only for some determined piece of business or case, as often as required (toties quoties), in the presence of the ordinary or his delegate done upon the Gospels of God (also by priests) and not otherwise and with the added promise of fulfilling faithfullly their duty, to which, howver, the excommunication, mentioned above, is not extended. There must be an

avoidance, moreover, by those who are set over those involved in this cases, lest anyone be admitted to a knowledge of the matters from helpers, unless in some way a party or an office to be performed by that person necessarily requires a knowledge of these matters.

* 13. The oath of keeping the secret must be given in these cases also by the accusers or those denouncing [the priest] and the witnesses. To none of these, however, is there subjection to a censure, unless by chance toward these same pesons some censure has been expressly threatened upon the person himself, for his accusation, his deposition or of his violation (Excussionis?) [of such] by act. The accused, however, should be most seriously warned that even he, with all [the others], especially when he observes the secret with his defender, is under the penalty of suspension a divinis in case of a transgression to be incurred ipso facto.

14. Finally, as for the publishing, the language, the confirmation, the custody of and the accidental nullity, in every way [these matters] must be observed which are prescribed by Canons 1642-43, 379-80-82 and 1680 respectively.

++9++

TITLE NUMBER ONE

THE FIRST KNOWLEDGE OF THE CRIME

15. Since the crime of solicitation takes place in rather rare decisions, lest it remain occult and unpunished and always with inestimable detriment to souls, it was necessary for the one person, as for many persons, conscious of that [act of solicitation], namely, the solicited penitent, to be compelled to reveal it through a denunciation imposed by positive law. Therefore:

16."According to the Apostolic Constitutions and especially of the Constitution of Benedict XIV Sacramentum Poenitentiae of June 1, 1941, the penitent must denounce the accused priest of the delict of solicitation in confession within a month to the Ordinary of the place or to the Holy Congregation of the Holy Office;, and the confessor must, burdened seriously in conscience, to warn the penitent of this duty." (Canon 904).

17. Moreover, according to the mind of Canon 1935 anyone of the faithful can always denunouce the delict of solicitation, of which he will have had a certain knowledge; also, the obligation of denunciation urges as often as the person is bound to it from the natural law itself because of the danger to faith or religion or other imminent public evil.

18."The faithful, however, who knowingly have disregarded the obligation to denounce the person by whom he was solicited, against the prescription (related above) of Canon 904, within a month, falls into an excommunication reserved latae sententiae, not to be absolved unless after he has satisfied the obligation or has promised seriously that he would so" (Can. 2368, § 2).

19. The duty of denunciation is a personal one and is to be fulfilled regularly by the person himself who has been solicited. But if he is prevented by the most serious difficulties from doing this, then either by

perhaps it has been joined with the crime of solicitation in sacramental confession. In decreeing penalties, however, against delinquents of this type, besides those which are found spoken of above, and the6y should also be kept before one's eyes (Canon 2359, § 2).

73. To have the worst crime, for the penal effects, one must do the equivalent of the following: any obscene, external act, gravely sinful, perpetrated in any way by a cleric or attempted by him with youths of either sex or with brute animals (bestiality).

74. Against accused clerics for these crimes, if they are exempt religious, and unless there takes place at the same time the crime of solicitation, even the regular superior can proceed, according to the holy canons and their proper constitutions, either in an administrative or a judicial manner. However, they must communicate the judicial decision pronounced as well as the adminsitrative decision in the more serious cases to the Supreme Congregation of the Holy Office.

++24++

FROM THE AUDIENCE OF THE HOLY FATHER, MARCH 16, 1962

Our Most Holy Father John XXIII, in an audience granted to the most eminent Cardinal Secretary of the Holy Office on March 16, 1962, deigned to approve and confirm this instruction, ordering upon those to whom it pertains to keep and observe it in the minutest detail.

At Rome, from the Office of the Sacred Congregation, March 16,. 1962.

Place of the seal A. Cardinal Ottaviani

310

Da: Eagle Strong Voice [hiddenfromhistory@yahoo.ca] Inviato: ven 09/10/09 22:25

A: cnovelli@alice.it

Cc:

Oggetto: Fw: vatican document ordering coverup of abuses - 1962

Allegati: | Visualizza dettagli

- News
- World news

Vatican told bishops to cover up sex abuse

Expulsion threat in secret documents

Read the 1962 Vatican document (PDF file)

- Buzz up!
- Digg it

- Antony Barnett, public affairs editor
- The Observer, Sunday 17 August 2003 01.27 BST
- Article history

The Vatican instructed Catholic bishops around the world to cover up cases of sexual abuse or risk being thrown out of the Church.

The Observer has obtained a 40-year-old confidential document from the secret Vatican archive which lawyers are calling a 'blueprint for deception and concealment'. One British lawyer acting for Church child abuse victims has described it as 'explosive'.

The 69-page Latin document bearing the seal of Pope John XXIII was sent to every bishop in the world. The instructions outline a policy of 'strictest' secrecy in dealing with allegations of sexual abuse and threatens those who speak out with excommunication.

They also call for the victim to take an oath of secrecy at the time of making a complaint to Church officials. It states that the instructions are to 'be diligently stored in the secret archives of the Curia [Vatican] as strictly confidential. Nor is it to be published nor added to with any commentaries.'

The document, which has been confirmed as genuine by the Roman Catholic Church in England and Wales, is called 'Crimine solicitationies', which translates as 'instruction on proceeding in cases of solicitation'.

It focuses on sexual abuse initiated as part of the confessional relationship between a priest and a member of his congregation. But the instructions also cover what it calls the 'worst crime', described as an obscene act perpetrated by a cleric with 'youths of either sex or with brute animals (bestiality)'.

Bishops are instructed to pursue these cases 'in the most secretive way... restrained by a perpetual silence... and everyone... is to observe the strictest secret which is commonly regarded as a secret of the Holy Office... under the penalty of excommunication'.

Texan lawyer Daniel Shea uncovered the document as part of his work for victims of abuse from Catholic priests in the US. He has handed it over to US authorities, urging them to launch a federal investigation into the clergy's alleged cover-up of sexual abuse. ← action?

He said: 'These instructions went out to every bishop around the globe and would certainly have applied in Britain. It proves there was an international conspiracy by the Church to hush up sexual abuse issues. It is a devious attempt to conceal criminal conduct and is a blueprint for deception and concealment.'

British lawyer Richard Scorer, who acts for children abused by Catholic priests in the UK, echoes this view and has described the document as 'explosive'.

He said: 'We always suspected that the Catholic Church systematically covered up abuse and tried to silence victims. This document appears to prove it. Threatening excommunication to anybody who speaks out shows the lengths the most senior figures in the Vatican were prepared to go to prevent the information getting out to the public domain.'

Appendix Five: Mass Graves in Canada – A List of Twenty Eight Burial Sites at former Indian residential schools

This list was compiled between 1995 and 2010 on the basis of eyewitness testimonies – including from those who dug the graves or helped bury children in them – as well as documents and letters from government and church archives, and physical and forensic surveys done at these locations
It does not represent a complete list of such burial sites, since many graves have been destroyed by the RCMP and other government and church agents. As well, a common method of disposal of bodies was to incinerate them in residential school furnaces, as other witnesses attest.

A. British Columbia

1. **Port Alberni:** Presbyterian-United Church school (1895-1973), now occupied by the Nuu-Chah-Nulth Tribal Council (NTC) office on Kitskuksis Road. Grave site is a series of sinkhole rows in hills 100 meters due west of the NTC building, in thick foliage, past an unused water pipeline. Children are also interred at the Tseshaht reserve cemetery, and in a wooded gully east of the Catholic cemetery on River Road.

2. **Alert Bay**: St. Michael's Anglican school (1878-1975), situated on Cormorant Island offshore from Port McNeill, Vancouver Island. Presently building is used by the Namgis First Nation. Site is an overgrown field adjacent to the building, and also under the foundations of the present new building, constructed during the 1960's. Skeletons were seen "between the walls" of the old facility by eyewitness Irene Starr (ibid).

3. **Kuper Island**: Roman Catholic school (1890-1975), offshore from Chemainus on Vancouver Island. Land is occupied by the Penelakut Indian Band. Former building is destroyed except for a front entrance staircase. Two grave sites: one immediately south of the former building, in a field containing a conventional cemetery; another at the west shoreline in a lagoon near the main dock, partly submerged by the ocean.

4. **Nanaimo Indian Hospital:** Indian Affairs and United Church experimental facility (1942-1970) on Department of National Defense land. Buildings now destroyed. Grave sites are immediately east of former buildings on Fifth avenue, adjacent to and south of Vancouver Island University .

5. **Mission:** St. Mary's Catholic school (1861-1984), adjacent to and north of Lougheed Highway and Fraser River Heritage Park . Original school buildings are destroyed, but many foundations are visible on the grounds of the Park. In this area there are two grave sites: a) immediately adjacent to the former girls' dormitory and present cemetery for priests, and a larger mass grave in an artificial earthen mound, north of the cemetery among overgrown foliage and blackberry bushes, and b) east of the old school grounds, on the hilly slopes next to the field leading to the newer school building which is presently used by the Sto:lo First Nation. Hill site is 150 meters west of building.

6. **North Vancouver**: Squamish (1898-1959) and Sechelt (1912-1975) Catholic schools, buildings are now destroyed. Children who died in these schools are interred in the Squamish Band Cemetery, North Vancouver.

7. **Sardis:** Coqualeetza Methodist-United Church School (1889-1940), then became an experimental hospital run by the federal government (1940-1969). Native burial site next to the Sto:lo Indian reserve and Little Mountain school, also possibly adjacent to former school-hospital building.

8. **Cranbrook**: St. Eugene Catholic school (1898-1970), recently converted into a tourist "resort" with federal funding, resulting in the covering-over of a mass burial site by a golf course in front of the building. Numerous grave sites are around and under this golf course.

9. **Williams Lake:** Catholic school (1890-1981), buildings now destroyed but foundations are intact, five miles south of the city. Grave sites reported north of school grounds and under foundations of a long tunnel-like structure.

10. **Meares Island (Tofino):** Kakawis-Christie Catholic school (1898-1974).Buildings are incorporated into the Kakawis Healing Centre. Body storage room is reported in the basement, adjacent to the burial grounds south of the school.

11. **Kamloops**: Catholic school (1890-1978). Buildings still intact. Mass grave south of the school, adjacent to and amidst an orchard. Numerous burials witnessed there.

12. **Lytton**: St. George's Anglican school (1901-1979). Graves of students flogged to death, and others, reported under the floorboards and next to the playground.

13. **Fraser Lake:** Lejac Catholic school (1910-1976), buildings now destroyed. Graves are reported under the old foundations and between the walls.

Alberta:

1. **Edmonton:** United Church school (1919-1960), presently the site of the Poundmaker Lodge in St. Albert. Graves of children are reported south of the former school site, under a thick hedge that runs north-south, adjacent to a large memorial marker.

2. **Edmonton**: Charles Camsell Hospital (1945-1967), building still intact. An experimental hospital run by Indian Affairs and United Church . Mass graves of children from the hospital reported south of the building, near the staff garden.

3. **Saddle Lake:** Bluequills Catholic school (1898-1970), building still intact. Skeletons and skulls were observed in a basement furnace. Mass grave reported adjacent to the school.

4. **Hobbema:** Ermineskin Catholic school (1916-1973), buildings gone. Five intact skeletons were observed in the school furnace. Graves under the former building foundations.

Manitoba:

1. **Brandon:** Methodist-United Church School (1895-1972). Building still intact. Burials reported west of the school building.

2. **Portage La Prairie**: Presbyterian-United Church School (1895-1950). Building destroyed, much rubble remains. Children are buried at the nearby Hillside Cemetery north of the school ruins.

3. **Norway House:** Methodist-United Church School (1900-1974). A "Very old" grave site is next to the former school building, demolished by the United Church in 2004.

Ontario:

1. **Thunder Bay:** Lakehead Psychiatric Hospital , still in operation. Experimental centre funded by the federal government. Women and children are reported buried adjacent to hospital grounds.

2. **Sioux Lookout:** Pelican Lake Catholic school (1911-1973). Burials of children are in a mound near to the school.

3. **Kenora**: Cecilia Jeffrey, a Presbyterian-United Church school (1900-1966). A large burial mound is east of the former school. Very extensive series of sinkholes are prominent, close to a lake.

4. **Fort Albany:** St. Anne's Catholic school (1936-1964). Children killed in the school electric chair are buried next to school.

5. **Spanish:** Catholic school (1883-1965). Numerous graves are reported.

6. **Brantford**: Mohawk Institute, Anglican Church school (1850-1969). Building still intact and used by local Mohawk band and businesses.A series of graves and prominent sinkholes are found in the forest immediately west of the main building. See separate report, *Appendix Six*, following.

7. **Sault Ste. Marie**: Shingwauk Anglican School (1873-1969), some intact buildings remain. Several graves of children are reported on the grounds of the old school.

Quebec:

1. **Montreal:** Allan Memorial Institute, McGill University , is still in operation since opening in 1940. MKULTRA experimental centre. Mass grave of children killed there are north of the main building, on the southern slopes of Mount Royal behind an old stonewall.

Appendix Six: The Mush Hole Inquiry – The first survey and excavation of a mass burial site near a former Indian residential school (The Anglican Mohawk Institute in Brantford, Ontario)

http://itccs.org/mass-graves-of-children-in-canada-documented-evidence/

Mass Graves of Children in Canada – Documented Evidence

A Special Report from The International Tribunal into Crimes of Church and State

The first documented evidence of the burial of children at a former Indian residential school

Issued by the ITCCS Central Office and Kevin D. Annett during the Ninth Annual Aboriginal Holocaust Memorial Week -

April 25, 2013

In late 2011 in Brantford, Ontario, history was made with the uncovering of forensic evidence of the burial of children at the oldest Indian residential school in Canada.

Despite subsequent attempts by the Church and Crown of England and their aboriginal agents to discredit and conceal this evidence of their crimes, this first unveiling of mass graves has prompted new disclosures of genocide across Canada.

After the first evidence of a mass grave near the Anglican-run Mohawk Institute in Brantford, Ontario was unearthed between September and November, 2011, these agencies that are responsible for the deaths of children at this, Canada's oldest "Indian residential school", mounted an enormous sabotage campaign to stop the dig and fog the evidence. That coverup eventually involved the Archbishop of Canterbury in London, Rowan Williams, the Anglican Primate in Canada, Fred Hiltz, and Buckingham Palace.

This sabotage temporarily halted the excavation of the Mohawk Institute graves – the first independent dig ever undertaken at Canadian residential schools. But the evidence uncovered confirmed that children are indeed buried there.

This report is a recapitulation of what was discovered at the Mohawk school, and reminds the world that forensic evidence has now substantiated that the Crown of England, the Vatican and the Canadian government and churches are responsible for the death of more than 50,000 children across Canada.

This report includes original field notes from the Mohawk Institute excavations, video recordings of the dig, and evidence of the bones and bits of school uniforms that were uncovered on the former school grounds, along with other corroborating material.

Background

In April, 2011, ten traditional elders of the Grand River Mohawk Nation issued a written invitation to Kevin Annett and the ITCCS to conduct an inquiry on their land into children who went missing at the nearby "Mush Hole": their name for the Mohawk Institute, founded in 1832 by the Crown and Church of England, where records indicate that on average 40% of the children died until it closed in 1970. (see Exhibit No. 1, in Appendix, below)

The Mohawk invitation authorized Kevin and his team to work with specialists to survey the old residential school grounds and search for the remains of children whom eyewitnesses claim were buried east of the Mohawk Institute building, which is still intact.

The survey and excavation work on the grounds of the former school began on September 29, 2011, and continued in its first phase for two weeks, until October 11. The second phase, which included intensive excavations that yielded the aforementioned bones and clothing, spanned four days between November 21 and 24, inclusive.

The project's core team included Kevin Annett and Lori O'Rorke with the ITCCS, four members of the Mohawk nation including two authorizing Mohawk elders, Cheryl and Bill Squire, a Ground Penetrating Radar technician, Clynt King, two consulting forensic and archaeological specialists, Kris Nahrgang of Trent University and Greg Olson with the Ontario Provincial Coroners' Office, and a senior forensic pathologist, Dr. Donald Ortner of the Smithsonian Institute in Washington, DC.

A third and final phase of this initial project occurred during January, 2012, involving interviews with key eyewitnesses who had access to Anglican church archives.

Previous Discovery of Children's Bones at the Mohawk Institute

Our project was initiated in part because of the discovery of children's bones near the former Mohawk Institute / "Mush Hole" school building in 2008, and previously, in 1982.

Tara Froman, curator of the Woodland Center – a museum adjacent to the still-standing former Mohawk Institute building – reported to Kevin Annett in April, 2011 that during the reconstruction of the floor of the

Woodland Center, sometime in 2008, an employee named Tom Hill found what turned out to be the forearm of an adolescent female.

This bone was analyzed by the Provincial Coroners' Office and then "locked away" by Barb Harris, an employee of the state-funded Six Nations Confederacy.

A similar incident had occurred during the actual construction of the Woodland Center in the spring of 1982, according to Tara Froman. That construction was stopped because the complete skeleton of a small child was found immediately west of the former Mohawk Institute building.

Froman says that she was sworn to silence about that discovery, and the remains were "taken away" by the Ontario Provincial Police, possibly into "deep storage" at the Royal Ontario Museum in Toronto.

The Mush Hole Dig: Phase One (September 29-October 11, 2011)

Phase One of the project involved interviews with Mush Hole survivors and the commencing of Ground Penetrating Radar (GPR) surveys on the grounds of the former school. The GPR operation was overseen by Clynt King, a technician employed by the local Six Nations Confederacy, a non-traditional state-funded organization.

A group of six survivors of the Mush Hole were gathered and interviewed for clues to the location of possible graves of children at or near the school building. Based on this information, the GPR survey began on the grounds immediately east of the building, on hilly and uneven terrain where school survivor Geronimo Henry reported seeing children buried in in the early 1950′s.

Sure enough, the GPR surveys immediately detected what GPR technician Clynt King referred to as "massive soil dislocation and abnormal disturbances" in the area east of and adjacent to the Mush Hole building. (see Exhibits No. 2 and No.3)

According to King, on the second day of the GPR survey, (September 30, 2011),

"It appears from the radar that at least ten to fifteen feet of soil has been displaced and covered over the original terrain east and southeast of the school building. This is definitely a subsurface anomaly, meaning it's earth that was dumped there."

Survivor Geronimo Henry (b. 1936) corroborated on the same day,

“None of that mound was there when I was in the Mush Hole (note: 1944-1953). It was all flat then. This has all been piled up, right where I saw them digging one night and burying a small kid.”

Significantly, in the same general area, Geronimo Henry also claims he saw fellow Mush Hole students being placed in an underground cistern as punishment. Henry states,

“Some of those kids went down in there and never came out again. I remember that happened to a girl who was only nine or ten.”

The cement cistern referred to by Geronimo Henry is about ten feet by sixteen feet in size, and stands immediately south of the main school building’s east (girls’) wing. The cistern’s concrete lid seal is broken, making the underground chamber accessible.

Members of the ITCCS team explored the underground cistern chamber on October 5, 2011 and discovered small, apparently animal bones that were scattered throughout the muddy floor of the concrete interior, along with chairs and other garbage. The team returned that night with a driller and bored into the underground wall facing the school building, finding much loose and displaced soil and a drainage pipe running from the school.

Random children’s graffiti was also detected on the walls, confirming that children had been in the cistern.

On the outside of the school building, opposite from the cistern on the north wall of the school, the top of an archway was also discovered. This archway was almost entirely covered by uneven, compacted soil which survivors Geronimo Henry and Roberta Hill claim had not been there in the 1950′s. It appears that the archway is the top of a buried doorway leading from a lower sub-basement area that has been concealed by soil deposits.

The existence of this sub-basement area is significant, in that other school survivors describe being taken as children for punishment to a chamber “under the basement”. This sub-basement chamber contained rings and shackles on the walls where one survivor who desires anonymity states that she saw children being confined in the year 1959 or 1960.

A cousin of Mohawk elder Yvonne Hill stated on October 6, 2011 that a sealed underground tunnel runs from the same sub-basement chamber through the school’s furnace room to a former Greenhouse on the grounds of the Woodland Cultural Center, and “that’s where they buried the kids who died”.

(NOTE: THE SAME SPOT AT THE WOODLAND CENTER IS WHERE SKELETAL REMAINS OF CHILDREN WERE UNEARTHED AND THEN CONCEALED IN 1982 AND 2008, SEE ABOVE). The furnace room's connection to the alleged underground tunnel may be related to the common practice in Indian residential schools of incinerating the bodies of children and newborns who had died or been killed on the premises.

The GPR survey of the Mush Hole grounds encompassed in total four grid areas to the north and northeast of the building. The total size of the surveyed grids was 400 square meters.

On Day 6 of the GPR survey (October 4), Dale Bomberry, head of Operations for the non-traditional, government-funded Six Nations Confederacy, suddenly denied further use of the GPR equipment to the ITCCS team. Clynt King was ordered by Bomberry to cease his activities and all of the data from the GPR survey was seized by Bomberry.

On Day 8 (October 6), Six Nations Confederacy chief Bill Montour was called to Ottawa for "consultations" with the government.

The same day, threats of physical violence were issued against Kevin Annett by three employees of the Confederacy – Tom Powless, Sean Toulouse and a cousin of Dale Bomberry. That evening, the underground cistern was opened and explored by unknown persons.

On Day 9 (October 7), members of the Men's Fire, a Mohawk security force working closely with the ITCCS team, discovered many boxes of residential school files in the basement immediately above the apparent sub-basement chamber described above. Within minutes, the Men's Fire members were stopped by Confederacy staff and photographed on video camera.

The same day, Chief Montour announced that no further support for the Mush Hole inquiry would be offered by the Confederacy, despite Montour having endorsed the survey and dig two days earlier (see Exhibit No. 4, Tekawennake Newspaper October 5, 2011, p. 2).

Consequently, this first phase of the inquiry was suspended on October 11 to allow the sponsoring Mohawk elders and the ITCCS team the chance to assess events and plan how to continue in the face of growing sabotage and resistance by government-funded "chief and council".

The Mush Hole Dig: Interregnum (October 11-November 21, 2011)

After a series of consultations between the ITCCS team and the sponsoring Mohawk elders, as well as the Men's Fire Group, it was unanimously decided to continue with the Mush Hole inquiry and excavations, based on what had been discovered until then.

Numerous attempts to contact GPR technician Clynt King and obtain the GPR survey data from the Mush Hole grounds were unsuccessful. King was reportedly "on extended vacation" and the Six Nations Confederacy refused to release the GPR survey data.

Accordingly, it was decided to proceed directly with a test excavation in the area most likely to contain burial sites, based on the GPR survey and eyewitness accounts.

An excavation team consisting of seven people was established, with the Men's Fire providing site security. The dig team was Kevin Annett (a trained student of archaeology), Cheryl Squire (representing the sponsoring elders), Nicole and Warren Squire, John Henhawk, Frank Miller (videographer) and Yvonne Fantin.

The need for security around the excavation was heightened by continual efforts to sabotage the inquiry on the part of government-paid aboriginal operatives led by Jan Longboat, a local resident. Longboat began approaching the sponsoring Mohawk elders with smears about Kevin Annett and even offers of money.

Consequently, and to build as much international and public support as possible, the excavation team was given absolute authority and permission by the sponsoring Mohawk elders to not simply recover remains on the Mush Hole grounds but to make the findings public, including by sharing them with the media.

This crucial authorization was openly declared and recognized to be part of the ITCCS team's mandate.

The excavations near the Mohawk Institute building commenced on November 21, 2011.

The Mush Hole Dig: Phase Two – November 21-24, 2011

The excavation team laid out a 30 by 30 foot excavation grid about fifty yards due east of the old school building, on lightly forested ground where witnesses Geronimo Henry and Roberta Hill had seen children buried. The grid was marked in 3 ft. increments and was located and aligned with a GPS locator.

On Day One of the dig, the first grid in the upper left corner of the site, designated Grid A1, was cleared of all underbrush and topsoil, and excavated to a depth of one foot.

Within this first top layer, Level One, two sizable bone fragments were discovered almost immediately, in association with many pieces of glass, coal and bricks. The bones were between two and three inches in length and one of them appeared to be part of a spine, either of animal or human origin. The other, longer bone had clearly been cut or chopped up. (See Exhibit 5)

On Day Two (November 22), new and significant evidence was obtained as a second level was opened between a depth of 12 and 24 inches. This evidence involved many small white and brown buttons made of bone and wood rather than plastic: clearly of a pre-1950 vintage.

These buttons were later positively identified by Mush Hole survivors Geronimo Henry, Roberta Hill and Lorna McNaughton as coming from the uniforms of girls at the school during the 1940′s.

The same style of buttons were continually found in association with more bone fragments, some as large as four inches in length, and several teeth. These bones and teeth, along with considerably more bits of brick and charcoal, proliferated the deeper the team dug, to a final depth of 22 inches. One of the bones had an apparent burn mark, and several other bones bore the signs of having been cut up.

In addition, other articles of clothing were unearthed at this Level Two, including the sole from an early-vintage shoe and pieces of a green-colored woolen blanket that survivor Roberta Hill verified as the kind used in the Mush Hole dormitories. One larger piece of blanket several square feet in size was discolored with a rust-colored stain.

Days Three and Four (November 23-24) unearthed even more significant evidence as the excavation extended to the base of Level Two to a depth of 22 inches; and to a length of 8 ft. 6 inches outside the first Grid A1 into Grid A2.

This evidence consisted of more bone and school button fragments entangled in the roots of a small tree that was uprooted in Grids A1-A2. The significance of finding school buttons tangled in the tree roots is indicated in the statement of Mush Hole survivor Roberta Hill:

"Whenever children died on our dorm they were buried east of the school, and a tree was planted on top of their grave. The staff used to talk about doing that among themselves."

A sample of these significant button artifacts excavated at the A1-A2 site is found in Exhibit 6.

After Day 4 of the dig, it was decided to temporarily halt the excavation to allow specialists the chance to analyze and identify the artifacts, and to issue a public statement about what we had unearthed.

Post-Excavation Analysis and Response: The Inquiry is Derailed

On December 1, 2011, a meeting of the dig team, the sponsoring Mohawk elders and two forensic specialists was held at the nearby Kanata Center, a half mile from the Mush Hole building and dig site. The Center, operated by traditional, non-government Mohawk elders at odds with the Six Nations Confederacy, served as the operations post for the inquiry.

The two forensic specialists, archaeologist Kris Nahrgang of Trent University and Greg Olson of the Provincial Coroner's Office, carefully examined the excavated bones from the A1-A2 site and came to the following conclusions about the bones:

1. Olson and Nahrgang both agreed that one of the unearthed bones was part of a small knee socket from "what is probably a small child four or five years old" (Olson). (see Exhibit 7) Olson said, "Personally, I am 95% sure that this is a human bone and I'd stake my reputation on it".

2. Both men agreed that the dig site should be excavated more to unearth additional evidence, and they recommended that "it is imperative" for a full-scale professional excavation to be launched at the Mush Hole grounds by the spring, after the ground had thawed.

3. Greg Olson recommended that a Provincial Coroner's Warrant be sought in the light of this probable discovery of human remains, in order to thoroughly search all Anglican church records and buildings for corroborating evidence. Olson pledged his willingness to publicly endorse and participate in such action.

However, less than one week later, on December 6, Greg Olson informed Kevin Annett by phone that he had been reprimanded by his "employer" – presumably the Provincial Coroner's Office – for partaking in the Mush Hole inquiry, and he was ordered not to do so again, "even during off-work hours". After that, neither he nor Kris Nahrgang – who refused to answer phone and email messages – continued their involvement with the dig or the ITCCS inquiry. (SEE EXHIBIT NO. 8 FOR COPIES OF ORIGINAL FIELD NOTES FROM THE MUSH HOLE SURVEY AND DIG).

In response, and following the instructions of the sponsoring Mohawk elders, on December 8, 2011, Kevin Annett mailed thirteen bone samples, including the knee socket identified by Greg Olson and Kris Nahrgang as "probably human", to Dr. Donald Ortner, the senior Forensic Pathologist at the Smithsonian Institute in Washington, DC.

Additional samples were sent to Dr. Ortner on January 10, 2012.

Dr. Ortner communicated by phone to Kevin on January 30 and said that "I tend to lean towards seeing the samples as animal remains", although he then qualified his statement with the remark,

"Some of them could easily be human, but they're too small to tell. I'd need to conduct more expensive tests to know for sure".

Dr. Ortner made it clear that he had only superficially glanced at the samples, but he promised to study them more thoroughly, and he agreed to work with the ITCCS team at the Mush Hole dig in the future.

On April 29, 2012, Dr. Don Ortner died suddenly of an apparent heart attack; he was 73 years old and in excellent health. Just prior to his death, Ortner had spoken to Kevin Annett on the phone and agreed to become involved in the next phase of the Mush Hole dig, by speaking to the Mohawk elders during early May.

Dr. Donald Ortner was a leading world specialist in the identification of diseases in human remains – such as the tuberculosis that the Mush Hole children were deliberately exposed to, and which killed off thousands of residential school students.

During the same period leading up to Dr. Ortner's death and the sabotage of the Mush Hole dig, between January and May, 2012, a continual campaign of fear and disinformation was launched on the internet and in the Mohawk community against the ITCCS inquiry and Kevin Annett.

This sabotage campaign was led by government operative Jan Longboat, Six Nations Confederacy chief Bill Montour and others in the pay of Longboat, including former dig team member Frank Miller, whom Longboat had, by her own admission, recruited with money payments. This campaign effectively halted the Mush Hole dig and inquiry.

Nevertheless, three Anglican church insiders approached the ITCCS team during the same period with vital information about this silencing and coverup campaign, as well as more evidence of crimes at the Mush Hole

Leona Moses

On December 2, 2011, Kevin Annett and elder Cheryl Squire were invited by Mohawk resident and former Anglican Church researcher Leona Moses to her home in Oshweken. Moses had contacted Cheryl Squire the day before on her own initiative. She stated to both Kevin and Cheryl as they entered her home,

"I want the truth to get out to the world. The church has been sitting on it for way too long".

These facts were shared by Leona Moses with Kevin and Cheryl over the next several hours:

1. While employed during 1998 by the Huron Diocese of the Anglican Church of Canada to examine their archives and records from that church's Mohawk Institute "Mush Hole" school in Brantford, Leona Moses (**LM**) found documents that showed that children were dying continually at the school over many years, and the church and government knew of these deaths and did nothing to stop or even investigate them.
2. These records were part of a designated "G 12 collection" held in the Huron College archives in London, Ontario under the authority of then-Huron Diocese Bishop Bruce Howe. The records have now been sealed from public access under present Bishop Bob Bennett.

3. LM personally read documents describing the regular practice of denying food and medical aid to children in the Mush Hole, of keeping parents ignorant of their sickened condition, and of temporarily improving food at the school only during official visits by government medical inspectors. These documents had been copied and sent to the Indian Affairs department in Ottawa.

4. After inquiring with Indian Affairs in Ottawa in 1998, LM was told by a department lawyer, "G 12 is closed to the public and can never be discussed". LM then asked her co-researcher Wendy Fletcher (**WF** / recently retired head of the Vancouver Shool of Theology) to help her access the records, and was told by WF, "There are over 30,000 documents in the Diocese archives that are sealed, and lots of them could bring down the church".

5. LM saw one "particularly damning document" in the archives that she called "a smoking gun": an "official looking thing, signed and sealed" (LM) dated from the year 1870. It was a formal agreement between the New England Company that established the Mush Hole, the Crown of England/Anglican Church, and non-Mohawk chiefs of the state-run Six Nations Confederacy. The agreement transferred authority over the Mush Hole school to the Confederacy, providing that the school targeted Mohawks for incarceration and extermination. The Confederacy chiefs agreed to cooperate in this plan.

6. LM saw this genocidal document only once, " and then it went missing, Wendy says into the G 12 collection". The regular Diocese archivist was then fired. LM was told after that, that to continue working, she would have to agree to being placed under a voluntary gag order or what then-Bishop Bruce Howe called an "oath of silence" for ten years. LM refused and resigned. WF agreed to be gagged by such an order, and served as the Diocese's "official researcher" after that.

7. Bishop Bruce Howe extended this "oath of silence" to all Diocese employees and clergy. Some clergy resigned or transferred out of the Diocese. WF told LM a few months after the latter had resigned that she, WF, had been threatened with a lawsuit if she disclosed anything in the G 12 collection. LM recalled,

"Wendy Fletcher feared for her life … I offered her sanctuary, especially after one of her secretaries died suddenly after helping Wendy dig deeper into the Mush Hole history in church archives when they were in London, England" (LM, 2 December 2011)

8. Before she resigned from the Diocese research committee, LM saw letters describing how Mush Hole Principal John Zimmerman (served 1936-1948) regularly took girls from the school to private homes of wealthy Brantford residents to rape and traffic them. LM met at least one local woman, a homeless Mohawk in Brantford, who was such a victim.

9. LM also saw documents describing that children in the Mush Hole were deliberately not given warm clothing or pajamas "as a matter of course", and that sickness and death from the cold was common. These deaths and conditions were regularly reported to the church by Mohawk parents, without any response or amelioration.

10. After his silencing of Diocese staff, Bishop Howe retired and was replaced by present Bishop Bob Bennett, who continued the policy of coverup and silencing. Bennett also ordered the destruction of school records showing the records of students and staff members.

11. Soon after the start of the ITCCS Mush Hole dig in late November, 2011, Bishop Bennett met with LM at her home and demanded to know what she had uncovered in the Diocese archives concerning staff and student records. Bennett confirmed to LM that the church was aware of all the crimes and the deaths of children but for that reason denied any public access to the evidence.

Bennett also described to LM a meeting held in 2006 at the Five Oaks United Church center at which a Member of Parliament, United Church clergy and "some doctors" described killings at the Mush Hole, including the murder of newborn children there and at the local Catholic residential schools.

12. Bishop Bennett also disclosed to LM that the Anglican, Catholic and United churches had made an agreement with the Canadian government whereby the latter (ie, taxpayers) would assume all of the financial liability for the residential school crimes, in return for which the churches would promise to disclose all of their evidence. But (to quote Bennett),

"We agreed among ourselves that we could never release certain kinds of information, even if it meant reneging on our promise"

13. After Bishop Bennett's remarks that indicated the Anglican church had committed deliberate fraud on the Canadian people, LM went to Canadian Anglican Primate Fred Hiltz and asked him to order Bennett to open the G 12 archive. Hiltz refused to do so, claiming, untruthfully, "I have no authority over the Bishops".

14. LM learned that the Mush Hole's founding agency, the New England Company based in London, England, still funds "Anglican Mohawks" and that the Queen's chaplain, Bishop John Wayne, has played a direct role in ordering the permanent sealing of the G 12 collection.

15. LM gave many of these facts to the Canadian media early in the year 2008, but only one newspaper, the Tekawennake in Brantford, printed some of her remarks. Teka editor Jim Windle did not explain why he edited LM's story and refused to share the story with the world media, as LM had requested.

Leona Moses reiterated again to Kevin and Cheryl before they left her home,

"The church must be brought to justice … please get this story out. I've been threatened by Bob Bennett if I keep speaking to you".

Two Anglican Church sources: Spring 2012

After news of the shut down of the Mush Hole dig circulated throughout the internet, two other Anglican church insiders approached Kevin Annett with information.

One of these insiders still worked in the Toronto Diocese office of the Anglican church, and another was an employee of the church in a liaison capacity with the Archbishop of Canterbury's office until the fall of 2009.

The present employee told Kevin that in mid January, 2012, Primate Fred Hiltz had been issued a direct order by Archbishop of Canterbury Rowan Williams to "permanently bury or destroy" any evidence that might implicate the church or "Her Majesty" in the death of children at the Brantford Mush Hole school. Hiltz commented on the request to his secretary, who passed in on to the employee.

The second, former church employee told Kevin that before he resigned from his position liaising with London, he had been told of a "serious leak" in the church archival system that implicated unnamed members of the Royal family with "mishaps" at an Indian school in Canada.

The former employee did not know whether this referred to the allegation from eyewitness William Combes that Queen Elizabeth and Prince Philip had been seen taking ten aboriginal children from the Kamloops Catholic residential school in October, 1964 during a verified state visit, after which none of the children were ever seen again. But the employee said,

"It was serious enough for the Archbishop to intervene personally and order a clean sweep of the archives in Canada and London".

Summary and Conclusion

In the light of these events and discoveries, the ITCCS Central Office has concluded the following:

1. The remains of children are interred on the grounds of the former Anglican Mohawk Institute Indian residential school in Brantford, Ontario.

2. These remains and other artifacts that have been unearthed on these grounds verify eyewitness accounts of how children who died at the Mohawk Institute were buried.

3. These children who died were the victims of a deliberate genocidal plan devised and implemented in 1870 by the Church and Crown of England and their accomplices in the Six Nations Confederacy and government of Canada.

4. The evidence of these deaths and burials has been deliberately concealed and destroyed by members of the Anglican Church and the Church and Crown of England, aided by members of the Six Nations Confederacy. This concealment amounts to a deliberate and ongoing Criminal Conspiracy and obstruction of justice.

5. The first independent inquiry into these deaths and burials was overtly sabotaged by these church and government bodies. Accordingly, the ITCCS and groups outside of Canada must intervene to continue the excavation of these buried remains at the Mohawk Institute in order to a) provide a proper burial for these remains, b) determine the cause of death and other facts surrounding these children, and c) use this evidence to bring further criminal charges against those persons and institutions responsible.

In early April, 2013, the ITCCS Central Office received a new invitation and endorsement by elders of the traditional Mohawk Nation to continue the Mush Hole excavation with their permission on the grounds of the former Mohawk Institute in Brantford.

In the light of the Common Law Court indictment and sentencing of the Crown of England, Canada and its churches for Crimes against Humanity on February 25, 2013 – a verdict based partly on the evidence acquired at the Mush Hole excavations in 2011 – Canada, the Crown and its police forces have lost any authority to prevent such a continued excavation on the grounds of the Mohawk Institute in Brantford.

Those indicted persons who have actively subverted the Mush Hole dig, including the Prime Minister of Canada, the Queen of England, the Archbishop of Canterbury, and Anglican Bishops Fred Hiltz, Bruce Howe and Bob Bennett, in fact face immediate arrest under outstanding Citizen Arrest Warrants for their complicity in obstructing justice.

Considering these developments, a new ITCCS forensic team equipped with professional specialists will be dispatched to Mohawk territory to proceed with this inquiry.

This team will be accompanied and protected by International Common Law Court officers who will provide security at the new Mush Hole excavations in conjunction with traditional Mohawk peace keepers. The Brantford excavation site and other locations are presently under close observation and lock-down by Mohawk traditional elders and Common Law Court officers.

These same Common Law Court officers will be armed with the power to arrest and detain not only the aforementioned church and crown officials and those who assist them, but anyone who disturbs or interferes with the excavation on the Mush Hole grounds.

We acknowledge and thank the traditional Mohawk people who are standing by this historic campaign and helping win justice for the missing children. We ask for the active support of all people of conscience.

ISSUED BY KEVIN D. ANNETT IN CONJUNCTION WITH ITCCS CENTRAL OFFICE, BRUSSELS
25 APRIL, 2013
Appendix containing Exhibit references and links

Exhibit 1: Invitation and authorization from Mohawk traditional elders to Kevin Annett and the ITCCS – April, 2011 (see first two photos below)
Exhibits 2 and 3: Ground Penentrating Radar (GPR) survey, Mush Hole grounds – September/October, 2011 - **https://www.youtube.com/watch?v=l0_j5cp-LbI**
Exhibit 4: Tekawennake Newspaper – October 5, 2011, p. 2 (see third photo below)

Exhibit 5: Bone samples, Mush Hole Dig – November, 2011

https://www.youtube.com/watch?v=5hNVyUiUNtc (Preview)

https://www.youtube.com/watch?v=sjM-cm-VIHQ

Exhibit 6: Button samples, Mush Hole Dig – November, 2011

https://www.youtube.com/watch?v=G04DuSJhBhw (Preview)

Exhibit 7: Probable human bone, Mush Hole Dig – November, 2011

https://www.youtube.com/watch?v=sjM-cm-VIHQ

Exhibit 8: Original field notes, Mush Hole Survey and Dig – September-November, 2011 (see fourth and photos below)

Exhibit 9: Sole Canadian media coverage of Mush Hole dig and discoveries – Tekawennake newspaper (see photos below)

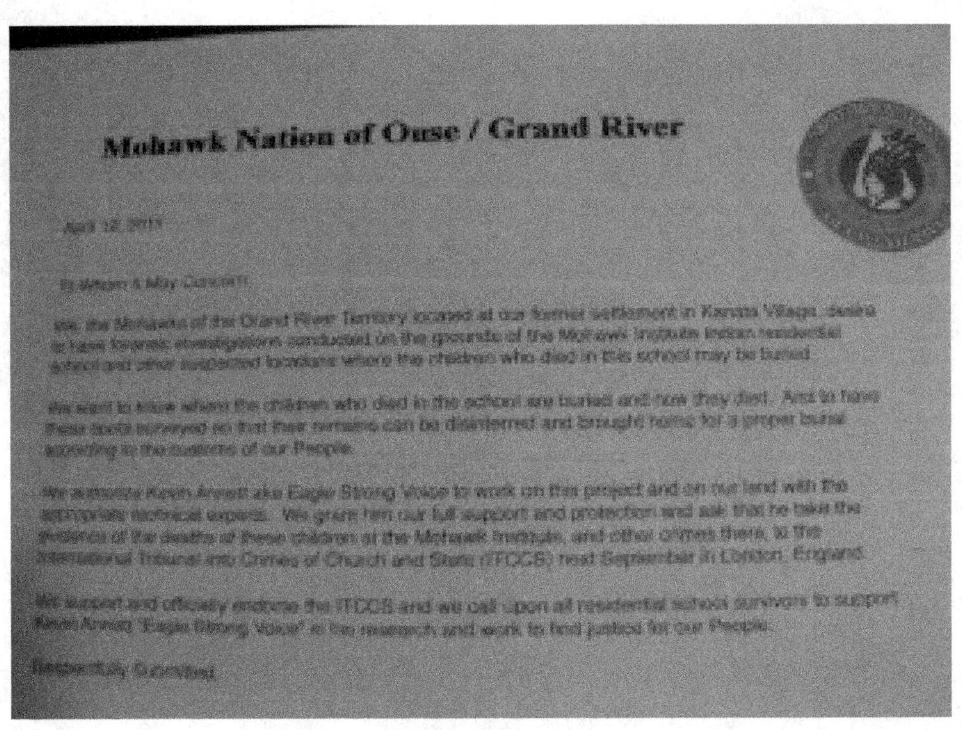

Mohawk Nation of Ouse / Grand River

April 12, 2011

To Whom It May Concern:

We, the Mohawks of the Grand River Territory located at our former settlement in Kanata Village, desire to have forensic investigations conducted on the grounds of the Mohawk Institute Indian residential school and other suspected locations where the children who died in this school may be buried.

We want to know where the children who died in the school are buried and how they died. And to have these [illegible] surveyed so that their remains can be disinterred and brought home for a proper burial according to the customs of our People.

We authorize Kevin Annett aka Eagle Strong Voice to work on this project and on our land with the appropriate technical experts. We grant him our full support and protection and ask that he take the evidence of the deaths of these children at the Mohawk Institute, and other crimes there, to the International Tribunal into Crimes of Church and State (ITCCS) next September in London, England.

We support and officially endorse the ITCCS and we call upon all residential school survivors to support Kevin Annett "Eagle Strong Voice" in his research and work to find justice for our People.

Respectfully Submitted

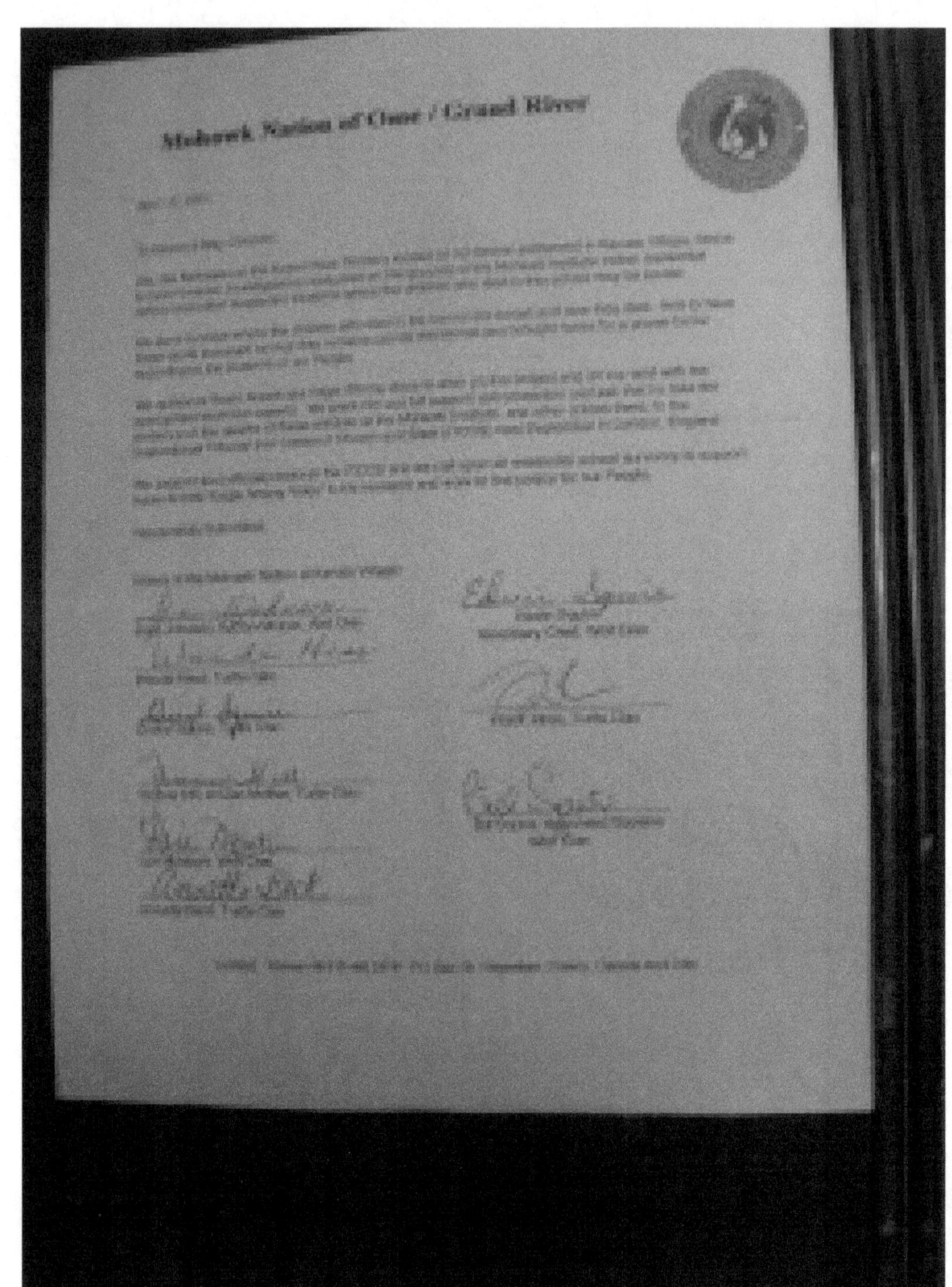

TEKAWENNAKE

CANADA'S OLDEST NATIVE WEEKLY – SINCE 1963

TWO VOICES – SIX NATIONS & MISSISSAUGAS OF THE NEW CREDIT NEWS

Forensic study of Mush Hole grounds begins

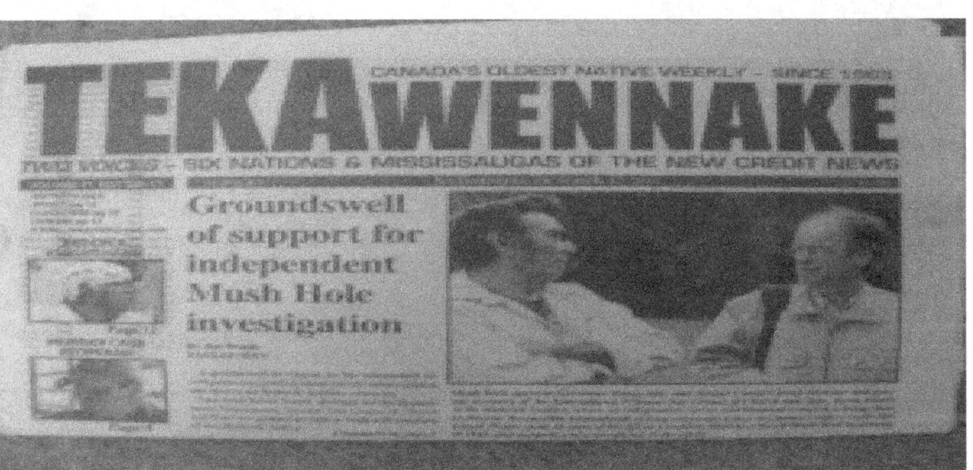

TEKAWENNAKE

CANADA'S OLDEST NATIVE WEEKLY – SINCE 1963

TWO VOICES – SIX NATIONS & MISSISSAUGAS OF THE NEW CREDIT NEWS

Groundswell of support for independent Mush Hole investigation

TEKAWENNAKE

CANADA'S OLDEST NATIVE WEEKLY – SINCE 1963

TWO VOICES – SIX NATIONS & MISSISSAUGAS OF THE NEW CREDIT NEWS

VOLUME 48, EDITION 17 | 20 PAGES | WEDNESDAY, NOVEMBER 30, 2011 | $1.00

E-MAIL: teka@tekanews.com

EAGLES SAG

Page 15

TEAM CANADA

Page 14

Possible child's remains uncovered at Mush Hole

By Jim Windle
EAGLES NEST

Mohawk researchers, with the aid of former United Church Minister, Kevin Annett, have unearthed what they believe to be at least one human bone fragment, that of a small child of around four or five years of age, judging by the size.

Also discovered were samples of small ivory and wooden buttons, which one former resident from the 1940's has identified as similar to those used on the uniforms issued to the girls who attended the former residential school.

The find was made Continued on page 2

At least one bone fragment found this week at the Mohawk Institute, which appears to be a small knee or shoulder socket, has caught the attention of a forensic archaeologist at the University of Northern British Columbia, who strongly believes it as being that of a small child, around three to four feet in height. The bone fragment was found along with several others in the same area and at the same depth as six or seven small ivory buttons and two wooden ones. The bone fragments found have been sent for positive forensic evaluation. The lab results will be returned within about 25 days. (Submitted Photo)

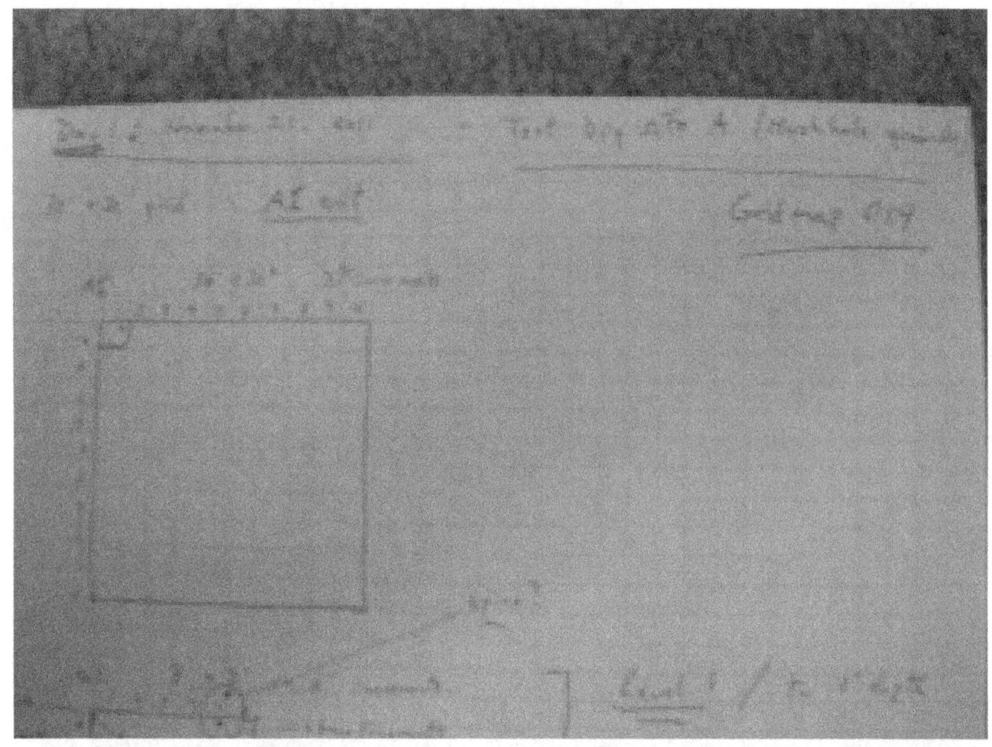

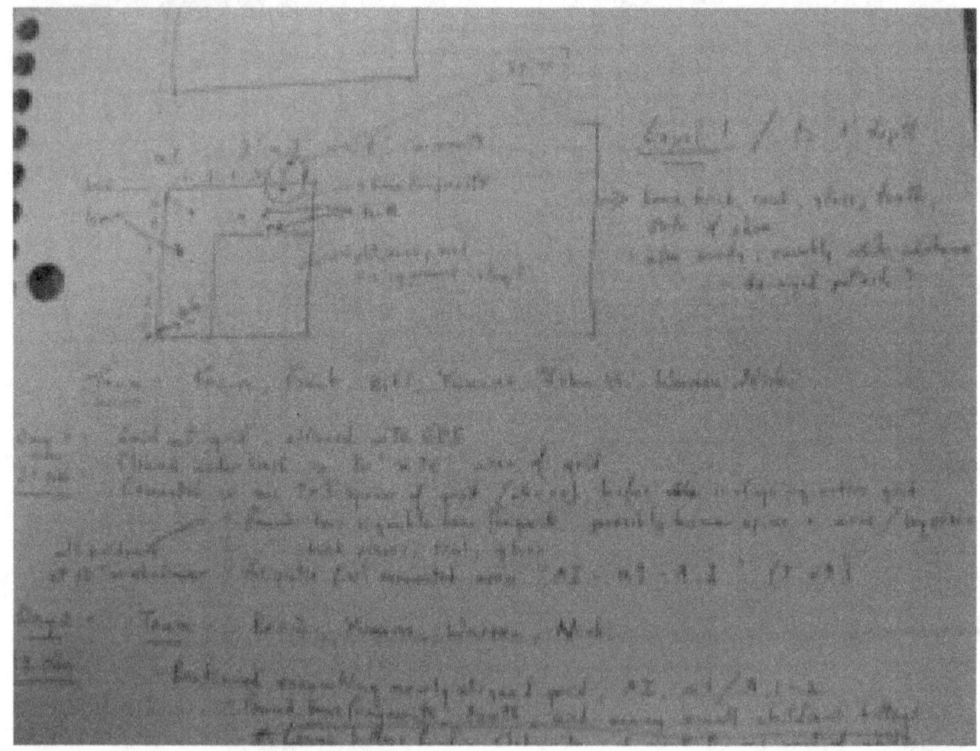

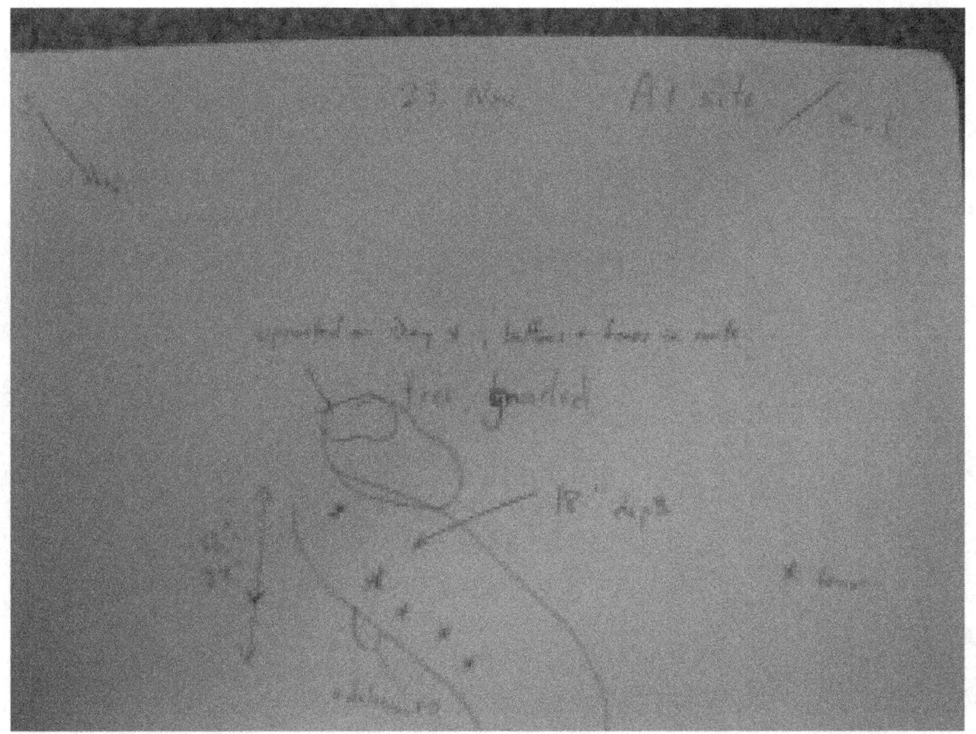

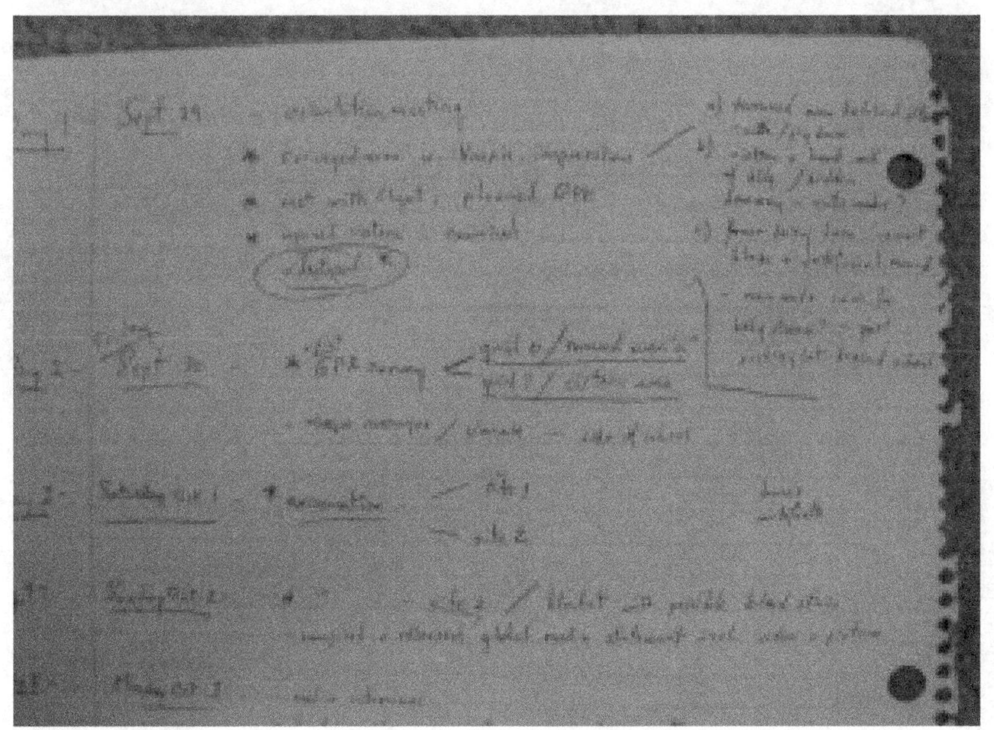

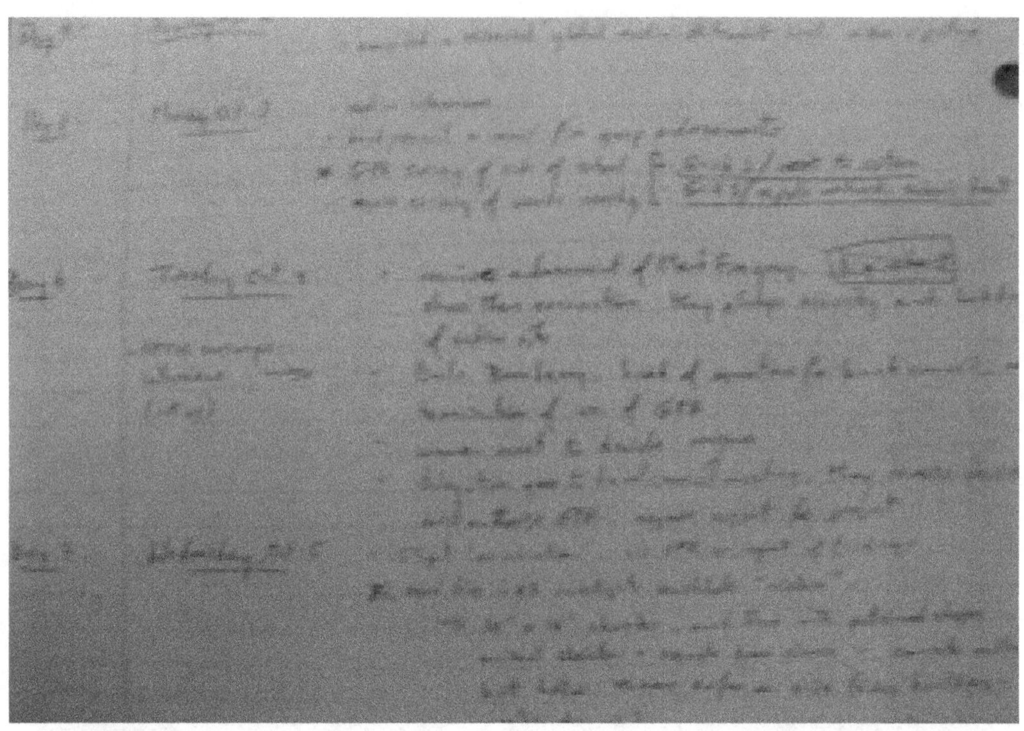

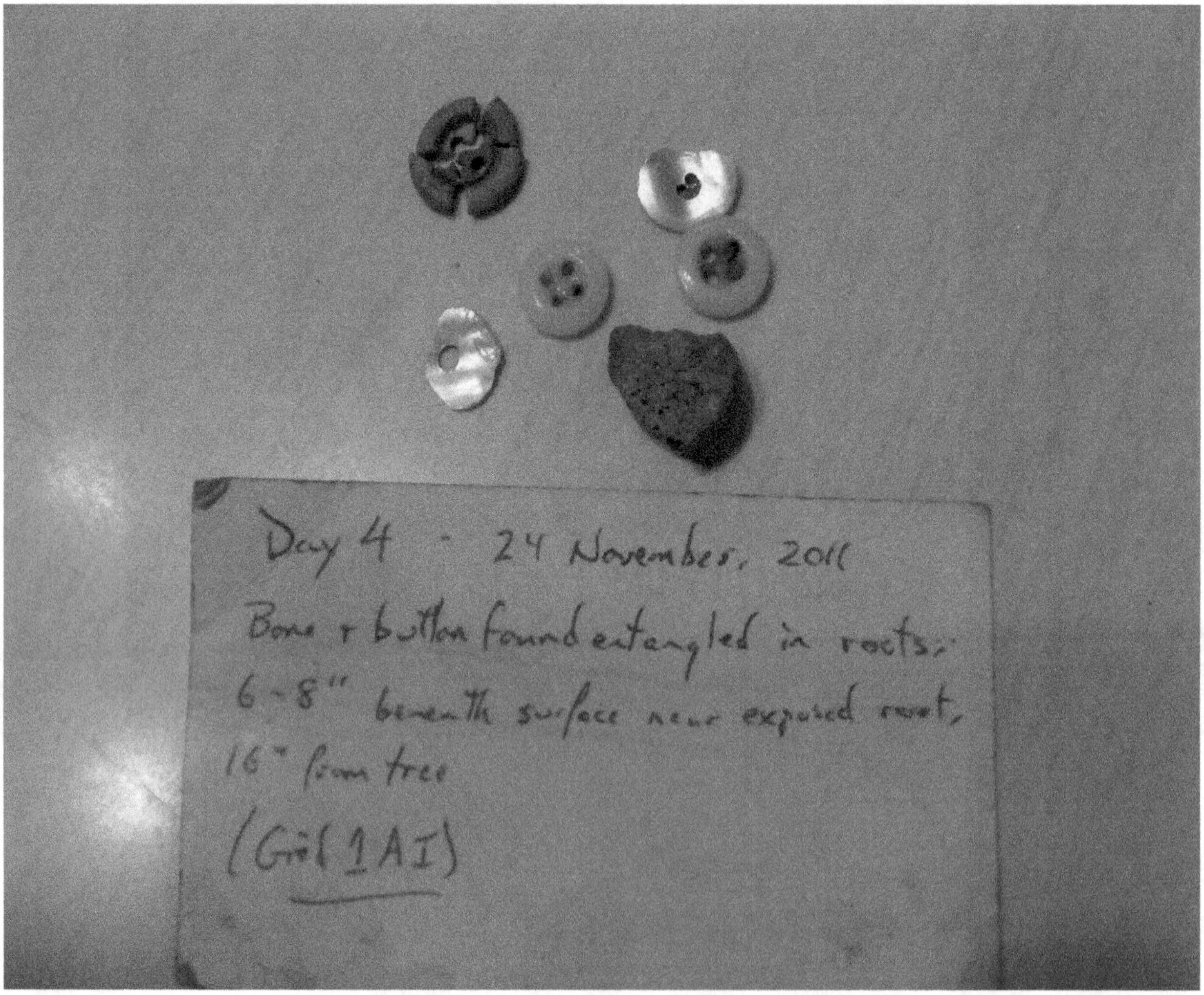

Day 4 · 24 November, 2011

Bone + button found entangled in roots; 6-8" beneath surface near exposed root, 16" from tree

(Grid 1 A I)

Appendix Seven: Missing people - A Memorandum on the Organized Disappearance and Murder of Women and Children on Canada's West Coast – A Summary from Eyewitnesses

Synopsis

1. An organized system of abduction, exploitation, torture and murder of large numbers of women and children appears to exist on Canada's west coast, and is operated and protected in part by sectors of the RCMP, the Vancouver Police Department (VPD), the judiciary, and members of the British Columbia government and federal government of Canada, including the Canadian military.

2. This system is highly funded and linked to criminal organizations including the Hell's Angels, the Hong Kong Triad, and unnamed individual "free lance" mobsters from Vancouver and the USA. It is funded in part by a massive drug trade, with which it is intimately connected.

3. This system is decades-old and has been supplied for many years with women and children from aboriginal reserves and residential schools, with the paid collusion of lawyers, clergy and officials of the Roman Catholic, Anglican and United Church of Canada, along with state-funded aboriginal leaders and officials of the Department of Indian Affairs.

4. This system is international in scope, Vancouver being one spoke in a wheel of pedophilia, sex slavery, human organ black markets, "snuff" films and violent child pornography that has outlets throughout the Pacific Rim world, particularly in China and Thailand.

5. This system relies upon a network of complicity extending to the highest levels of power in Canada and other nations, involving coroners, judges, doctors, clergy, politicians and social workers, as well as the media. It also relies upon a network of "body dumping grounds" and mass graves, located in remote rural areas or on aboriginal reserves and both church and Crown land, where human remains are regularly disposed of by RCMP officers.

6. This system is kept in place because of a practice and philosophy of unofficial tolerance and protection by the established police, judicial, military, church and governmental institutions in Canada and elsewhere. The crimes committed by individual officers of the police, churches, court and government against women and children caught in this system are known and tolerated by these institutions.

Eyewitness Accounts

Eyewitness #1: Caucasian woman, age forty nine, domiciled in Vancouver at 2618 West 8th Avenue, ph: **778-386-7024**. Given name of witness is Annie PARKER, who claims to have personal knowledge of the allegations made herein. Statement video-recorded on 16 February 2006, in Vancouver.

1. The witness states that during the spring of 2000, she was severely assaulted by an officer of the RCMP, Bruce MICHAELSON, in her Vancouver home after requesting RCMP assistance to deal with harassment from her ex-husband. MICHAELSON tortured the witness and compelled her to join what she terms "the hooker game", where she learned the facts alleged herein.

2. The alleged "hooker game" is a protected system run by Vancouver police and RCMP officers in which prostitutes are arrested, drugged, raped and sometimes filmed as part of violent pornographic and "snuff" movies, in which they are tortured and killed on film. The women killed in this manner are then disposed of at special body dumping sites monitored by the police.

3. The witness claims that there are two levels of the "hooker game": the simplest level involves the arrest, drugging and raping of prostitutes, then releasing them. The witness estimates that at least one-quarter of all Vancouver policemen take part in this level of the "hooker game", and that the rest of the police force as well as the Mayor and Chief of Police are aware of it. The higher level of the game involves the use of prostitutes in snuff and pornographic films, and in torturing and murdering them. While unaware of the details of the more extreme level of the game, most police know of its existence but do not betray it or its practitioners for fear that their involvement in the lower level of the game will be exposed.

4. The witness claims that the drug most commonly used on victims of the "hooker game" is SCOPALAMINE, a hypnotic barbituate often termed a "rape drug", in which the victim is "zombified", obeying any command, and then is unable to remember the events for some time. However, memory can return, and the fear of this occurring has prompted MICHAELSON and other participants in the more extreme game to murder the victims and dispose of their bodies. MICHAELSON is the key actor in this body disposal system, according to the witness.

5. Soon after the assault of the witness by MICHAELSON in the spring of 2000, she was taken by MICHAELSON to one of the locations of the "hooker game": a "clubhouse" for policemen in either the penthouse of the Century Plaza Hotel or in the basement of the Hotel Georgia in downtown Vancouver. Witness claims that this clubhouse hosts a "pornographic film studio where woman are raped and tortured on film". MICHAELSON is described by the witness as "a pimp and drug dealer for all the Vancouver cops and their friends ... a lot of the dealing goes on at the clubhouse."

6. Witness states that MICHAELSON works out of a North Vancouver RCMP detachment and is on the city drug squad, having access to large volumes of illicit drugs that he sells to policemen and others.

7. At one of the clubhouses described in Point No. 5, the witness was introduced by MICHAELSON to Willy PICTON and Steven PICTON, who ran and continue to run a pornography and snuff film business from Port Coquitlam (alias "Piggy's Palace"). The witness was subsequently taken by Steven PICTON to the Port Coquitlam site (alias "Piggy's Palace") on several occasions to engage in sex and drugs. At this site, she witnessed young girls being drugged and raped, including on film, after being brought to the site by RCMP officers. Witness describes seeing three RCMP officers, including MICHAELSON, at Piggy's Palace, engaged in drugs and in raping women. Witness states that "ten of the twelve recently murdered women were last seen in the company of RCMP guys."

8. At Piggy's Palace the witness also met Jean-Guy BOUDRAIS or BEAUDRAIS, whom witness claims is the serial killer responsible for the murder of many of the women in the downtown eastside of Vancouver over the past ten years. Witness states that BOUDRAIS is a close associate of MICHAELSON, obtains women and drugs from him, and relies on MICHAELSON to dispose of his victims after he has raped, tortured and killed them. Witness says that BOUDRAIS works for a computer programming company tied to the Canadian military or the federal government, and gives seminars in Ontario and Montreal , where he is domiciled. Witness claims that BOUDRAIS, like MICHAELSON, is a Freemason.

9. Witness claims that Steven PICTON is the ringleader of the snuff film operation that formerly operated out of Piggy's Palace, and which has now moved to an undisclosed location in Coquitlam. One of PICTON's associates operates a front for snuff films out of a company named "Goodbye Girls" at 999 West Broadway in Vancouver. Witness claims that snuff film victims' bodies are weighted with cement blocks and dumped in Beaver Lake in Stanley Park .

10. Witness claims that a snuff film network in Vancouver involves MICHAELSON, a CBC cameraman named Gerry DUNNE associated with Pogo Productions, a film maker named Dave COLLINS who owns Lions Gate Studios, an underworld enforcer named LARRY, a porn film star named Tom TASSE, and the PICTON brothers. TASSE worked in a snuff film studio in the basement of a North Vancouver home a few blocks from MICHAELSON's RCMP office. Snuff films sell for up to $250,000 and have eager buyers in Asian countries and the USA .

11. Witness was told by MICHAELSON that he acts as the main supplier of women and drugs for this snuff film network and for the "hooker game" with the assistance of three "dirty cops": a local policeman named Bob KRISKO, and two

RCMP officers named DAVE and STEVEN. Both of the latter cops are associated with the Missing Women's Task Force and use this position to prey on and rape/murder street women in Vancouver .

12. Witness claims that both DAVE and STEVEN are also associated with BOUDRAIS and have raped and murdered women with him, including Brianne VOTH, age 19, who was abducted, raped and drowned in 2004 in Coquitlam by BOUDRAIS and STEVEN, in association with a prostitute named Stella MALLOWAY.

13. Witness was told by MICHAELSON that either DAVE or STEVEN own a cabin that serves as a body dumping site for women killed by them, BOUDRAIS and others. The cabin is located ten minutes' drive west of Horseshoe Bay on the Sea to Sky Highway , in a hunting camp off a dirt road. Bodies are dumped in a metal cistern at this site.

14. Witness states that MICHAELSON introduced her to BOUDRAIS in 2002 and BOUDRAIS abducted her and drove her to this body dumping site. When witness began screaming and claimed that others knew she was with him, BOUDRAIS returned her to Vancouver after raping her. While threatening witness not to talk, BOUDRAIS told her that he and DAVE and STEVEN murder on average four to six women every year.

15. After this attack by BOUDRAIS, witness began to seek outside help, including by contacting the FBI (see Point No.16 below), and as a consequence was nearly killed by MICHAELSON in retaliation. On January 9 of either 2003 or 2004, MICHAELSON broke into the Kitsilano apartment of the witness and broke her ribs, jaw and arm with a baseball bat. MICHAELSON then tied her up, put her in trunk of his car and drove her to the policemen's "clubhouse" in the Hotel Georgia basement. MICHAELSON then said to the witness, "Now I'll show you what we do to hookers", and proceeded to torture her with dental instruments, including on her genitalia, branding her cult-style with an insignia. MICHAELSON then told the witness "We own you now", and put her to work as a prostitute and lure to attract other women into the game.

16. The witness went to Vancouver General Hospital for treatment after her torture, and was treated at the Oak street clinic by a Dr. Jean McLENNAN or McLAREN. A report of her injuries was filed by this doctor with the Vancouver Police Department that same week.

17. The "hooker game" receives judicial protection from at least one judge, a justice GROBBERMAN, who prior to being a judge served in the provincial Attorney-General's office under the very man, Ernie QUANTZ, who organized a judicial cover-up on behalf of several prominent pedophiles during the 1980's. The witness claims seeing other judges and Prime Minister Paul MARTIN at the policemen's clubhouse in downtown Vancouver during the same evening that MICHAELSON and the PICTON brothers were present, and while drugs and prostitutes were being used. Also in attendance that evening were members of the Canadian Security Intelligence Service (CSIS) and Canadian military officers.

18. After she was attacked by BOUDRAIS, the witness phoned the FBI and asked for an investigation of BOUDRAIS, which occurred in 2005. The FBI investigators were misdirected by MICHAELSON to a false witness who shared the same first name as the witness, and as a result the FBI claimed that there was no evidence against BOUDRAIS. VPD detective Rabinovitch who assisted the FBI also claimed that BOUDRAIS could not be found even though he was circulating openly in Vancouver at the same time. One of the FBI investigators told the witness, however, that BOUDRAIS's description matched those of the Green River Killer, a serial rapist and murderer in the USA who is still at large.

19. Witness claims that MICHAELSON provides security for foreign diplomats in Vancouver and film industry stars, including Eddie MURPHY, to whom MICHAELSON introduced the witness in 2002. Witness claims that MURPHY raped and sadistically assaulted her, slicing her skin with a knife and leaving permanent scars on her shoulder and neck. (See videotaped interview) Witness states that MURPHY was also responsible for the death of two women during the years 2002-3 in Vancouver: a 21 year old Asian porn actress and a prostitute, both of whom were provided to MURPHY by MICHAELSON, and whose bodies were disposed of by the latter after MURPHY had tortured and raped them, and then overdosed them on drugs.

20. Witness states that she reported the attack on her by MURPHY to a Detective SCOTT with the VPD, along with the claim of MURPHY's murder of the two women, but when MICHAELSON learned of the complaint he tortured the witness with a knife, carving her neck and face, (see videotaped interview) and threatened to kill her if she pressed charges against MURPHY. Witness then withdrew her complaint. Detective SCOTT subsequently confirmed to the witness that MURPHY was responsible for the murders but they had not enough evidence to prosecute him.

21. Witness believes that MICHAELSON and his associates are "hunting prostitutes of intelligence" and are engaged "in a kind of ethnic cleansing ... they target Indians and girls as young as twelve or thirteen." She believes there is a connection between MICHAELSON's network and the disappearances of aboriginal women along the Highway of Tears in northern British Columbia.

22. Witness states that she is kept under constant electronic surveillance by MICHAELSON and his associates, and that her apartment keys have been copied by them to allow their regular access. This is "standard procedure when it comes to women they have hooked into the game", according to the witness.

23. All of the facts described herein by the witness were related by her in person to Linda Malcolm, a police woman with the VPD in January of 2006, as part of the Missing Women's Task Force. No action has been forthcoming.

Further background on Eyewitness #1:
Annie PARKER states that she was raised in North Bay, Ontario and was used in a child pedophile ring in that city by her father, LEN PARKER, who was a prominent Freemason and newspaper editor who was associated with the NORAD military base in the same city. Annie PARKER says her father raped and tortured her throughout her childhood, and was involved in "mind control research" at the aforementioned NORAD base. He often spoke to her about the so-called "Marionette Syndrome", whereby a subject is rendered into a mentally docile puppet as the result of extreme torture and trauma. He told the witness that these experiments were being done on children at the NORAD base by American researchers, and that the local pedophile ring existed to provide test subjects to these researchers, as well as child prostitutes to judges and politicians.

The witness also claims that, in 1961, when she was four years old, she and an aboriginal girl named Rosemary, who was six, were abducted and jailed in a farmhouse owned by Freemasons where they were serially raped. Rosemary had been abducted from the local Indian reserve. During the rapes, Rosemary tried to help the witness escape from the barn and was caught and killed, and then her skull was displayed in the local Freemason Hall. The witness feels forever indebted to Rosemary for saving her life, and is committed to helping children like her.

Eyewitness #2: Caucasian woman, mid fifties, normally domiciled in Powell River, B.C. but presently living in hiding in Alberta. Given name is Dagmar STEPHENS. As a former nurse, human resources social worker and child apprehension court worker in the Powell River and Zeballos area, the witness claims to have personal knowledge of the allegations made herein. Statement made during the week of 2-7 February, 2006, by telephone.
1. Witness states that she was recently forced out of the coastal community of Powell River , B.C. and had her life threatened because of her firsthand knowledge of the role of local RCMP, church officials and doctors in the murder of local women and children, and in the importation of illegal drugs and armaments from overseas.

2. Witness is a former social and court worker who worked in the aboriginal community and among youth between 1982 and 2004. She was a member of the Powell River United Church until forced from its congregation by ministers Dave NEWELL and Cameron REID after she claimed that local church members were importing drugs and engaging in pedophilia. (Note: REID was one of the two church officials who handed Rev. Kevin ANNETT his summary dismissal notice in 1995 after ANNETT began to uncover church crimes among native people in Port Alberni)

3. Witness has firsthand knowledge that Dr. Harvey HENDERSON of the Zeballos health clinic is deliberately addicting aboriginal people to a lethal drug named Oxycotin, a synthetic heroin that induces suicidal behavior. He is doing so at the behest of officials of the state-funded Nuu-Chah-Nulth Tribal Council (NTC) in Port Alberni, BC, in order for the land of his

murdered patients to be bought up cheaply by NTC officers. HENDERSON has himself bought much native land on the Ahousat reserve on Flores Island, which he services as a doctor and where he freely distributes the Oxycotin drug. In 2005, all of the suicides among the Ahousats occurred while HENDERSON was working there. HENDERSON lives in Sayward, BC, north of Campbell River.

4. In 2004, witness observed the unloading of drugs and armaments off a black seaplane in the Okeover Inlet near Powell River, under the oversight of Bob PAQUIN, former officer in Quebec secret police and convicted pedophile, Tracy ELKINS, former officer in the South African army, and Colin McCORMACK and Roland LEWIS, local businessmen and associates of the Mayor, coroner and RCMP. Witness claims that these men operate local drug importation with RCMP protection, and deal drugs to local youth and aboriginals. All three are local Freemasons and members of Catholic Knights of Malta, along with Stu ALFGARD, local coroner and pedophile.

5. Witness claims that a similar drug drop off point is at Bliss Landing seaport and helicopter pad, north of Powell River, where Americans regularly fly in drugs.

6. Witness began to run afoul of this group when, in 1986, her local youth group resolved to confront drug use in Powell River schools, and found immediate resistance to their efforts from the school administration, churches, and social services. Witness then asked parents and local police to support them, which they did; an undercover squad of police began to monitor the activities of aforementioned suspects. But within one year, during 1988, all seven of these undercover policemen died, including head cop Bruce DENNISTON, and their deaths were all ruled as being caused by cancer by coroner and pedophile/drug importer ALFGARD.

7. Witness claims that in 2002, a local Anglican minister named KAREN died suddenly after speaking out publicly about the role of the local Masonic Lodge in suspected drug dealing and pedophilia. Her fellow activist in this exposure, Foursquare Baptist church pastor Gord FRALIC, quickly moved out of town after KAREN's death and relocated to Kelowna.

8. Witness is presently residing in Alberta in fear of her life, after being directly threatened and attacked by Tracy ELKINS, former South African army officer and principal drug dealer in Powell River area. Witness states that ELKINS assaulted her and drugged her son after witness continued to investigate local drug importing networks. Witness claims that BC politicians and Powell River residents Gordon WILSON and Judy TYABJI were made aware of all of these facts and declined to support her or the anti-drug educational work of her youth group.

Eyewitness #3: Aboriginal man in his mid forties, resident and maintenance worker employed at the Musqueam Indian Reserve off 51st Avenue on the west side of Vancouver, adjacent to the University of British Columbia. Given name of witness is Leslie GUERIN; domiciled at 3908 KeKait Place , Vancouver, cell phone No.: **778-772-5640.** Initial statement made on videotape during the period 9 May – June 6, 2005, with additional statements made during period of 3 December – 18 January, 2006, in Vancouver.

1. Witness is a member of the Musqueam First Nation in Vancouver who has worked as a maintenance worker and laborer on the Musqueam Reserve since 1990. He is a confidant and associate of many Musqueam officials and politicians. In this position, witness claims to have firsthand and personal knowledge of the allegations he makes herein.

2. Summary of allegations of witness: The Musqueam Reserve has operated as a mass grave and body dumping site since at least 1989. It is also a center of illegal drug and armaments importing through the adjoining Celtic Shipyards, and is connected to native-run pedophile rings that extend to northern B.C. and southern Alberta . The Musqueam band council leaders, especially the GUERIN, SPARROW and GRANT-JOHN families, are involved in these criminal activities in conjunction with officials of the RCMP, the First Nations Summit and the federal government of Canada.

3. The Canadian government provides political and judicial protection for these crimes since the pedophile and body disposal activities by the PICTON brothers and others take place at the behest and in the interest of the government of Canada. The government and police also side with and protect the SPARROW and GUERIN families in their efforts to

attack and undermine other families at Musqueam in order to seize their land and other effects, even when these methods result in deaths. One of these methods of terrorizing other Musqueams utilized by the SPARROW-GUERIN-JOHN clique is to seize their children and transport them off the reserve, including into pedophile rings connected with the provincial government's Ministry of Children and Families. This clique conducts criminal activities on the Musqueam reserve, including drug dealing, strong-arming of dissidents or critics, illegally selling salmon and other fish as well as cigarettes and alcohol, wrongfully evicting band members from their homes and dis-entitling them of their land and DIA payments.

4. Witness claims that the Musqueam Reserve has functioned as a body-dumping and mass burial site since at least 1989, when he personally observed Willie PICTON deposit and bury large garbage bags in a pit directly opposite the Musqueam First Nation office on the reserve. (See his statement, Exhibit A).Witness claims that he subsequently disinterred the contents of these bags and found numerous bones that upon examination proved to be human, including parts of pelvis, skull and femur. Witness retains samples of these remains in his possession while other samples, including an adult female humerus, are held at Simon Fraser University.

5. Corollary evidence of this allegation was provided by the witness in the form of a letter (Exhibit B) by Musqueam Housing Officer A. Glenn GUERIN dated 29 October 2004, which states that Dave PICTON, brother of Willie, was employed by the Musqueam band under contract for three of four months during 1989 or 1990, to provide land fill for a street extension.

6. Witness states that the activities of Willie and Dave PICTON on the Musqueam reserve were fully known and approved by all the band councilors at Musqueam, including Wendy SPARROW, aka Wendy GRANT-JOHN, federal Department of Indian Affairs official and wife of accused pedophile-drug dealer Chief Ed JOHN, who is domiciled at the Musqueam reserve and owns adjoining Celtic Shipyards.

7. Witness reported the activities of the PICTON brothers at Musqueam in 2002 to the Vancouver police (VPD), after the " Piggy Palace " story was reported in local media. But Ed and Leona SPARROW stopped the subsequent police investigation of the remains deposited at Musqueam by the PICTONs after arranging a cover-up with VPD Constable Scott ROLLINS (Badge #2028) and Officer Jodine KELLER. Leona SPARROW was also seen attending parties at the PICTON's "Pig Farm" in company of RCMP.

8. The following media were contacted by the witness and informed of the remains deposited by the PICTONs at Musqueam, but declined from investigating: Mike CLARKE, City TV, Kelly RYAN, CBC radio, Gerald BELLETT, Vancouver Sun, and Karen Urguhart, The Province. Also notified by witness was William MACDONALD, Office of the Police Complaints Commissioner in Vancouver.

9. After more than two years, on November 3, 2004, witness and fellow Musqueam band member Jim KEW made a formal complaint to the VPD Complaints Commissioner about the refusal of police to investigate either the burial site at Musqueam or the apparent role of the PICTONs in burying the remains. (Exhibit C) No response has been received from the VPD at any level.

10. Witness reports seeing Uzi guns and other automatic weapons being unloaded from containers at Celtic Shipyards, 3150 Celtic Avenue, in the summer of 1988, under the supervision of SPARROW relatives Joe BECKER and Wayne GUERIN. BECKER spoke to witness at the time and referred to the importing of drugs through the same shipyard in vessels using false bow fronts. Witness worked as a security guard at Celtic Shipyards between 1995 and 2001, and observed similar unloading of guns and drugs during these years.

11. Witness claims that same Joe BECKER works as an enforcer for Musqueam band officials, including the GUERIN and SPARROW families, along with Walter Dunstan CAMPBELL, whom witness says was arrested with the body of a dead woman in his car trunk, but was quickly released. CAMPBELL also operates protection system for child porn film operation at Carrall and Hastings streets, which in 2004-5 operated behind the front of a bank.

12. Witness claims that other Musqueam officials involved in this child porn film operation include Robert GUERIN, Andrew CHARLES, Frank and Jason MALLOWAY (see Point No. 12 in Testimony #1, re: Stella MALLOWAY), a non-native drug dealer named "DA SILVA", and Chief Ed JOHN. CHARLES, JOHN and CAMPBELL, along with Ed SPARROW, were responsible for the gang rape and beating of Marlon LOUIE, a band member, during 2003 after LOUIE had discovered a "hit list" of the Musqueam "goon squad" headed by Joe BECKER and Walter Dunstan CAMPBELL.

13. BECKER and CAMPBELL head this enforcement "goon squad" on Musqueam reserve that includes former Canucks hockey player Gino OJICK, who owns Musqueam Golf Course Café. Witness claims that OJICK attempted to kill him with poison in 2002 after witness went to the VPD with allegation about PICTON brothers' activities at Musqueam.

14. Witness claims that the main security officer for the Musqueam reserve, ex-Edmonton policeman David LAVALLEE, is part of this enforcement/goon squad. LAVALLEE left the Edmonton police under a cloud of suspicion concerning his involvement in the rape and disappearance of local women and children.

15. Witness claims that the members of this enforcement/goon squad are responsible for the deaths of numerous Musqueam band members, often through staging fake car accidents or executing people with drug overdoses. These deaths occur in order to seize the homes and land of the murdered persons, and secure the power of the SPARROW-GUERIN clique. One such murder occurred in 2000 when a young native woman named GANARJEE was evicted for not being able to pay her property taxes, which had been wrongfully increased by the GUERIN-SPARROW clique. She then became homeless on Hastings street, was addicted to drugs by CAMPBELL, and then "overdosed" and died. The SPARROW family then received her home and property.

16. Witness claims that GANARJEE's property was seized by lawyer Marvin STORROW of Blake, Cassells and Graydon law firm in Vancouver, who works closely with the SPARROW clique and their relative Chief Ed JOHN. (Note: STORROW represented JOHN in a 2002 BC Supreme Court lawsuit that silenced JOHN's critics and imposed a gag order on any media reporting of the accusations of criminal actions by JOHN.) STORROW has a long history of involvement with the Musqueam band and the SPARROW family (see Exhibit D) and has strong ties with the federal Liberal party. Leona SPARROW who is associated with the PICTONs and concealed their activity at Musqueam (see Point No. 6) has worked for STORROW's law firm.

17. Other lawyers and firms associated with the SPARROW clique and their activities include Lou HARVEY and Smithe-Radcliffe law firm. HARVEY is an old associate of STORROW and has helped to steal and illegally transfer Musqueam land into the control of Squamish politicians working for the federal government.

18. Witness claims that the SPARROW clique evade federal laws limiting the commercial sale of salmon by aboriginal people, and completely monopolize an illegal black market in fish operating out of the Musqueam reserve. Wendy GRANT-JOHN (a former SPARROW) operates her own fish store, Longhouse Seafoods in the Dunbar region of Vancouver, which illegally sells sockeye and other salmon. The enforcement/goon squad silence band criticism of these acts.

19. Similarly, in a written statement dated December 26, 2005, the witness claims "For the record, all the elders whom have died, it's Wendy's family (who) lives in each and every home that comes from another unexpected death ... they (the SPARROW clique) have a group of people monitoring each band member and so they wait for a window of opportunity to strike. They pick targets in the community and slowly tear them apart – deliberately destroy lives."

20. The witness has drawn three separate maps of the Musqueam reserve that identify the location of two major body dumping and burial sites (Exhibit E, 1-3).

Witness #4: Retired aboriginal man in his late fifties, a band councilor and member of the Musqueam band and a friend of Witness #3. Given name is Arthur STOGAN sr, he is a direct descendent of the hereditary chiefs of the Musqueam people. Resides on the reserve, phone **604-263-6295**. His lifelong residence at Musqueam and involvement as a band councilor gives him a personal knowledge of the facts he alleges herein. Initial statement made on videotape during the period 9 May – June 6, 2005, with additional statements made during period of 3 December – 18 January, 2006, in Vancouver.

1. Witness affirms all that witness #3 alleges in his statement, adding that he and his extended family are being targeted by the SPARROW clique for their opposition to the crimes described. In particular, witness claims that his grandchildren have been deliberately seized by Ministry of Children and Family (MCF) officials and sent into foster homes operated by known pedophiles in order to silence the witness and force him into conformity. (See Exhibit F) (Note: MCF was run by SPARROW relative and Musqueam enforcer Ed JOHN during 2000-2001 when he served in the provincial government).

2. Witness claims that after the death of his father, Vincent STOGAN, the hereditary chief of the Musqueam, in 2000, attacks against he and his family were made by the SPARROW clique on the reserve, especially after the witness began to speak out against that clique's corrupt and nepotistic practices. These attacks culminated in February of 2004, when all fourteen of the witnesses' grandchildren were seized by Xyolhemeylh, the Child Protection Society of the Sto"lo First Nation near Chilliwack \. Witness was denied any visiting rights, even though one of his grand daughters was placed in the home of a convicted pedophile by Xyolhemeylh worker Loretta ROSZA, who also falsified reports and made false claims about the children. ROSZA is associated with Wendy GRANT-JOHN (SPARROW) through the Sumas First Nation. Both the Chilliwack and Mission detachments of the RCMP refused to investigate complaints by the witness regarding these actions. (Exhibit F)

3. Witness states that another reason for this attack on he and his family is his discovery of evidence that the present SPARROW clique and their relatives cooperated with the federal government in destroying traditional records and histories of the Musqueam and Coast Salish people during the 1970's, as part of the effort to ethnically cleanse west coast aboriginal people and steal their land. A letter from the Department of Indian Affairs dated September 22, 1972 states that individual records of native people in B.C. were to be destroyed under the scrutiny of Chief Clarence Joe, a SPARROW relative. (see Exhibit G)These records included evidence of original land ownership and genealogy.

4. Witness states that there is a direct link between criminal and pedophile networks involving aboriginal politicians in both Musqueam and Cowichan nations because of traditional kinship ties across Georgia Straight. Witness claims that Joe BECKER, Delbert GUERIN and Andrew CHARLES are linked to Cowichan chiefs who are heavily involved in the drug trade, illegal fishing and pedophile rings operating out of Nanaimo, centred around the HARRIS family of the Chemainus First Nation.

5. In December of 2005, the witness compiled these allegations into a letter to Amnesty International, and sent with this letter forensic samples of the alleged human remains unearthed by Witness #3 at the Musqueam burial site visited by the PICTONs. This letter and package were returned to the witness unopened. Both witness and Witness #3 live in daily fear for their lives.

Witness #5: An aboriginal man, age fifty five, who is traditional hereditary chief of the Chemainus Nation in Oyster Bay, BC, on Vancouver Island. Given name is Steven SAMPSON Jr., he resides on his traditional family land near Shell Beach. He has lived all of his life in proximity with the people described in his statement, and as a traditional chief and a former activist in the American Indian Movement and the Red Power Movement, he has direct and personal knowledge of the facts alleged herein. Statement made during the period 3-19 June, 2005, in Shell Beach.

1. Witness claims that the present leadership of the Chemainus First Nation is deeply involved in illegal activity, and are responsible for murders on the local reserves. This leadership revolves around George HARRIS and George, Ed and Peter SEYMOUR, whom witness claim operate the local drug and child trafficking and child porn networks in conjunction with Nanaimo criminal Willie CURRIE. CURRIE operates a local equivalent of the PICTON "Pig Farm" in a house on Jingle Pot Road in Nanaimo, where he has raped and murdered numerous young girls, including Lisa Marie DEYONG in 2004.

2. Witness states that George HARRIS is closely connected to the GUERIN-SPARROW clique in Musqueam, and engages in illegal fishing and drug importation practices with them across Georgia Straight. The parents of HARRIS, Irene and Lawrence HARRIS, were Catholic church-sponsored "watchmen" who transported children into the Kuper Island

Residential School during the 1940's and '50's, and who were descended from collaborating puppet "chiefs" set up by Catholic missionaries in the 19th century.

3. Witness claims that the HARRIS clique have tried to force him and his family off their land for years, through physical intimidation, murder, poisoning their water, and attempting to kill off the SAMPSON blood line through involuntary sterilizations inflicted on both of the witness' sons, Troy and Steve.

Witness #6: Aboriginal woman in her mid-fifties, given name is Bernice WILLIAMS (native name SKUNDAAL), of Haida and Nuu-Chah-Nulth ancestry. Member of the Downtown Eastside Womens' Centre in Vancouver, and an activist since the 1970's with native and womens' groups across B.C. Statement made on April 3 and April 28, 2006, in Vancouver, B.C.

1. Witness claims that a Vancouver police officer named Dave DICKSON is responsible for the rape and murder of numerous aboriginal women in the downtown eastside. DICKSON holds a senior position of responsibility in the Missing Womens' Task Force and is very prominent in the downtown eastside of Vancouver, serving on community liaison boards.

2. Witness claims that she has been attacked on several occasions by policemen and women associated with DICKSON because of her investigation into the missing women. In February, 2006, witness was attacked without warning by five policemen in an alley of the two hundred block east Hastings, was struck in the head, pepper-sprayed and handcuffed, and was being forced into a police van for a "midnight ride", during which she expected to be killed. Witness screamed for help and a local resident saw the attack, and raised a furor, at which point the police let the witness go.

3. Witness confirms the statements of Witness #1, Annie PARKER, concerning the identity of Bruce MICHAELSON and other police connected to the disappearance, torture, rape and murder of women in Vancouver.

4. Witness claims that the disappearance of Vancouver aboriginal women as part of the aforementioned "Hooker Game" is directly connected to the murder of women in northern B.C. along the so-called "Highway of Tears", and is being actively covered-up by government, judges and police in B.C.

5. Witness claims that she and her associates at the Downtown Eastside Women's' Centre (DEWC) face continual harassment by the police and by former DEWC senior staff, some of whom actively resisted their efforts to expose the murderers of aboriginal women in Vancouver. Witness claims that these staff and others are aware of the identity of these murderers and are working with city police and others to conceal their identity.

Addendum

Statement of Grant Wakefield, alleged former field agent of the Canadian Security Intelligence Service (CSIS) – Witness #7.

1. Witness contacted Kevin Annett and spoke with him by payphone in Vancouver on two occasions during May of 2010. Given name was Grant WAKEFIELD, domiciled in New Westminster, given phone numbers 604-540-7638 and 778-789-5051, email g.wakefield@me.com .

2. Witness began by stating that all the information he would share is documented and contained in the "PICTON master file secreted in the Superintendent's office at the RCMP's E Division headquarters on 47th avenue in Vancouver." Others who were given the same information include lawyer Cameron WARD, RCMP psychologist Mike WEBSTER and a Moira WEBSTER, along with CBC TV reporter Natalie CLANCY. Courts in Vancouver consistently "lost" files on PICTONS. WARD and CLANCY both given hard evidence of RCMP involvement in killing of women but ignored it.

3. Witness claimed to be a former field agent for CSIS who was assigned to infiltrate the PICTON brothers' farm in Coquitlam, aka "Piggy's Palace" (PP), during the 1990's because of the supposed presence there of "paramilitary right wing" groups. Discovered close involvement of RCMP officers with Hell's Angels and both Dave and Willy Picton at PP, where women were taken, raped and killed on film. Cannibalism was also practiced and filmed. Also found that "top politicians and military leaders" frequented PP and "a wealthy home in Port Coquitlam where the actual killings were done": a "19th century type building that looks like an institution"; the building has no recorded owner but has a Masonic past. The Pictons "were just the clean-up crew after the killings and snuff films were made" at this other building. RCMP brought female victims to both locations routinely.

4. Witness found that Ian DONALDSON, Q.C., Picton defense lawyer, and Randi CONNOR, Crown Counsel who staid first charges against Willy Picton and told RCMP to not reveal evidence of PP, were both share holders in ETERNAL HOLDINGS (EH), a numbered company on the Vancouver Stock Exchange that owned the land where PP situated. At time of the first disclosure of PP crimes – 1997 – the land was purchased by EH at below market price. EH now operates as PALLADUM LTD., connected to on line porn, which is connected to a Mark MERRICK of Edmonton who owns bestgore.com, linked to child porn and snuff films. MERRICK claims to charge $2 million for each snuff film. PICTONs also owned land in Powell River (see Testimony #2 of Dagmar STEPHENS).

5. Other snuff film companies include LIONS GATE FILMS (LGM), another name for LIONS GATE SECURITY (LGS). LGS formerly was WHITE KNIGHT SECURITY (WKS) which provided security at PP along with an RCMP Inspector BIDDLECOME. LGS officers included Don ADAM, RCMP, who initially headed investigation at PP, and Jim or Kim BROWN, RCMP, close friend of Dave PICTON and tied to "well connected senators" like CAMPBELL. BROWN was involved in PP investigation and on Vancouver Missing Womens' Task Force despite being on film images raping women at PP and having violent porn images on his computer. Crown Counsel CONNOR ordered the film of BROWN at PP buried along with evidence that RCMP badges and uniforms were found at PP. Voir Dire court session in 2005 revealed this evidence and its suppression by CONNOR, but courts sealed the evidence by order of a Judge STONE. Incident known to reporter Stevie CAMERON who never reported it in her articles and book "The Picton File". CAMERON is a cousin or close relative of Senator CAMPBELL.

6. EH was also connected to GOOD TIMES FOUNDATION (GTF), a licensed charity formed in 1992 at time of Dave Picton's first arrest. Hell's Angels money involved in creating GTF which was likely the holding company for PP land. GTF participants often present at PP including Mayor of Coquitlam, two members of provincial government (MLA's), military, police and judges, former RCMP officer, Vancouver Mayor and Chief Coroner and now Senator Larry CAMPBELL, former Prime Minister Paul MARTIN (who appointed Campbell to Senate). Witness saw all these individuals at PP.
7. Others connected to PP include Luc MAGNOTA, employee of MERRICK's Best Gore snuff film company and a room-mate with Tim Gay BOWHAM, a convicted serial snuff film killer from USA (sentenced June 2009). MAGNOTA named by RCMP as having female body parts in his car, but never arrested or questioned. Vancouver police officer DICKSON part of PP ring as well but also on the Vancouver Missing Womens' Task Force. *(See statement of Witness #6, above, confirming identity of DICKSON).*

8. The Coqutilam local fire department tried closing PP on several occasions and every time was stopped by RCMP. A Vancouver downtown eastside hotel also used by PP participants and BIDDLECOME to rape women, probably Patricia Hotel on east Hastings street. (This is the same hotel that banned Kevin ANNETT from staying there without giving cause in 2010 after he interviewed Witness).

9. RCMP officer Catherine GALLIFORD tried reopening PICTON case and was warned not to, was physically and sexually assaulted by male RCMP officers, later tired to sue them but was rebuffed and threatened by different judges. Since 2004 GALLIFORD worked on Missing Womens' Task Force but then quit suddenly without explanation.

Affirmation

I, Kevin Daniel Annett, of 360 Columbia Street in Vancouver, B.C., do solemnly declare and swear that these statements and the facts alleged herein were shared with me by each of the persons named as witnesses in this memorandum, and were recorded by me on video camera on the dates given.

___*(signed in the original)*_____________________________

Rev. Kevin Daniel Annett, M.A., M.Div.
May 26, 2006
Vancouver, B.C.

hursday, June 21, 2001 — The Province • News A3

Roadblock on serial killer: Cop

Ex-inspector suing force blames stubbornness of cops investigating cases of 30 missing women in Vancouver

Stories by Andy Ivens
Staff Reporter

Vancouver police kept mum about a possible serial killer preying on women because of stubbornness and the high cost of tracking him, former detective inspector Kim Rossmo charged yesterday.

Rossmo, the plaintiff in a wrongful dismissal trial against the police force, testified his expertise as a doctor in criminology was routinely dismissed by VPD investigators working on the case of 20 to 30 women who've gone missing from the city's skid row since 1998.

Most of the missing women are prostitutes.

Rossmo named Deputy Chief John Unger — one of two defendants in the case — as his principal nemesis during a five-year stint when Rossmo piled up awards and garnered prestige for the VPD for his ground-breaking work in the field of geographic profiling.

And he accused police Insp. Fred Biddlecombe of being a roadblock in the investigation of the missing women.

Rossmo said the major crime division bore him out of its investigation, even after he was called to a meeting in November 1998 to look at the missing women case.

He said Biddlecombe "threw a small temper tantrum" when he was brought in.

"Insp. Biddlecombe threatened not to send people to meetings, or share information," Rossmo testified.

At the time, he said, he suggested going to the media, partly to save the department any embarrassment if it was proven a serial killer was operating, as Rossmo still suspects.

"I suggested [telling the media] there is a possibility a serial killer is at work on the Downtown Eastside," he said, adding that his suggestion was immediately shot down.

"One positive was that major crime [division] tried to locate as many missing as possible."

Although he never used his geographic profiling talents on the case, Rossmo said the experience was like being on a 747 jetliner when someone tells the pilot there's smoke in the cabin.

"If the captain says, 'Prove to me there's a fire,' you know he's either a fool or incompetent."

Rossmo said he was not alone in his feelings that not enough has been done to solve the missing-women case.

"Many people in the VPD feel the same about this — frustration."

He cited sex, race and the low social status of the missing women as reasons the VPD went slow, likening the situation to the story of the emperor's new clothes.

"For 18 months, women mainly in the sex trade were disappearing," noted Rossmo. "If you have a serial killer running around, you have to do something about it. Nobody wants to do anything."

Deputy Chief Unger and Chief Terry Blythe declined to comment on Rossmo's bombshell.

They are witnesses in the case and it would be improper for them to talk to the press before giving their testimony.

— The Prov

Kim Rossmo is reassured by his lawyer Murray Tevlin outside court yesterday

Appendix Eight: A Joint Plan for Genocide – The 1910 Contract to operate the Indian residential schools jointly by the government of Canada and mainline churches.

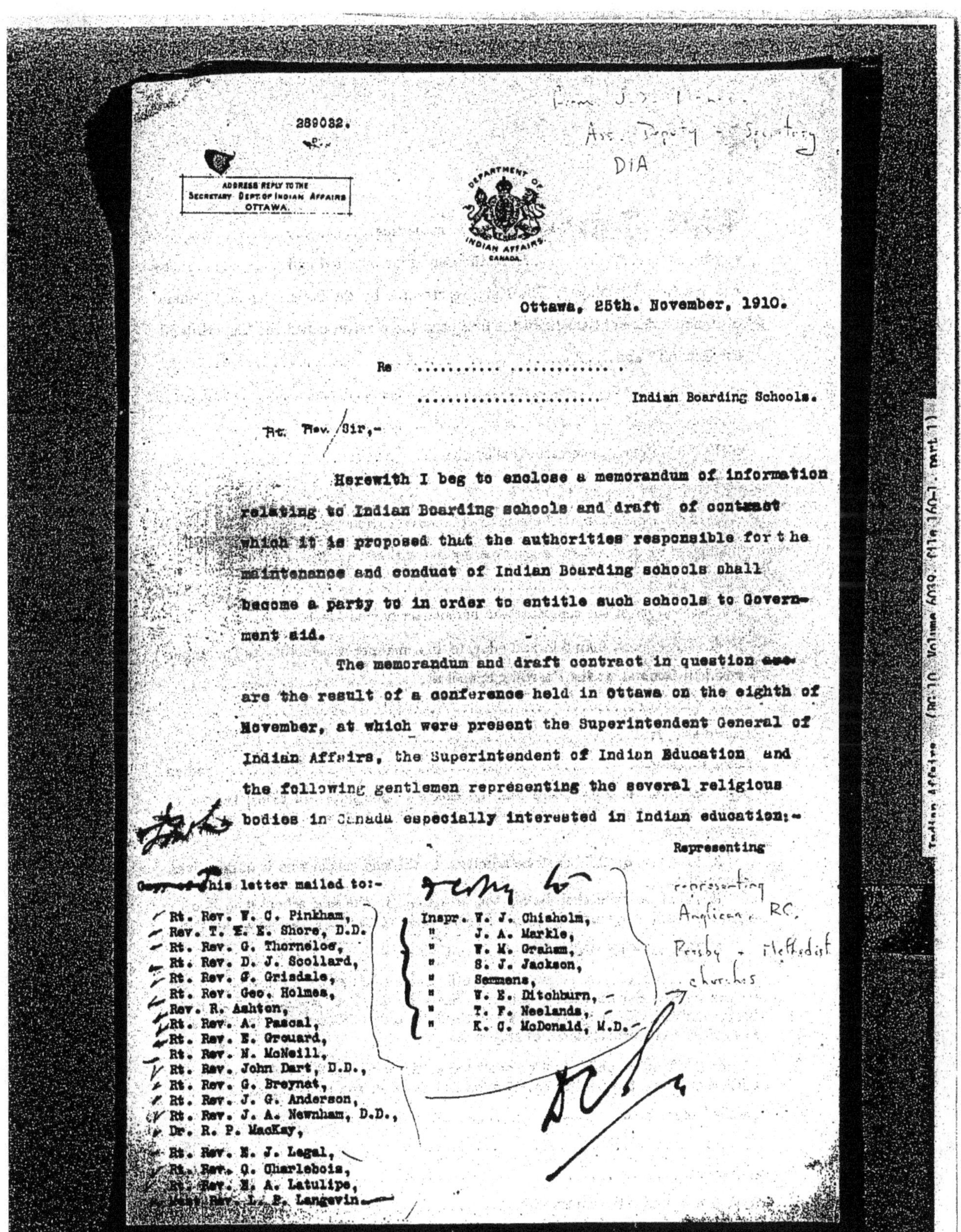

289082.

ADDRESS REPLY TO THE SECRETARY DEPT. OF INDIAN AFFAIRS OTTAWA.

DEPARTMENT OF INDIAN AFFAIRS CANADA

From J. D. McLean Asst. Deputy & Secretary DIA

Ottawa, 25th. November, 1910.

Re ....

.... Indian Boarding Schools.

Rt. Rev. Sir,-

Herewith I beg to enclose a memorandum of information relating to Indian Boarding schools and draft of contract which it is proposed that the authorities responsible for the maintenance and conduct of Indian Boarding schools shall become a party to in order to entitle such schools to Government aid.

The memorandum and draft contract in question are the result of a conference held in Ottawa on the eighth of November, at which were present the Superintendent General of Indian Affairs, the Superintendent of Indian Education and the following gentlemen representing the several religious bodies in Canada especially interested in Indian education:-

Representing

Copy of this letter mailed to:-

Rt. Rev. W. C. Pinkham,
Rev. T. E. E. Shore, D.D.
Rt. Rev. G. Thorneloe,
Rt. Rev. D. J. Scollard,
Rt. Rev. S. Grisdale,
Rt. Rev. Geo. Holmes,
Rev. R. Ashton,
Rt. Rev. A. Pascal,
Rt. Rev. E. Grouard,
Rt. Rev. N. McNeill,
Rt. Rev. John Dart, D.D.,
Rt. Rev. G. Breynat,
Rt. Rev. J. G. Anderson,
Rt. Rev. J. A. Newnham, D.D.,
Dr. R. P. MacKay,
Rt. Rev. E. J. Legal,
Rt. Rev. O. Charlebois,
Rt. Rev. E. A. Latulipe,
Most Rev. L. P. Langevin.

Inspr. W. J. Chisholm,
" J. A. Markle,
" W. M. Graham,
" S. J. Jackson,
" Semmens,
" W. E. Ditchburn,
" T. F. Neelands,
" K. C. McDonald, M.D.

representing Anglican, RC, Presby, Methodist churches

This Agreement made this..............................

day of......................one thousand nine hundred and..............by and between His Majesty The King, represented by the Superintendent General of Indian Affairs of Canada, of the first part, (hereinafter called the 'Superintendent General') and...

....

....

of the second part, (hereinafter called the..................................

..........................).

WITNESSETH that the said parties have covenanted and agreed, and by these presents do covenant and agree, to and with each other as follows:—

I. The..for and in consideration of the compensation hereinafter named agree:—

1. To support, maintain and educate, in a manner satisfactory to the Superintendent General, at the Boarding School at..............................

....

known as..

not more than...Indian pupils, and not to allow more than an excess of one pupil for every twenty or fraction of twenty of the above number of pupils to remain in the said school at any one time.

2. (*a*) That no child shall be admitted to the said school who is under seven years of age.

(*b*) That no child shall be allowed to remain in the said school who is over eighteen years of age unless by special permission of the Superintendent General.

3. That no child shall be admitted to the school by the..................

.................................until, where practicable, a physician, to be named by the Superintendent General, has reported that the child is in good health and suitable as an inmate of said school, and the Superintendent General has authorized the acceptance of such child.

letters re- indiscriminate admission of TB kids

4. (*a*) That no child shall be admitted to the said school without the special authority of the Superintendent General unless he or she is the child of a duly enrolled member of..

....Band of Indians or...irregular Band of Indians now under the supervision of.........................., Indian Agent.

* 13. To maintain the buildings at the said school and the school premises when they are the property of the.. in good condition and repair, the whole to the satisfaction of the Superintendent General.

14. To observe appropriately the King's Birthday, Victoria Day, Dominion Day and Thanksgiving Day at the said school.

15. To have school-room exercises on five and industrial exercises on six days in each week, legal holidays excepted; and excepting also a vacation not to exceed one month between the first day of July and the first day of October in each year, unless some other course is expressly sanctioned by the Superintendent General. During the vacation the pupils may, in the discretion of the.......... ....be permitted to visit their homes, but the Superintendent General will not pay any part of the cost of transportation either going or returning. *

16. To make to the Superintendent General such reports upon the said school as he may from time to time require.

17. To permit the Superintendent General and any person or persons named by him for that purpose to inspect the said school, school buildings and premises, and to afford the Superintendent General and such person or persons every facility for making such inspection thorough and complete.

18. To make any change or alteration in the school building or premises or in the management or control of the said school rendered necessary to comply with the intent and spirit of the agreement, and to remove for cause from the said school any teacher, officer, employee or pupil when required so to do by the Superintendent General.

19. Not to assign this contract or any interest therein without first obtaining the written consent of the Superintendent General.

II. The Superintendent General, in consideration of the faithful performance by the...of the above covenants and stipulations, agrees:—

1. To pay the.. at the rate of..per annum for each pupil, but the number of pupils so to be paid for shall not exceed.............. ....in accordance with the restrictions hereinbefore set out; the payments shall be made quarterly and each quarterly payment shall be computed on the average attendance of each pupil; provided, however, that the said grant shall be allowed and paid during the vacation; but no payments will be made until returns have been received by the Superintendent General duly certified by the.. that the said school has been maintained and managed according to the true intent and meaning of this contract.

* 2. To provide the pupils of the said school with medicines, school-books, stationery and school appliances.

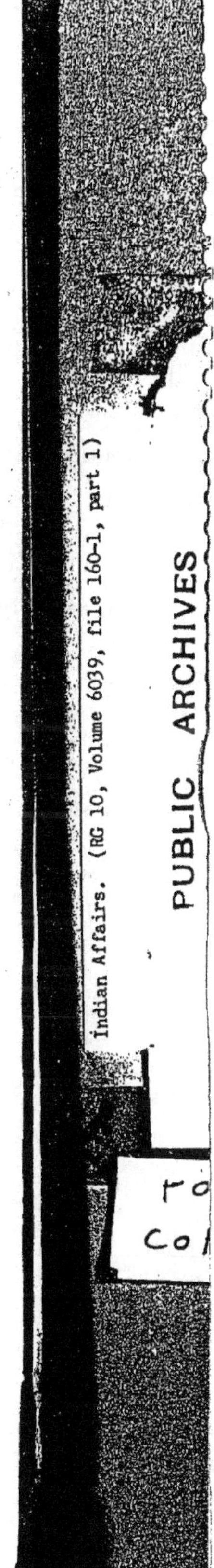

jointly w churches

4

3. To maintain the buildings at the said school and the school premises, when they are the property of the Government, in good condition and repair, and provide for proper sanitation and sanitary appliances.

III. The Superintendent General shall have the right to cancel and rescind this contract if in his opinion the.. has failed to comply with any of the covenants and stipulations of this contract by giving six months' notice in writing to the................................ and such notice shall be sufficiently served by sending it by registered mail addressed to the.. at..

* any examples of?

IV. Pursuant to the statute in that behalf, it is hereby expressly agreed that no member of the House of Commons of Canada shall have any share or part in this agreement or any benefit to arise therefrom. — Alberni M.P.?

V. Should the amount voted by Parliament and applicable towards payment by the Superintendent General of the grant for each pupil in the said school hereinbefore provided for or towards payment of anything to be supplied, provided or done by the Superintendent General under this contract, be at any time expended during the continuance of this contract, the Superintendent General may give the..notice to that effect, and thereafter the..shall not be entitled to any payment under this contract, and the Superintendent General and His Majesty shall not be liable to supply, provide or do anything under this contract for which the expenditure of money may be necessary, until the necessary funds shall have been voted by Parliament in that behalf, and in no event shall the..have, make or prefer any claim against the Superintendent General or His Majesty for any damages or compensation.

VI. In this contract the word.. shall mean and include the...and ....and the words 'Superintendent General' shall mean the Superintendent General or acting Superintendent General of Indian Affairs for the time being; and the words 'His Majesty' include His Majesty's heirs and successors.

VII. This contract, unless rescinded by the Superintendent General under the provisions hereinbefore mentioned, shall continue in force for a term of......

Indian Affairs. (RG 10, Volume 6039, file 160-1, part 1)

........................years to be computed from the......................

day of.................................19 .

IN WITNESS WHEREOF the undersigned have hereunto subscribed their names and affixed their seals the day and year hereinbefore written.

WITNESS:

....[Seal]

For the party of the First Part.

....[Seal]

For the party of the Second Part.

Appendix Nine: Rules and regulations governing an Indian residential school - the United Church facility in Port Alberni in 1962

UNITED tab 0194

ALBERNI RESIDENTIAL SCHOOL September 24, 1962

Lines of Communication, General Policy, and Staff Duties

1. The staff of the Alberni Residential School is appointed by the Principal, except in the case of the Vice-Principal and Director of Christian Education whose appointments are made by the Board of Home Missions, and in the case of the teaching staff which is appointed by the Regional Superintendent of Schools and/or the District Superintendent of Indian Schools. Such appointments, however, are made with the concurrence of the Principal, and his recommendations, which are given consideration. * church control of senior staff

2. The non-teaching staff of the School will be in accordance with the numbers suggested by the Board of Home Missions, but such numbers may be increased or decreased at the discretion of the Principal, according to the immediate needs of the establishment.

3. The salaries paid to the staff members will depend upon seniority, value of services and general contribution. Increases will be made at the discretion of the Principal but at no time by total exceed the overall sum authorized.

4. Appointments - The Principal is appointed by the Minister of Citizenship and Immigration, in agreement with the Board of Home Missions, Toronto.) - joint appointment of Principal

5. Duties - The Principal is responsible to the above-named authorities for the physical, mental, moral, religious, and educational needs of the students in his charge. He is responsible for the disbursement of funds allotted to him according to the scales laid down and his own discretionary powers. * — line of authority + responsibility

5 a. Residences, teacherages and accomodations are the sole responsibility of the Principal in allocation and furnishing. ← * Principal solely responsible for school

6. Any member of staff who attempts to usurp, flout, or falsely attribute any remark to the Principal, or in any way undermine the authority of the Principal by word or deed, shall do so on pain of dismissal or suspension from duties. ← institutionalized cover-up

7. Any member of staff wishing to communicate with higher authority, to the press, or to the radio, or by any other means of communication to the general public, may do so only with the concurrence of the Principal. If such communication appears to be in direct conflict with the policy of the school, and/or the Indian Affairs Branch, the matter shall be discussed with or by the Principal and the Local Advisory Committee, whose joint consultation shall produce such decisions which shall be final. ? ***

8. The Principal has the authority to instantly dismiss any staff member guilty of (a) gross misconduct, (b) negligence or dereliction of duty, or (c) conduct detrimental to the general well being of his charges. In the case of (a), an appeal may be made to the Local Advisory Board who shall in consultation with the Principal decide the issue, such decision shall be final and binding. If such an appeal is made, the appellant shall be suspended until a decision be made. — no habeas corpus - presumption of guilt

9. The in the case of teaching staff guilty of (a) they shall be instantly suspended and reported to the District Superintendent of Schools, his superior, or his deputy. In the case of (b) or (c) their conduct shall be reported to the above authorities and recommendations be made.

10. The Vice-Principal - The Vice-Principal is second in charge to the Principal. He is responsible to the Principal that rules governing the general and specific policy of the school as laid down, be followed. In the absence of the Principal, he is in sole charge of the school, calling upon the Local Advisory Board for such advice and assistance as may be needed.

11. The Vice-Principal has the authority, delegated by the Principal to instantly suspend any staff member guilty of gross misconduct etc. as defined in (a) (b) (c) of para. 8.

12. In the case of teaching staff guilty of (a) (b) (c) he shall consult with the senior teacher and plan a course of action in line with general policy acting with or without the general agreement of [illegible] that the general routine of the school as laid down is strictly observed. He is responsible for the training and recreation of the students as laid down in policy.

15. The Vice Principal is in charge of the senior residence when in residence. He is responsible that the occupants of the residence conduct themselves always in a manner that is seemly, and in accordance with the accepted rules of good conduct and reasonable behaviour. He shall report any serious dereliction of such rules to the Principal, and deal with minor infractions in such fashion as he shall deem necessary. ✓

16. The Vice Principal may make such changes in, and with staff knowledge, to the staff accommodation, except by structural alteration. He may make changes in furniture, beds, lockers, etc. in dormitories in consultation with the matron, and the knowledge of the supervisors if in his opinion, such changes appear desirable and leading to improvement. Major changes shall first be discussed with the Principal.

17. The Vice Principal shall be responsible for such book-keeping as may be decided by the Principal. ← *church in charge of financial records

18. The Vice Principal may make certain purchases in connection with school requirements in consultation with the Matron and Principal. He may authorize purchase of gasoline and arrange allocation of school vehicles.

The House-Mother – "Matron"

19. The House-Mother is third in the line of communication. The H.M. is responsible to the Principal and in his absence the Vice Principal for the physical well being of all students. In matters of sickness, she shall make such arrangements as she shall deem necessary for the recovery of patients in her charge. *

20. The H.M. is responsible to the Principal for the general cleanliness of the students, of the dormitories and their maintenance thereof. She shall be responsible for the general appearance of the women supervisors in matter of dress, general behaviour and attitudes. ✓

21. She shall see that sufficient food, varied in nature according to the accepted standards of dietary practice be ordered, having due regard for the amount of money available for food. She shall ensure that all kitchen equipment is clean and maintained in a satisfactory condition. She shall see that all rooms adjacent to and in connection with the kitchen be clean, tidy, and frequently inspected. (define?)

22. The H.M. shall be in charge of all domestic staff and do her best to ensure a high standard of cleanliness and good cooking and baking practice.

23. She shall see that all domestic staff are uniformed to an accepted standard.

24. The House-Mother shall give such counselling advice to the girls as may be needed and shall ensure that all possible is done for their mental and moral welfare.

25. The H.M. shall endeavour to promote healthy relationships between staff members, and endeavour to inculcate a cheerful spirit of co-operation and service to others by example and precept.

26. The H.M. shall, in co-operation with the Principal and Vice Principal, promote social parties for both students and staff during the festive season and at such other times as she may feel to be propitious.

27. The H.M. shall be responsible for the maintenance of up-to-date time keeping records regarding domestic and supervisory staff, and ensure that adequate free time be allocated. staff lists

Assistant Matron

28. The Assistant Matron shall assist the matron in matters of supervising, nursing and general duties as required by the matron. In the absence of the matron, she shall perform such duties as are normally carried out by the matron.

Nurse

29. The Nurse shall be responsible to the Principal and Matron for the physical welfareof patients under treatment. She shall maintain such stocks of medical equipment as may be needed to operate an efficient dispensary and first aid station. Such stocks carried are to consist only of those recommendedby the school doctor, and the Principal. * medical care not independent of Principal

30. The Nurse shall inform the Principal of the daily state of patients in her care. She shall recommend to the Principal when the advice of the doctor should be sought in cases of a doubtful diagnosis or severe injury. In the absence of the Principal, she shall act on her own initiative. The care of her patients shall be her prime consideration. * Principal informed of injury or illness

31. The Nurse shall keep a true record of all students needing or having received medical care. The Nurse shall report doubtful cases, or suspected cases of malingering, to the Principal.

Head Supervisor

32. The Head Supervisor shall be responsible to the Vice Principal for the direction of the male supervisors and the rota of duties thereof.

33. The H.S. shall bring to the notice of the V.P. any serious breach of school rules pertaining to students or supervisors. He shall by precept and example convey to his fellow supervisors and the students under his control, a model worthy of their emulation. He shall ensure that both supervisors and students are completely familiar with fire drill policy.

34. The H.S. shall not enter into any argument or disagreement with his fellow supervisors if by so doing he places himself or his superiors in an unworthy light.

35. The H.S. may not move, or cause to be moved, any dormitory or recreation room fitting without discussion and permission from the V. P. or Principal.

36. The H.S. may not physically handle any student, neither may he strike or chastise any student as punishment. * ← why this prohibition only re- Head Supervisor? (not on Principal etc.)

Supervisors

37. Supervisors shall be under the general direction of the V.P. and the H.S. Supervisors shall be responsible to the House Mother for the general well-being of their charges in matters of physical health and personal cleanliness.

*conflicting lines of authority = harder to trace authorization for wrongdoing or violence

38. The female supervisors shall bring to the Matron (H.M.) any problems affecting the well-being of the girls in their charge.

39. Supervisors may not use any electrical equipment other than that supplied for cleaning, maintenance, and recreation without prior permission from the Principal, or V.P.

(E)

40. Supervisors may not tamper with or allow the tampering with, any electrical equipment by the students. They may not plug in leads except into the outlets supplied. No unauthorized connections are allowed under any circumstances.

- why emphasis on electricity
- faulty wiring a norm?
- indication of substandard housing being the norm?

41. Supervisors are responsible for complete familiarity with school policy, rules and regulations, and in all matters pertaining to their duties.

42. Supervisors may not physically handle, or assault any student. Any extremely difficult or recalcitrant cases shall be brought to the notice of the H.S., V.P. or Principal.

43. Supervisors shall not permit any student to operate any piece of electrical equipment unless it is under his complete surveillance. Neither may he permit any student to operate the dumb-waiter.

(E)

44. When no written rule provides for a contingency arising, sound common-sense shall prevail.

blank cheque

45. Supervisors may not permit students the use of keys to gain access to any store-room or place where clothing or food is kept or any materials or articles of equipment.

← suggests hunger + ill-clothing as norm

Engineer

46. Is responsible to the Principal for the efficient operation of the boiler systems in the school. The Engineer shall maintain his equipment in sound working order. He shall recommend to the Principal any repairs requiring outside contracts.

47. The Engineer is responsible that the electrical equipment, wiring, lighting and all systems on the electrical side be maintained in a safe and efficient manner.

(E)

48. He shall make such effective repairs in accordance with the electrical standards as laid down by authority. He shall not permit the installation of any wiring circuits except by express permission of the Principal. He shall report any illegal electrical wiring or equipment installed or used by any person or staff member. He shall report to the Principal any major defects beyond his capacity to repair because of insufficient knowledge or lack of equipment. He shall make periodic inspections

(E)

49. The Engineer is responsible for the plumbing in the school. He shall maintain all equipment in working condition constantly. He shall acquaint the Principal or Vice Principal of any defects occurring due to neglect or misuse. He shall make arrangements with the Principal for necessary outside contracts and requisitions.

50. The Engineer may not allow any misuse of plumbing equipment or fittings and shall report any such cases coming to his notice. He shall make periodic inspection of all equipment under his control and report the effectiveness of such equipment. He is mainly responsible for all fire fighting equipment.

The Maintenance Man

51. Is responsible to the Principal for the maintenance of the fabric of the school building. He shall keep in good repair all furniture, fittings both fixed and mobile. He shall maintain all doors including fire doors, locks, fittings, windows and their glazing, screens and their fittings in good working order. He shall in conjunction with the Engineer test, and maintain to a high standard of efficiency all fire-fighting equipment. He shall be in charge of transportation of fire-fighting equipment.

52. The Maintenance Man shall maintain all paint work to reasonable levels of paint stocks carried. He shall report any defect by neglect or misuse to the Principal. He shall make frequent inspection to minimize any wilful damage to any fitting or equipment, under his control. He may not make any alteration to existing equipment, or structural repairs or alterations except by permission of the Principal. He may not build, move, or change the appearance of any locker, cupboard, door or such equipment except by permission of the Principal. He may not make, build or construct any cupboards, shelves, lockers, fixed or movable structures except by permission of the Principal. suggests /sabotage?

53. He shall at all times maintain his workshop, tools and equipment in a tidy and workmanlike manner as befits a skilled craftsman.

54. He shall report an make recommendations to the Principal, any alterations large and small, which in his opinion may be carried out to the benefit of the shcool.

55. He shall maintain a work book and work sheet, and shall follow the priority order in which work is to be carried out.

56. He shall assist the Principal in the compilation of requisitions according to stock needs, repairs, and alterations.

57. The Maintenance Man is responsible only to the Principal or Vice Principal as defined. He may in emergency make such repairs as will safeguard the fabric and or equipment of the shcool. *

Director of Christian Education

58. The Christian Educator is responsible to the Committee of Presbytery via the Principal, for the religious welfare of the students. ← church supervision + appointment

59. The C.E. shall outline and maintain a regular programme of Christian Education in accordance with the accepted standards and traditions of the United Church of Canada.

60. The C.E. shall confer with the Principal when any change of programme is desired other than that which is regularly conducted.

61. The C.E. may invite staff members to conduct services. He shall in such cases give advice in regard to the structure of such services which shall be in accordance with the United Church of Canada teachings.

62. The C.E. shall follow closely the requirements of the Committee with regard to the Christian education in the reserves.

Appendix Ten: Germ Warfare in British Columbia – The Case of John Sheepshanks and the Chilcotin people

In the fall of 2008, Tom Swanky, a former librarian in Quesnel, British Columbia released archival material he had research for over a decade concerning the earliest years of European occupation of the province. The material was entitled ***"The Tragedy of British Columbia: Genocide at its Founding".*** It relied on period newspapers and government correspondence to show that the leading politicians, traders, church officials, doctors and military men of the first colony on Canada's west coast actively killed off large sectors of the indigenous population.

Swanky's exhaustive study shows that this killing occurred primarily through the deliberate spreading of smallpox to Indians in targeted territories desired by white settlers, by the use of infected blankets and smallpox inoculations. He also demonstrates that a common element linking all of the chief conspirators in this domestic germ warfare is that they were all members of the Anglican Church of England and the colonial government, and were all shareholders in the Hudson's Bay Company and its subsidiary, the Puget Sound Agricultural Company (PSAC), which hungered for aboriginal lands.

Swanky begins by showing how the largest Indian war in Canada after the Riel Rebellion – the Chilcotin War of 1862-1868 – was an attempt by the Chilcotin (Tsilhqot'in) Indians to halt the men who were disseminating smallpox among their people. These men included Rev. John Sheepshanks, an Anglican missionary and a key actor in the germ warfare that would exterminate over 90% of the Chilcotins in a few years. For Sheepshanks almost singlehandedly inoculated the Chilcotin villages around the present day city of Quesnel and devastated this populace.

Across British Columbia, the pattern of this germ warfare remained the same: the highest concentration of Indian deaths from smallpox followed on the heels of their inoculation by Sheepshanks and others, and after the very men disseminating the disease had applied for "pre-emption" of the lands occupied by the Indians being inoculated well before they were killed off by the disease. (Normally, land could only be pre-empted if they contained no inhabitants).

For example, on the central coastline near Bella Coola during 1861 and 1862, over three quarters of the several thousand Indians were dead from smallpox after being inoculated by Anglican missionaries; 1500 had died in just a four week period. Just before their annihilation, the Attorney General for the province, George Carey – a long time trading partner with the PSAC – had stated in the legislative Assembly *"There is no settlement in Bella Coola, nor shall there be."*

Several of Carey's business partners – John and Robert Miles and Duncan MacKay, all PSAC shareholders – had during 1860 applied for pre-empted lots of 160 acres each on the land still occupied by the Bella Coola Indians: nearly a year before the smallpox wiped out most of them. Obviously, these unlawful pre-emptions occurred in the knowledge that there would soon be no Bella Coolas on the land.

In his memoirs, Francis Poole – an officer in the Royal Engineers and a business partner of George Carey – wrote, *"I led the party that introduced smallpox in Bella Coola and Fort Alexander ..."* William Downey, another PSAC partner, wrote in 1893, *"In the year 1862, smallpox was carried by whites into Bella Coola."*

During the same period, Rev. John Sheepshanks conducted the same genocidal operation in the central interior. Early in 1862, another Royal Engineer, Colonel Moody of New Westminster (then the provincial capital) ordered Lt. Henry Palmer to go among the populous Chilcotin Indians and "lay out reserves for several new town sites." Moody – a PSAC investor - then put his friend John Sheepshanks – who served as chaplain to the Royal Engineers – in touch with a Dr. Seddall, who provided the missionary with smallpox inoculations. Sheepshanks then joined up with Lt. Palmer.

According to the Colombian newspaper of April 29, 1863,

"The good missionary Reverend Sheepshanks stated at a public meeting that during his tour of the Interior during July of last year, he had vaccinated all the Indians he could find."

Within two months of Sheepshanks' mass inoculation of the Chilcotins, nearly all of them were dead or dying from smallpox. In what is now the town of Quesnel, his partner Lt. Palmer had already pre-empted most of the Chilcotins' land on behalf of Col. Moody and his business associates.

John Sheepshanks was rewarded for his murder of so many Indians by his eventual appointment as Bishop of Norwich and a seat in the House of Lords in London, which he held until his death in 1908. In his memoirs, Sheepshanks remarked ominously,

"The noble savage is being improved off the face of the earth ... I cannot now dwell upon the causes of the disappearance of these people, though alas! Some of them I know right well."

John McLain, one of Sheepshank's associates also commented much after the fact, when recalling his sojourn among the Chilcotins as a land speculator, *"I got a blanket well-infected with smallpox, carefully put it between a saddle blanket and a sweat pad ... I succeeded. They all died of smallpox."* *(From his memoir* *Only in Nazko* *, 1908)*

At exactly the same time, a third area of British Columbia was experiencing the same germ warfare. William Manson, a factor with the Hudson's Bay Company in Kamloops, kept an official journal in which he noted the following incidents as he disseminated smallpox:

June 24, 1862: Vaccinated many Indians of the North River
July 12: Smallpox raging among the North River Indians
July 29: Vaccinated South Branch Indians
August 2: Indians begin dying along the south branch
August 18: Indians refuse contact and further vaccinations
September 28: Smallpox is raging among all the Indian bands

By October of 1862, smallpox had devastated Indian tribes in a huge arc encompassing the west coast, northern and central Interior villages. In the Chilcotin area alone, over 5000 Indians had died of the disease in less than six months, while only four whites had died from it: for only the Indians had been inoculated.

Significantly, this arc of mass death corresponded exactly to the path of travel of smallpox-disseminators like Sheepshanks, John Poole of the Royal Engineers and Alex MacDonald of PSAC. In fact, over 90% of all interior Indians died during this brief period, and all of their land had been previously pre-empted by Sheepshanks' business partners in PSAC.

Nearly all of the senior government officers in British Columbia at this time were company shareholders, including Governor Douglas, Speaker of the Assembly Dr. John Helmcken, Chief Justice Cameron and thirteen Members of the Legislature. All of these men were loyal Anglicans.

The "official" history books still teach that the Chilcotin Indian wars were the result of savages taking vengeance on whites who camped near their territories. Smallpox, John Sheepshanks and the Puget Sound Agricultural Company are never mentioned.

"Colonization is civilization ... If we, the superior race, take the land of other races, wemust utterly destroy the previous inhabitants."
- Sir Edward Bulwer-Lytton, co-founder of British Columbia, Member of theLegislative Assembly, in his book *The Coming Race* (1868)

"All men must die. The Indians obeyed the mandate perhaps a little earlier thanotherwise they might. The diseases not only killed many but made the living diseased,rendered the women barren or their offspring incapable of living. This is the real and truecause of their disappearance. Socially, probably their death is of little consequence; politically, it does not seem they were intended to set the world on fire. What of the breedremain will require a great deal of crossing to make a superior race. The British have beenthrough the process."-
Dr. John Helmcken, Speaker of the British Columbia Legislature, Hudson'sBay Company Director, dispenser of smallpox, from his *Reminiscences* (1898)

"I may have to employ the Colorado Solution and order every white man to kill every indian in the province – Premier Frederick Seymour, 1868

Source: *The True Story of Canada's War of Extermination on the Pacific* by Tom Swanky (2012)

To: Colonel Henry Bouquet

You will Do well to try to Innoculate the
Indians by means of Blankets, as well as to try
Every other method that can serve to Extirpate
this Execrable Race. I should be very glad your
Scheme for Hunting them Down by Dogs could take Effect
Effect, but England is at too great a Distance
to think of that at present.

From: Lord Jeffrey Amherst, 16 July 1763

src: British Manuscript Project, 1941-1945, the United States Library of Congress, microfilm reel 34/41, item 114

Photograph courtesy BC Archives Call Number F-05146

Rev. John Sheepshanks (1834-1909)

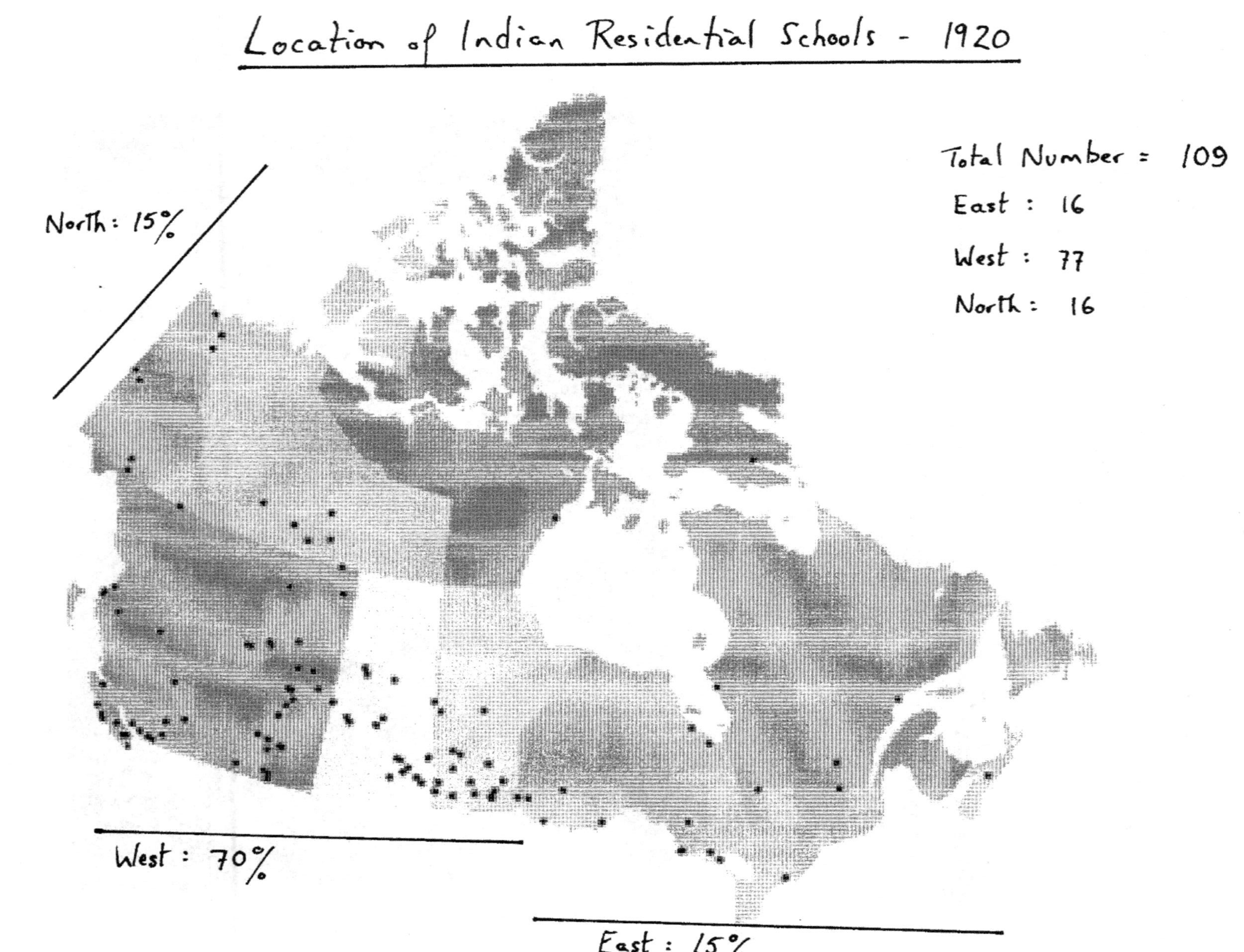

http://ecommunity.pwsd76.ab.ca/file.php/863/moddata/resource/17717/ss_09/mm/m3/ss9_m3_s1_l3_007_schools/images/irs_m... 1/26/2013

Scalping Proclamation, Nova Scotia, 1756*

Issued by Governor Charles Lawrence

We, by and with the Advice and Consent of His Majesty's Council, do hereby Authorize and Command all Officers, Civil and Military, and all His Majesty's Subjects, to annoy, distress, take and destroy the Indians inhabiting different parts of this Province, wherever they are found, and all such as may be aiding or assisting them.

And We hereby promise, by and with the Advice and Consent of His Majesty's Council, a Reward of Thirty Pounds Sterling for every Male Indian Prisoner, above the age of sixteen, brought in alive, or for a scalp of such Male Indian Twenty-five Pounds Sterling, and Twenty-Five Pounds Sterling for every Indian Woman or Child brought in alive: Such rewards to be paid by the Officer commanding at any of His Majesty's Forts in this Province, immediately on receiving the Prisoners or scalps above mentioned, according to the intent and meaning of this Proclamation.

Note: This Nova Scotia law has never been repealed

www.miqmaq.com ***, 2001***

War Crimes in Nazi Germany and Canada: A Comparison

Annual Death Rate in Auschwitz: **15% - 25%** (1)

Annual Death Rate in Canadian Indian residential schools: **35% - 65%** (2)

Number of persons convicted for these deaths at Auschwitz and other Nazi death camps: **209** (3)

Number of persons convicted for these deaths at Indian residential schools: **None**

"The so called ill treatment in our detention centers, stories of which were spread everywhere, were not, as some claim, inflicted methodically, but were excesses committed by individual camp guards and men who laid violent hands on the detainees. – Rudolf Hoess, SS Commandant at Auschwitz, at his trial in 1945

The abuses experienced by students at our Indian schools were almost benign in nature. They were not the result of a deliberate or a systematic policy but were isolated acts of individuals. – Brian Thorpe, Secretary of British Columbia Conference of the United Church of Canada, March 3, 1996

……………..

Sources:

(1) Body Disposal at Auschwitz: The End of Holocaust Denial by John C. Zimmerman (1999)

(2) Department of Indian Affairs statistics including the Indian school survey of Chief Medical Officer Dr. Peter Bryce, November 1907 and quoted in the Globe and Mail, April 24, 2007. See also www.hiddennolonger.com .

(3) Statistical Tables of the Nuremberg Trials; Telford Taylor, U.S. Assistant prosecutor, author of "The Nuremberg War Crimes Trials", International Conciliation, No. 450, p. 371, April 1949.

I Saw

By William Combes, March 24, 2000

A Kamloops residential school survivor and eyewitness to the abduction of ten children by Elizabeth Windsor on October 10, 1964 - William was killed by lethal injection in St. Paul's Catholic hospital, Vancouver, February 25, 2011 just before his scheduled appearance at a Tribunal in London, England

I saw angelic babies weep, weeping and crying themselves to sleep.
One night in the dormitory I crept to numerous beds,
"Little ones" I asked "What's the matter?"
"I miss my mommy and daddy. I'm hungry!" they cried. Many told me "Billy! I need food"
I and my friend Georgy got together late at night.
We put dummies in our beds, climbed down the fire escape to raid the kitchen and the orchard.
One night around midnight we froze in fright,
I saw – We saw figures and a strange light.
"Georgy! What's that?" I asked. "This is no fun!"
Georgy responded tearfully, "They're burying another one" (Baby)
I almost screamed.
"Shh" Georgy said. "We might be caught, we'll join the dead" (ones).
Today I have nightmares of that fearful night, waking up sweaty, cold and in dire fright.
I saw figures with shovels and flash lights,
Digging a hole by an apple tree to bury little ones.
For the dead weep and plea, "Set me free, set me free; Billy, Georgy, feed me!"
Today I cry at night, still hearing babies' plea:
"Feed me, feed me, or I might die!"
I and Georgy brought the food – My dreams I can draw
of the truths and sufferings of the Kamloops Indian residential school.
I SAW! I SAW! I SAW!

Testimonies

https://www.youtube.com/watch?v=kae1KlXk13Q

https://www.youtube.com/watch?v=RBUd3UXt6fI

https://www.youtube.com/watch?v=CReISnQDbBE

Bibliography

Books

Allen, Richard, The Social Passion: Religion and Social Reform in Canada (University of Toronto Press, 1973)

Alvarez, Alex, Governments, Citizens and Genocide: A Comparative and Interdisciplinary Approach (Indiana University Press, 2001)

Annett, Kevin, Hidden No Longer: Genocide in Canada, Past and Present (3rd ed.,Vancouver, 2010)
Unrepentant: Disrobing the Emperor (O Books, London, 2010)
Unrelenting (Amazon, 2016)

Aquinas, Thomas, Summa Theologica, Book Two (Paris, 1267)

Arnett, Chris, The Terror of the Coast: Land Alienation and Colonial War on Vancouver Island and the Gulf Islands, 1849-1863 (Talon Books, 1999)

Black, Edwin, War against the Weak: Eugenics and America's Campaign to create a Master Race (New York, Thunder's Mouth Press, 2003)

Bryce, Dr. Peter, The Story of a National Crime: Record of the Health Conditions of the Indians of Canada from 1840-1921 (Ottawa, 1921)

Choquette, Robert, The Oblate Assault on Canada's Northwest (University of Ottawa Press, 1995)

Cooper, John, Raphael Lemkin and the Struggle for the Genocide Convention (Herald Press, 2008)

De Las Casas, Bartolomeo, A Brief Account of the Devastation of the Indies (Madrid, 1542)

Goldhagen, Daniel, Hitler's Willing Executioners: Ordinary Germans and the Holocaust (Harvard University Press, 1995)

Gramsci, Antonio, The Prison Notebooks (Pathfinder Press, 1971)

Hunter, Sara, Always Remember Love: Memoirs of a Survivor of Nazi Medical Experimentation in post-war Canada (self published, Victoria, 1999)

Lea, Henry Charles, The Inquisition of the Spanish Dependencies (New York, 1908)

Lemkin, Raphael, Axis Rule in Occupied Europe (Washington, 1944)
Totally Unofficial Man: The Autobiography of Raphael Lemkin (self-published, 1959)

Lindquist, Sven, Exterminate All the Brutes: The Origins of European Genocide (New Press, 1992)

Marx, Karl, Capital, Volume One (London, 1888)

Miller, Alice, For Your Own Good: Hidden Cruelty in Child Rearing and the Roots of Violence (Noonday Press, 1983)

Newcomb, Steve, Pagans in the Promised Land (Fulcrum, 2008)

Nicholson, Rob, Stolen Innocence: Institutionalized Child Trafficking in British Columbia (Kelowna, 1998)

Rubenstein, Richard, The Cunning of History: The Holocaust and the American Future (Harper, 1975)

Ryerson, Stanley, The Founding of Canada: Beginnings to 1815 (Progress Books, 1960)

Siggins, Maggie, Riel: A Life of Revolution (Harper Collins, 1995)

Sproat, Gilbert Malcolm, The Nootka: Scenes and Studies of Savage Life (Smith Elder, 1868)
Stannard, David E., American Holocaust (Oxford University Press, 1994)

Swanky, Tom, The Tragedy of British Columbia: Genocide at its Founding (Quesnel, 2008)

Walker, Williston, A History of the Christian Church (Charles Scribners, 1959)

Zimmerman, John C., Body Disposal at Auschwitz: The End of Holocaust Denial (University of Nevada press, 1999)

Journal Articles

"Health Protection or Population Control?" by Lynn McLean, in Alive, August 1996

"The Evidence of Christian Nationalism in Federal Indian Law: The Doctrine of Discovery, Johnson v. McIntosh, and Plenary Power" by Steve Newcombe, in New York University Review of Law and Social Change, Vol. XX, No. 2, 1993

"The Nuremberg War Crimes Trials – Statistical Tables" by Telford Taylor, Deputy American Prosecutor, in International Conciliation, No. 450, April 1949, pp. 371.

Government Legislation and Reports

The Quarterly Review of the Department of Indian Affairs, Ottawa

The Indian Act of Canada (RSC 1989)

An Act Incorporating the United Church of Canada (14-15 George V, Assented July 19, 1924 in the House of Commons, Ottawa)

The Sexual Sterilization Act of the Province of Alberta (1928) and the Sexual Sterilization Act of British Columbia (1933)

Report of the Canadian Department of External Affairs, Ottawa, 1948

The Royal Commission of Inquiry into Aboriginal Peoples, Ottawa, 1997

The Crimes against Humanity and War Crimes Act, c. 24 (Assented June 29, 2000 in the House of Commons, Ottawa)

Church Records and Reports

Crimen Sollicitationas, "On the Crime of Solicitation", Vatican City Closed Archives, 1929 and 1962

Papal Bulls *Romanus Pontifex* (1455) and *Inter Catera* (1493), Rome

Mission to Nootka, 1874-1900: Reminiscences of the West Coast of Vancouver Island by Bishop A.J. Brabant (Sydney, 1900)

Record of Proceedings of 1st and 2nd General Councils of the United Church of Canada, 1925, 1926

Annual Reports of the United Church of Canada and the Anglican Church of Canada

Archival Material

Microfilmed records of the Department of Indian and Northern Affairs (INAC) and the Department of Indian Affairs (DIA), RG 10 series on Indian Residential Schools, Vol. 7733, University of British Columbia Library, Vancouver

Microfilmed records of INAC, RG 10 series, Vancouver Island University, Nanaimo

Written and videotaped Proceedings of the IHRAAM Northwest Tribunal into Indian Residential Schools, June 12-14, 1998, Vancouver

Videotaped interviews, written statements and notarized affidavits of 358 residential school survivors made between February 1995 and October 2015, and held as a public trust in the archives of Kevin Annett and the International Tribunal into Crimes of Church and State (ITCCS)

Miscellaneous

News clippings and other media reports too numerous to document, but referred to in Notes

Documentary film **Unrepentant: Kevin Annett and Canada's Genocide** (2006); Winner of Best Director Award, New York Independent Film Festival (2006), Best Documentary, Los Angeles Independent Film Festival (2007), Best Documentary, Creation Aboriginal Film Festival, Edmonton (2009)

Contact

The International Tribunal for the Disappeared of Canada (ITDC) has three Canadian field offices in Vancouver, Winnipeg and Toronto.

The ITDC central office can be contacted at disappearedofcanada@gmail.com . It is affiliated with the central office of the International Tribunal into Crimes of Church and State in Brussels. (www.itccs.org)

All communications and interviews will be conducted in the strictest confidence.

We owe respect to the living. To the dead we owe only the Truth.
- Voltaire

CPSIA information can be obtained
at www.ICGtesting.com
Printed in the USA
LVHW061509070721
692093LV00010B/557